T0285176

Spying Through a Glass Darkly

Espionage and counter-intelligence activities, both real and imagined, weave a complex and alluring story. Yet there is hardly any serious philosophical work on the subject. Cécile Fabre presents a systematic account of the ethics of espionage and counterintelligence. She argues that such operations, in the context of war and foreign policy, are morally justified as a means, but only as a means, to protect oneself and third parties from ongoing violations of fundamental rights. In doing so, she addresses a range of ethical questions: are intelligence officers morally permitted to bribe, deceive, blackmail, and manipulate as a way to uncover state secrets? Is cyberespionage morally permissible? Are governments morally permitted to resort to the mass surveillance of their and foreign populations as a means to unearth possible threats against national security? Can treason ever be morally permissible? Can it ever be legitimate to resort to economic espionage in the name of national security? The book offers answers to those questions through a blend of philosophical arguments and historical examples.

NEW TOPICS IN APPLIED PHILOSOPHY

Series editor
Kasper Lippert-Rasmussen

This series presents works of original research on practical issues that are not yet well covered by philosophy. The aim is not only to present work that meets high philosophical standards while being informed by a good understanding of relevant empirical matters, but also to open up new areas for philosophical exploration. The series will demonstrate the value and interest of practical issues for philosophy and vice versa.

Spying Through a Glass Darkly

The Ethics of Espionage and Counter-Intelligence

CÉCILE FABRE

OXFORD
UNIVERSITY PRESS

OXFORD

UNIVERSITY PRESS

Great Clarendon Street, Oxford, OX2 6DP,
United Kingdom

Oxford University Press is a department of the University of Oxford.
It furthers the University's objective of excellence in research, scholarship,
and education by publishing worldwide. Oxford is a registered trade mark of
Oxford University Press in the UK and in certain other countries

© Cécile Fabre 2022

The moral rights of the author have been asserted

First published 2022
First published in paperback 2024

All rights reserved. No part of this publication may be reproduced, stored in
a retrieval system, or transmitted, in any form or by any means, without the
prior permission in writing of Oxford University Press, or as expressly permitted
by law, by licence or under terms agreed with the appropriate reprographics
rights organization. Enquiries concerning reproduction outside the scope of the
above should be sent to the Rights Department, Oxford University Press, at the
address above

You must not circulate this work in any other form
and you must impose this same condition on any acquirer

Published in the United States of America by Oxford University Press
198 Madison Avenue, New York, NY 10016, United States of America

British Library Cataloguing in Publication Data
Data available

Library of Congress Cataloging in Publication Data
Data available

ISBN 978-0-19-883376-5 (Hbk.)
ISBN 978-0-19-891217-0 (Pbk.)

Links to third party websites are provided by Oxford in good faith and
for information only. Oxford disclaims any responsibility for the materials
contained in any third party website referenced in this work.

To Eric and Martin

Acknowledgements

I read my first spy novel, Ian Fleming's *Goldfinger* (in French translation), about thirty-five years ago. Since then, spy fiction (be it in novel, movie or TV series form) has been one of my favourite genres, alongside crime fiction. Over the last four years, I have *had* to read spy novels, watch spy movies and sit through years' worth of television series. Of all my books so far, this one has been the most enjoyable to research and write, though at times and for reasons that will become apparent throughout, uncomfortably so. Unless I decide to write on the ethics of policing, it is unlikely that I will ever again combine my research with my love for so-called popular culture and so have the chance to indulge in the latter entirely without guilt. Partly for this reason, my elation at having finished this book is tinged with regret.

Early draft chapters were presented at the following venues, whose organizers and participants I thank here: the Stockholm Institute for Ethics of War and Peace (June 2016); the Oxford Blavatnik School of Government (October 2016); the PPE Student Society in Warwick (November 2016); the Oxford Moral Philosophy Seminar (February 2017); the All Souls College Lunchtime Seminar (March 2017); the Edmond J. Safra Center for Ethics Conference (May 2017); the Oxford Philosophy Society (February 2018); the Annual Conference of the British Society for Ethical Theory (July 2018); UCL's Legal Philosophy Forum and Political Philosophy Seminar (April 2019); the Oxford-Queens Political and Legal Theory Workshop (June 2019); the University of Sheffield (October 2019); Fordham Law School (October 2020); Temple University and the University of Manchester (November 2020); the Stockdale Center for Ethical Leadership at the US Naval Academy (April 2021).

A number of friends and colleagues have supplied comments on the project. I am indebted to Kimberley Brownlee, Alejandro Chehtman, Mark Cornwall, Janina Dill, Gideon Elford, Toni Erskine, William Evans, Andrew Hurrell, Kasim Khorasanee, Cécile Laborde, Seth Lazar, Meira Levinson, Jeff McMahan, Kieran Oberman, Simon Palmer, Mitt Regan, Brianna Rosen, Thomas Simpson, Thomas Sinclair, Daniel Statman, Victor Tadros, and Albert Weale. Theodor Meron helped me with the wording of the title. The bulk of Chapter 6 appeared in August 2020 as a standalone article in *Law and Philosophy*, under the title 'The Morality of Treason'. (Fabre, C. The Morality of Treason. Law and Philosophy 39, 427–61 (2020). https://creativecommons.org/licenses/by/4.0/legalcode.) An anonymous reviewer for the journal provided excellent suggestions for improving the paper. Seumas Miller's detailed comments on the book's opening chapters and David Miller's and Andy Owen's probing and constructive remarks on the antepenultimate draft proved extremely helpful in the latter stages of the writing process.

A workshop on that draft was held via Zoom on 25 September 2020. My four commentators, Ross Bellaby, Jonathan Parry, Massimo Renzo and Carissa Veliz, did a superb job at highlighting many of the weaknesses in the book. The participants who joined us from different continents handled the format with great patience. The book is the better for their rigorous feedback. Ross's own book on the ethics of intelligence convinced me that the topic was worth pursuing at length. Massimo and Jonathan agreed with characteristic generosity to take part in the workshop even though they had already seen some draft chapters in rougher form. Carissa persuaded me over the years that her account of privacy is essentially correct, which led me to make substantial revisions to my own. (She also regularly draws my attention to good spy novels. I am grateful to her for that too.)

At Oxford University Press, Peter Momtchiloff, the Philosophy Commissioning Editor, and Kasper Lippert-Rasmussen, the editor for the series *New Topics in Applied Philosophy*, have been unfailingly supportive. Tony Coady supplied pages of comments on the penultimate draft. An anonymous reader for the Press helped me see what I needed to do in order to turn the book into something more than the sum of its chapters. I know that I have not been able to do everything that those two readers have asked of me, but I hope that I have gone some way towards addressing their concerns. Finally, I am grateful to Louise Larchbourne, Céline Louasli, and Vasuki Ravichandran for steering the book through the production and copy-editing stages.

Amongst the many people who have provided feedback on the book, some used to work in intelligence. Their encouragements and insights have been invaluable, though at their request and for obvious reasons, I have not specifically acknowledged some of the points they have made to me. I can only hope that the world of which I attempt to make normative sense here is not too far away from the world in which they operated.

Be that as it may, that world is somewhat removed from my professional home, All Souls College. I joined the College in 2014 on the basis of a research proposal which contained only one sentence on the importance of intelligence work for the conduct of foreign policy. Little did I (and the College) know that I would turn that sentence into a book. It is a pleasure, once again, to record my debt to the Warden and Fellows for the unparalleled privileges of Fellowship.

Last and foremost, my brothers, Eric and Martin, have been a source of fun and support, through thick and thin, for as long as I can remember. We also share an abiding love for spy and crime fiction. I suspect that they will not read this book, as they are somewhat impatient with philosophy. (Fair enough.) Nevertheless, I dedicate it to them, with love and gratitude.

Contents

Introduction

For now we see through a glass, darkly; but then face to face: now I
know in part; but then shall I know even as also I am known.

St Paul, *1 Corinthians* 13: 12–13

Some time in the second millenium BC: as the Book of Numbers tells the story (at
13: 17ff.), Moses sends out one man from each of the twelve tribes of Israel, with
instructions to 'go and spy the land' of Canaan. Caleb returns with the favourable
news that Canaan is ripe for the taking; the others report that its fortified cities
and strong population make it an impossible target. The Israelites decide not to
invade the land, for which they incur the wrath of God and condemn themselves
to wandering in the desert for forty years—in possibly one of the earliest and most
spectacular intelligence failures 'on record'.

November 2017: the *Financial Times* alleges that Britain's Government Communications Headquarters (aka GCHQ) is concerned about possible links between
the Russian software company Kaspersky Lab, whose founder is a former Soviet
military officer, and the Russian government. Kaspersky Lab's anti-virus software
has been offered for free by Barclays Bank to hundreds of thousands of customers.
The concern is that the Russian security services are using the software to hack into
the computers of government employees and military personnel who bank with
Barclays. All main parties categorically reject the allegations as untrue, although
it emerges that American and Israeli intelligence services reportedly have similar
concerns.[1]

Between the land of Canaan some time in the second millenium BC and the
headquarters of a private company in 2017 Russia, espionage activities weave a
complex story. From Julius Caesar's agents in Britain to the spies scouting medieval
market towns under the cloak of their clerical habit, from Francis Walsingham's
spy network to the Sun King's ciphers, from the cryptanalysts of Bletchley Park to
the Cold War's intelligence battles, from the National Security Agency (aka NSA)'s
wiretapping scandal to the infiltration of ISIS cells by Chechen forces loyal to
President Putin—one could tell hundreds of anecdotes. As John Le Carré's iconic
character George Smiley vividly tells it,

---

[1] See S. Jones and M. Arnold, 'UK Spymasters Raise Suspicions over Kaspersky Software's Russia
Links', *The Financial Times* (12/11/2017).

'Why spy? . . . For as long as rogues become leaders, we shall spy. For as long as there are bullies and liars and madmen in the world, we shall spy. For as long as nations compete, and politicians deceive, and tyrants launch conquests, and consumers need resources, and the homeless look for land, and the hungry for food, and the rich for excess, your chosen profession is perfectly secure, I can assure you.'[2]

Books (both fiction and non-fiction), articles, special journal issues, and policy papers number in the dozens of thousands.[3] However, there is very little serious *philosophical* work on espionage. This often comes as a surprise to current and previous officers from Western intelligence services, many of whom (as some of the empirical works I will cite throughout this book attest) are deeply concerned with the ethical issues raised by their professional activities. Indeed, the websites for the British, American, and French services put ethical norms at the forefront of those agencies' activities. The fact that those norms are observed in the breach as well as in the observance is beyond dispute—a point to which I shall return. But it is also undeniable that the intelligence community, at least in Western democracies, wants to be seen as acting ethically—and not, it seems, purely for public relations reasons. It is odd that philosophers should have neglected espionage, particularly as they have had quite a bit to say on war, of which it is an important component.

I do not have a good explanation for such neglect. At any rate, and promisingly, two recent and important book-length normative accounts of war assert that agents are under a duty to seek evidence that would enable them to ascertain whether they are fighting justly.[4] My aim is to develop this point in the context of war and foreign policy more broadly construed. I ask, in that context, what we are morally permitted and obliged to do in order to procure the information we need in the face of third parties' wish that the information should remain unavailable. That question has a counterpart, to wit: what we are morally permitted and obliged

---

[2] J. Le Carré, *The Secret Pilgrim* (Penguin Books, 2011), 208–9.

[3] I will refer to a number of those works throughout the book. For a wonderful one-volume, global history of espionage, see C. Andrew, *The Secret World: A History of Intelligence* (Allen Lane, 2018).

[4] See A. A. Haque, *Law and Morality at War* (Oxford University Press, 2017), 129; V. Tadros, *To Do, To Die, To Reason Why: Individual Ethics in War* (Oxford University Press, 2020), 15. For notable exceptions to philosophy's neglect of intelligence activities, see T. Pfaff and J. R. Tiel, 'The Ethics of Espionage,' *Journal of Military Ethics* 3 (2004): 1–15; M. Quinlan, 'Just Intelligence: Prolegomena to an Ethical Theory,' *Intelligence and National Security* 22 (2007): 1–13; T. Erskine, ' "As Rays of Light to the Human Soul"? Moral Agents and Intelligence Gathering,' in L. Scott and P. Jackson (eds.), *Understanding Intelligence in the Twenty-First Century—Journey in the Shadows* (Routlege, 2004); R. W. Bellaby, *The Ethics of Intelligence* (Routledge, 2014); D. Cole, *Just War and the Ethics of Espionage* (Routledge, 2015); D. Omand, 'Ethical Guidelines in Using Secret Intelligence for Public Security,' *Cambridge Review of International Affairs* 19 (2006): 613–28; D. Omand and M. Phythian, *Principled Spying—The Ethics of Secret Intelligence* (Oxford University Press, 2018); T. Simpson, 'The Morality of Unconventional Force,' in J. Galliott and W. Reed (eds.), *Ethics and the Future of Spying* (Routledge, 2016); J. Goldman (ed.), *Ethics of Spying: A Reader for the Intelligence Professional*, vol. 1 (Scarecrow Press, 2005) and J. Goldman (ed.), *Ethics of Spying: A Reader for the Intelligence Professional*, vol. 2 (Scarecrow Press, 2010).

to do in order to thwart outsiders' attempts to procure information which *we* want to keep secret. These two questions are at the heart of, respectively, espionage and counter-intelligence. In both war and peace, we see only through the glass darkly. Our foes' and friends' aims and intentions are worryingly opaque to us, as we want ours to remain opaque to them. When we spy on our foes and friends, we do not merely find out who they really are and what they do. We expose ourselves to the risk that they too will uncover our secrets. As we polish the glass in order the better to see them, we enable them the better to see us and thus the better to threaten us.

I defend the following claims. First, espionage and counter-intelligence (for short, intelligence activities) are morally justified as a means, but only as a means, to thwart violations of fundamental rights or risks thereof, in the context of foreign policy writ large, subject to meeting the requirements of necessity, effectiveness, and proportionality. Second, more strongly, intelligence activities which are justified on those grounds and under those conditions are sometimes morally mandatory. In the course of defending those claims, I scrutinize a range of acts which are the bread and butter of those activities: deception, treason, manipulation, exploitation, blackmail, eavesdropping, computer hacking, and mass surveillance.

My central question is related to another question, to wit, whether an agent may harm another person given that she does not know all the relevant facts. The ethics of decision-making under conditions of uncertainty has garnered considerable attention of late. In the context of war, for example, philosophers have asked whether a soldier may kill someone who appears to be a civilian when there are signs that she might be a combatant under disguise.[5]

Those two questions are related in the following ways. Suppose that the Prime Minister has to decide whether to impose economic sanctions on a repressive and belllicose regime. She does not know whether sanctions will be effective. If they are not effective, she is not morally entitled to impose them. She can reduce the level of uncertainty under which she operates by procuring more information, p, via her intelligence services, about that regime's officials. But now suppose that she merely suspects, and does not know for sure, that having p will help her determine whether she may justifiably impose sanctions. Under those circumstances, she must thus decide whether to procure p. The question at the heart of this book, then, is whether she is morally permitted, indeed obliged, to procure p before she imposes sanctions, and if so what her intelligence agents are morally permitted or

---

[5] See, e.g., S. O. Hansson, 'Decision Making Under Great Uncertainty,' *Philosophy of the Social Sciences* 26 (1996): 369–86; Haque, *Law and Morality at War*; S. Lazar, 'Deontological Decision Theory and Agent-Centered Options,' *Ethics* 127 (2017): 579–609; S. Lazar, 'In Dubious Battle: Uncertainty and the Ethics of Killing,' *Philosophical Studies* 175 (2018): 859–83; M. J. Zimmerman, *Living with Uncertainty—The Moral Significance of Ignorance* (Cambridge University Press, 2008). The uncertainty of which I speak here is uncertainty about the non-moral facts at issue, as distinct from moral uncertainty.

obliged to do in order to get it for her, including in those many cases in which it is not clear that *p* is what she needs. Although the question of what one is morally permitted or obliged to do under conditions of uncertainty and the question of what one is morally permitted or obliged to do to reduce uncertainty are related in the way I have just indicated, they remain different questions. This book in effect seeks to show that the latter question is worth exploring in greater depth than has been the case so far.

I define espionage as the act of seeking to acquire information about third parties which is thought to be needed for the conduct of foreign policy, and which there are reasons to believe those parties would rather keep secret. Espionage is one form, amongst many, of intelligence-gathering. An investigative journalist who seeks to ascertain whether a foreign regime is planning a military aggression on another country and who is planning to publish her findings in her newspaper is not conducting espionage activities against that regime. That same journalist would be taking part in an espionage operation if she acted at the behest of her country's intelligence services and passed on her findings to them.

I define counter-intelligence as the act of protecting oneself from third parties' espionage activities. As we shall see, the distinction between espionage and counter-intelligence is not hard and fast: in order to protect our secrets effectively, we might need to know how other parties intend to acquire them, which is itself a secret; and in order to know that, we might need to mount an espionage operation.

Throughout, I focus on what individuals who are engaged in espionage and counter-intelligence are morally allowed or obliged to do, be they government ministers allowing intelligence agencies surreptitiously to collect vast amounts of data on civilian populations, intelligence officers bugging foreign diplomats' cars or recruiting assets in foreign countries, state employees pondering whether to sell official secrets to a foreign power, or (less often) ordinary citizens stumbling upon secret information.

My definition of espionage might seem odd. The *Oxford English Dictionary* defines the verb 'to spy' (perhaps from Old French *espier*, or perhaps Old High German *spehôn*) as 'To watch (a person, etc.) in a secret or stealthy manner; to keep under observation with hostile intent'. On the first limb of that definition, the mere acquisition of sensitive information about (e.g.) a community's national security apparatus does not constitute espionage: what makes it so is the resort to stealth. At the same time, the second limb implies that the act of spying need not be done by stealth. On my construal, what matters is that one should seek to acquire information which, we have reasons to believe, the other side does not want us to have.

I say 'which we have reasons to believe'. We might well be wrong. Even if we are—even if the other side does want us to have the information we seek—we can still be aptly described as engaging in espionage. Suppose that a British military officer is a mole for Russia's Foreign Intelligence Service (aka SVR.) He passes to his handlers highly classified information about Britain's latest cyber-warfare operations. Unbeknownst to him, however, Britain's Security Service (aka MI5), which is in charge of British counter-intelligence, is fully aware of that fact. Instead of arresting him, MI5 agents mount a counter-intelligence operation of misdirection: they feed him information which is accurate and which they want the Russians to have, but which is not particularly important. It would be odd to deny that the mole and his handlers are carrying out espionage activities.[6]

I do not mean to provide an exhaustive account of what intelligence agencies do. In particular, I say nothing about covert operations, the provision of military assistance by intelligence operatives, or the use of intelligence officers as conduits for back-channel diplomacy. Espionage and counter-intelligence as I define them here raise enough difficult issues on their own to warrant a book-length treatment. Moreover, I restrict my inquiry to foreign policy broadly understood—which includes war but also diplomatic relations in general, the imposition of economic sanctions, treaty negotiations, and so on. I do not address the ethics of espionage as an instrument of domestic law enforcement or policing, or as carried out by private businesses in the course of their operations.

Admittedly, those boundaries (between domestic and foreign, conducting a foreign policy and thwarting criminal activities, the public and the private) are often blurred. On the first count, for example, the FBI in the US and MI5 in the UK spied on left-wing groups in their respective countries from the late 1940s onwards in the context of the Cold War. Further back, it is impossible to understand the lengths to which Francis Walsingham went to foil English Catholic plots against Elizabeth I without understanding the broader geopolitical context of the European Reformation and Counter-Reformation. Those two cases fall within the remit of this book. By contrast, the deployment by the London Metropolitan Police of undercover officers in green activist movements as late as the 2000s does not.[7]

Those cases involve a state's intelligence agencies. In cases involving supra-state organizations and non-state actors, the boundaries between the domestic and the foreign are harder to draw. At one end of the scale, the United Nations receive and analyse intelligence from their member states, yet it makes little sense to speak of the UN's domestic or foreign policy. Contrastingly, the European Union conducts

[6] For a clear and detailed overview of various counter-intelligence practices, see W. R. Johnson, *Thwarting Enemies at Home and Abroad* (Georgetown University Press, 2009); H. Prunckun, *Counterintelligence—Theory and Practice* (Rowman & Littlefield, 2012). Some scholars and practitioners distinguish counter-intelligence from counter-espionage, and define the former as protecting oneself from another party's intelligence activities, and the latter as detecting and neutralizing that party's spies. I use the term 'counter-intelligence' to cover both of these. When I do not need to differentiate between espionage and counter-intelligence, I use the word 'intelligence', as in 'intelligence operations' or 'intelligence activities'.
[7] On the FBI and MI5, see, e.g., C. Andrew, *The Defence of the Realm: The Authorized History of MI5* (Penguin Books, 2012); T. Weiner, *Enemies: A History of the FBI* (Penguin Books, 2012). On Walsingham, see, e.g., S. Alford, *The Watchers—A Secret History of the Reign of Elizabeth* (Penguin Books, 2013); J. Cooper, *The Queen's Agent* (Faber and Faber, 2011).

a foreign policy and its member states engage in ever-growing (if sometimes tense) intelligence-sharing activities against external threats; yet it seems odd to construe EU-wide police cooperation as a domestic matter.[8]

At the other end of the scale, some non-state actors which act as quasi-states resort to espionage and counter-intelligence. Although it may seem odd to describe them as having a foreign policy, the term is apt, at least to the extent that they seek to further territorial-cum-political ends and that they cooperate with, or fight, political actors (be they states or not) whom they have some justification for construing as external to them. It would not make sense to exclude them from my inquiry. This is why I use the term 'political community' rather than 'state', and 'leadership' rather than 'regime' or 'government', unless the context warrants otherwise.[9]

Consider next the distinction between conducting a foreign policy and thwarting criminal operations. Transnational terrorist movements often mesh with criminal networks. Suppose that the Metropolitan Police learns from one of its undercover officers in the London end of a transnational drug network that some of the proceeds of the drug trade are used by the London cell of a transnational terrorist group. The group is backed by a foreign power that is notoriously hostile to the UK. The Met passes on the information to MI5. In this example, my focus is on the London–Syria 'terrorism angle' and MI5's activities, not on the drug angle and the Met (even though some of my conclusions regarding undercover spying are likely to apply to undercover policing.)

Consider finally the distinction between public and private actors. It is widely alleged that governments carry out or facilitate economic espionage, on the grounds that the strength of their economy depends on private firms' ability to compete on the global market. It is also widely alleged that private firms spy on governments and on one another. I do not attend to the second of those allegations in this book. But to the extent that much of a political community's critical infrastructure is owned or managed by private companies, the latter's ability to resist attacks by foreign organizations *is* crucial to citizens' welfare. Moreover,

---

[8] On the role of intelligence-gathering in UN peacekeeping operations, see A. W. Dorn, 'United Nations Peacekeeping Intelligence,' in L. K. Johnson (ed.), *Oxford Handbook of National Security Intelligence* (Oxford University Press, 2010). For a sceptical take on the UN's intelligence capacities, see S. Chesterman, *Shared Secrets: Intelligence and Collective Security—Lowy Institute Paper 10* (2006). On intelligence cooperation between sovereign states, whether in the form of bilateral arrangements or under the auspices of multilateral institutions—notably the EU—see, e.g., J. van Buuren, 'Analyzing International Intelligence Cooperation: Institutions or Intelligence Assemblages?,' in I. Duyvesteyn et al. (eds.), *The Future of Intelligence–Challenges in the 21st century* (Routledge, 2015); B. Fägersten, 'European Intelligence Cooperation,' in I. Duyvesteyn et al. (eds.), *The Future of Intelligence—Challenges in the 21st century* (Routledge, 2015). On the disclosure and withholding of information in the context of global governance, see A. Carnegie and A. Carson, *Secrets in Global Governance—Disclosure Dilemmas and the Challenge of International Cooperation in World Politics* (Cambridge University Press, 2020).

[9] On intelligence activities carried out by nonstate actors, see, e.g., J. R. Harber, 'Unconventional Spies: The Counterintelligence Threat from Non-State Actors,' *International Journal of Intelligence and CounterIntelligence* 22 (2009): 221–36; C. A. Wege, 'The Changing Islamic State Intelligence Apparatus,' *International Journal of Intelligence and CounterIntelligence* 31 (2018): 271–88.

as the example of the Kaspersky Lab suggests (assuming that the story is true), governments also use private companies as vehicles to attack foreign powers. Those last two sets of cases fall squarely within the remit of the book.

In some respects, this might seem a strange project. For is it not obvious (some readers might think) that procuring intelligence about other foreign policy actors is morally permitted, particularly in war, as a means to protect ourselves from wrongful harms at the hands of such actors? Is it not obvious that we may use against foreign actors the very same tools which they are using against us?

Not really. Espionage has always elicited strong moral condemnation. This is partly due to the fact that intelligence agencies have long engaged in deeply problematic activities such as sabotage, targeted killings, and *coups d'état*. But it is also because the act of spying itself is troublesome: as we shall see, procuring information about a political community and its members which (we think) the latter would rather that we not have is morally problematic. Moreover, the spies who work on our behalf and at our behest often must manipulate, deceive, exploit, and blackmail individuals who, they believe, have or can access have the information we need. That information, moreover, is often about individuals. For example, our intelligence services might find out that a building hosts a putative hostile community's cyber-command, and that a group of hackers in that building is planning an attack or trying to infiltrate our critical infrastructure. Even if they can get that information without deceiving or manipulating anyone, they will need at the very least to place suspects under surveillance, at the expense of their privacy. One need not accept Kant's over-dramatic description of spying as 'that infernal art' or John Le Carré's fictional denunciation of spies as 'a squalid procession of vain fools' to find it difficult to condone those practices. We cannot hope to give them proper justification unless we consider the ends to which they are deployed.[10]

Before I describe the book in greater detail, a remark on methodology. I make extensive use of empirical examples, as befits the subject matter. With respect to this particular topic, however, empirical examples pose specific methodological difficulties. Much of the recent material is classified, and much of what intelligence agents tell us about their work, for example when they speak out in the media or write their memoirs, is not to be taken at face value. To deal with this difficulty, I proceed as follows. When I can strengthen a philosophical point with an example which does not depend for its illustrative power on the fact that it reflects current practices, I look to historical accounts backed by declassified material.

[10] I. Kant, 'Perpetual Peace: A Philosophical Sketch,' in H. Reiss (ed.), *Kant—Political Writings* (Cambridge University Press, 1991 [1795]), § 6; I. Kant, 'Metaphysics of Morals,' in H. Reiss (ed.), *Kant—Political Writings* (Cambridge University Press, 1991 [1797]), §§ 57–8; J. Le Carré, *The Spy Who Came in from the Cold*, new ed. (Penguin Classics, 2014), 243. My point here echoes Seumas Miller's plea that an adequate normative account of the police (as an institution) must address not merely the investigative means police officers employ but the ends which they are meant to serve. See S. Miller, *The Moral Foundations of Social Institutions—A Philosophical Study* (Cambridge University Press, 2010), 262–4.

When I need as contemporary an example as I can find, I rely on extensive secondary literature and reports from reputed media and journalists, with appropriate expository caveats. To help forge a route through an overwhelmingly abundant empirical literature, I use histories of intelligence agencies,[11] handbooks and often-cited collections of essays,[12] and unofficial accounts from former insiders or well-connected outsiders.[13]

Those varied and fascinating sources help bring the philosophical material to life. However, there is a risk that by illustrating moral justifications for espionage with real-life examples, the book might give the impression of being too uncritical of intelligence agencies. I am not uncritical—on the contrary. The claim that intelligence activities are morally justified only as a means to thwart violations of fundamental rights and subject to meeting the requirements of necessity, effectiveness, and proportionality implies that activities which fail to meet any of those conditions are morally impermissible. It is entirely possible—perhaps even likely—that much of what intelligence agencies have done and are currently doing is morally wrong, at the bar of the account I defend here.

If this is so, the question is what to do with those institutions. I do not pursue it here. This is a book of applied moral and political philosophy. I do not have much to say about the best way to institutionalize morally justified espionage practices. Nor do I take a view on whether domestic and international law ought to reflect the moral principles I defend here. I do not lack interest in those institutional and legal issues. However, and at the risk of frustrating some readers, I do believe in some division of labour.[14]

Let me now turn to the book's outline. In the first chapter, I set the stage for the arguments to follow. First, I provide an overview of the ethics of spying in classical moral and political thought and review the scant contemporary literature. I distinguish between three normative approaches to espionage and counter-intelligence: (a) the dirty-hands approach, which sees espionage as a necessary

---

[11] For example, in the UK, see Andrew, *The Defence of the Realm*; K. Jeffery, *MI6—The History of The Secret Intelligence Service 1909-1949* (Bloomsbury Publishing, 2010); R. J. Aldrich, *GCHQ: The Uncensored History of Britain's Most Secret Agency* (Harper Press, 2011). On the KGB, see C. Andrew and V. Mitrokhin, *The Mitrokhin Archive: The KGB in Europe and the West* (Penguin Books, 1999); C. Andrew and V. Mitrokhin, *The Mitrokhin Archive II: The KGB and the World* (Penguin Books, 2005).

[12] For example, L. Scott and P. Jackson (eds.), *Understanding Intelligence in the Twenty-First Century—Journey in the Shadows* (Routledge, 2004); W. K. Wark (ed.), *Twenty-First Century Intelligence* (Routledge, 2005); C. Andrew, R. J. Aldrich, and W. K. Wark (eds.), *Secret Intelligence—A Reader* (Routledge, 2009); L. K. Johnson (ed.), *The Oxford Handbook of National Security Intelligence* (Oxford University Press, 2010); P. Gill and M. Phythian, *Intelligence in an Insecure World* (Polity Press, 2012); R. Dover, M. S. Goodman, and C. Hillebrand (eds.), *Routledge Companion to Intelligence Studies* (Routledge, 2014); I. Duyvesteyn et al. (eds.), *The Future of Intelligence—Challenges in the 21st century* (Routledge, 2015).

[13] For example, and in addition to the works cited in n. 11, T. Weiner, *Legacy of Ashes: The History of the CIA* (Penguin Books, 2007); Weiner, *Enemies*; O. Kalugin, *Spymaster* (Smith Gryphon Ltd, 1994).

[14] The best recent normative account of the relationship between the morality and the law of war is Adil Ahmad Haque's. The best recent institutional account of just war theory is Allen Buchanan's. See Haque, *Law and Morality at War*; A. Buchanan, *Institutionalizing the Just War* (Oxford University Press, 2017).

evil; (b) the contractarian approach, which defends those practices by appeal to norms to which the relevant parties consent, or would consent under certain circumstances; (c) the just war theory approach, which applies just-war principles to espionage and counter-intelligence. I argue that none of these approaches are fully satisfactory, although they provide building blocks for my own. Second, I set out the book's normative foundations, by providing an account of the fundamental rights the defence of which justifies espionage and counter-intelligence, and an account of the conditions under which harming in defence of rights is generally justified.

If espionage consists in appropriating the intelligence we need from actors who, as far as we can tell, do not want us to have it, counter-intelligence consists in defending the intelligence that we have from actors who, as far as we can tell, would very much like to get it. Accordingly, I begin my defence, in Chapter 2, with an account of political secrets. Most political communities prohibit the disclosure and appropriation of certain kinds of information, and impose on those who breach the relevant laws criminal sanctions ranging from prison sentences to the death penalty. The underlying thought is that there is a particular kind of information, relating to national security and political agency, which a political community is warranted in not making available to non-members (or, as I shall sometimes call them, outsiders.) A normative inquiry into the ethics of espionage and counter-intelligence must ask, as a first step, whether political actors have a right that such information remain and be treated as secret. On the face of it, the claim that they do seems straightforward. As we shall see, however, it raises a number of difficulties to which we shall have to remain attentive throughout the book.

In Chapter 3, I make a first pass at defending espionage. I argue that espionage is justified—in fact, mandatory—as a means, but only as a means, to thwart violations of fundamental rights in the context of foreign policy writ large. Those claims apply to the practice of spying on both friends and foes.

In Chapter 4, I bring to bear my defence of secrecy and espionage on the acquisition of secret intelligence from private economic actors—in other words, economic espionage. I argue that citizens have a right to secrecy in respect of economic information as pertains to their community's privatized critical infrastructure. However, the same considerations which support and restrict espionage to morally justified military, security, and political ends also support and restrict it to morally justified economic ends.

In the remainder of the book, I examine the means by which intelligence activities are carried out. I spend more time on the ethics of so-called human intelligence (HUMINT) than on the ethics of the technological means used by intelligence agencies (TECHINT). Even though the use of non-human sources has grown exponentially in the last two decades, intelligence agencies have been routinely criticized in the last twenty years for their excessive reliance on technology, not least because information provided by satellite images or cyber-means often needs to be contextualized by and triangulated with that emanating from human sources. Revealingly, the website for Britain's Secret Intelligence Service (aka MI6) has a fascinating explanation of what intelligence consists of, which places the human factor at the heart of its operations.[15]

And so we begin, in Chapter 5, with deceptive tactics. *Pace* Kant, who reviled espionage because it necessarily (on his view) involves deception, I argue that intelligence agencies and their operatives are sometimes justified, and in fact morally obliged, to resort to a whole range of deceptive means, including outright lying, as a means to acquire secret information about other political communities and to protect their own secrets. I focus on cases in which the individual agents who participate in the relevant deception operations act at the behest of their own political community.

In Chapter 6, by contrast, I turn to another form of deception—one which elicits even greater condemnation—to wit, the deception carried out by traitors. More often than not, intelligence services recruit from within the enemy. After providing a conceptual account of treason, I argue that treason is sometimes permissible, indeed mandatory—not merely between enemies but also (sometimes) between declared allies.

Chapter 7 completes my inquiry into the ethics of HUMINT. It scrutinizes the means by which intelligence agencies recruit their assets, sources, and informants. It begins by considering the latter's motives. Those motives range widely; they include greed, bitterness, susceptibility to flattery, the need to belong, and ideological commitments. I express considerable scepticism towards the view that spying out of ideological commitments is morally better than spying out of negatively valenced psychological dispositions. I then review three concerns about the recruitment and handling of human sources, namely that they are manipulative, exploitative, and coercive. I outline cases in which those concerns are warranted and cases in which they are not.

The last two chapters turn to the technical side of espionage and counter-intelligence. In Chapter 8, I consider the use of cameras, bugging devices, and computers. I investigate whether there are salient moral differences between on the one hand, resorting to human sources and on the other hand, intercepting signals and conducting remote observation and detection. I bring out the issues at stake by rehearsing some historical examples. I then offer a contrastive moral assessment of HUMINT and TECHINT, and consider whether cyber-intelligence, namely the use of computers to target other computers, raises distinct moral issues. I argue that it does not.

In Chapter 9, I tackle the ethics of mass surveillance in contemporary societies as a means to unearth who, amongst our own and foreign populations, might pose

---

[15] See https://www.sis.gov.uk (accessed on 17/08/2021).

a threat. I provide a brief overview of practices of mass surveillance as described by Edward Snowden and mount what I take to be the best possible case in their favour. I consider and offer a partial rejection of the claim that mass surveillance constitutes an unacceptable violation of the right to privacy. I then consider and partly endorse the claim that mass surveillance practices entrench existing unfair inequalities.

Those chapters address a wide range of issues. The Epilogue brings these together into a brief summary and outlines areas for further inquiry.

1
Building Blocks

1.1 Introduction

This chapter sets the stage for the remainder of the book. Section 1.2 provides an overview of the ethics of spying in classical moral and political thought. Section 1.3 examines three possible approaches to espionage: (a) the dirty-hands approach, which sees espionage as a necessary evil; (b) the contractarian view that espionage is best defended by appeal to normative conventions to which all agree; and (c) the view that the most fruitful way to construct an ethics of espionage is through the lenses of just war theory. None of those approaches are fully satisfactory, though they provide building blocks for my own. Section 1.4 sets out the normative principles on which the book rests.

1.2 'Spiders' Webs': Classical Moral and Political Thought

Espionage goes hand in hand with government, and its practices and processes have thus often tracked governance practices and processes. Roughly put, in Europe, the bureaucratization of espionage gathered pace in the sixteenth to the nineteenth centuries with the development of the modern state. Contrastingly, medieval rulers tended to rely on loose networks of ambassadors, messengers, pilgrims, clerics, and merchants. There are parallels in the Ancient World.[1]

---

[1] On debates about espionage in medieval Europe, see, e.g., J. R. Alban and C. T. Allmand, 'Spies and Spying in the Fourteenth Century', in C. T. Allmand (ed.), *War, Literature, and Politics in the Late Middle Ages* (Liverpool University Press, 1976). For a panoramic account of intelligence activities in early modern Europe, see D. Navarro Bonilla, "Secret Intelligences' in European Military, Political and Diplomatic Theory: An Essential Factor in the Defense of the Modern State (Sixteenth and Seventeenth Centuries)', *Intelligence and National Security* 27 (2012): 283–301. The Republic of Venice provides a fascinating example of a complex and increasingly bureaucratic approach to espionage, alongside reliance of informal networks of political and economic patronage. On this particular case, see I. Iordanou, *Venice's Secret Service—Organizing Intelligence in the Renaissance* (Oxford University Press, 2019). On the eighteenth century, see G. Rothenberg, 'Military Intelligence Gathering in the Second Half of the Eighteenth Century—1740–1792', in K. Neilson and B. J. C. McKercher (eds.), *Go Spy the Land—Military Intelligence in History* (Praeger, 1992). On espionage in the ancient Near East, particularly Carthage, see, e.g., R. Sheldon, 'Hannibal's Spies', *International Journal of Intelligence and CounterIntelligence* 1 (1986): 53–70. On intelligence in Ancient Rome, see R. Sheldon, *Intelligence Activities in Ancient Rome—Trust in the Gods, but Verify* (Routledge, 2005) and A. Ferrill, 'Roman Military Intelligence', in Neilson and McKercher (eds.), *Go Spy the Land—Military Intelligence in History* (Praeger, 1992).

It would be foolish to try and trace within the confines of a short section the rich history of espionage. Instead, I offer a brief overview of some of the main issues which those who have written on espionage in moral and political thought have raised. There is not that much material to go on. Vitoria, Gentili, Grotius, and Vattel are rightly regarded as founding fathers of modern theoretical thinking on war. Yet Vitoria's major work on war is silent on the use of spies. Gentili briefly states that it is appropriate to deny spies the privileges of combatancy and to punish them harshly, but that it is also entirely right to use them. Grotius merely notes that sending spies into enemy territory for a just cause is just at the bar of the law of nations and permitted by the law of war; at the same time, it is appropriate to refuse entrance to, or to expel, ambassadors who are suspected of spying. Vattel, for his part, argues that the sovereign is not constrained by the laws of war and the laws of nations not to use spies, though he may not demand of his subjects that they should so serve him.[2]

When the classics mention espionage, they express considerable moral ambivalence—and this across times, places, and intellectual and moral traditions, be it in sixth-century China, the Ancient Mediterranean world, the Western Middle Ages, Japanese military thinking in the seventeenth century, or nineteenth-century European thought.[3] Spying is sometimes referred to as one of the world's three oldest professions, alongside prostitution and mercenarism. Interestingly, all three have in common that they are often regarded as a necessary evil: prostitutes give their clients what they need and cannot get elsewhere; mercenaries enable rulers to fight wars when they cannot find willing soldiers; spies provide rulers with the information they need about their opponents at home and rivals abroad. Let us not delude ourselves that we will never need prostitutes, mercenaries, and spies—or so the argument goes; but let us not delude ourselves either that theirs is a noble calling. On the contrary: it is shameful, repugnant even, because it consists in selling what ought to be given for free, or in acting from ignoble motives, or in lying and deceiving—or all of those. The Bible itself evinces doubts about spying. In the Book of Numbers, as we saw in the Introduction, the founders of the twelve

---

[2] F. Vitoria, 'On the Law of War,' in A. Pagden and J. Lawrance (eds.), *Political Writings* (Cambridge University Press, 1991 [1539]); A. Gentili, *De Jure Belli Libri Tres*, ed. J. Rolfe (Clarendon Press, 1933 [1588–9]), Bk II, ch. 9; H. Grotius, *The Rights of War and Peace*, ed. R. Tuck (Liberty Fund, 2005 [1625]), Bk III, ch. IV, § XVIII-3. On Grotius' account, the case of ambassadors who are suspected of spying against the sovereign to whom they are accredited is more complex: there are grounds for expelling them but only if they confess or if their own sovereign admits that they are spies. (See *The Rights of War and Peace*, Bk II, ch. XVIII, § III-2. On this issue, see also A. Gentili, *De Legationibus Libri Tres* (Oxford University Press, 1924 [1585]), Bk II, ch. 4.) For Vattel's view, see E. De Vattel, *Le droit des gens—Principes de la loi naturelle appliquée à la conduite et aux affairs des nations et des souverains* (Carnegie Institute, 1916 [1758]), Bk III, ch. X, § 179–80.

[3] For an accessible panoramic account, see S. Musco, 'Intelligence Gathering and the Relationship Between Rulers and Spies: Some Lessons from Eminent and Lesser-known Classics,' *Intelligence and National Security* 31 (2016): 1025–39.

tribes of Israel are explicitly and matter-of-factly mandated by Moses to spy on the land of Canaan and its inhabitants, so as to ascertain whether an attempt at conquest might succeed. In the Book of Joshua (at 2 and 6: 17, 22–5), Joshua sends two of his men to spy on the city of Jericho. The King of Jericho is warned of the strangers' arrival and sends his soldiers after them. They find shelter in the house of a prostitute, Rahab. When Joshua breaches the walls of Jericho and sacks the city, he spares her life and that of her kin, in return for her kindness to his spies. There is no suggestion in the text that Joshua should not have spied on Jericho nor, interestingly, that Rahab should not have helped his men against her community.[4] Yet, in Genesis (at 42: 9–11), when Joseph, governor of Egypt, accuses his brothers, who do not recognize him, of spying on him and his land, they reply: 'Nay, my lord, but to buy food are thy servants come. We are all one man's sons; we are true men, thy servants are no spies.'

Notwithstanding those doubts, the thought that rulers have no choice but to use spies is not under dispute. It is couched in two different ways. On one view, loosely drawn from Machiavelli's works, rulers have prudential reasons for using spies. In so far as a ruler depends for this greatness on his ability to win wars and as his ability to win wars depends on the quality of the information he has about the enemy, it is in his interest to employ spies.[5]

On another view, as articulated by the military strategist and general Sun Tzu in the sixth century BC, the ruler who does not resort to espionage commits a moral wrong. Sun Tzu's classic treatise *The Art of War* ends with a ringing endorsement of spies who, we are told, 'are a most important element in war, because on them depends an army's ability to move'. Sun Tzu's defence is unambiguously moral. War is so costly to the sovereign's soldiers and subjects, particularly his poorest subjects, that he is under an obligation to try and shorten it by acquiring knowledge of the enemy's intentions and dispositions. Given that the only way to acquire such knowledge is by using spies, a sovereign who refuses to use spies, notably on the grounds that they are too expensive to maintain, is 'completely devoid of humanity.'[6]

---

[4] The story of Rahab is fascinating. She is a prostitute and thus supposed to be of loose morals. She deals with the King's pursuers with guile: she admits that they were at her house as there is no point, and in fact greater danger, in denying it; but she claims that she has no idea who they were, and sends the pursuers on a false trail. She is described (in the King James translation) as kind to the spies: she is after all risking her life for them. Yet at the same time she pleads for her and her parents' lives, extracting from them a promise that they will intercede with Joshua on her behalf. For all she knows, though, they might be lying to her, and she might have risked her life for nought. Those few verses have all the ingredients of a classic life-and-death intelligence dilemma.

[5] In *The Art of War*, Machiavelli refers to spies by name once, to admonish the ruler to guard himself against them. Other maxims can be interpreted as tacitly endorsing the resort to espionage. (See N. Machiavelli, *The Art of War*, ed. C. Lynch (Chicago University Press, 2003 [1521]), 157–8.) My point in the main text is a reconstruction of what he would in all likelihood have said on the issue if pressed to do so explicitly.

[6] S. Tzu, *The Art of War*, ed. S. B. Griffith (Oxford University Press, 1963 [sixth century BC]), ch. 13, §§ 27 and 2 respectively.

Compare with Hobbes' wonderfully evocative view in *De Cive*:

The first requirement therefore of a commonwealth's defence is that there be someone to collect *intelligence* and so far as possible *forecast* the plans and movements of all those who have the capacity to do it harm. Reliable *intelligence agents* are to those who exercise sovereign power as rays of light to the human soul. . . . Hence they are as necessary to the safety of a commonwealth as rays of light to the safety of a man. Or we may use the analogy of spiders' webs, whose incredibly fine threads spread out in all directions and convey outside movements to the spiders sitting in their little cavities inside. Without *intelligence agents* sovereigns have no more idea what orders need to be given for the defence of their subjects than spiders can know when to emerge and where to make for without the threads of their webs.

The metaphor of the spider's web whose threads tie the ruler to his spies is not uncommon: one also finds it in Sun Tzu. On Hobbes' view, moreover,

[since] princes are obliged by the law of nature to make every effort to secure the citizens' safety; it follows not only that they are permitted to send out spies, maintain troops, build fortifications and to exact money for the purpose, but also that they may not do otherwise.[7]

The laws of nature compel the sovereign, to whom we have entrusted the task of protecting us from threats to our security, to deploy spies, both internally (lest some people be tempted to sow the seeds of discord within the realm) and externally (lest foreign princes be tempted to attack us.) A sovereign who fails to use spies might not be 'completely devoid of humanity'; but she is in breach of her obligations at the bar of the laws of nature.

Interestingly, there is no suggestion in Sun Tzu's and Hobbes' writings, and more widely in the classics, that the moral status of the ends to which spies are deployed makes any difference to the permissibility and obligatoriness of espionage. Any ruler, irrespective of her ends, must endeavour to protect her subjects and must thus employ spies. No less interestingly, the sovereign's moral obligation is one which she owes to her subjects or fellow citizens, not to the enemy's. That being said, for all that the ruler depends on spies, she must remain aware that the information which they give her might not be reliable and that, even if it is reliable, it will often admit of different interpretations and suggest radically opposed courses of action. One of the most trenchant critiques of intelligence

---

[7] T. Hobbes, *On the Citizen*, ed. R. Tuck and M. Silverstone (Cambridge University Press, 1998 [1642]), ch. XIII, §§ 7 and 8 respectively. For a discussion of Hobbes' view, see Erskine, ' "As Rays of Light to the Human Soul"? Moral Agents and Intelligence Gathering'.

along those lines comes from Clausewitz, who warns that intelligence obtained in war is uncertain, changeable, and contradictory.[8]

My reconstruction of those arguments in favour of the acquisition of intelligence about the enemy straightforwardly applies to counter-intelligence operations. In just the same way as the ruler must employ spies, she must protect herself from her enemies' spies, on two counts: prudentially put, her greatness depends on her enemies' inability to conquer her and thus to procure the information it needs; non-prudentially put, in so far as she owes it to her subjects or is commanded by the laws of nature to minimize their suffering, and in so far as minimizing their suffering requires defeating the enemy, she owes it to them or is commanded by the laws of nature to thwart the latter's espionage efforts.

Rulers must avail themselves of spies, yet spies themselves are not immune from moral opprobrium—on the contrary. As Joseph's brothers insist, true men—men who do not deceive and who are faithful to their kin—do not spy on others. In the Lieber Code, a spy is defined as 'a person who secretly, in disguise or under false pretense, seeks information with the intention of communicating it to the enemy' (art. 88). A ruler's messenger or ambassador, a cleric, a pilgrim, a merchant, indeed a journalist, can be labelled a spy so long as he attempts to deceive his targets as a means to procure such information.

As I make clear in the Introduction, I do not define espionage as an inherently deceitful practice. Nevertheless, there is a close connection between spying and deception: rulers would not need to spy on their enemy if the latter were openly declaring its intentions and advertising its strengths and weaknesses. Given that it is not willing to do so, one of the best ways to get that information is by subterfuge. Hence the ambivalence about spies which we find in medieval commentators who conceive of war as a chivalric contest between moral equals. Hence, too, Montesquieu's unambiguous statement that spies have no place in a constitutional monarchy, and Kant's objections to spying on the grounds that it is deceitful. By Kant's lights, the deception inherent in espionage makes it especially wrongful in wartime. It undermines trust between belligerents and increases the risk that belligerents will fight wars of mutual annihilation, thereby jeopardizing prospects for peace. It inevitably leads to peacetime espionage, which vitiates trust between peacemakers and thereby destroys whatever peace has been painstakingly achieved.[9] Moreover, some forms of subterfuge are morally worse than others. Sun Tzu distinguishes between five categories of spies: (a) 'native spies', namely

---

[8] C. von Clausewitz, *On War*, ed. M. Howard and P. Paret (International Finance Section, Dept. of Economics, Princeton University, 1984 [1832]), 117–18.

[9] Montesquieu, *The Spirit of the Laws*, ed. A. M. Cohler (Cambridge University Press, 1989 [1748]), II–II–12; Kant, 'Perpetual Peace: A Philosophical Sketch', § 6; Kant, 'Metaphysics of Morals', §§ 57–58.

local populations; (b) 'inside spies', namely officials from the enemy; (c) 'doubled spies', namely spies in the employ of the enemy whom one manages to turn; (d) 'expendable spies', namely spies whom one denounces to the enemy without their knowledge, with the aim of having them feed false information to the enemy upon being arrested; (e) 'living spies', namely our own spies whom we send into enemy territory and who come back with information.[10] Three out of five kinds of spies belong to the enemy: there is an intimate connection between espionage and treason.

That said, the tradition is not uniformly condemning of the deception involved in espionage. For example, Gentili approves both of the deceptive use of the enemy's own agents against him and of Rahab's lies. Vattel holds that the sovereign may recruit his spies from the enemy itself, thus inducing them to commit treason; he may also use double agents. In so doing, he is encouraging the commission of 'abominable crimes', and it would be preferable not to resort to such means. But in so far as he is endangering neither prospects for peace nor the state's security, he may so act.[11]

Spies, whether traitors or not, are punished harshly. Indeed, as the Lieber Code tersely states in article 88, 'the spy is punishable with death by hanging by the neck, whether or not he succeeds in obtaining the information or in conveying it to the enemy.' Spies know this all too well, of course. How, then, might the ruler recruit and retain them? Sun Tzu again: by treating them well, with liberality and generosity. Outright coercion is generally not favoured: flattery, material inducements and appeals to the justness of the cause, are.[12]

To the extent that classical thinkers discuss espionage, they are more preoccupied with what we would now regard as human sources, or human intelligence, than with what we might call, somewhat loosely, the technology of spying such as opening letters and decoding ciphers; nor do they spend much time, if at all, pondering the ethical issues raised by rulers' systematic surveillance of their own subjects. To some extent, this might reflect the relatively rudimentary tools of which rulers could avail themselves, and those writers' (and their era's) relative lack of concern for what we nowadays describe and value as the private sphere. Yet, as we shall see, some of their prescriptions do not depend for their strength on the means – technology or humans – by which secrets are acquired and protected; and many of their concerns, for example to the effect that espionage breeds distrust, are equally if not more salient in the age of computers.

---

[10] Sun Tzu, *The Art of War*, §§ 22–5.
[11] Gentili, *De Jure Belli Libri Tres*, Bk II, ch. 5, esp. § 240 and § 248; De Vattel, *Le Droit des Gens*, Bk III, ch. 10, §§ 180–2.
[12] Sun Tzu, *The Art of War*, §§ 14–16. See also Musco, 'Intelligence Gathering and the Relationship between Rulers and Spies,' 1034–5.

1.3 Three Contemporary Approaches to Espionage

The contemporary philosophical literature on espionage is not that much more developed than classical moral and political thought. In this section, I review three approaches. The first is not one which philosophers of espionage have explicitly taken, though it melds the well-developed dirty-hands literature with some of the moral concerns about espionage which we find in classical moral and political philosophy. Hence its inclusion here. The other two approaches—the contractarian approach and the just war theory approach—dominate the field.

1.3.1 Dirty Hands

Intelligence officers deceive, bribe, and/or manipulate their targets as a means to get the information they want. They exploit their vices and vulnerabilities. They encourage them to deceive their colleagues, friends, spouses, and children, indeed to commit treason. They are ordered by their masters to do all of this—and are paid for it. No wonder espionage, for all its glamorous, James-Bondish, trappings, has a bad name. No wonder it feels dirty.

It is tempting, thus, to construe espionage and counter-intelligence as paradigmatic illustrations of the so-called dirty-hands problem. In his seminal article on the problem, Michael Walzer invites us to consider the case of the newly elected president of a country in the grip of a colonial war, who has campaigned and won on a committed anti-war and anti-torture platform. The president is told that the rebels have hidden a number of bombs throughout the capital city. The rebels' leader, who knows where the bombs are, has been captured. The president orders the country's security services to have him tortured.[13]

The case exhibits all three elements of a classic dirty-hands scenario: (a) an official is presented, *qua* official, (b) with a choice between two courses of action, both of which are morally unpalatable; (c) he chooses torture, thereby dirtying his hands, on the grounds that breaching the moral prohibition on torture is not as bad as allowing hundreds of people to die.

On the dirty-hands view of espionage, intelligence officers dirty their hands to the extent that, (a) *qua* officials, they must (b) choose between on the one hand not lying, betraying, blackmailing, etc., at the cost of being left in the dark, and on the other hand committing those acts as a means to procure and protect sensitive information; and that (c) they choose to do the latter.

---

[13] M. Walzer, 'Political Action: The Problem of Dirty Hands,' *Philosophy & Public Affairs* 2 (1973): 160–80, 166–7. For a very good summary of the debate, see C. A. J. Coady, 'The Problem of Dirty Hands,' in E. N. Zalta (ed.), *Stanford Encyclopedia of Philosophy* (Fall 2018).

A dirty-hands case is not the same as a moral dilemma, which presents agents with a situation in which, no matter what they do, they can never be deemed to have done the right thing. The spy dirties his hands and so by implication acts wrongly along one dimension, but may nevertheless act rightly *all-things-considered*. Moreover, a dirty-hands case is not the same as a moral conflict, which presents agents with a choice between two incompatible options. Having to choose saving one patient rather than another, when there is a medicine shortage, is a moral conflict; but the doctor does not dirty her hands by choosing as she does. The spy, by contrast, does, in that he must do wrong *in order* to do right or *in order* that right should prevail.[14]

On some views, the very notion of a dirty-hands case is incoherent. Either one may never do wrong, along any dimension, in which case the president ought not to order the act of torture notwithstanding the resulting loss of lives; or one must always choose the morally optimal course of action (which saving hundreds of lives surely is), in which case the president cannot be deemed to act wrongly by ordering the torture.[15]

Neither view strikes me as plausible. Without wanting to re-tread familiar territory, *not* acting, and thereby allowing evil to occur, is not a particularly clean way to lead one's life: there are serious moral costs to agential abstinence. At the same time, the claim that one is morally justified in φ-ing is compatible with the claim that one *is* breaching a moral prohibition against φ-ing.[16]

If so, the dirty-hands problem is relevant to espionage and counter-intelligence activities. Many of the things which intelligence officers do are presumptively wrongful, and the burden of proof thus lies on the shoulders of those who wish to show that agents are justified in so acting. But as we shall also see in s. 1.4.2, the presumption of wrongfulness can be lifted or overridden. To anticipate briefly: it is lifted when the individuals who are deceived, betrayed, blackmailed, or manipulated into providing secret information have acted or failed to act in ways such that they are liable to be so treated. If they are liable, their right against such treatment is not infringed. The presumption is overridden when the ends pursued

---

[14] See, e.g., Michael Stocker and Stephen de Wijze. See M. Stocker, 'Dirty Hands and Ordinary Life,' in P. Rynard and D. P. Shugarman (eds.), *Cruelty and Deception* (Broadview Press, 2000); S. de Wijze, 'Dirty Hands: Doing Wrong to do Right,' in I. Primoratz (ed.), *Politics and Morality* (Palgrave Macmillan, 2006).

[15] The contrast between those two views is sometimes presented as a dispute between, roughly put, Kantian and Machiavellian ethics. This is not entirely apt: there is a non-Kantian way of defending the first view, which appeals to the divine law, and there is a non-Machiavellian way of defending the second view, which appeals to Ross' notion of *prima facie* duties. See, respectively, G. E. M. Anscombe, 'Modern Moral Philosophy,' *Philosophy* 33 (1958): 1–19; K. Nielsen, 'There is No Dilemma of Dirty Hands,' in I. Primoratz (ed.), *Politics and Morality* (Palgrave Macmillan, 2006).

[16] On being justified in φ-ing yet also breaching a duty not to φ, see B. A. O. Williams, 'Politics and Moral Character,' in S. Hampshire (ed.), *Public and Private Morality* (Cambridge University Press, 1978). In the specific context of dirty hands, see M. Hollis, 'Dirty Hands,' *British Journal of Political Science* 12 (1982): 385–98; A. P. Cunningham, 'The Moral Importance of Dirty Hands,' *Journal of Value Inquiry* 26 (1992): 239–50; Stocker, 'Dirty Hands and Ordinary Life'; Wijze, 'Dirty Hands'.

by intelligence officers are sufficiently weighty to provide them with a justification for so treating those individuals even though the latter are not liable to such treatment. In the former case, there is no moral remainder and intelligence officers do not dirty their hands; in the latter case, there is a remainder, and they do dirty their hands. We shall revisit this point at various junctures throughout the book.

1.3.2 Contractarianism

Another way to frame an ethics of espionage appeals to contractarian political morality. Roughly put, social-contract theories divide into those who rely on the Hobbesian premise that individuals are self-interested maximizers, those who rely on the Lockean premise that individuals are one another's moral equals and ought to treat one another as such, and those who pin their colours to the mast of Rawlsian morality. All three theories locate the source of political authority in consent. On the Hobbesian view, the consent at issue is that of individuals who realize that it is in their interest to entrust the sovereign with the task of protecting them from internal and external threats. On the Lockean view, the consent at issue is that of individuals who realize that the only way to ensure that all are treated equally is to have each consent to the sovereign's authority. On the Rawlsian view, the consent at issue is the hypothetical consent of citizens who are rational, are under moral duties to respect and protect one another's and foreigners' fundamental interests, and are motivated to fulfil those duties.

All three interpretations of contractarianism have been pressed into the service of just war theory and yield conclusions with respect to wartime and peacetime espionage. Thus, some proponents of prudential contractarianism have argued that the laws of war are underpinned by norms (standardly, the *jus gentium*) which are essentially conventional in nature. So construed, those norms are the product of a shared understanding between political communities of rational and moral agents who understand that, absent an overarching sovereign such as the state, it is realistic to assume that some of them will go to war, and that it is in their own and mutual interest to minimize bloodshed and preserve prospects for peace.[17] Hence the following contractarian account of espionage. On the one hand, self-interested maximizers realize that some of them will engage in espionage and that it is in their own and mutual interest to constrain this practice in such a way that it does not destroy all prospects for peaceful international relations. On the other hand, spies themselves have over time developed shared understandings of what count

---

[17] For prominent contemporary defences of this view as applied to war, see G. I. Mavrodes, 'Conventions and the Morality of War,' *Philosophy & Public Affairs* 4 (1975): 117–31; Y. Benbaji and D. Statman, *War by Agreement* (Oxford University Press, 2019). For its application to spying, see Simpson, 'The Morality of Unconventional Force'.

as acceptable modes of behaviour: planting a mole, yes; coercing a possible asset into becoming a heroin addict and exploiting his addiction to get him to betray his country, no. Espionage, on that view, is a game, a craft, whose rules are well understood by its players and mark it off from other human activities.[18]

Some proponents of egalitarian contractarianism, for their part, have recently defended espionage as follows. Individuals who treat one another as moral equals recognize that in just the same way as their consent is a necessary condition for laws and policies to be legitimate, so is the consent of others. Moreover, the point is universalizable to all other human beings, irrespective of borders. Within borders, individuals consent to the state doing to them what is necessary to protect their freedom and security. By the principle of universalization, they must accept that everyone else in the world consents to exactly the same provisions, and that other states might do to them what their own state does to others. Espionage is one way in which states help protect their citizens, in both peacetime and wartime. By consenting to enter into a political contract under the authority of the state, individuals consent to being spied upon by their own state, and to have their state spy upon the civilian populations of enemy states, if and when necessary for peace; by the same token, they also consent to being spied upon by other states. There are limits, however, to that to which they consent. In particular, they do not (or at any rate cannot be expected to) consent to espionage that is not necessary for the protection of their liberties.[19]

The Rawlsian approach draws on egalitarian contractarianism, though it differs from it in some important ways. Individuals are rational and moral agents. As rational agents, they have an interest in the protection of their fundamental rights. As moral agents, they owe it to one another to protect the fundamental rights of both their compatriots and foreign citizens, and are motivated to fulfil that duty. They do so by setting up institutions such as a health-care system, an education system, a justice system, armed forces, and, relevantly, intelligence agencies. By dint of their duty to protect one another's rights, they are under a duty to support those (just) institutions at home and abroad. The professionals who work in those institutions are under a moral obligation to abide by norms of conduct which are designed to ensure that everyone's rights are respected and protected. Not only are those professional norms thus grounded in fundamental rights; they are also shaped by what citizens, on whose behalf those professionals act and who might themselves be the target of their activities, *would* consent to, given that they want both to protect their own interests and to fulfil their moral duty of protection.

---

[18] The view I describe here is closely related to some interpretations of the law of espionage. See, e.g., A. Lubin, 'The Liberty to Spy', *Harvard International Law Journal* 61 (2020): 185–243. As Lubin observes, the dominant view amongst legal scholars is that there is no such thing as a law of espionage.

[19] See Pfaff and Tiel, 'The Ethics of Espionage'. They explicitly ground their arguments in Lockean contractarianism. See also T. Pfaff, 'Bungee Jumping off the Moral High Ground: Ethics of Espionage in the Modern Age', in J. Goldman (ed.), *Ethics of Spying: A Reader for the Intelligence Professional*, vol. 1 (Scarecrow Press, 2005); Bellaby, *The Ethics of Intelligence*, 37.

To illustrate, suppose that a given mode of intelligence collection would enable agencies to identify potential terrorists with a relatively high degree of success but would also be very intrusive on ordinary citizens' privacy. Suppose further that those citizens would not consent to being subjected to this tactic, precisely on those grounds. Not only must intelligence agencies rule out its use against their fellow citizens; the latter, by virtue of the norm of reciprocity, cannot reasonably endorse its use against foreigners. Conversely, suppose that this tactic imposes only minor costs on those citizens, such that they would consent to being subjected to it for the sake of catching terrorists. By virtue of the norm of reciprocity combined with their duty to support the fundamental rights of foreign citizens as well as the just institutions which the latter set up, they are under a duty to tolerate the use of such a tactic by foreign intelligence agencies against them. On this view, the fact that citizens would or would not consent to a particular mode of intelligence collection enables us to ascertain what is morally justified conduct.[20]

There are well-known difficulties with all three variants of contractarianism. First, in response to prudential contractarianism, it does not follow from the fact that a practice is mutually beneficial to those who subscribe to it that it is morally right. It matters whether parties in the practice stand on a footing of relative equality or are locked in an asymmetrical or exploitative relationship. For example, consider current norms of espionage, which license the wholesale collection of geosatellite intelligence by the military in wartime, and prohibit intelligence agents from blackmailing or bribing enemy civilians into betraying their country. It may be that citizens of countries with sophisticated surveillance technologies and citizens of technology-poor countries benefit from the current convention, relative to a baseline of wholesale prohibition on both forms of intelligence-gathering. But the technologically poor would most likely do better than under the current convention either if blackmail were conventionally permitted alongside wholesale collection of geosatellite intelligence, or if the former were still forbidden but the technologically strong were subject to more stringent constraints on the use of technologies. Moreover, the technology-weak are also weak in other respects (economically, financially, etc.), often as a result of considerable injustice over time at the hands of the technologically strong. If a consequence of their overall weakness is that they are not in a position to get the technologically strong to agree to a set of espionage rules which are more to their advantage than extant conventions, we are licensed to suspect that those conventions are morally problematic.

Second, the fact that political communities have developed shared understandings of what count as acceptable and unacceptable espionage practices does little

---

[20] The main proponent of this approach, as I summarize it here, is Michael Skerker. See M. Skerker, 'Moral Concerns with Cyberespionage', in F. Allhoff, A. Henschke, and B. J. Strawser (eds.), *Binary Bullets* (Oxford University Press, 2016); M. Skerker, 'The Rights of Foreign Intelligence Targets', in S. Miller, M. Regan, and P. Walsh (eds.), *National Security Intelligence and Ethics* (Routledge, 2021).

to show that those practices are, in fact, morally acceptable. Construing espionage as a game, as it sometimes is and as much spy fiction does, obscures the fact that those supposedly shared understandings are contested within and outside those communities. For example, the practice of using honeytraps to blackmail enemy agents into betraying their country might be regarded as wholly acceptable by one intelligence service yet condemned by another. We cannot evaluate whether those criticisms are plausible other than by appealing to nonconventional moral principles.[21]

Third, in response to egalitarian contractarianism, even if there is a sense in which we do, or indeed should, consent to the authority of the state, and even if our consent endows its decisions with legitimacy, it does not follow that we do, would, or should consent to whatever the state—or, rather, our leaders—decide to do for the sake of our security. I suspect that proponents of egalitarian contractarianism would agree and would, for example, reject interrogational torture precisely because it violates the principle of fundamental equality. As soon as they make this concession, however, contractarians give the game away. For if one can rule out certain practices as impermissible on the grounds that they violate the principle of fundamental equality, one can evaluate all relevant practices at the bar of that principle, irrespective of the fact that individuals do, would, or should consent to it.

Fourth, both variants of contractarianism consider and justify the practice of espionage in isolation from the moral status of the policy which it is supposed to serve. It matters not, from their point of view, whether the information so gathered is used in the service of a just foreign policy or, on the contrary, to work out the most effective ways of killing thousands of innocent civilians in war, of imposing the most devastating and unjustified sanctions, or of gaining an unfair advantage in trade negotiations. That too is something which the game analogy obscures. As we shall see in Chapters 3 and 4, however, it really does, and should, matter.

Fifth, the Rawlsian approach is not vulnerable to some of the objections deployed against standard contractarianism. In particular, it constrains what the technologically powerful can do to the technologically weak. Suppose that while our agencies can use sophisticated and targeted modes of intelligence collection, our enemy has only very crude and very invasive means at its disposal—so invasive that we would not consent to their use. If our agencies know that our enemy will resort to those means in retaliation for our own intelligence efforts, they ought to refrain. More generally, the Rawlsian approach draws no fundamental distinction between citizens' obligations to one another and their obligations to foreigners.[22]

---

[21] For a similar point as applied to the war convention, see, e.g., L. K. McPherson, 'The Limits of the War Convention', *Philosophy & Social Criticism* 31 (2005): 147–63.

[22] Skerker, 'The Rights of Foreign Intelligence Targets'.

However, it suffers from two problems. First, for all that it relegates consent to the role of a heuristic device, it still relies on speculating about what *would* be tolerable to a citizenry. This seems a poor guide to ascertaining what they may justifiably impose on foreign citizenries. Its proponents might be tempted to respond that the reason why we can speculate that citizens would find a particular tactic tolerable is, precisely, that it *is* tolerable. However, while this move might perhaps block the first objection, it would open the door to a second one, namely that appealing to consent is unecessary. What matters is what makes a tactic morally permissible or mandatory—period.[23]

1.3.3 Just War Theory

A third way of framing an ethics of espionage and counter-intelligence appeals to just war theory. This is not surprising, given the role which espionage activities play in war. In just the same way as just war theory teaches us to distinguish between *jus ad bellum*, *jus in bello*, and *jus post bellum*, it should teach us to distinguish between *jus ad explorationem* or, as some scholars would have it, *jus ad intelligentiam*, *jus in exploratione/in intelligentia*, and *jus post explorationem/post intelligentiam*. On this view, the constituent principles of each of those *jura* of war, such as just cause, last resort, proportionality, and discrimination are also constituent principles of the *jura* of espionage.[24]

Just war theory sets out when the resort to war is justified and what combatants may and must do once the war has started. However, just war theory is not as useful as we might think for understanding espionage and counter-intelligence. In wartime, those operations are one tool amongst the many used by belligerents and thus fall squarely within the remit of *jus in bello*, in the same way as the use of this or that type of weapons. In peacetime, they are one tool amongst the many used by foreign-policy actors in the pursuit of their goals. In that context, just war theory seems inapposite, since it is not meant to theorize the use of

---

[23] In his response to this objection, Skerker argues in defence of consent that which tactics and which sets of norms are best suited to protecting rights evolve over time and are contingent on the nature and level of threats which need countering. I take the point but I do not see why appealing to consent, as opposed to ascertaining how best to specify general moral principles by reference to the context in which they apply, does the job.

[24] For the use of just war theory as a framework to understand the morality of espionage, see, e.g., A. Gendron, 'Just War, Just Intelligence: An Ethical Framework for Foreign Espionage', *International Journal of Intelligence and Counter Intelligence* 18 (2005): 398–434; Omand, 'Ethical Guidelines in Using Secret Intelligence for Public Security'; Quinlan, 'Just intelligence'; W. C. J. Plouffe, 'Just War Theory as a Basis for Just Intelligence Theory: Necessary Evil or Sub–Rosa Colored Self–Deception', *International Journal of Intelligence Ethics* 2 (2011): 77–116; Bellaby, *The Ethics of Intelligence*; D. Perry, *Partly Cloudy—Ethics in War, Espionage, Covert Action, and Interrogation*, 2nd. (Rowman & Littlefield, 2016). Proponents of the application of just war theory to the field of espionage have not explored what a *jus post intelligentiam* might look like. Nor will I.

peacetime instruments of policy. What we need is a normative account of justified and unjustified foreign policy in general, of which an ethics of espionage is but one element.

Moreover, just war theory has a simplifying and thereby distorting impact on attempts to articulate and defend an ethics of espionage and counter-intelligence. It is too quick simply to say that, in just the same way as war must have a just cause, or be proportionate, so must espionage. By their very nature, those operations are for the most part pre-emptive: whether in wartime or in peacetime, their main aim is to collect intelligence in order to thwart threats *before* they materialize. In contrast, to wage war is for the most part to respond to ongoing attacks. Furthermore, and more importantly still, when we attempt to justify war, we attempt to justify killing. But to spy, and to protect one's secrets, is not to kill. If and to the extent that intelligence operations harm their targets, they do so in less obvious and more complex ways, to which a normative account of espionage must be sensitive.

We should resist the temptation of mechanistically applying the constitutive principles of just war theory to anything that resembles or is connected to war. Instead, we should develop and specify for whatever context at hand—here, intelligence activities—principles for the ongoing and preemptive imposition of defensive harm in general. Such is my aim here.[25]

1.4 Foundations

In this section, I lay the normative foundations on which those principles rest: an account of the rights and duties which all individuals wherever they reside have *vis-à-vis* one another; and an account of when individuals are justified in harming one another in defence of those rights. It is beyond the scope of this book to provide a thorough defence of either. I believe that they are relatively uncontroversial. My aim in the chapters that follow is to show what conclusions they yield for the morality of espionage and counter-intelligence.

[25] For a thoughtful discussion of similarities and differences between just war theory and what they call *jus ad intelligentiam* and *jus in intelligentia,* see Omand and Phythian, *Principled Spying,* ch. 3. Of those two authors, Phythian pays particular attention to the preventive nature of intelligence activities. See also Pfaff, 'Bungee Jumping off the Moral High Ground'. For an even more sceptical view of the usefulness of just war theory in the present context, see S. Miller, 'Rethinking the Just Intelligence Theory of National Security Intelligence Collection and Analysis: The Principles of Discrimination, Necessity, Proportionality and Reciprocity', *Social Epistemology* 35 (2021): 211–31.

1.4.1 Fundamental Rights

I take it for granted that all individuals, wherever they reside in the world, owe it to one another, wherever they reside in the world, to treat one another with equal concern and respect. This foundational principle—the principle of fundamental equality—implies that individuals have rights against one another to fair treatment, and not to be harassed, humiliated, objectified, and instrumentalized. It also implies that they have moral rights against one another to the freedoms and resources which they need in order to lead a flourishing life—as set out in the Universal Declaration of Human Rights of 1948 and subsequent international declarations and covenants. Drawing in part on (*inter alia*) Martha Nussbaum's influential approach, I assume that individuals flourish to the extent that they have and enjoy the following capabilities: bodily integrity, basic health, and average longevity; the ability to engage in a range of meaningful relationships; the ability to frame and revise a conception of the good life with which they identify; some degree of control over the material resources they need to achieve those ends and over their social and political environment. It also implies, finally, that individuals owe it to one another to protect one another from violations of their fundamental rights.[26]

Throughout the book I call those rights *fundamental rights*, rather than *human rights*, for there is no reason to suppose in principle that only human beings have those rights. I also assume that rights protect interests—though I do not defend that view here. Rights, moreover, include claims to the performance of the corresponding duties, permissions (or liberties) to exercise those rights, powers to change our moral relationship with those third parties, and immunities against third parties' attempts to change our moral relationships with them. Rights can be forfeited or overridden: they are *pro tanto* rights, not absolute rights—as are duties, powers, and permissions. This should be taken as a given throughout the book.[27]

The principle of fundamental equality and its aforementioned implications need elaboration. First, it is in the spirit if not always in the letter of international declarations and convenants to rule out as presumptively impermissible any conduct or act which offends against the dignity of the individual—including conducts and acts which are not tantamount to infringing freedoms or withholding resources.

Second, I adopt a non-experiential account of harm: that of which I am not aware and which I do not experience can harm me. I take it that a plausible account

---

[26] There are many iterations of the capabilities approach and its concomittant conception of human flourishing. See, in particular, M. C. Nussbaum, *Creating Capabilities—The Human Development Approach* (Harvard University Press, 2011).

[27] The *locus classicus* for the claim that rights comprise claims, powers, immunities, and permissions is W. N. Hohfeld, *Fundamental Conceptions as Applied in Judicial Reasoning* (Yale University Press, 1919). For a classic defence of the interest theory, see J. Raz, *The Morality of Freedom* (Clarendon Press, 1986), ch. 7.

of what we may and may not do to one another must yield the conclusion that to kill someone instantaneously without his being aware of it is to harm him. To reject non-experiential accounts is to leave oneself unable to account for that claim. Some might object that one can account for the wrongfulness of instantaneous and unspotted killing without presupposing that the victim is thereby harmed. I struggle to see how one could plausibly deny that the victim's interest in remaining alive is set back, and that so setting back this particular interest of hers is harmful to her.

Third, rights to resources and their correlative duties need spelling out in ways some of which are omitted from international declarations and covenants yet which are in the spirt of their underlying principle—namely the principle that individuals owe it to one another to provide assistance to one another. If you cannot get the resources which you are owed as a matter of justice, I am at the very least under a duty not to prevent you from getting those resources. More strongly still, under certain circumstances, I am under a duty to give them to you. This applies to the basic necessities of life as well as to the resources we need to protect ourselves from unwarranted harm (for example, guns). It also applies to the personal services which we can offer such as our time, energy, and the deployment of our mental and physical abilities. Duties of assistance, whichever form they take, are subject to a no-undue-sacrifice proviso: there are limits to what we may reasonably be expected to do for one another's sake.[28]

Fourth, duties to provide individuals what they need as a matter of right often require large-scale coordination. This has the following implications. For a start, although those duties are borne by all of us across borders, they are best devolved to institutions with the requisite capacities, such as the state or the community on whose territory those in need reside. As a British citizen residing in the United Kingdom, I do not have stronger *fundamental* duties to provide assistance to my fellow citizens than I do to help someone who is similarly in need of my help and is a citizen of, for example, Colombia. But I have an instrumental duty to help the former rather than the latter via the institutions of the British state, just as Colombian citizens have instrumental duties to one another, which they discharge via the institutions of the Colombian state.[29]

---

[28] The literature on duties to provide assistance to those in need, which include a duty to protect them from unwarranted harm, is huge. See, e.g., C. Jones, *Global Justice—Defending Cosmopolitanism* (Oxford University Press, 1999); A. Ripstein, 'Three Duties to Rescue: Moral, Civil, and Criminal,' *Law and Philosophy* 19 (2000): 751–79; R. W. Miller, 'Beneficence, Duty and Distance,' *Philosophy & Public Affairs* 32 (2004): 357–83; S. Caney, *Justice Beyond Borders: A Global Political Theory* (Oxford University Press, 2005); T. Pogge and D. Moellendorf (eds.), *Global Justice: Seminal Essays—Global Responsibilities I* (Paragon House, 2008); G. Brock, *Global Justice: A Cosmopolitan Account* (Oxford University Press, 2009).

[29] For a classic defence of this view, see R. E. Goodin, 'What Is So Special about Our Fellow Countrymen?,' *Ethics* 98 (1988): 663–86. The view is compatible with interstate transfers of resources, indeed those transfers are mandated by justice.

Moreover, duties to provide assistance include duties to set up and grant us access to institutions with the requisite capacities. Our right to clean water is worthless if our community's critical infrastructure cannot deliver clean water. Our right to a decent minimum income is worthless if we live in a society in which banks are central and cannot access our bank accounts. While individuals have the aforementioned fundamental rights irrespective of their membership of a given political community and prior to the establishment of those institutions, those rights need to be rendered more precise, by the institutions tasked with their realization, in the light of the specific social, political, and economic context in which they are claimed and exercised.

Fifth, and relatedly, in addition to fundamental rights, whose conferral does not ultimately depend on their holders' membership of this or that community, individuals can have special rights. These are rights which originate in a particular relationship or in a particular act. On the former count: you and I, as British citizens, have special rights against one another *qua* British citizens—for example, that we both vote in UK general elections so as to help maintain the health of our democratic system. On the latter count: if I promise you that I will φ, my promise confers on you a right against me that I should φ, and imposes on me the relevant duty. If my political community concludes a diplomatic treaty or trade agreement with yours, we acquire rights and duties *vis-à-vis* one another which we would not have otherwise.[30]

Sixth, those institutions' officials have a number of rights, powers, and duties *qua* officials. Those rights and duties are grounded in and derive their normative force from individuals' fundamental moral rights. This does not imply that the rights, powers, and duties of officials are exactly the same as the rights of citizens in which they are grounded. On the contrary, officials have powers to issue directives which citizens lack. But those powers are justified in virtue of the deeper claim that citizens have a right that those relationships be so changed. Similarly, state officials' powers to issue directives are protected by rights that third parties not interfere with their morally justified exercise of those powers: those rights are held by state officials and by those on whose behalf they act. Fundamental moral rights, thus, are both constraints on officials' conduct and the rationale for officials' rights, powers, and duties and, ultimately, for the relevant institutions. To put the point in the language of legitimacy, it is both the ground for and a condition of an institution's legitimacy—of its officials' powers and rights to issue authoritative commands and to enforce those commands—that it should be able and willing to

---

[30] For the distinction between general and special rights, see H. L. A. Hart, 'Are There Any Natural Rights?,' *The Philosophical Review* 64 (1955): 175–91. The point about treaties applies to those treaty clauses which are not merely declarative—that is to say, which specify general rights or create new rights. For an extended discussion, see C. Fabre, *Cosmopolitan Peace* (Oxford University Press, 2016), s. 4.2.1.

secure individuals' fundamental rights and enable them to fulfil their fundamental moral duties.[31]

1.4.2 Defensive Harm

Justified Harm and Uncertainty

In s. 1.3.3, I resisted the view that the ethics of espionage and counter-intelligence is best framed through the lenses of just war theory. Instead, I suggested that we frame it by appeal to general principles for the ongoing and preemptive imposition of defensive harm. This is the task I set myself for the remainder of this book. In this section, I set out the account of justified defensive harm on which I rely. I do not defend it in full (this would take a book of its own). I hope that it has enough rough intuitive plausibility to get most readers on board.[32]

All individuals have a presumptive right not to be harmed, but they can sometimes become liable to defensive harm: that is to say, it is permissible deliberately to harm them in self-defence or in defence of others without thereby infringing their right. An important philosophical question is that of the basis on which agents are liable to defensive harm.

I take it for granted that contributing to a morally unjustified threat to another party's fundamental rights—for short, to an unjust venture—can make someone liable to harm. The devil lies in the details of an agent's contribution and of the bearing it has on the harm one may deliberately impose on her. I may be morally justified in deliberately killing a lethal attacker on the grounds that he would otherwise kill me while, for example, wrongfully invading my country. But I am not morally justified in deliberately killing enemy civilians on the grounds that their regime would not be able to conduct an unjust war were it not for the fact that they pay taxes. Nor, *a fortiori*, am I morally justified in killing those taxpayers on the grounds that their regime is in a position to pursue an unjust albeit non-lethal foreign policy thanks to their willingness to pay taxes. Even so, there are harms short of death which I may deliberately inflict on them, such as some form of economic sanctions.

---

[31] My brief account has important similarities to Seumas Miller's normative theory of social institutions. See Miller, *The Moral Foundations of Social Institutions*, chs. 1–2.

[32] The literature on defensive harm in general, and its application to war in particular, is vast. For recent accounts, see (non-exhaustively) D. Rodin, *War and Self-Defense* (Clarendon Press, 2002); J. McMahan, *Killing in War* (Oxford University Press, 2009); C. Fabre, *Cosmopolitan War* (Oxford University Press, 2012); H. Frowe, *Defensive Killing* (Oxford University Press, 2014); S. Lazar, *Sparing Civilians* (Oxford University Press, 2015); Haque, *Law and Morality at War*; A. Walen, *The Mechanics of Claims and Permissible Killing in War* (Oxford University Press, 2019); J. Quong, *The Morality of Defensive Force* (Oxford University Press, 2020); Tadros, *To Do, To Die, To Reason Why*; F. M. Kamm, 'Failures of Just War Theory: Terror, Harm, and Justice', *Ethics* 114 (2004): 650–92; F. M. Kamm, *The Moral Target: Aiming at Right Conduct in War and Other Conflicts* (Oxford University Press, 2012).

Contribution to an unjust venture is not the only basis for liability to defensive harm. Wrongfully failing to protect someone from a rights violation is another. Suppose that you are under an unjustifiable threat from Bloggs and that I am under a duty to protect you from it, subject to my ability to do so and so long as the costs I thereby incur are not excessive: my duty to protect you instantiates the general duty to offer assistance to those in need. If I refuse to do my duty, I am liable to steps being taken to force me to do so, and you have a justification for taking those steps.

It is also sometimes permissible to harm another person deliberately even though he is not is not liable to being harmed. Suppose that a police car is justifiably chasing a known killer who will commit another murder unless he is apprehended. Although the police driver is taking all reasonable precautions, his car veers out of control at a pedestrian. The pedestrian will die unless she shoots the police driver. This case raises at least two questions: (a) is someone who subjects another person to a justified lethal threat liable to defensive harm? (b) if he is not, is it morally permissible to harm him and if so on what grounds? I believe that the driver is not liable to defensive force but that the pedestrian is justified in killing him: agents who have not done anything to warrant being under threat of grievous harm are permitted to confer greater weight on their morally weighty interests (of which one's survival clearly is one) than on the goals of third parties who, albeit justifiably, threaten those interests. In this case, neither party violates the other's right not to be killed: rather, they both justifiably infringe it. The analogous case, in war, is that of a tactical bomber who, in the course of a justified military mission, is about to kill innocent civilians as collateral damage. The civilians are justified in giving priority to the morally weighty end of *their* survival over his, and in shooting him down in self-defence. But to the extent that the pilot and the driver are not liable to defensive harm, their right not to be killed has been infringed (albeit justifiably.)

It is one thing to establish that someone is unjustifiably contributing to an unjust venture or is failing to do his part in thwarting that venture, or that there is a justification for harming him notwithstanding the fact that he has not done or failed to do those things. It is another to say that harming him is justified all-things-considered. Three widely accepted conditions must be met: the defensive harm must be necessary, effective and proportionate. By the requirement of necessity, I mean the following: one may impose a harm or risk thereof on another person in pursuit of a morally justified end only if there is no lesser morally weighted harm h the imposition of which would bring about one's morally justified ends. By the requirement of effectiveness, I mean the following: one may impose a harm or risk thereof on another person in pursuit of a morally justified end only if one's course of action stands a reasonable chance of succeeding. By the requirement of proportionality, I mean the following: one may impose a harm or risk thereof on another person in pursuit of a morally justified end only if the good one thereby brings about (in the form of that justified end) outweighs the harm. Those three requirements constrain both the deliberate and the merely foreseen and collateral imposition of harm.[33]

With those points in hand, I posit that an agent G is morally justified in harming another B if and only if:

(a)   either B unjustifiably contributes to the violation of some agent's fundamental rights (be it G herself or another party), or B unjustifiably fails to protect that agent from such rights violations, or harming B (who is not liable to such harm) brings about, or is a collateral cost of justifiably pursuing, a morally weighty end;

(b)   G's course of action is necessary, effective, and proportionate.

So far, so simple: the facts are such that B does not have a justification for acting or for failing to act as he does and that G's response would meet the requirements of necessity, effectiveness, and proportionality. Now suppose that G does not know for sure whether B is committing a rights violation or whether her chosen course of defensive action is necessary, effective, or proportionate. What, then, may or must G do? Faced with G's predicament, we have two options. We can say that she is permitted to harm B only if she meets the aforementioned requirements as a matter of fact—period. To G's request for advice ('What's the right thing to do?'), we answer 'well, under the circumstances, φ seems the right thing to do, but it may well turn out not to be the case and so it might turn out that you acted wrongly. But you are not blameworthy.'

This is not satisfactory. G sometimes is justified in inflicting defensive harm on B—even if, *objectively speaking*, she is not justified in so acting. Put differently, it does not seem outlandish to answer her request as follows: 'under those circumstances, φ is the right thing to do. Even if it turns out that B was not posing a threat, or that he was but that killing him was not necessary to advert the threat, you were justified in doing φ in the light of the best available evidence; for if the facts had been as suggested by the evidence, you would have been objectively justified in acting as you did.'[34]

I cannot provide a full account of the ethics of decision-making under conditions of uncertainty. For my purposes in this book, the following five points suffice.

---

[33] One of the most lively debates in defensive ethics turns on whether effectiveness and necessity are internal to liability—whether, that is, an agent is liable only to necessary and effective defensive harm, or whether those constraints operate externally. I have no wish and, fortunately, no need, to enter the fray. On the internalist side, see J. McMahan, 'The Morality of Military Occupation,' *Loyola International and Comparative Law Review* 31 (2009): 101–23; on the externalist side with respect to necessity, see H. Frowe, *The Ethics of War and Peace*, 2nd. (Routledge, 2016). For a hybrid view, see J. M. Firth and J. Quong, 'Necessity, Moral Liability, and Defensive Harm,' *Law and Philosophy* 31 (2012): 673–701; J. Quong, *The Morality of Defensive Force*, ch. 5.

[34] I draw here on Parfit's familiar distinction between fact-relative, belief-relative, and evidence-relative conceptions of rightness and wrongness. See D. Parfit, *On What Matters—vol. 1* (Oxford University Press, 2011), 150–62. See also McMahan, *Killing in War*, 162–9.

First, the fact that G is uncertain about the non-moral facts of the matter does not make it any less the case that she is objectively under an obligation not to harm B if B is not liable to be harmed, if harming him is not necessary, etc.

Second, I postulate that, under conditions of uncertainty, G is subjectively justified in harming B by φ-ing if and only if she has formed a belief on the basis of the best available evidence that B commits a rights violation or unjustifiably fails to protect another party from such rights violations, or that there is a weightier justification for φ-ing, or that φ-ing meets the requirements of necessity, effectiveness, and proportionality.

Third, the phrase 'the best available evidence' refers to information (a) which increases the probability that the conjecture it is meant to support is true, (b) which is there for G to procure, and (c) which she is under an epistemic duty to procure in order for her belief to be justified. The claim that G is under an epistemic duty to procure evidence is not the same as the claim that she is under a moral duty to do so. Suppose that G is the Prime Minister. She is told that terrorists have hijacked a plane and are en route to crash into one of several government buildings somewhere in the country. To confuse matters, the terrorists have managed to 'hide' their aircraft amongst four others currently flying in the country's airspace. G could order that all five planes be shot down, at the cost of the lives of 1,500 innocent passengers. She would much rather not do so. She is also told that the only way to get the terrorists to disclose which plane they are flying is by torturing their leader's five-year-old son and 'broadcasting' the torture to the terrorists. The evidence—which aircraft has been highjacked—is available for her to procure. She is under an epistemic duty to procure the evidence in order to form a justified belief as to which aircraft has been hijacked. Suppose that, were she to order that the child be tortured, his father would disclose that he and his men have hijacked aircraft *A1*. On the account of evidence-based justification for defensive harming I have just offered, G is (subjectively) morally justified in ordering that *A1* be shot down only if she has the child tortured, since only then is she epistemically licensed to hold the relevant belief. However, she is not (I assume) morally justified in torturing the child. If she does her duty and refrains from having the child tortured, she is not epistemically licensed to form the belief that *A1* or indeed any of the other four aircrafts has been hijacked, and she is therefore not subjectively morally justified in shooting the plane down.

With this interpretation of 'best available evidence' in hand, together with the distinction just offered between epistemic and moral justification, this book can be framed as an answer (in part) to the following question, in the context of foreign policy writ large: are individuals morally permitted, indeed obliged, to procure the information which they are under an epistemic duty to procure given that if they do not procure it, their beliefs are not epistemically justified and, consequently, the foreign policy decisions they take on the basis of those beliefs are not (subjectively) morally justified? As we shall see, the amount and range of evidence which they are morally permitted or obliged to secure before they act depend on the magnitude of harms and risks they would incur and inflict in doing so.[35]

Fourth, I set aside one of the thorniest questions raised by the ethics of harming under uncertainty, namely: is an agent subjectively justified in harming another person only if her epistemic reasons for believing that the facts so warrant reach a certain threshold of probability or reasonableness, or does her justification need only to be indexed to expected moral utility, or is it a combination of both? I cannot settle this here. I favour a hybrid approach, according to which one is not subjectively justified in harming another person unless one's epistemic reasons in favour of doing so are undefeated by countervailing reasons—or, as I shall sometimes put it, unless one has a reasonable belief that one is objectively justified in inflicting such harm.[36]

Finally, suppose that G is mistaken: for example, B is not posing a wrongful threat. Her belief is epistemically justified but false. Even though G was subjectively justified in harming B, the fact that she was not objectively justified leaves a moral remainder in those cases in which B is not responsible for the evidence being as it was. Suppose, conversely, that G is objectively justified in harming B but that she acts on an impulse and ignores the relevant evidence. She does the objectively right thing by fluke, and has gone morally amiss—or so I shall argue in Chapter 3.

In sum, when evaluating G's conduct, we need to be sensitive to the facts of the matter, to the evidence at G's disposal, and to what G does with that evidence. G is *fully justified* in harming B when she is objectively and subjectively justified in so doing. Unless I say otherwise, when I say that an agent is justified in φ-ing, I shall mean that she is fully justified.

Defensive Harm and Institutions

I averred above (a) that individuals have fundamental rights to respectful treatment and to the freedoms and resources needed for a flourishing life; (b) that those rights correlate into duties to (*inter alia*) set up institutions with the requisite capacities for coordination; (c) that individuals have a right to be protected from violations of those fundamental rights.

Taken together, points (b) and (c) entail that individuals owe it to one another to set up institutions whose task it is to enforce their fundamental rights: the police, the judiciary, the military and, of course, intelligence agencies. It would be a mistake, however, to construe this book as a professional ethics manual for

---

[35] On the difficulties inherent in providing a plausible account of 'best available evidence', see Zimmerman, *Living with Uncertainty*, 35–36. In the remainder of the book, when I say 'may', 'must', 'justified', I mean morally so, not epistemically so—unless otherwise specified.

[36] For defences of the threshold approach, see, in particular, H. Frowe, 'A Practical Account of Self-Defence', *Law and Philosophy* 29 (2010): 245–72; J. McMahan, 'Who is Morally Liable to be Killed in War', *Analysis* 71 (2011): 544–59. For a sustained critique of the approach and endorsement of moral expectabilism, see Lazar, 'In dubious battle'. For a defence of a hybrid view on which I draw here, see Haque, *Law and Morality at War*, ch. 5.

intelligence officers. Professional ethics develops and defends norms of conduct which apply to occupiers of institutionalized professional roles (doctors, lawyers, police officers, soldiers, businesspeople, etc.) Those norms delineate professionals' rights and duties. They are rooted in general moral principles (e.g. do no harm), but are specified by reference both to what the relevant institutions are meant to do (e.g. apprehend criminals) and to the broader cultural, social, and political context in which they operate. Consider for example the claim that US intelligence professionals, *qua* professionals, are under a duty not to use torture. On this view, the prohibition against torture is sometimes grounded in the general prohibition on violently degrading treatment, in the ends which intelligence agencies are meant to serve (help uncover threats against national security, for which torture is counterproductive), and in the claim that torturing is antithetical to American public culture.[37]

I do not deny that norms, and the rights and duties which they set out, can be shaped by institutional contexts. However, my aim is to develop a normative account of intelligence activities which might serve as a benchmark for evaluating and, when appropriate, reforming institutional practices (though, to reiterate, I leave those institutional questions aside). If it is to serve that purpose, my account cannot hew too closely to extant professional ethics. Moreover, the rights and duties which it defends are not held and borne only by intelligence professionals. As we shall see, many of the individuals who carry out intelligence activities are not members of intelligence services. One cannot defend the view that they are morally entitled to carry out deceptions operations or that they are morally obliged to betray their political community by appealing to professional ethics.

Defensive Harm and Foreign Policy

Take two political communities, Green and Blue. Suppose that Blue's leadership embarks on a foreign policy *vis-à-vis* Green which consists in systematically violating the fundamental rights of Green's citizens. Subject to the aforementioned requirements, Green's leadership may be objectively justified in taking harmful steps to protect those rights, on behalf of its fellow citizens and residents. When it harms those members of Blue who unjustifiably contribute to or unjustifiably fail to thwart Blue's foreign policy, it does not violate *their* right not to be harmed. When it harms (deliberately or foreseeably) those members of Blue who are

---

[37] For this particular claim about torture, see J. Waldron, *Torture, Terror and Trade-Offs: Philosophy for the White House* (Oxford University Press, 2010). For a professional-ethics book on the ethics of spying addressed to US intelligence officers, see J. M. Olson, *Fair Play: The Moral Dilemmas of Spying* (Potomac Books, 2006). Important normative accounts of the police include the following: J. Kleinig, *The Ethics of Policing* (Cambridge University Press, 1996); S. Miller and I. A. Gordon, *Investigative Ethics: Ethics for Police Detectives and Criminal Investigators* (Wiley-Blackwell, 2014); L. W. Hunt, *The Retrieval of Liberalism in Policing* (Oxford University Press, 2018).

innocent of those rights violations, it is objectively justified in infringing their right not to be harmed.

Suppose now that Green does not know for sure that the facts which would make its course of action objectively justified obtain. However, to the best of Green's available evidence, Blue is conducting a foreign policy of systemic rights violations. Subject to the aforementioned requirements, Green's leadership is subjectively justified in taking harmful steps to protect those rights, on behalf of its fellow citizens and residents.

Consider the situation from Blue's point of view. Suppose, first, that Blue's leadership does not have evidentiary grounds for forming the belief that its foreign policy protects its own citizens' fundamental rights. It is neither objectively nor subjectively justified in so acting. Blue and Green are not morally on a par.

Suppose, next, that Blue has good evidentiary grounds for believing that its foreign policy serves to protect its *own* rights—that it is responding to what it has good reasons for believing is Green's own systematic rights-violating policy. From the point of view of subjective permissibility, Blue and Green are on a par. But Green's assessment, and not Blue's, is correct. Green is justified, not just at the subjective bar of its epistemic situation but objectively so, in harming Blue. Unlike Blue, it is fully justified in so acting. We have another scenario in which Green and Blue are not symmetrically situated, morally speaking, relative to one another.

If those points are correct, the moral status of the foreign policy which Green and Blue pursue has a bearing on our overall moral assessment of Green's course of action. It matters that Green is objectively and not merely subjectively justified in pursuing this policy while Blue is not. *Pace* contractarianism, individuals in general and intelligence officers in particular who stand on opposite sides of a conflict are not always on a par.

The phrase 'the moral status of Green's policy' needs disambiguating. The fact that Green is pursuing a morally justified policy at time t_1 is no guarantee that its policy will remain overall just at t_2. Conversely, the fact that Blue's foreign policy is unjust at t_1 does not preclude the possibility that it might become just at t_2. Moreover, even if Green pursues just foreign policy ends at t_1, some of its actions in pursuit of those ends might be unjust. Finally, its foreign policy *vis-à-vis* Blue might comprise several distinct ends, of which the major ones might be justified while the subsidiary ones might be unjust.[38]

With those points in hand, I can restate the book's central thesis more precisely. In its initial formulation, the thesis was stated thus: intelligence activities are morally justified (and sometimes mandatory) only as a means to protect oneself and third parties from violations of fundamental moral rights or risks thereof in

---

[38] For extensive discussion in the context of war, see, e.g., S. Bazargan, 'The Permissibility of Aiding and Abetting Unjust Wars,' *Journal of Moral Philosophy* 8 (2011): 513–29; V. Tadros, 'Unjust Wars Worth Fighting For,' *Journal of Practical Ethics* 4 (2016): 52–78.

the context of foreign policy writ large. More precisely put: intelligence activities are morally justified

(a) either, and if so objectively so, as a means, and only as a means, to protect oneself and third parties from actual ongoing violations of fundamental moral rights or risks thereof in the context of foreign policy writ large, subject to meeting, as a matter of fact, the requirements of necessity, effectiveness, and proportionality;
(b) or, and if so subjectively so, as a means, and only as a means, to protect oneself and third parties from what one has reasons to believe in the light of the best available evidence[39] are ongoing violations of fundamental moral rights or risks thereof in the context of foreign policy writ large, subject to the (subjectively construed) aforementioned requirements.

When they are both objectively and subjectively justified, we can say that they are *fully* justified. I am interested in full justifiability. For the sake of expository simplicity, when I say that intelligence activities are justified as a means and only as a means to thwart rights violations, this is what I shall mean.

Three final expository points. First, when I speak of rights violations, I always have in mind violations of fundamental (moral) rights. Second, I shall use the shortcut 'unjust foreign policy' to denote a policy of violations of fundamental rights in the context of peacetime and wartime foreign relations. Third, I develop my arguments by using as my examples two political communities, Green and Blue. Unless otherwise stated, I use those labels to denote (depending on the context) those communities' leadership, intelligence officers and other agents acting on behalf those communities' citizens, and citizens themselves. By 'citizens', I mean nationals and long-term residents of sovereign states as well as members of political communities with aspirations to sovereign statehood.

1.5 Conclusion

Spies lie, cheat, and betray as a means to procure the information their paymasters want and to protect the information they want to keep secret. Neither the language of dirty hands, nor contractarian political morality, nor the framework of just war theory are of decisive help as we try to make sense of the intuition that in some cases, involving the defence of fundamental moral rights, intelligence activities are morally justified. Yet, as I shall now show, there are wrongs *and* rights in attempting to see through the glass darkly.

---

[39] Here, the best available evidence is evidence one has, not for resorting to defensive measures, but for undertaking intelligence activities. This raises a worry about infinite regress which I will tackle in s. 3.4.

2

Political Secrets

2.1 Introduction

Espionage consists in acquiring information about another party against their presumed or explicit wishes, while counter-intelligence consists in protecting information about oneself from another party's attempt to acquire it against our presumed or explicit wishes. To defend both is to show that one may justifiably acquire and protect supposedly *secret* information. The secrets which intelligence agencies and their political paymasters collect and use pertain in the main to foreign political communities' critical security apparatus, their political agency, their economic interests, and their members' personal lives; the secrets which they seek to protect pertain to their own similar goods.

Defending espionage and counter-intelligence would be easy if citizens had no right that any of such information should remain secret. As I argue in this chapter, however, they do. My stated plan is likely to elicit two contrasting reactions. On the one hand, some might argue that in the wake of *(inter alia)* Edward Snowden's and Chelsea Mannings' revelations and subsequent calls for greater transparency on the part of our governments, what we need is less secrecy, not more. I agree: our governments all too often hide ongoing and past abuses under its cloaks. But even if we need less secrecy, it does not follow that we need none at all. On the other hand, some might counter that the chapter's main thesis is too obviously true to need defending. After all, the unauthorized appropriation of state secrets is treated as a serious criminal offence and as a reason to expel foreign 'diplomats'. Neither measure tends to elicit controversy; nor does the principle on which they rest, to wit, that political communities are warranted in keeping some kinds of information secret.

Seemingly obvious claims often prove harder to justify than we might think. Such is the case here. Section 2.2 provides a descriptive account of the right to secrecy. Sections 2.3 and 2.4 offer a defence of the right to secrecy as pertains to security and political agency—or political secrets. I postpone secrecy in respect of their economic interests and personal lives until Chapters 4 and 9, respectively.

Two preliminary points before I start. First, my concern is with secrecy as hiding information on the grounds that one does not wish it to be known, as distinct from the practice of withholding information as a means to induce another party to form false beliefs—what Amy Gutmann and Dennis Thompson aptly call 'deceptive secrecy'.[1] Deceptive secrecy takes us into the territory of the ethics of (active) deception in politics. I shall revisit it in Chapter 5.

Second, my aim is to prepare the grounds for my defence of foreign espionage and counter-intelligence. I do not seek to provide a full account of political secrecy.[2] Nor do I tackle every single challenge which one may raise against the institutional practices and culture of secrecy which pervade most regimes, including liberal democracies. I focus on the kind of information which intelligence agencies routinely seek to procure and protect, and merely seek to make a qualified case in favour of the view that not all such information is an apt candidate for full transparency.

2.2 Secrecy

2.2.1 Defining Secrecy

Recall Moses' decision to send spies out to Canaan. Here were his instructions, as related to us in Numbers (13: 17–20):

> Get you up this way southward, and go up into the mountain:
>
> And see the land, what it is, and the people that dwelleth therein, whether they be strong or weak, few or many;
>
> And what the land is that they dwell in, whether it be good or bad; and what cities they be that they dwell in, whether in tents, or in strong holds;
>
> And what the land is, whether it be fat or lean, whether there be wood therein, or not. And be ye of good courage, and bring of the fruit of the land. Now was the time of the first ripe grapes.

None of this information was secret. The land of Canaan was there for all to see, as were the robustness of its cities and the strength of its inhabitants. Yet Moses' men clearly were spies. Likewise, much of the information which intelligence agencies collect is available from open sources such as newspapers, social media, and official reports. Nevertheless, secrecy is an apt basis on which to frame their activities. If it were possible for the targets of intelligence agencies to hide that information, they often would do so, and we may therefore appropriately ask whether they have a claim that it be treated *as if* it were kept secret. Moreover,

---

[1] A. Gutmann and D. Thompson, *Democracy and Disagreement* (Harvard University Press, 1996), 117. It may be that, although my reason for withholding information from you about x is that I do not want you to know x, I know that I will induce you to form a false belief of some sort. I need not address this complication here.

[2] For a book-length philosophical account of secrecy (in fact, to my knowlege, the only such account), see S. Bok, *Secrets: On the Ethics of Concealment and Revelation*, 2nd ed. (Vintage Books, 1989).

much of the information which intelligence agencies and their governments want is in fact secret. Hence the need for an account of secrecy.

Suppose that I am in possession of a vital piece of information, p, about my country's nuclear arsenal—say, the launching codes. You work for a foreign power's intelligence services. We need to know what it takes for me to be described as successfully keeping the codes secret from you, and what it takes for you to be described as treating the codes as secret.

I successfully keep the codes secret from you if I deliberately do not disclose them to you *and* if you do not manage to appropriate them regardless: non-disclosure is not sufficient for secrecy. Thus, for a long time, British governments would not publicly acknowledge that Britain had such institutions as the Secret Service and the Intelligence Services—long past the point when they had stopped actively hiding their existence and even as the information had become widely known—what is sometimes called an 'open secret', in other words, no secret at all.[3] At the same time, disclosure is not sufficient for the information no longer to be a secret. Suppose that I decide to betray my country for yours. I disclose the codes to you while, unbeknownst to me, you are asleep. They remain a secret to you.

For your part, you treat p as a secret if you intentionally refrain from apprising yourself of it either on the grounds (you surmise) that I have decided not to disclose it to you or that I would not want you to know about and/or disclose it, or on the grounds that, whatever I might wish, you believe that p should not be made public. You fail to treat p as a secret if, though you do not apprise yourself of it, you communicate it to third parties. Return to the case where I actively and knowingly betray my country for yours. I give you an encrypted USB stick containing vital information about my country's critical infrastructure. If you pass on the stick to your service, it is no conceptual defence against a charge of breaching secrecy to protest that you did not decode the information. At the very least, you have appropriated the USB stick, knowing what it contains, though not the details thereof. There is a sense in which you have appropriated the information. Even if (contrary to what I have just argued) it is best to say that you have only appropriated the stick and not its content—, you have disclosed to your service the fact that the stick contains vital information and have given them the opportunity to appropriate the information. Although (as we shall see later) the distinction between appropriation and disclosure is important, thwarting both is necessary for secrecy.[4]

---

[3] On the gradual unveiling of MI5 in the late 1980s—culminating in the passing of the Secret Service Act in 1989, see Andrew, *The Defence of the Realm*, 753–8. Similarly, the existence of MI6, was not officially acknowledged until the early 1990s.

[4] For other definitions of secrecy, see, e.g., S. Bok, *Secrets: On the Ethics of Concealment and Revelation*, 2nd ed. (Vintage Books, 1989), ch. 1; T. L. Carson, *Lying and Deception—Theory and Practice* (Oxford University Press, 2010), ch. 2; J. E. Mahon, 'Secrets v. Lies: Is There an Asymmetry?', in E. Michaelson and A. Stokke (eds.), *Lying—Language, Knowledge, Ethics and Politics* (Oxford University Press, 2018). My working definition differs from theirs in various respects which I need not rehearse here.

Finally, a statement of the form 'A successfully keeps a secret from B' is relatively easy to understand if A and B are both individuals. A statement of the form 'The Americans and the British are successfully keeping the details of the Manhattan Project secret from the Soviets' is harder to parse. Suppose that in January 1945, a British scientist lets information about the Project slip to someone who, unbeknownst to him, has pro-Soviet sympathies. We would not conclude that the Americans and the British have failed to keep the existence of the Project a secret. So long as relevantly situated British and American officials intentionally fail to disclose that fact to relevantly situated Soviet officials and that the latter do not know about the Project, they have successfully kept that fact secret from the latter. The clause 'relevantly situated' is crucial. Take a junior British civil servant in the Agriculture ministry who has the good sense while on a trip to Moscow not to gossip about what he has heard on the grapevine about 'our chaps doing really exciting work in nuclear physics'. Compare him with the head of the British nuclear programme showing similar restraint at an Allied summit. The former is not aptly described as keeping the Manhattan Project secret; the latter is.[5]

2.2.2 The Right to Secrecy

To keep a piece of information secret, or to wish that it be so treated by third parties, is one thing. Whether there is a right to secrecy is another. In this subsection, I offer a conceptual analysis of the claim that X has a right against Y that some information be treated as a secret, such as to impose on Y a duty not to seek to appropriate and/or to disclose that information.

Rights-holders
Our concern is with information about (loosely put for now) a political community and its members. The right to secrecy is held by the latter: as we saw in s. 1.4.1, the rights which a community's officials have in relation to the secrecy of that information are grounded in, and derive their normative force from, the rights held by individual citizens.

The content of the right
To say that citizens have a right to secrecy is to say that their interest in the relevant information remaining hidden is important enough to hold third parties under some duty. In the context of this book, secrecy protects two kinds of information. On the one hand, it protects information the unauthorized appropriation and

---

[5] As it turns out, the Soviets knew about the Project, thanks to moles. (See s. 2.3.2.) For an interesting discussion of the number and position of officials who need to remain silent in order for a secret to be characterized as a political secret, see D. E. Pozen, 'Deep Secrecy', *Stanford Law Review* 62 (2010): 257–339 at 268–75. Although Pozen is concerned with defining 'deep secrets', his account is useful for secrets in general. I am grateful to Seumas Miller for penetrating comments on this subsection.

disclosure of which would jeopardize individual goods, to wit, goods which are central to individuals' flourishing, whose existence and production do not depend on joint collaborative efforts, and which those individuals can enjoy single-handledly. Bodily integrity is a paradigmatic example of such a good. Citizens have a right that information the disclosure of which might threaten their lives and limbs be kept secret.

On the other hand, secrecy protects information about collective goods, to wit, those goods which are shared by citizens of the same political community. There are different kinds of collective goods. Some goods, such as clean air, are collective in that, although their contribution to the quality of one person's life is independent of their contribution to the quality of life of another person, they are necessarily jointly produced. We cannot have clean air unless most of us do our bit at controlling pollution, but its contribution to my quality of life is independent of its contribution to yours. Other goods, such as friendship, are collective in that their contribution to the quality of life of one person depends on the fact that they also contribute to the quality of life of another, relevantly situated agent. My friendship with you makes my life go well only if it also makes your life goes well: otherwise, we cannot call it a friendship. Finally, some goods, such as democratic agency, are collective in the sense that we cannot access them unless others do too. I have access to the good of democratic agency over the territory known as the United Kingdom of Great Britain and Northern Ireland only if other British citizens have it too. If all my fellow British citizens were to die tomorrow in a nuclear explosion of which I were the sole survivor, I could not enjoy the good of democratic agency over the United Kingdom, for there would be no political community left about which decisions must be made.[6]

Information which it is in the interest of members of a political community to keep secret need not be solely about their own goods. It can be information to the effect that they have information about other communities' and their members' individual and collective goods. Suppose that Green's government has information to the effect that Blue's government is seeking to extract unfair concessions in their upcoming round of trade negotiations. The fact that Green is cognizant of Blue's negotiating position is itself a piece of information which it might wish to keep secret on the grounds that its disclosure would undermine its own negotiating position and thereby its members' collective political agency. Similarly, even if Green's information about Blue is based on material which is available from open sources and which Blue has not tried to keep secret, Green's analysis of Blue's likely negotiating position is itself something that it might want to keep secret—and, precisely for that reason, that Blue might want to obtain.

[6] For illuminating discussions of collective goods on which I draw here, see J. Waldron, 'Can Communal Goods be Human Rights?', in his *Liberal Rights—Collected Papers 1981–1991* (Cambridge University Press, 1993); J. Waldron, 'Safety and Security', in his *Torture, Terror and Trade-Offs*; Miller, *The Moral Foundations of Social Institutions*, ch. 2.

Duties and duty-bearers

The last conceptual feature of the right to political secrecy pertains to the content and bearers of its correlative duties. Regarding their content, I noted in s. 2.2.1 that thwarting appropriation and disclosure is crucial to secrecy. By implication, to say that an agent has a right to secrecy in relation to *p* is to say that third parties are under duties not to appropriate or disclose *p* without her consent. The two can sometimes come apart. Our government might have a justification for appropriating the military secrets of hostile power Aggressor. But if disclosing those secrets to another party would lead the latter to mount an unjust attack on Aggressor, it might owe it to the latter not to do so. Conversely, suppose that our government wrongfully appropriates the military secrets of our peaceful neighbour Neutral. It does not follow that our government may not disclose that information to third parties if it nevertheless obtains it. If it finds out that Neutral is morphing into a hostile power with aggressive intentions against another country, it might well have a very strong reason to disclose the truth (indeed, under some circumstances, it might even be under a duty to do so).

In this particular example, the relevant information is not available to the general public. But even if it is, there might still be a duty not to appropriate and disclose it. For example, in January 2018, the Australian intelligence community was rocked by the revelation that hundreds of classified files had been found in a cabinet made available for purchase at a government second-hand sale. In some sense, those files were public. It does not follow that the lucky buyer of the cabinet would have been morally justified in disclosing the files to all and sundry: there might well be very good reasons as to why he or she did their duty by notifying the Australian authorities.[7]

Duty-bearers, for their part, include not merely the citizens and officials of the political community from which one wants to keep secrets. They include one's own. Suppose that Green would like to procure some secret information about Blue. One way in which Blue's authorities can protect it is by denying their fellow citizens and some of their own officials access to it. To say, thus, that Blue's citizens have a right to secrecy against Green is to say, by implication, that they have a right against one another as well as against their officials that they not seek to help Green acquire Blue's secrets. The more closely and relevantly situated an official is to the relevant information, the stronger her case for knowing about it and yet the more stringent her duty not to disclose it. Yet, the less closely and relevantly situated

---

[7] A. Topping, 'Top secret Australian government files found in secondhand shop', *The Guardian* (31/01/2018). In line with my definition of espionage in the Introduction to this book, had the purchaser of the cabinet passed on its content to a foreign government, they would have committed an act of espionage (or, possibly, treason, depending on their relationship with Australia (see Chapter 6)). Had they leaked it to the media, they would not. A similar incident happened in the UK in June 2021, as this book was about to enter production: a member of the public stumbled upon classified documents from the Ministry of Defence which had been left at a bus stop, and contacted the British authorities. (See M. Wolfe-Robinson, 'Classified Ministry of Defence papers found at bus stop in Kent', *The Guardian* (27/06/2021).)

she is to the information, the less she needs to know about it, the more stringent her duty not to appropriate it and the less serious her failure not to disclose it. Suppose that the British junior civil servant from the Agriculture Ministry, while on his trip to Moscow, lets slip in an unguarded moment what he has heard on the grapevine about Britain's defence nuclear programme. He merely engages in gossip. By contrast, were the head of the British nuclear programme to show similar lack of restraint, he arguably would not merely be gossiping: he would be guilty of gross misconduct. Were the same junior civil servant surreptitiously to try and obtain the files of foreign scientists who have worked on the programme in the past, he might well be charged with a serious crime; not so, perhaps, with the head of the programme, so long as he could show good cause in connection with his institutional position. The compartmentalization of secrecy takes on different forms depending on the nature of the information at stake and the institutional position of duty-bearers.

We now have a handle on the concept of the right to political secrecy. I now defend the claim that citizens have such a right in respect of information regarding their security and their democratic political agency.

2.3 Security

2.3.1 The Argument

Consider first the security argument. To say that Blue's members have a right to security is to say that their interest in it is strong enough to be protected by a right that others not undermine it. If the appropriation and disclosure of certain kinds of information about themselves or their community would jeopardize their security, then (the argument goes) they have a right that the information remain or be treated as secret.

The security argument holds that security can be compromised even if the information is merely accessed, and not used. The opposite move is often made by proponents of intrusive surveillance measures, who challenge law-abiding citizens to explain what they can possibly fear from surveillance operations if they have nothing to hide. That move is not convincing. Just as the slave of a benevolent master cannot properly trust that his master will never at any point turn against him, individuals whose means of defence are known to would-be attackers cannot fully trust that the threat which the latter pose will not materialize, when the only reason why it does not materialize is that the attackers choose it to be so. Under those conditions, they *do* have something to fear.[8]

---

[8] The point I am making here about safety echoes Philip Pettit's claim that the slave of a benevolent master does not enjoy undominated freedom. See P. Pettit, *Republicanism—A Theory of Freedom and Government* (Oxford University Press, 1999).

What does it mean, though, for individuals to enjoy the good of security? In an illuminating piece, Jeremy Waldron notes that individual security is much more than physical safety. It refers to the 'protection of one's basic mode of life and economic values, as well as reasonable protection against fear and terror, and the presence of a positive assurance that these values will continue to be maintained in the future.'[9] Furthermore, in so far as someone's own security so construed in part depends on her fellow community members' own security so construed, we can speak of collective security as a state of affairs where individuals together enjoy, and produce the conditions for, individual security.[10]

The security argument for secrecy at the very least applies to those goods information about which must remain unaccessed lest our military security would be undermined. This includes information about material things such as installations and equipment, as well as scientific research that is relevant to the military.

The argument also applies to information about goods the enjoyment of which is part and parcel of our individual and collective security—in a nutshell, the community's critical infrastructure. Therein lies the problem. As Moses' story reminds us, there are swathes of information about Blue's security and its components which potential or actual enemies might use against Blue—such as Blue's morale in crisis, the size of Blue's population, the density of its populated areas, the strength of its economy, the size of its mountains, or the shape of its coastline. The more expansive one's conception of security—beyond the strictly military and towards the more plausible construal of security as encompassing a community's critical infrastructure—the greater the difficulty. On the one hand, the appropriation and disclosure of what appears to be trivial information might be unwarrantedly harmful to Blue. On the other hand, to say that Blue's members have a right to secrecy in respect of any information which might be used to undermine their security proves too much: for any information could be so used, and so no one, whether a member of Blue itself or an outsider, could be said to enjoy meaningful freedom of expression, since no one would be at liberty to say anything about Blue without prior permission; nor could anyone have meaningful opportunities to acquire knowledge about Blue's history, geography, politics, etc.

Faced with this difficulty, we need to chart a course between information which can and should be regarded as secret on security grounds, and information which ought to be available to all. As we do so, we can usefully distinguish between goods which are part and parcel of Blue's state and security apparatus; goods which are part of Blue's ability to function as a political community; and goods which have no bearing on Blue's political institutions, security apparatus, or critical infrastructure.

---

[9] Waldron, 'Safety and Security', 130.
[10] Waldron, 'Safety and Security' 150–60.

Military hardware and installations, troops, intelligence and security services are paradigmatic examples of the first kind of good, and there clearly is a presumptive case for treating any information about these as secrets. Which goods count as such is contingent on the military technology in use. At the beginning of the twentieth century, when British fears of German expansionism reached fever pitch, the War Office prepared for a possible invasion of Germany by a British Expeditionary Force and commissioned a survey of the areas where the Force might deploy. The survey included information about bicycle shops.[11] Cyclist battalions were formed and incorporated in the Territorial Force in 1908; throughout the First World War, they would be used at the front for reconnaissance and intelligence-gathering missions. Hence the importance of knowing where to find spare parts in enemy territory. This does not apply today.

Examples of the second kind of goods include, *inter alia* and to reiterate, the resilience of the population, the shape of Blue's territory, the stability of its political institutions and the robustness of its critical infrastructure (such as its telecommunications system, power grid, water and gas supplies, banking institutions, health care resources, emergency services, transports, access to food and oil). Sustained attacks on those goods, particularly on its critical infrastructure, would bring Blue to its knees.[12] It may not matter much that Blue's enemies should know how many power plants, banks, and hospitals Blue has, and where those facilities are. But what clearly matters is that they should not be able to penetrate those facilities, whether physically or virtually. If this is correct, then the right to secrecy (as justified by appeal to security) is not a right that individuals not seek to engage in (e.g.) street photography (thereby recording whether this or that building is a bank or hospital) but, rather, a right that they not seek information the appropriation and disclosure of which would jeopardize Blue's key institutions. Return to the Canaanites: perhaps they would not have objected to a stranger merely finding out that their cities are heavily fortified, but they would certainly have objected to a putative enemy seeking to ascertain that very fact before attacking them.

Finally, examples of the third kind of goods, which have no bearing on Blue's security and political and critical infrastructure, are likely to be very trivial, and Blue's security thus is no grounds for presumptively regarding information about those goods as a secret a priori. I say 'a priori' because the security context within which Blue finds itself matters too, such as whether Blue is at war, whether it faces threats of a non-conventional nature and, if so, how likely it is that the threats will materialize into an attack.

---

[11] Andrew, *The Defence of the Realm*, 13.

[12] In the UK context, the Centre for the Protection of National Infrastructure provides a good overview of what the UK government regards as the main threats to national security (https://www.cpni.gov.uk/ (accessed on 17/08/2021).) In the US, that information is provided by the Department of Homeland Security (https://www.dhs.gov/cisa/overview (accessed on 17/08/2021).)

2.3.2 A Complication

The security argument must show which kind of information about which kind of good is sensitive enough to warrant protection under the cloak of secrecy. It must also show why the good of security justifies holding this or that party as the bearer of the relevant duties. The claim that potential attackers (Green, in my example) are under those duties is relatively easy to defend. As we saw in section 2.2.2, however, secrecy may need to extend to Blue's own members as a means to protect them from informational invasions by Green. In political communities such as states and their extensive bureaucracy, this provides a rationale for restricting access to sensitive information not just to (say) the civil service but, in some cases at least, to certain officials within the service, indeed, within intelligence services, to a select few. The problem here is that excessive secrecy—notably secrecy between different parts of an organization—can jeopardize officials' ability to protect their fellow members from wrongful threats against their collective security. The VENONA Programme illustrates the point well. Starting in 1943, a team of American cryptanalysts from the US Army's Signal Intelligence Service intercepted several thousands of telegrams sent by Soviet intelligence agencies to their agents in the West, notably the US and Britain, during and after the Second World War. The Programme's cryptanalysts were able to reveal that the Soviets had a mole in the Manhattan Project, uncovered the Rosenbergs' activities, and found patchy information about the existence of a ring of British spies with access to British intelligence—the network later known as the Cambridge Five. VENONA was so secret that only a handful of officers had full access to the decrypts, and that even officers who were fully aware of the existence of the programme would not share relevant information with other similarly aware officers from different services. Therein lay the Programme's weakness. Had secrecy not been as tight, some of the clues pointing to Kim Philby as one of the members of the Cambridge Five might have been interpreted correctly much earlier than they were. The story of VENONA illustrates the need for constantly re-evaluating judgements about the sensitivity of a particular piece of information—precisely on security grounds.[13]

---

[13] Andrew, *The Defence of the Realm*, 365–79. See also Aldrich, *GCHQ*, ch. 3. The Venona Programme ended in 1980, and remained classified until 1995, at which point the NSA (the successor to the Army's Signal Intelligence Services) released some of the decrypts. For a discussion of the dangers of secrecy for secrecy itself, along similar lines, see S. Bok, *Secrets: On the Ethics of Concealment and Revelation*, second ed. (Vintage Books, 1989), 194–6. Another very good example of the ways in which inter-agency secrecy has been highly damaging to collective security is 9/11. For a concise summary, see Andrew, *The Secret World*, ch. 30.

The uses and abuses of secrecy raise another deep difficulty which I do not have the space to discuss in this book, namely the conflict between the imperative of protecting secrets for the sake of national security and demands for transparency in the criminal justice system. I shall return to this point briefly in the Epilogue of the book. For an illuminating discussion of the uses and abuses of political secrecy by various US administrations, and for policy proposals to deal with those abuses, see (in the American context) R. Sagar, *Secrets and Leaks: The Dilemmas of State Secrecy* (Princeton

2.4 Democratic Agency

2.4.1 The Argument

Collective security properly understood provides a justification for treating certain types of information as secret. To the extent that the appropriation and disclosure of such information threaten individual and collective security and thereby democratic agency, the latter offers yet further grounds for secrecy. Moreover, attacks on agency (be it personal or political) warrant attention in and of themselves, whether or not they take the form of or lead to attacks on security. In this section, thus, I argue that individuals have a democratic right to secrecy.

By democratic rights, I mean rights the protection of which is a necessary condition for a political community to *count* as a democracy: for example, the right to vote in free, regular, and open elections; the right that there be a formal connection between citizens' vote and the outcome of the voting procedure; the right that the outcome of the voting procedure not be unwarrantedly thwarted *ex post*.

Now, information the unauthorized appropriation or disclosure of which would stymie citizens' exercise of their democratic agency can legitimately be protected by a right to secrecy. Citizens' interests in political participation, in there being a formal connection between their individual preferences and political decisions, and in those political decisions not being thwarted by outsiders, are important enough to be protected by the whole panoply of democratic civil and political rights. By implication, their interest in sensitive information about the processes and outcomes of their democratic political agency not being disclosed and appropriated is important enough to be protected by the relevant right. It is precisely because the latter protects the exercise of democratic agency that it is aptly construed as a democratic right. To illustrate, suppose that my interest in casting a vote and in that vote being appropriately counted is important enough to be protected not merely by a right to do so but also by a right to do so electronically (should I be unable to go to the polling station). If so, it is also important enough to be protected by a right that the cyber-security measures taken by the government to ensure the integrity of the online voting sites and electronic vote-counting machines not be disclosed to all and sundry. The point applies to the act of hiding the very existence of those measures, should this prove necessary to ensure their effectiveness.[14]

University Press, 2013); Pozen, 'Deep Secrecy', and—more generally—R. W. Bellaby, 'Too Many Secrets? When Should the Intelligence Community be Allowed to Keep Secrets?', *Polity* 51 (2019): 62–94; R. W. Bellaby, 'The Ethics of Whistleblowing: Creating a New Limit on Intelligence Activity', *Journal of International Political Theory* 14 (2018): 60–84.

[14] It has been objected to me that to confer on citizens a democratic right against their community's offficials that the latter not disclose democracy-protecting information implies that citizens also have

In this particular example, secrecy protects the integrity of democratic procedures and, thereby, of democratic agency. No less clearly, in just the same way that untimely disclosure often jeopardizes individuals' ability to bring their plans to completion, so it does in the realm of politics in general, and foreign relations in particular. Most obviously, officials might not be able to embark on difficult and politically controversial diplomatic negotiations if they know that everything they say is monitored by foreign intelligence agencies. For example, the Oslo Peace Process, which led to mutual recognition by Israel and the PLO in 1993, started as a backchannel process of negotiations under the auspices of the Norwegian authorities. By definition, diplomatic backchannels are supposed to remain secret: their role is precisely to allow officials from political communities in conflict to negotiate with one another without fear of, most immediately, coming to harm and, less immediately, of untimely and destructive exposure. Of course, secrecy might not work. Indeed, it is sometimes said that in this particular case, backchannel negotiations, though crucially important to the peace process at first, in the end proved counter-productive, as secrecy bred distrust, which in turn prompted yet more secret talks, which in turn fostered ever greater distrust—locking both parties in a vicious cycle of mutual hostility. The point remains, however, that secrecy may sometimes help, and that when it does, the relevant parties have a right to it.[15]

The democratic agency argument also holds in less fraught cases. Suppose that Blue's and Green's respective leaderships wish to conclude an agreement over access to underwater natural resources in compliance with the relevant international laws and treaties, and that they have a democratic mandate from their citizenries to do so. Blue cannot be sure that, if it chose fully to disclose its negotiating strategy, strengths and weaknesses, so would Green—and vice-versa. Blue cannot be sure that Green would not take advantage of asymmetrical knowledge (in its favour) to impose on Blue unfair terms, and vice-versa. They thus each have a strong interest in keeping some of the details of their negotiating strategy secret from the other. To the extent that Blue's and Green's negotiations

---

the democratic right to authorize those officials to disclose such information, at the cost of democracy itself. As this is too high a cost, citizens do not have a democratic right to secrecy. The objection does not work. The claim that one has a right to φ is compatible with the claim that one is under a duty to φ. For example, I have a right not to leave my house, which imposes on you a duty not to force me out. I can at the same time be under a duty not to leave my house—for example on the grounds that I am infected with a highly contagious and lethal virus. By parity of reasoning, one can coherently hold that citizens have a democratic right to secrecy and maintain that they are under a duty, indeed a democratic duty, to keep the relevant information secret.

[15] On the Norwegian backchannel in the Oslo Peace Process, see A. Wanis-St John, *Back Channel Negotiation—Secrecy in the Middle East Peace Process* (Syracuse University Press, 2011). The Northern Ireland peace process provides another interesting example of backchannel negotiations. See, e.g., E. O'Kane, 'Talking to the Enemy? The Role of the Back-Channel in the Development of the Northern Ireland Peace Process', *Contemporary British History* 29 (2015): 401–20; N. O. Dochartaigh, 'Together in the Middle: Back-channel Negotiation in the Irish Peace Process', *Journal of Peace Research* 48 (2011): 767–80; D. Omand, *How Spies Think—Ten Lessons in Intelligence* (Penguin Books, 2019), ch. 8.

are independently justified and originate in democratic political procedures, their respective citizenries have a right that the relevant information be kept secret. Their right is aptly construed as a democratic right, which they hold against each other. Here is a real-life example of a breach of that right. In 2004, Australia and Timor-Leste embarked on negotiations over reserves in oil and natural gas located in the Timor Sea. Timor-Leste, which had acquired its independence from Indonesia in 2002, had an annual GDP of c.440 million dollars, and, with half of its population under the global poverty line, was heavily dependent on access to oil; Australia was and is one of the most developed economies in the world, with an annual GDP in 2004 of c.600 billion dollars. The negotiations resulted in a treaty under the terms of which each party had an equal share of exploitation revenues. In the light of the enormous economic disparities between the two countries, the terms were more favourable to Australia than to Timor-Leste. Unbeknownst to the government of Timor-Leste, however, the Australian Secret Intelligence Service (aka ASIS) had bugged the offices of some of its key officials, including the Prime Minister. As a result, the Australian government had access to key information about Timor-Leste's negotiating position. When the espionage operation was disclosed to the then-goverment of Timor-Leste by an ASIS whistleblower under cover of anonymity ('Witness K'), Timor-Leste launched proceedings against Australia at the International Court of Justice, on the grounds that the treaty had been secured via a breach of faith and was invalid. In the end, Timor-Leste and Australia renegotiated the treaty, giving the former much more favourable terms than under the initial agreement. In acting as they did during the 2004 negotiations, the Australian authorities violated Timorese citizens' democratic right to secrecy.[16]

It might be objected that my argument proves too much. For it seems to imply, implausibly, that thwarting the outcome of democratic procedures is always a violation of a democratic right. In response: this would indeed be implausible. For a start, and to anticipate on my defence of espionage in Chapter 3, citizens and officials lack the right to vote for and pursue grievously wrongful policies—in the same way as individuals in a private capacity lack the right to commit grievous wrongdoing against other agents. Moreover, in just the same way as individuals, in a private capacity, lack the right not to be thwarted in their pursuit of any of their permissible endeavours, so do they as citizens of a democratic community. However, this point is compatible with the claim that they have a right to secrecy in respect of their permissible endeavours. To illustrate, I do not have a right that, once I open my restaurant, you not set up your own restaurant next door

---

[16] For annual GDPs by country, see the World Bank's website. On the Australia-East Timor spying scandal, this 2019 article from *The Guardian* offers a good summary of the basic facts: C. Knaus, 'Witness K and the "outrageous" Spy Scandal that Failed to Shame Australia', *The Guardian* (09/08/2019). Thanks to C. A. J. Coady for drawing my attention to this case.

and thereby cause me to go bankrupt. If, however, I have weighty reasons for not disclosing to you that I plan to open up a restaurant, I have (it seems to me) a *pro tanto* claim that you not seek to appropriate that information against my wishes, in particular by using covert means. By analogy, my claim in this section is merely that to the extent that citizens of a democratic polity have a democratic right to pursue a particular foreign policy end and that they have good reasons for wishing to keep its details secret, they have a democratic right that third parties not seek to appropriate and disclose the relevant information.[17]

2.4.2 Secrecy and Democratic Accountability

Secrecy raises an obvious and serious difficulty for democracy. On the one hand, in an indirect democracy, citizens delegate to officials the rights of government broadly construed, which include the right to conduct foreign and military policy. In order to act effectively, the executive branch and the administrative agencies which it tasks with implementing this policy must keep information secret not merely from foreign powers, but, in order to maintain such secrecy, also from citizens and their elected representatives. This requires that they should foster a certain culture of secrecy. On the other hand, and precisely on democratic grounds, citizens must be able to call their officials to account for their political decisions—including the decision to classify and restrict access to this or that piece of information. Yet, in order to call state officials to account for their informational decisions, citizens need to know precisely what they have chosen to protect as a political secret and why, which implies that such information cannot remain secret and, more widely, that state officials' activities must be transparent. Democratic agency requires secrecy and yet at the same time demands that officials' decisions be made public.[18]

The most common answer to the problem relies on a distinction between deep and shallow secrets. The government treats a piece of information about policy *P* as a deep secret when it keeps secret not just the content of *P*, but the very fact that there is such a thing as *P* in the first instance. Suppose that the government so effectively hides from citizens the very fact that there is an intelligence budget that citizens do not even know that it is worth asking whether such a thing exists.

---

[17] I am grateful to Gideon Elford for pressing me on this point.

[18] For particularly good articulations of the problem, see, e.g., C. Kutz, 'Secret Law and the Value of Publicity', *Ratio Juris* 22 (2009): 197–217, Gutmann and Thompson, *Democracy and Disagreement*, ch. 3; D. F. Thompson, 'Democratic Secrecy', *Political Science Quarterly* 114 (1999): 181–93. For an illuminating account of the publicity requirement as first set out by Immanuel Kant, and for a defence of a variant thereof, see D. Luban, 'The Publicity Principle', in R. E. Goodin (ed.), *The Theory of Institutional Design* (Cambridge University Press, 1996). For a recent and sceptical discussion of the requirement in the social contract tradition, see C. Naticchia, 'Transparency and Executive Authority', in C. Finkelstein and M. Skerker (eds.), *Sovereignty and the New Executive Authority* (Oxford University Press, 2019).

Those 'unknown unknowns' (in Donald Rumsfeld's unfairly ridiculed phrase) are deep secrets. Contrastingly, suppose that the government does not hide the fact that there is such a thing as a military intelligence budget but refuses to disclose what that budget is. The military budget is a shallow secret.[19]

On this proposal, shallow secrets entail a loss of democratic accountability but are acceptable as a means of preserving democratic agency, whereas deep secrets wholly undermine democratic accountability and agency and must therefore be eschewed.[20] If individuals do not know that a particular decision is made by officials acting on their behalf (let alone what that decision is), they have no means of challenging it. Deep secrets leave citizens, elected representatives, and judges wholly at the mercy of the executive branch of government—in a way that shallow secrets do not.

The proposal will not always work. Not treating an information as a deep secret will more often than not render the shallow secret ineffective or irrelevant. Suppose that our government keeps secret not just the kind of anti-encryption techniques our intelligence services are devising, but the very fact that it is devising such techniques and thus the very fact that there is cause for wondering whether it is doing so. Under pressure from the media, it divulges the fact that it is doing so. That it is devising encryption techniques is no longer a deep secret. As a result, our enemies start communicating via old-fashioned dead drops: information about encryption techniques, which we have taken pains to keep secret albeit of a shallow kind, is now irrelevant, and our security is under renewed threat. We may have made some gains at the bar of democratic accountability, but at a very high and, on some views, possibly unacceptable cost.[21]

Moreover, even if we are reasonably confident that desisting from keeping deep secrets would not render shallow secrets useless, we still need to ascertain how much of the relevant information can be safely disclosed. In some cases, this seems fairly straightforward. We might say for example that citizens ought to know that their leadership routinely uses killer drones in conflict zones—so that they can reflect on the moral justifiability of this policy—but that, even if it turns out that the policy is justified, they ought not to know the details of each

---

[19] Rumsfeld made the point at a Department of Defense News Briefing on 12/02/2002. (The transcript is available at https://www.youtube.com/watch?v=REWeBzGuzCc (accessed on 17/08/2021).) In fact, the phrase was used fairly routinely within US intelligence and defence circles before he popularized it. See also Pozen, 'Deep Secrecy'. For a recent and interesting application of the point to the specific context of security and intelligence operations, see M. Skerker, 'A Two-Level Account of Executive Authority', in C. Finkelstein and M. Skerker (eds.), *Sovereignty and the New Executive Authority*.

[20] On the right to keep shallow secrets as a corollary of the democratic right to rule, see, e.g., D. Mokrosinska, 'Why States Have No Right to Privacy, But May Be Entitled to Secrecy: A Non-consequentialist Defense of State Secrecy', *Critical Review of International Social and Political Philosophy* 23 (2020): 415–44.

[21] Rahul Sagar develops a similar line of criticism to mine, with particular focus on judges' ability to 'moderate secrecy'. See Sagar, *Secrets and Leaks*, 73–4.

drone operation. In other cases, however, the level of generality at which a policy ought to be described when made public can itself be a matter of controversy. For example, the US Intelligence overall budget was released to the public for the first time in 2011 and 2012, following a law to that effect passed in 2007. But the precise ways in which the budget is allocated remain classified information. Until 2007, successive US administrations would claim that it was enough, for the sake of democratic accountability and agency, that American citizens should know that there were intelligence programmes: knowing how much funding those programmes received in total was deemed too specific. Since 2007, the latter piece of information has been deemed to stand at the disclosable level of generality, whereas detailed allocation decisions are not. Were we to challenge the US administration's understanding of where to draw the line between those different levels of generality (and thus of disclosability), we would have to know why this or that piece of information is regarded as non-disclosable for being too specific, which would defeat the case for secrecy altogether.

Save for those cases in which no one could plausibly claim that hiding a piece of information from all and sundry is the only or most effective way to protect our security and agency, there is little prospect for a theoretical solution to the accountability conundrum. The solution lies in the proper vetting and ethical training of intelligence officers; in fostering constant awareness amongst citizens and officials of the dangers of a culture of excessive secrecy; and in the normatively directed institutional design of intelligence oversight. For example, it is imperative that ethical classification guidelines be designed and robustly enforced, and that officials be trained in following those guidelines and questioning abuses. Relatedly, it is also imperative that institutions be set up to monitor which officials should be given oversight of which kind of sensitive information, in order to minimize the risk that secrecy will be abused. In some contexts, the courts might be better placed than elected representatives ultimately to render judgement on the appropriateness of classification decisions; in other contexts, not so. Finally, it is imperative that whistle-blowers be given adequate protections.[22]

2.4.3 Secrecy and Non-democratic Regimes

Illiberal and undemocratic regimes (dictatorial regimes for short) use secrecy as a means to oppress their population. Do those regimes, and indeed the individuals for whose sake they claim to act, have a right to secrecy? One might think not:

---

[22] Sagar, *Secrets and Leaks*; Mokrosinska, 'Why states have no right to privacy, but may be entitled to secrecy'. On the importance of fostering norms of professional integrity, Miller, *The Moral Foundations of Social Institutions*, 188–96.

secrecy, under those circumstances, undermines rather than protects security and political agency. What those individuals acutely need is transparency, not secrecy.

However, even in communities run by dictatorial regimes, individuals need secure access to and enjoyment of a number of goods, such as water installations, energy sources, financial institutions, and health services. It clearly is in their interest that sensitive information about those goods should remain secret. Proponents of transparency might concede this point and yet object that my argument in this chapter does not apply to information about those regimes' military and security apparatus—that is to say, to the means which the regime uses in order to oppress its population. They would be on stronger grounds. Nevertheless, even dictatorial regimes are sometimes justified in protecting their populations from wrongful threats—be they internal or external. Their apparatus has two purposes: oppression and protection. Secrecy both protects and oppresses those populations; transparency might both help them fight their regime, and yet make it harder to protect themselves from wrongful threats.

The question, then, is whether the fact that the military and security apparatus is used to oppress a population dictates in favour of transparency unless the case for secrecy on protective grounds is met, or whether the fact that it is used to protect that population dictates in favour of secrecy unless the case for transparency on those very same grounds is met. In the case of dictatorial regimes, the justificatory burden which must be met in order to lift the presumption in favour of secrecy surrounding that apparatus is much lower than in the case of democratic regimes—and the more dictatorial the regime, the more so. Or, put conversely, in such cases, the justificatory burden which must be met in order to lift the presumption in favour of transparency is much higher than in the case of democratic regimes. Even so, the fact that dictatorial regimes must meet a higher justificatory burden in order to impose secrecy does not show that they can never meet it.

2.5 Conclusion

No one, except perhaps Julian Assange and his followers, advocates full publicity, and for good reasons: no one should want it to be known how exactly our civilian and military leadership will deploy our armed forces in case of an attack on our territory; in fact, it is safe to presume that Assange himself would not have wanted hackers to disclose to all and sundry the access codes to the Ecuadorian Embassy in Britain while he was in residence there. At the same time, no one, except perhaps the North Korean leadership, advocates full informational control over all aspects of their domestic and foreign policy, and for good reasons. The issue, rather, is what kind of information may be justifiably treated as secret from whom, by whom, and why. In this chapter, I have provided a qualified defence of secrecy and the right thereto, by appealing to the values of democratic agency and security.

In Chapters 4 and 9, I will supplement my defence by appealing to the importance of (respectively) economic interests and privacy.

Let us suppose, then, that both Blue's and Green's citizens have a *pro tanto* right to secrecy. This raises the following two questions: whether they are morally justified and if so, by what means, in seeking to acquire one another's secrets; whether they are morally justified and if so, by what means, in seeking to protect their own secrets from each other's attempts at acquisition.

The second question is the question of counter-intelligence. Faced with what it plausibly regards as Blue's attempts to appropriate those secrets, Green will typically conduct defensive and offensive counter-intelligence operations. As I define it in this book, defensive counter-intelligence consists in (e.g.) encoding one's communications, classifying information so as to restrict access thereto, and detecting attempts by the other side to breach one's secrets. Offensive counter-intelligence, by contrast, consists in counter-attacking the other side, by (e.g.) using its attempt to break one's codes to infiltrate and neutralize its own systems, or by deceiving them about the effectiveness of their espionage operations. I shall address the ethics of counter-intelligence in later chapters (with one exception). Beforehand, we must consider whether, and if so, on what grounds, acquiring political secrets without the consent of their holders—in other words, espionage—is morally justified.

3
Defending Espionage

3.1 Introduction

We have just seen that there are swathes of information which members of a political community have a right to keep secret. By implication, they are justified in protecting those secrets. In subsequent chapters, I shall consider some of the means by which they may do so. In this chapter, I examine the grounds on which outsiders may justifiably procure those secrets against their bearers' consent. Section 3.2 argues that a political community may justifiably spy on another political community, but only as a means to thwart rights-violations. Section 3.3 argues that it is under a duty to spy to that end and as a means to minimise the risks that it itself will commit rights-violations. Section 3.4 exposes an infinite regress at the heart of my defence of espionage and offers a tentative solution to the problem. Section 3.5 considers the controversial practice of espionage between allies.

Note that I merely seek to provide grounds for the permission and the duty to resort to espionage. It may be that, all-things-considered and in particular once one takes into account the means by which intelligence agencies conduct such operations, they are not justified all-things-considered in so acting. I leave those issues aside for now. Accordingly, the permission and duty to spy which I defend here are only *pro tanto*.

3.2 The Permission to Spy

3.2.1 The Argument

Citizens and officials acting on their behalf who use or plan to use some information p to commit serious rights violations do not have a right that p should remain secret. Suppose that Blue's forces have attacked Green without just cause. Green's leadership has to decide whether to retaliate and, as the war goes on, how to fight. Assuming that its defensive war meets the requirements of necessity, effectiveness, and proportionality, Green's forces are morally justified in destroying Blue's military infrastructure and in killing its invading soldiers.[1] By the same

---

[1] For contemporary defences of such a claim, see, e.g., K. Draper, *War and Individual Rights: The Foundations of Just War Theory* (Oxford University Press, 2016); Fabre, *Cosmopolitan* War; Frowe, *Defensive Killing*; McMahan, *Killing in War*; Rodin, *War and Self-Defense*.

token, Green's leadership is morally justified in authorizing its intelligence services to gather such information about Blue's war-fighting abilities as would enable its forces to tailor their defensive actions to the threat which they are facing. Analogously, if you attempt to kill me without just cause, not only am I morally justified in killing you in self-defence: I am morally justified in trying to ascertain how many guns you have at your disposal for this, surely, is not privileged information which you are entitled to prevent me from acquiring.

The point is not restricted to war. Suppose that Blue embarks on a policy of unwarrantedly undermining foreign leaders, including Green's leaders, who refuse to align themselves with Blue's national interests, and with seriously harmful consequences for those leaders' populations. In so far as Blue acts unjustly, Green may justifiably appropriate information which Blue lacks a right to keep secret and which Green needs in order to tailor its response.

Furthermore, the permission to spy extends to multilateral cases. Suppose that Blue is violating its obligations under a mutually agreed-upon (and morally justified) treaty or international agreement—say, a convention against nuclear proliferation.[2] As we saw in s. 1.4.1, international agreements do not only create rights and obligations *de novo*. They often reaffirm, or declare, general rights such as the fundamental rights I defended there; they also specify the content of the obligations which correlate with those rights. As declarative and specifying instruments, the obligations which they contain correlate with fundamental rights; ensuring compliance with rights-affirming treaties thus falls within the remit of my rights-based justification for spying.

Finally, suppose that Blue seeks unwarrantedly to acquire sensitive and secret information about (e.g.) Green's water infrastructure, raising fears that it might target it in a cyber-operation. In order to protect itself from Blue's intelligence agencies, Green must procure secret information about those agencies. It may justifiably do so. Unwarranted espionage provides its targets with a just cause for offensive counter-intelligence.[3]

---

[2] For the same point as applied to international law as relating to espionage, see S. Chesterman, "The Spy Who Came in From the Cold War'—Intelligence and International Law,' *Michigan Journal of International Law* 27 (2006): 1077–130, 1090–3; Lubin, 'The Liberty to Spy,' 30–2. See also (from the point of view of IR theory) C. D. Baker, 'Tolerance of International Espionage: A Functional Approach,' *American University International Law Review* 19 (2004): 1091–113.

[3] In a series of single-authored and jointly authored articles, Seumas Miller describes this point as a principle of retrospective reciprocity. I am not entirely sure that the language of reciprocity is apt: *lex talionis* seems to capture the thought better. Miller also believes that liberal democracies whose national security apparatus is targeted by the intelligence agencies of authoritarian regimes have far greater latitude, with respect to their operations of counter-intelligence, than when they are targeted by fellow liberal democracies. I do not think that the nature of the regime is morally decisive in this particular respect. (S. Miller, 'Rethinking the Just Intelligence Theory of National Security Intelligence Collection and Analysis'; P. F. Walsh and S. Miller, 'Rethinking "Five Eyes" Security Intelligence Collection Policies and Practice Post Snowden', Intelligence and National Security 31 (2016): 345–68.)

Sometimes, Green may justifiably appropriate such information even though its targets still have a right that it be kept secret. Suppose that Green's intelligence services spy on Blue's officials with a view to getting information about Blue's resilience against cyber-attacks. In the course of their espionage operation, Green's services find out how Blue prevents third parties from mounting cyber-attacks on its water supplies. Blue's residents have a right that Green's services not seek to appropriate this particular bit of information. For even if their leadership is pursuing unjust foreign policy ends—indeed even if they themselves support such ends—they are not liable to having sensitive information about their water supply appropriated and disclosed. At the same time, Green may justifiably appropriate information about Blue's military computer networks, precisely because it is trying to ascertain how to protect itself from Blue's unjust foreign policy. Green's appropriation of civilian secret information is best construed as justified collateral damage.

By contrast, espionage in the service of an unjust foreign policy is generally not justified. This applies to Blue, but also, under some circumstances, to Green. As we saw in s. 1.4.2, the fact that Green's main foreign policy ends *vis-à-vis* Blue are just at t_1 does not preclude the possibility that some of the policy's constitutive phases or Green's subsidiary ends are unjust, or that those main ends might become unjust at t_2. Suppose that Green is planning to impose comprehensive economic sanctions on Blue in order to get the latter to abandon its WMD programme, but that it has not disclosed its intentions to Blue. Suppose further that comprehensive sanctions are morally wrong on the grounds that they cause disproportionate lethal collateral damage to innocent civilians. Or suppose that Green is planning to take advantage of ongoing diplomatic negotiations on nuclear disarmament (its main policy end) to extract otherwise unfair terms from Blue in concurrent trade negotiations (its subsidiary end). Green may not resort to espionage as a means to gather the information it needs to further those unjust ends.

Moreover, Green lacks a right that Blue not seek to appropriate information about, respectively, its sanctions policy and its negotiating stance. Contrastingly, Blue, which has a *pro tanto* justification for countering Green's unjust subsidiary ends, may justifiably spy on Green to that end.

I said two paragraphs ago that espionage in the service of unjust ends is *generally* not justified: there are exceptions. Suppose that Blue mounts an unwarranted cyber-attack against Green. It ought to stop, and thus is under an obligation not to conduct intelligence operations in support of the attack. However, thanks to the information it gathers, it is in a position to shorten its attack, thereby causing lesser harms. Although Blue's government ought not to order its intelligence agencies so to act, those agencies are second-best justified to comply and take part in those operations so as to achieve the morally weighty end of inducing it to desist.[4]

---

[4] I apply to the case of spies Tadros' argument that individual soldiers are justified on those grounds in participating in an unjust war. (See Tadros, 'Unjust Wars Worth Fighting For,' 66–70.) The example

3.2.2 Three Objections

My defence of the permission to spy is likely to elicit three objections. The first objection holds that I am not permissive enough. I disallow espionage as a means merely to ascertain what other political communities are up to, yet it does not seem preposterous of Green to seek to investigate, for example, whether Blue's growing economic power might pave the way to a more hostile attitude, albeit not one that is necessarily wrongful.[5]

I disagree, at the bar of the arguments for the right to political secrecy which I mounted in Chapter 2. I will not rehearse them here. Suffice it to say that to take rights seriously is to commit oneself to the view that one may harm the interests which they protect only in response to rights violations or justified rights infringements. Not any reason will do.

The second objection, by contrast, holds that I am too permissive. After all, governments often frame and justify their foreign policy ends by appealing to the protection of fundamental rights. For example, it is entirely conceivable that acquiring secret information about foreign countries' latest military development programme will enable Green to improve its own military hardware and thus to protect itself and third parties from rights violations at some point in the future. It is hard to see how one can object to Green's espionage activities by my lights. But if this is true, there seems to be few moral limits to espionage activities.[6]

In general, the protection of rights, albeit necessary, is not a sufficient condition for justified harm imposition. Thus, even if one knows for sure that one will face such a threat in the future and that one can parry the threat now by going to war, it does not follow that one is justified in going to war. Considerations of necessity, effectiveness and proportionality come into play. So do they in the case of espionage. Moreover, suppose that it is objectively the case that Green would successfully protect itself or third parties from rights violations by spying on Blue now, and that its operation meets the requirements of necessity, effectiveness, and proportionality. Even so, the further away (in time) the prospect of those violations occurring, the weaker (typically) Green's grounds for forming the requisite justified beliefs, and the more willing should Green be to assume that the facts are not such as to make it fully justified to spy on Blue.

On another construal, the 'too permissive' objection notes that political communities which pursue unjust foreign-policy ends are morally permitted on my account to procure information which will in fact enable them more efficiently to pursue those ends. In all likelihood, Blue will not know in advance

---

in the text illustrates the general problem of what C. A. J. Coady calls 'extrication morality'. (C. A. J. Coady, 'Escaping from the Bomb: Immoral Deterrence and the Problem of Extrication,' in H. Shue (ed.), *Nuclear Deterrence and Moral Restraint* (Cambridge University Press, 1989).)

[5] Thanks to Seumas Miller for pressing me on this point.

[6] Thanks to Cécile Laborde for pressing me on this point.

of spying on Green *whether* it will be subjected to wrongful retaliatory measures or unfair diplomatic negotiations. For example, in order to know whether Green is planning to impose unfair terms on Blue, the latter might need intelligence about the overall direction of Green's foreign policy, including negotiating terms which Green would be morally justified in imposing on Blue and willing to accept. To say that Blue is justified in accessing intelligence which helps promote their justified foreign policy ends *vis-à-vis* Green and which the latter therefore have no claim that they not access, is to say, in effect, that Blue is justified in acquiring intelligence about Green *tout court* even though it might use it to further its *ab initio* unjust ends.

The objection misfires. It does not undermine the claim that Blue is justified in acquiring Green's (relevant) political secrets *only* as a means to minimize the risk that it will commit rights violations. Likewise, the fact that I might wantonly kill you by using the knife I have just bought does not undermine the claim that I am morally justified in buying that knife in the first instance as a means, but only as a means, to pursue just, or at any rate not unjust, ends (such as protecting myself from a wrongful attack or chopping my vegetables.)

The third likely objection draws on the empirical literature on espionage, some of which claims that intelligence failures vastly outweigh successes. We encountered that claim in Clausewitz's writings (s. 1.2). To contemporary critics, intelligence operations are ineffective in one or several of the following ways: they make no difference to final outcomes; they make no difference to leaders' ability to do the right thing; they are counter-productive. Here are some reasons why. Intelligence acquisition often *is* unreliable. Getting and checking the accuracy of the information which spies provide to their leaders might take so much time as to impede more successful decisions. Possessing intelligence is useless unless it is properly channelled, analysed, and acted upon. Thus, Stalin had many advance warnings of Hitler's plan to invade the Soviet Union, yet this did very little to help the Soviet military prepare for it. Relatedly, intelligence is politicized by leaders who all too often want to be told what they want to hear rather than what they actually need to know, and intelligence analysts are not always able and willing to resist those pressures. Finally, intelligence activities often engender in political and military leaders misplaced confidence that they are pursuing the right course of action; they also afford those leaders a basis for manipulating their citizenries. On some accounts of the intelligence operations which led to the invasion of Iraq by the US-led coalition in 2003, these are a textbook case of intelligence failure.[7]

---

[7] The literature on intelligence failures is enormous. For an accessible summary of the US-Iraq cases, see P. Gill and Phythian, *Intelligence in an Insecure World*, ch. 7. On Soviet intelligence in the lead-up to WWII, see, e.g., Andrew and Mitrokhin, *The Mitrokhin Archive*, 117–24; J. Haslam, *Near and Distant Neighbors—A New History of Soviet Intelligence* (Oxford University Press, 2015), ch. 5. For criticisms of intelligence in general, see, e.g., P. Knightley, *The Second Oldest Profession: Spies and*

If those warnings are factually correct, we should take them seriously: as we saw in s. 1.4.2, agents are morally permitted to harm or to risk harming another person only if they stand a chance of achieving their morally justified ends in so doing. However, we should not overestimate the force of the objection. While intelligence failures are there for us all to see, intelligence successes tend not to be reported. Moreover, the crucial issue is that of the likelihood that intelligence agencies always have been, currently are, or necessarily will be, ineffective in those ways. So long as there is a reasonable chance that procuring intelligence will enable Green to pursue its rightful ends, it may justifiably do so.

Furthermore, the charge of ineffectiveness is often conflated with the objection that espionage is counter-productive, in the sense that it impairs rather than enhances political actors' ability to make the right decisions. If and when it is, those actors' decisions to pursue intelligence activities are morally wrong on the grounds that the harms to which they contribute are disproportionate overall. But if this is correct, espionage is no different on this count than war. If the risk that a war might be a disproportionate response to rights-violations does not warrant a pacifist stand on war in general, the risk that some espionage operations might be disproportionately harmful should not lead us to reject espionage in general either.

Some pacifists would retort that *this is precisely their point*: given that war is always likely to be a disproportionate response to violations of fundamental rights (a judgement borne out by historical facts), we should reject any decision to go to war, no matter what. If so, drawing a parallel between war and intelligence activities will not work. Indeed, those pacifists might further press, given that intelligence activities are likely to be a disproportionate response to rights-violations, we should reject intelligence activities in general.

This view implies that we should dismantle both the armed forces and intelligence agencies.[8] I am not ready to bite this particular bullet. A full rejection of

Spying in the Twentieth Century (Penguin Books, 1988); J. Keegan, *Intelligence in War—Knowledge of the Enemy from Napoleon to Al-Quaeda* (Pimlico, 2004). For a more nuanced view on intelligence failures, see, e.g., R. K. Betts, 'Analysis, War, and Decisions: Why Intelligence Failures are Inevitable,' *World Politics* 31 (1978): 61–89; R. K. Betts, 'Surprise Despite Warning,' in Andrew, Aldrich, and Wark (eds.), *Secret Intelligence—A Reader*; Gill and Phythian, *Intelligence in an Insecure World*, ch. 7. On the difficulties inherent in intelligence analysis, see, e.g., A. Fatić, 'The Epistemology of Intelligence Ethics,' in J. Galliott and W. Reed (eds.), *Ethics and the Future of Spying* (Routledge, 2016); J. E. Sims, 'Philosophy, theory and Intelligence,' in R. Dover, M. S. Goodman and C. Hillebrand (eds.), *Routledge Companion to Intelligence Studies* (Routledge, 2014); P. Jackson, 'On Uncertainty and the Limits of Intelligence,' in L. K. Johnson (ed.), *The Oxford Handbook of National Security Intelligence* (Oxford University Press, 2010); D. Omand, *Securing the State* (Hurst & Co., 2010), ch. 6; Omand, *How Spies Think*. On intelligence *successes* in war, see U. Bar-Joseph and R. McDermott, *Intelligence Success and Failure—The Human Factor* (Oxford University Press, 2017). On the dispositions, attitudes, and traits of character which impede the acquisition of knowledge, with reference to the 2003 invasion of Iraq, see Q. Cassam, *Vices of the Mind* (Oxford University Press, 2019), esp. ch. 1

[8] For a powerful argument to that effect regarding the military establishment, see N. Dobos, *Ethics, Security, and the War-Machine—The True Cost of the Military* (Oxford University Press, 2020). Thanks to C. A. J. Coady for pressing me hard on this.

pacifism in general would take me far beyond the scope of this book. I am also not persuaded that the historical record bears out the pacifist's pessimistic conclusion with respect to intelligence activities. Even if we ought to be pacifists with respect to war, and even if, by implication, we should reject intelligence activities in so far as they are part of war, it does not follow that we ought to reject them altogether, including in the service of morally justified ends calling for actions short of war.

3.3 The Duty to Spy

I have defended the permission to spy as a means to protect oneself, and third parties, from rights violations. In this section, I argue that political communities are under a duty to resort to it—on two grounds.

First, suppose that Green is under a duty to thwart foreign actors' unjust policy. For example, it is under a duty to intervene militarily in the affairs of another political community or to resort to economic sanctions. If one is under a duty to φ and if one needs information in order to discharge that duty, one is under a *(pro tanto)* duty to acquire such information.

Second, Green is under a duty to spy as a means to minimize the risk that it itself will commit rights violations. Even if Green embarks on a rights-protecting foreign policy, there is always a risk that it will violate rights. It behoves it to minimize that risk. In so far as procuring the relevant information would help, Green ought to do so. This is the point made so forcefully by Sun Tzu and Thomas Hobbes. However, my defence of the duty to spy differs from theirs. I agree that public officials fail in their duty to their fellow citizens (including soldiers) if they do not take the necessary steps to protect them. However, I contend that the duty to spy is owed by Green to *anyone* who might be adversely affected by its foreign-policy decisions— whether those individuals contribute to Blue's unjust foreign policy ends or are innocent bystanders.[9]

---

[9] See also J. W. Lango, 'Intelligence about Noncombatants: The Ethics of Intelligence and the Just War Principle of Noncombatant Immunity', *International Journal of Intelligence Ethics* 2 (2011): 50–76. For recent discussions of the duty to inform oneself about the likelihood that one will fulfil one's other duties, see, e.g., G. Rosen, 'Culpability and Ignorance', *Proceedings of the Aristotelian Society* 103 (2003): 61–84; H. M. Smith, 'The Subjective Moral Duty to Inform Oneself before Acting', *Ethics* 125 (2014): 11–38. Smith uses a slightly different example from mine in the previous paragraph. See also S. Lazar, 'Risky Killing—How Risks Worsen Violations of Objective Rights', *Journal of Moral Philosophy* 16 (2019): 1–26. On the morality of risk imposition in general, see, e.g., R. Kumar, 'Risking and Wronging', *Philosophy & Public Affairs* 43 (2015): 27–51; D. McCarthy, 'Rights, Explanation, and Risks', *Ethics* 107 (1997): 205–25; J. Oberdiek, *Imposing Risk—A Normative Framework* (Oxford University Press, 2017); J. J. Thomson, 'Imposing Risks', in *Rights, Restitution, and Risk: Essays in Moral Theory* (Harvard University Press, 1986). A separate point: refusing to inform oneself (alongside related dispositions such as being unreceptive to available evidence, unwarranted confidence in one's own judgements, etc.) are epistemic vices independently of the fact that they are also moral vices. For an illuminating account of epistemic vices, see Cassam, *Vices of the Mind.*

Consider Green's duty to Blue's residents. Suppose that Green justifiably seeks to stymie Blue's WMD programme. Blue has so far resisted all attempts by Green to inspect its facilities and refused to engage in diplomatic negotiations. Green concludes that a targeted strike on the building which contains the IT mainframe for the WMD programme would be a necessary, effective, and proportionate response. Suppose that Green's leadership has information from one source that the WMD mainframe is located in a particular building, and information from another source that the building hosts the mainframe for Blue's health-care system. Only spies located *in situ* can help Green ascertain what the site is.

Let us suppose that the site contains the civilian mainframe. Were Green to bomb it, thousands of patients who depend on the good functioning of the mainframe would be grievously harmed and dozens of civilian IT workers would be killed. Were its leadership to order the bombing without sending spies out to check even though it is in a position to do so, it would unecessarily subject those individuals to the risk of being killed unwarrantedly. Deliberately killing the innocent grievously wrongs them; doing so when one did not need to do so is far worse.

Suppose now that the site hosts the mainframe for the WMD programme. Were Green to bomb it without checking what it is, it would be objectively justified in so doing: military workers are legitimate targets on account of their contribution to Blue's unjust ends. Nevertheless, it would wrong those agents by proceeding without having first checked that they *are* legitimate targets. For to treat someone with the respect he or she is owed as a moral agent does not merely require that one should harm him deliberately only if he has acted in such a way as to warrant it: it also requires that one should do so *on those grounds*. As Thomas Nagel puts it in his seminal article on war, 'hostile treatment of any person must be justified in terms of something about that person which makes the treatment appropriate.'[10] This is why—according to Nagel and, indeed, the entire just war tradition—deliberately attacking innocent civilians is morally wrong: in so far as they are innocent, there is nothing about them which warrants hostile treatment. But—I submit—the point also applies to attacking agents who are legitimate targets. To attack agents without any information regarding what, if anything, there is about them which warrants such treatment is to fail to treat them with the respect which they are owed. A legitimate target cannot complain that Green is attacking him *tout court*, but he can complain that Green is attacking him without evidence—so long as Green could reasonably be expected to get such evidence.

Ex hypothesi, the information which Green needs in order to minimize the risk that its officials will wrongfully harm Blue's residents is kept secret by Blue's leadership itself. Under those circumstances, some readers might be tempted to

---

[10] T. Nagel, 'War and Massacre,' *Philosophy & Public Affairs* 1 (1972): 123–44.

object that Blue's residents have no grievance against Green if Green fails to take steps so as to acquire the relevant information.

I disagree. Blue's decision to treat the information as a military secret does not exonerate Green from all responsibility for the fact that the risk eventuates. If Green can ask its agents to check, *in situ*, what the site exactly is without exposing those agents or other individuals to undue risks of harm, it ought to do so. More generally, the fact that someone wrongfully fails to do at t_1 what would enable another party not to cause wrongful harm at t_2 does not exonerate the latter from taking steps so as to mitigate the former's dereliction of duty.[11]

Consider now Green's duty to its own residents and officials. Green's leadership clearly is under a duty to Green's residents to ascertain whether bombing Blue's WMD facilities would expose those individuals to unnecessary, ineffective, or disproportionate retaliatory harm at the hands of Blue. To be sure, Blue's leadership would be causally responsible for those harms were it to subject Green to (e.g.) terrorist attacks or harmful economic sanctions, in retaliation for Green's justified bombing campaign against its WMD programme. However, Blue's leadership would act in response to Green's prior decision to bomb their facilities. As an intervening agent, Blue does not bear sole responsibility for the ensuing wrongful harms: Green's leadership bears some of the responsibility and it thus behoves it to try and establish how likely it is that Blue's leadership will respond in this way.[12]

Furthermore, Green's leadership is under a duty to its own officials, *qua* officials, to spy on Blue. Green is justified in resorting to harmful measures only in pursuit of just foreign-policy ends. When its leadership is not in possession of all the facts, it ought to act on the basis of beliefs which are formed in the light of the best available evidence. The weaker and less reliable the evidence, the less likely it is that Green's officials tasked with implementing those harmful measures will be objectively justified in committing those harmful acts—and the more likely it is that they will be aptly charged with violating the rights of Blue's residents and officials not to be harmed in these ways. Were Green's leadership not to procure the needed information, it would expose its officials to the moral burden of harming individuals who, in fact, ought not to be harmed. Green's leadership is under a duty to those officials to spare them from needlessly incurring such burdens—a duty which it can discharge by instructing its spies to gather the relevant information about Blue.

---

[11] I address some of the harms which can accrue to intelligence officers and in particular to assets in the field in s. 5.6.

[12] On the shared responsibility of intervening and non-intervening agents, see, e.g., M. J. Zimmerman, 'Intervening Agents and Moral Responsibility,' *The Philosophical Quarterly* 35 (1985): 347–58; V. Tadros, 'Permissibility in a World of Wrongdoing,' *Philosophy & Public Affairs* 44 (2016): 101–32. In the case mentioned in the previous paragraph, Blue is not an *intervening* agent. Those cases highlight different ways in which responsibility for wrongful harms can be shared.

I have assumed so far that Green is pursuing just, rights-protecting, foreign-policy ends *vis-à-vis* Blue. Consider now Blue's situation. Even though its main foreign-policy ends are *ex hypothesi* unjust, it too is under a duty to resort to espionage as a means to minimize the risk that its officials will violate the fundamental rights of another party. Suppose that Blue is unjustifiably developing a new weapons programme, and that Green is justifiably attempting to thwart it by mounting a cyber-attack on Blue, from a location which it seeks to keep secret. Suppose that Blue's leadership have information to the effect that Green's cyber-weapons headquarters are located in a particular building. They also have contradictory information from another source that the building hosts Green's civilian IT mainframe. If Blue's spies report back that the building's computer mainframe is a civilian facility, Blue will desist from bombing it, thereby sparing the lives and limbs of civilians who depend on it as well as of the workers who work there. If the spies report back that the building hosts Green's cyber-command, Blue will have it bombed, killing all inside.

Depending on the nature of the site, spying on Green in breach of the latter's justified decision to keep the information secret might give Blue the opportunity *not* to kill Green's civilian IT workers, thereby respecting their right not to be killed. It might also give Blue licence, *by its own lights*, to kill Green's military IT workers, in violation of their right not to be killed. In the light of that fact, what must Blue do?

Suppose that, as a matter of fact, the site is a military site. If Blue has it checked, Green's military IT workers will die, and without adequate justification. From those workers' point of view, it makes no difference whether Blue kills them on the grounds that they work for the military or without having checked that this is what they are and that it is permitted to kill them by its own lights. In this particular case, it is not apt to say that Blue is under a duty to those workers to conduct espionage activities so as to check the nature of the site.

It might be thought that this claim is in tension with my earlier claim that Green owes it to Blue's IT workers to check that they are legitimate targets, even though those workers have lost their right not to be killed. If Green is derelict, I argued, those workers can legitimately complain that Green failed to treat them with the respect they are owed, even though they lack a right not to be killed. It might thus be thought that Green's military IT workers, who in the case under scrutiny here have a right *not* to be killed, also have a grievance if Blue proceeds to kill them without checking whether it may do so by its own lights.

It is not clear to me however what wrong exactly is done to those workers, given that Blue is morally mistaken in thinking that they may be killed in the first instance. Analogously, imagine a negligent Nazi commander who does not bother to check whether the unarmed civilians he is about to have exterminated are Jewish and so may justifiably be killed by his lights. Suppose that they are Jewish. I fail to see in what way exactly the commander's failure to procure the evidence he needs in order to act by his own lights is a failure of respect *vis-à-vis* those victims.

In any event, the crucial point is that *if* the site is a civilian site, Green's civilian IT workers will be spared. If the unarmed civilians are Aryan, so will they. If only for that reason, Blue, or the Nazi commander, ought to check: as we saw in s. 3.3, deliberately harming the innocent is a serious wrong to the latter. Doing so when one could avail oneself of the morally correct option not to do so is far worse.

Finally, Blue's leaders sometimes owe it to their population to spy on Green. To reiterate, it is wrong to implicate agents in the commission of rights violations. So to implicate them either by ordering them so to act and subjecting them to penalties for failing to comply, or by claiming to act on their behalf or at their behest, is also morally wrong. Failing to reduce the probability that they would be so implicated when one could do so by informing oneself of the appropriateness of a particular policy is wrong. It is especially wrong if, as a result of being so implicated, Blue's population is rendered more vulnerable to Green's harmful retaliatory foreign policy. But even if Green would spare those civilians, Blue's leadership is still under the stated duty to their fellow citizens: think of the protest, in the purest form, 'not in my name'.

It might seem that those considerations decisively tell against the view that there is a moral difference between those who stand on opposite sides of an intelligence war. Both sides are under a duty to minimize the number of occurrences on which they will violate rights; neither side knows whether it will be subjected to such violations at the hands of the other; and both sides need to procure information in order to establish how best to meet their duty, to ascertain whether it is vulnerable to wrongful harms, and to determine how best to protect itself. It seems that there is very little to distinguish between Green and Blue with respect to their espionage-related activities, and that their spies are morally on a par.

However, Green and Blue—more specifically, their agents—differ from one another, morally speaking, in one important respect. So long as Blue is pursuing unjust foreign policy ends, its first-best duty is to cease and desist. Granted, given that it will not do so, it is under a duty to take steps so as to reduce the likelihood that its officials will inflict wrongful harms. It is also under a duty to minimize its residents' vulnerability to Green's wrongful acts. Those points notwithstanding, Blue is derelict in its duty to conduct just foreign-policy ends. Its decision to deploy spies, and those spies' acts, though in one sense morally justified as a second-best moral option, nevertheless is morally tainted. It is in that sense that there remains a moral asymmetry between intelligence agents on different sides of a conflict: some dirty their hands, while others keep theirs clean. The question, then, is whether the fact that a duty to spy is a first-best or a second-best duty makes a difference to the stringency of the restrictions under which those communities and their intelligence agencies must operate. I shall return to this issue in subsequent chapters.[13]

[13] For a recent discussion of the moral status of second-best reasons in the context of war killing, see J. Parry and D. Viehoff, 'Instrumental Authority and Its Challenges: The Case of the Laws of War,' *Ethics* 129 (2019): 548–75.

Two final points. First, in s. 2.2, I noted that the right to secrecy correlates with a duty not to appropriate information and a duty not to disseminate it, and that those duties can sometimes come apart. To say that an agent no longer has a right to secrecy, thus, may mean either that the other party is no longer under a duty not to collect the information, or that it is no longer under a duty not to disclose it, or both. The rationale for the duty to spy sometimes also supports a duty to share the information so acquired with the agencies or (if appropriate) the leaders of other political communities directly. In fact, intelligence-sharing is an essential part of statecraft, whether it is practised openly or secretively. By the same token, tensions and disagreements about the degree to which intelligence is and ought to be shared are a constant feature of diplomatic relations writ large. Of course, there is no guarantee that the information will be used to rightful ends. The British authorities rightly decided not to reveal to the Soviets that they had cracked Enigma, so fearful were they that the Germans had penetrated the Soviet military intelligence services. Ironically, at the same time, John Cairncross, who was working at Bletchey Park and then at MI6, and belonged to the Cambridge Five ring, was keeping his Soviet masters informed of those developments. Nevertheless, the British decision not to disclose was morally right. More recently, a number of American intelligence experts have expressed concerns that some of the United States' intelligence partners in the Middle East, South East Asia, and Colombia may have been penetrated by terrorist organizations. In Britain, concerns have been raised about the risks that, by sharing intelligence with the United States, British intelligence agencies such as GCHQ are complicit in illegal drone killings. Nevertheless, there also are cases in which intelligence-sharing has thwarted serious attacks and concommitant rights violation and where a refusal to cooperate would have constituted a dereliction of duty.[14]

Second, given that thanks to spying, Blue might end up sparing some of Green's residents from having their rights violated, it may well be imprudent as well as, in the end, morally wrong of Green's officials always to engage in *counter*-intelligence operations against Blue—and vice-versa. The following two examples from the

---

[14] On the risks and benefits of intelligence-sharing in general, see, e.g., Carnegie and Carson, *Secrets in Global Governance*; C. Clough, 'Quid Pro Quo: The Challenges of International Strategic Intelligence Cooperation,' *International Journal of Intelligence and CounterIntelligence* 17 (2004): 601–13; S. Lefevre, 'The Difficulties and Dilemmas of International Intelligence Cooperation,' *International Journal of Intelligence and CounterIntelligence* 16 (2003): 527–42; J. E. Sims, 'Foreign Intelligence Liaison: Devils, Deals, and Details,' *International Journal of Intelligence and CounterIntelligence* 19 (2006): 195–217; Chesterman, 'The Spy Who Came in From the Cold War'; R. J. Aldrich, 'Transatlantic Intelligence and Security Cooperation,' *International Affairs* 80 (2004): 731–53. Aldrich's article has a good discussion of the Enigma case. It also mentions as an example of successful intelligence-sharing a pan-European operation which led to the arrest of a number of Al-Qaeda members in early 2001. On the aforementioned concerns about penetration by nonstate actors, see, e.g., Wege, 'The Changing Islamic State Intelligence Apparatus.' On concerns about Britain's involvement, via intelligence-sharing, in violations of international law, see, e.g., A. Ross and J. Ball, 'GCHQ documents raise fresh questions over UK complicity in US drone strikes', *The Guardian* (24/06/2015).

Cold War nicely illustrate the point. In 1955, the British double agent George Blake, who was a MI6 officer, revealed to his Soviet paymasters that the British were digging underground tunnels to tap phone landlines in Soviet-controlled areas of Berlin. The phone taps together with the fact that the Soviets knew about these provided both sides reassurance that neither was planning a wholesale attack—which in turn helped stabilize Anglo-Soviet relations in the early years of the Cold War. It is a good thing that the Soviets did not employ full counter-intelligence measures and prevent the British from installing the taps (and, indeed, that the British did not manage to arrest Blake early on, thereby preventing him from disclosing to the Soviets what he knew). The NATO war games of 1983 tell a similar story: thanks to a Soviet mole within NATO, the Soviet authorities were told that the Alliance was not in the process of attacking the USSR. This may have been one of the reasons why, despite their growing alarm at what they thought was a NATO nuclear first strike, they decided not to counter-attack.[15]

3.4 The Problem of Uncertainty

We must now address an obvious difficulty. I noted in s. 1.4.2 that we want to know whether agents are objectively and subjectively justified (for short, fully justified) in inflicting harm on another party—here, the harm attendant on having secrets appropriated or disclosed. More often than not, Green does not have enough evidence to ascertain whether Blue is conducting, or preparing to conduct, an unjust foreign policy, and what it may justifiably do in response—for example, whether it could justifiably impose economic sanctions on Blue. Hence its need and justification for going on a fishing expedition. The difficulty arises when Green does not have evidence that having a particular piece of information p would be conducive to forming the relevant justified belief and to making the objectively and subjectively right decision. We might conclude that it may justifiably procure another piece of information p^*, if doing so would reduce its level of uncertainty as to whether or not having p would help reduce its uncertainty as to whether it may impose sanctions. But what if it does not know whether having p^* would help in this way? Well, then, perhaps it may justifiably procure some other piece of information p^{**}, as a means to ascertain whether having p^* would help reduce its level of uncertainty as to whether p^* would help determine whether it may procure p. But what if it does not know whether p^{**} would help? And so on.

---

[15] On the Berlin tunnel taps, see Aldrich, *GCHQ*, 175–6. (Blake was eventually arrested in 1961, but in 1966 escaped, and fled to Moscow, where he lived until his death in December 2020.) On the 1983 NATO war games, see T. Downing, *1983—The World at the Brink* (Abacus, 2018) and Omand, *How Spies Think*, ch. 8. Omand makes the general point of this paragraph in *Securing the State*, 134–6. As a former member of the Joint Intelligence Committee and Director of GCHQ, he should know.

The difficulty is that Green's justification for breaching secrecy is not available to its agents unless and until they breach secrecy, which raises the spectre of infinite regress. Here is a possible solution. In the light of the account of subjective permissibility sketched out in s. 1.4.2, Green must have a reasonable belief that it is objectively justified in spying on Blue—that is to say, its epistemic reasons for forming that belief must be undefeated by other reasons. If Green lacks such belief, it must work on the assumption that Blue is not liable to being spied upon. Even if, as a matter of fact, it is objectively justified in spying on Blue, it is not subjectively and therefore not fully justified in doing so.

When, then, might Green be justified in spying on Blue? In domestic law enforcement, police officers normally have to show a judge why they need to obtain information about a particular individual, in order to get a warrant to obtain that information in a particular way (for example, by entering their property). If they lack reasonable grounds for believing that a crime was or is about to be committed, they may not obtain the information (at least, not in ways which breach the agent's presumptive rights to property, privacy, and so on.) Typically, they adduce two grounds for forming that belief, both of which are relevant here. First, they have been supplied with information by informants or, more generally, members of the community. Think, for example, of parents worried about their son's increasing radicalization and taking their concerns to the police. By analogy, in the intelligence context, Green's services might be given information by some citizen of Blue which might warrant further and more intrusive investigation.

Second, law enforcement officials rely on open sources. By analogy, suppose that Green and Blue have long been locked into a dispute over contested territory alongside the border that separates them. Military tensions have flared up on a regular basis for a number of years. Open sources provide Green's services with reasons to believe that Blue's leadership are planning to annex part of Green's territory. For example, news reports and open-sky satellite images seemingly indicate that Blue's leadership has been massing troops close to the border. Blue's leadership is perfectly aware both of how Green's leadership is likely to interpret this information, and unwilling to provide anything but feeble denial of aggressive bellicose intentions. Blue's conduct, together with open-source evidence, provides Green with the information p^* which it needs in order to go and look for further evidence p. Under those circumstances, Green's belief that Blue has bellicose intentions is reasonable, and Green is fully justified in seeking to procure p.[16]

---

[16] See also R. W. Bellaby, *The Ethics of Intelligence*, 34. For the view that knowingly acting in such as way as to cause another party to believe, reasonably, that one poses a serious threat to them makes one liable to defensive harm, see, e.g., Quong, *The Morality of Defensive Force*, 43–4. For the view that the requirement of reasonable cause does not apply to intelligence activities with the same stringency as it applies to police operations, see Omand and Phythian, *Principled Spying*, 26. I am grateful to Alejandro Chehtman for helping me clarify my thoughts on this. The scenario which I am describing here reflects recurrent flare-ups between Russia and Ukraine on the latter's eastern border.

In some cases, the harms that would eventuate were Green wholly ignorant of the threat it faces and therefore unprepared for it would be so great that it is permissible to investigate whether there is such a threat, even in the absence of grounds for forming the requisite belief. Weapons of mass destruction are a paradigmatic example. Even if setting up a nuclear programme is not, in itself, morally wrong (at least as a response to other actors' decision to have one), setting it up with a view to using as a first-strike and indiscriminate instrument is morally wrong. And even if one does not intend so to use it, the transborder risks inherent in an uncontrolled nuclear explosion and in the uranium falling into the wrong hands are such that third parties do have a claim to know about it. If I am right, Japanese officials were entitled to investigate whether the United States were developing nuclear weapons even if they merely suspected, on however flimsy a basis, that such programme existed. Saddam Hussein did not have a right that the United Nations not attempt to uncover such a programme. In the latter case, the point is not that Saddam Hussein's regime was under a duty to comply with verification protocols such that its failure to do so meant that it no longer had a right that the United Nations not seek to uncover the relevant information. The point is that it did not have that right in the first instance.

3.5 Between Allies—'A Waste of Energy'?

I have assumed throughout this chapter that Green and Blue are in more or less declared conflict with each other. This assumption is not wholly faithful to espionage practices. In his history of GCHQ, Richard Aldrich records ways in which, in the 1960s, the organization would insert backdoor traps in the Swiss code-breaking computers bought by the French and German governments. Fifty years later, Edward Snowden revealed that GCHQ and its American counterpart, the NSA, had mounted extensive surveillance operations on the United States' and the United Kingdom's allies, notably Germany and France, prompting Chancellor Merkel to protest that spying amongst allies is a 'waste of energy'. In response to outraged protestations from the French, American (and French) commentators acidly pointed out that France's services had a long history of doing exactly the same to the Americans. It further emerged that Germany's Federal Intelligence Service (aka BND) had conducted espionage operations against successive American administrations for a number of years.[17]

---

[17] Aldrich, 'Transatlantic Intelligence and Security Cooperation' 209ff, and 519–23; L. Harding, *The Snowden Files* (Faber and Faber, 2014), especially ch. 12. For a contemporary account of the US–French spying 'scandal', see K. Willsher, 'France summons US ambassador over "unacceptable" spying', *The Guardian* (24/06/2015). On the Germans' operations against the US, see, e.g., J. Huggler, 'German intelligence accused of "spying on USA"', *The Daily Telegraph* (22/06/2017). P. Oltermann and S. Ackerman, 'Germany asks top US intelligence official to leave country over spy row', *The*

These countries profess to regard one another as allies and are supposed to join forces against common external threats, in particular by sharing intelligence. France, Britain, and the United States were founding members of NATO and part of its integrated command system in the early 1960s. West Germany became a member in 1955 and was joined by East Germany in 1990 upon the reunification of the country. Espionage between allies is not restricted to peacetime operations: the fact that the USSR became an ally of Britain and the United States in 1941 did not dampen its leaders' appetite for infiltrating their intelligence services—in fact, quite the opposite.[18]

The fact that Green and Blue are allies places them under a duty not to spy on one another, for at least three reasons. First, to the extent that an alliance is not one of pure expediency but is instead rooted in a commitment to the same moral and political values or similar geopolitical goals, its parties are under a duty to one another to trust one another and not to act in such as way as to jeopardize that alliance. To the extent that espionage and counter-intelligence operations undermine that trust, they ought to be avoided. Second, to the extent that an alliance creates mutually understood expectations that its parties will not spy on one another, the latter are under a duty not to act in breach of those expectations. Third, to the extent that an alliance confers benefits on its parties (not least the benefits of intelligence sharing), the latter are under a duty not to betray one another by spying on one another.

Here, as always, the duty is a *pro tanto* duty. Circumstances may change. For example, one of the allies might be derelict in its duty to the other to share intelligence that is relevant to the pursuit of their common ends. An alliance might be purely expedient and understood as such by its parties, each of which expects the other to break it at the first good opportunity. The 1939 pact of non-aggression between Germany and the USSR comes to mind. Finally, even if neither party is anticipating betraying the other, today's ally might turn out to be tomorrow's enemy. Granted, the fact that Green and Blue are allies implies that Green must overcome a higher evidentiary hurdle in order to ground its belief that it is under threat from Blue. But this does not undermine the claim that it is under some circumstances justified in spying on Blue.

3.6 Conclusion

I have argued that political communities are sometimes morally justified, indeed are under a duty, to engage in intelligence activities against other political commu-

---

Guardian (10/07/2014). For the claim that espionage between allies is sometimes morally justified, see K. Macnish, *The Ethics of Surveillance: An Introduction* (Routledge, 2017), 82–4.

[18] Andrew, *The Defence of the Realm*, 263–82; Andrew and Mitrokhin, *The Mitrokhin Archive*, ch. 7.

nities as a means to conduct a rights-respecting foreign policy or, less ambitiously, as a means to minimize the risk that they will conduct an unjust foreign policy, and (relatedly) as a means to protect themselves from unwarranted espionage activities. They are not justified in doing so as a means to pursue an unjust policy, save in those cases in which they would, in so doing, bring about the morally weighty end of minimizing rights violations (in which case they are only second-best justified in so doing.)

To claim that a party is *pro tanto* justified or required to spy on another party and/or to counteract the latter's own intelligence activities is one thing. To claim that it is all-things-considered permitted or required to do so is another, and depends on careful scrutiny of the means by which it does so. I shall explore a wide range of such means in subsequent chapters. Beforehand, I turn to economic espionage.

4

Economic Espionage

4.1 Introduction

Perhaps you will, at some point today, make yourself a nice cup of tea. It is likely that in whole or in part your tea leaves will have been imported from India. India acquired its dominant position as a tea-manufacturing country in the nineteenth century. The East India Company, in effect the British Government's agency for managing India, was anxious to break China's stranglehold on tea production. It dispatched the Scottish botanist and plant hunter Robert Fortune to China's tea-growing regions with instructions to steal the secrets of its production.[1]

Perhaps you own a Huawei phone and are planning to upgrade it to a 5G-enabled handset as soon as models become available. Depending on where you live, you may well be sorely disappointed: at the time of writing this, the company has been blacklisted in various ways by a number of governments, who are concerned that it is working too closely with the Chinese state and is enmeshed in the latter's espionage operations against Western economic (as well as geopolitical) interests.

Both cases involve economic espionage—to wit, the practice of acquiring secret economic intelligence from private economic actors. It is a tried and tested tool of statecraft. Rulers have long resorted to it to a variety of ends: helping their own firms gain a competitive commercial advantage; strengthening national security; promoting their citizens' vital interests; and advancing their geopolitical and strategic aims on the world stage. To give but one example, the Republic of Venice arguably had the most developed network of economic spies of the 15th and 16th century: as a mercantile city, its political survival depended on it. More recently, since the end of the Cold War, economic espionage has witnessed exponential growth as the machinery of the state has become more complex, as the boundaries between the political and the economic spheres have become more porous, and as the world has become more globalized and more connected, not least via the Internet: as we shall see later on (s. 8.4.1), major operations of cyber-espionage have involved both political and economic intelligence-gathering.[2]

---

[1] S. Rose, *For All the Tea in China* (Hutchinson, 2009).

[2] For fascinating discussions of the Venice case, see C. Andrew, *The Secret World*, ch. 8; Iordanou, *Venice's Secret Service*. For an excellent account of economic and industrial espionage which charts its rise, describes its many guises, and reviews states' attempts to counter it, see H. Nasheri, *Economic Espionage and Industrial Spying* (Cambridge University Press, 2005). For a shorter account, specifically

There is little scholarly work in that area. The stupefyingly large empirical liter-ature on espionage tends to concentrate on state-on-state intelligence activities. Economic espionage, it is fair to say, has a bad reputation in the media and has been neglected by academia. My aim is to start filling the gap, by providing a qual-ified defence of state-sponsored economic espionage against private businesses (henceforth, for short, economic espionage). Section 4.2 offers a defence of the right to economic secrecy. Section 4.3 mounts a defence of economic espionage as the acquisition of economic secrets. Section 4.4 responds to four objections.

I restrict the scope of the chapter as follows. First, I leave consideration of the moral status of the means by which states appropriate secret economic intelligence (as well as military-cum-geopolitical intelligence) until subsequent chapters. As we shall see, those means are limited only by their agents' imagination, from (allegedly) planting listening devices in business-class aircraft cabins, to steal-ing laptops, blackmailing business executives, infiltrating business conventions, and hacking into computer networks. Furthermore, in their quest for economic intelligence, states often employ private intelligence firms alongside their own intelligence agencies. I will not consider the ethics of the privatization of espionage. Such arguments as may be deployed for or against private spies parallel arguments for and against the use of mercenaries in war.[3]

Second, I set aside business-on-business, and business-on-states, espionage activities (aka corporate or industrial espionage). I also set aside cases in which a state spies on a private company in order to access data about its political opponents—as the Chinese authorities are alleged to have done in 2010 by target-ing the Gmail accounts of Chinese human-rights activists. Rather, I am concerned with the acquisition of secret information about firms' operations, strategy, and resources in so far as it is relevant to the defence of fundamental rights against for-

---

about economic espionage in the United States until the mid 2000s, see H. Rishikoff, 'Economic and Industrial Espionage: Who is Eating America's Lunch and How to Stop it?', in J. E. Sims and G. L. Burton (eds.), *Vaults, Mirrors, and Masks: Rediscovering U.S. Counterintelligence* (Georgetown University Press, 2009). For a concise summary of interesting, pre-1945 cases, see B. Champion, 'A review of selected cases of industrial espionage and economic spying, 1568–1945', *Intelligence and National Security* 13 (1998): 123–43. See also G. Corera, *Intercept: The Secret History of Computers and Spies* (Weidenfeld & Nicolson, 2015), esp. ch. 10 and, for a discussion of Huawei, ch. 11. In one of the latest developments in the history of espionage, it was alleged in the summer of 2020 that China-backed and Russia-backed hackers had attempted to hack into the servers of American, British, and Canadian public organizations and private corporations involved in developing a COVID vaccine. (See, e.g., C. Bing and M. Taylor, 'Exclusive: China-backed hackers 'targeted COVID-19 vaccine firm Moderna', *Reuters* (30/07/2020). H. Warrell, C. Cookson, and H. Foy, 'Russia-linked hackers accused of targeting Covid-19 vaccine developers', *The Financial Times* (16/07/2020).)

[3] On the means employed by economic spies, see, e.g., H. Nasheri, *Economic Espionage and Industrial Spying* (Cambridge University Press, 2005), ch. 1; E. Javers, *Broker, Trader, Lawyer, Spy: The Secret World of Corporate Espionage* (HarperCollins, 2010); F. W. J. Rustmann, *CIA Inc.—Espionage and the Craft of Business Intelligence* (Brassey's Inc., 2002). The United States' National CounterIntelligence and Security Center has a particularly useful document on economic espionage in cyber-space, which is available at https://fas.org/irp/ops/ci/feec-2018.pdf (17/08/2021).

eign threats.[4] For the sake of expository simplicity, I focus on economic espionage against foreign and global firms, although some of my arguments apply *mutatis mutandis* to cases in which a state's agencies target domestic firms. Contrast the following two cases. In the first case, the French domestic intelligence service places undercover officers in a French-owned IT firm under contract with a key player in the maintenance of France's nuclear reactors on the grounds that one of its employees might be selling secrets to a foreign power. In the second case, France's external service runs agents in a Chinese IT firm with close links to China's nuclear industry on the grounds that French nuclear security is under threat from China. Suppose that the French authorities are correct in their assessment of the situation. Considerations which support their decision to run an agent in the Chinese firm also support their decision to run one in the French firm. It is the second case that concerns me here. (This is a purely hypothetical, though plausible, case. I am using France as an example because the French state is widely cited in the scant empirical literature as one of the most effective and ruthless 'economic spies' in the world.)

One final and related caveat. I assume for the sake of argument that appropriately constrained forms of capitalism are not inherently unjust. The fact that private individuals and businesses own capital goods, that the law enforces private property rights, and that the production and allocation of goods and services are governed by market supply and demand does not, in itself, render this mode of organizing economic activity unjust. On the contrary, I assume that private ownership (including of capital goods) and the market are morally legitimate institutions, so long as certain conditions obtain. It is a foundational tenet of this book that all individuals, wherever they reside in the world, have fundamental rights to the freedoms and resources they need to lead a flourishing life (s. 1.4.1). I take it for granted that businesses are under moral duties to respect individuals' fundamental moral rights, wherever those individuals are located in the world, and thus that some degree of state regulation of and interference with private economic activities is morally justified. Some readers will undoubtedly claim that I concede too much to capitalism. Perhaps I do. If so, my arguments can be read as a counter-claim to opponents of economic espionage whose objections are grounded, precisely, in their defence of capitalism. *Even if* capitalism is morally justified—I argue—it does not follow that economic espionage is not.

4.2 Economic Secrets

Collective security and democratic agency are collective goods. As we saw in Chapter 2, appropriating secret information about those goods without the

---

[4] On this particular example—one of many involving China—see a recent document from the Council on Foreign Relations, 'Operation Aurora', available at https://www.cfr.org/interactive/cyber-operations/operation-aurora (accessed on 17/08/2021).

relevant authorization is usually deemed a criminal offence. Interestingly, in some jurisdictions, appropriating economic intelligence without the consent of the relevant economic agents is also regarded as a criminal offence. In the United States, for example, the 1996 Economic Espionage Act stipulates that stealing trade secrets is a federal crime, whether the intention is to benefit a foreign state or to harm the owners of that secret and whether the act is carried out by private actors or at the behest of foreign powers. In June 2018, the United Kingdom enacted legislation aimed at enforcing the 2016 EU Trade Secrets Directive, thanks to which existing albeit piecemeal protections as afforded in civil courts are now codified. That said, under English law, the theft of trade secrets is not regarded as a criminal offence.

Those laws seem to recognize a legal right to economic secrets. As I suggest in this section, there is also a *pro tanto* moral right thereto, which it pays to decompose into its constitutive elements: (a) the content of the right; (b) the right-holder; (c) the grounds for the conferral of the right.

Economic information about a firm divides into operational information and proprietary information. Operational information includes, *inter alia*, information about the firm's financial health, size, strategy, outputs, pricing policies, and customers' lists. Proprietary information includes, *inter alia*, technical drawings, computer source codes, and chemical formulas. To say that there is a right to economic secrecy is to say that the right-holder has a right that some economic information of both kinds not be appropriated and disclosed without her consent.

The right to economic secrecy thus protects whomever has the relevant interests. In the first instance, the interest-bearers and, thereby, the rights-holders, are businesses and/or their individual agents. By 'a business', I mean a firm or a corporation which is privately owned and whose aims are to manufacture goods and/or provide services, and to sell its products for a profit on open markets. Businesses are neither quite like a state-governed political community, nor quite like a voluntary association such as a club. Unlike the former, whose members do not by and large choose to join (save for at least some immigrants), a business comprises individuals who by and large so choose (albeit, for some of them, under economic duress). Moreover, whereas a firm's employees are not the source of their managers' authority, citizens of liberal democracies are the source of the authority of their legislature and government. Unlike a club-like voluntary association, whose members relate to one another on a footing of equality, relationships between members of a firm are relationships of authority and power.[5]

---

[5] Political theorists have not devoted much attention to firms and corporations. Two exceptions are A. A. Singer, *The Form of the Firm—A Normative Political Theory of the Corporation* (Oxford University Press, 2019); E. Anderson, *Private Government: How Employers Rule Our Lives (and Why We Don't Talk about It)* (Princeton University Press, 2017).

A business's employees, directors, managers, and shareholders all have interests in its ongoing robustness—be it an indirect interest in earning a living from it (whether or not one enjoys one's work), or (in some cases) a direct interest in nurturing and developing it. Furthermore, a business's consumers may also have interests in its ongoing health—or, at any rate, if not in a particular instance of a business, at least in the sector of which it is a part: we may not worry too much about one large food retailer going bankrupt, but we should and would worry if all food retailers were to collapse. Finally, individuals who are neither shareholders, employees, managers, nor consumers of a particular business may sometimes have an interest in the latter's robustness: think of large corporations whose business activities are so central to and interwoven in our daily lives, even when we do not ourselves buy its products, that they are deemed to be 'too big to fail': if they are at risk of failing, they will receive tax-funded state aid at the expense of the provision of other public goods. If those interests are important enough to be protected by rights, then those rights are held, jointly, by all of us, even if we are not directly involved in those corporations. By implication, if some individuals have an interest in operational or proprietary information about a particular business remaining secret and if that interest is important enough to be protected by a right, then those individuals are aptly described as the holders of that right.

The claim that some agent has a *pro tanto* right to economic secrecy stands in need of justification: one must establish why that agent has an interest in operational and/or proprietary information about a business remaining secret, and why that interest is important enough to be protected by rights against unauthorized appropriation and disclosure.[6]

The mere fact that an agent rightfully owns something confers on her a right to control some information about that thing. Not *all* information passes the test though. There are good reasons for imposing on firms a duty to disclose who owns them and to make their annual financial accounts and returns publicly available— the kind of information, in other words, which, in the UK, businesses are required to provide to the state under the terms of the 2006 Companies Act. Nevertheless, with that qualification in hand, property rights provide a basis for the right to economic secrecy in so far as secrecy protects information about (*inter alia*) goods

---

[6] In one of the few book-length philosophical treatments of secrecy, Sissela Bok considers various defences of trade and corporate secrecy, notably, as I do here, agency, property, and security. She does not fully commit herself to defending or indeed rejecting the view that agents are sometimes warranted in keeping economic information secret; rather, she highlights considerations for and against—though it is fair to say, I think, that she leans against it. (Bok, *Secrets*, ch. 10.)

Some readers might object that the right to economic secrets is not a genuine moral right but, rather, is a morally justified legal mechanism for protecting some interests: were there other or better means of protecting those interests (the objection goes), one would not commit a wrongdoing by (e.g.) not developing a patent regime. I am inclined to think that there is a moral right to economic secrecy. In any event, the points I make below in its defence can be recast as moral justifications for the legal right. (I am grateful to David Miller for pressing me on this point.)

in which economic agents have such rights. To the extent that those individuals have property rights over those goods and that secrecy helps protect access to those goods, they have a right to the relevant secrets. By analogy, the claim that I own my house implies that I have a right to keep the deactivation code for its alarm system secret.

The point applies to operational and proprietary information. In the latter case, the rights at issue are rights to intellectual property—that is to say, property over intangible goods such as processes, data, working methods, works of art, inventions, and so on. Intellectual property is protected by a number of mechanisms, such as copyrights regimes, patents regimes, and trade secrecy. Trade secrets, in particular, protect economic agents from the unauthorized appropriation and disclosure of data, products, and processes which are not generally known within that domain of activity, and whose commercial value derives precisely from the fact that they are secret.[7]

Defences of trade secrecy tend to take broadly Lockean or utilitarian forms.[8] According to the Lockean argument, inventors and investors have a strong interest—strong enough to be protected by a right—in enjoying the fruits of their creation or investment. Unauthorized appropriation and disclosure by their competitors of the processes by which they have come to produce those goods undermine that interest. Inventors and investors have a strong interest in being protected from such risks—strong enough to be protected by rights to secrecy. The argument is broadly Lockean in that it relies on the assumption that economic agents have a right to the fruit of what they independently own—their labour, investments, etc. The utilitarian argument, by contrast, makes no reference to creators' and investors' existing rights. It holds that trade secrecy, by giving those agents a competitive advantage over their rivals, gives them incentives to continue to produce, thereby maximizing general welfare.

Both arguments for trade secrecy have limits. It is key to the utilitarian argument that trade secrecy should help maximize general welfare. It is part and parcel of Lockean justifications for property rights that they are subject to various provisos. While a full defence of trade secrecy is beyond the scope of this book, the presumption in favour of capitalism tilts the balance in favour of intellectual property rights in general, and of the right to secrecy over proprietary information in particular.

---

[7] This widely accepted definition of trade secrecy can be found in article 39 of the Trade-Related Aspects of Intellectual Property Rights Agreement—itself adopted by the members states of the WTO at the conclusion of the WTO's founding negotiations (or Uruguay Round) in 1994.

[8] For thorough accounts and scrutiny of those various arguments, see, e.g, S. V. Shiffrin, 'Lockean Theories of Intellectual Property', in S. R. Munzer (ed.), *New Essays in the Political Theory of Property* (Cambridge University Press, 2001); J. Wilson, 'Could There be a Right to Own Intellectual Property?', Law and Philosophy 28 (2009): 393–427; A. Lever (ed.), *New Frontiers in the Philosophy of Intellectual Property* (Cambridge University Press, 2012); Bok, *Secrets*, ch. 10. Bok is sceptical about the property argument for trade secrecy, though her scepticism seems to target the move from an individual right to secrecy to a business corporation's right thereto.

Some readers will undoubtedly protest that I concede too much to capitalism (to put the criticism roughly.) Perhaps they are right. Even so, appeals to intellectual-property rights ground only a limited right to economic secrecy—limited, that is, both to economic agents who own the relevant goods and information (such as business owners, shareholders, inventors, etc.), and to what can be owned. It does not support conferring the right on other economic agents such as employees and consumers, or on non-economic agents who nevertheless have a strong interest in a business's success and robustness; nor does it support the claim that there is a right to economic secrecy with respect to operational information about those aspects of economic life which are not well captured by the language of ownership. To justify the right to economic secrecy in such cases, we must look elsewhere.

Consider, first, what we may call economic agency. Economic agents have an interest in successfully availing themselves of opportunities to set up, develop, grow, and contribute to businesses. In a capitalist system, this implies that employ-ees, managers, and directors have an interest in the business's ability to operate on the open market, whether or not they own it. To the extent that keeping key information secret enables businesses to gain or maintain a competitive advantage, such as (for example) operational information about expansion plans and investments in various sectors, those economic agents have an interest in this particular kind of secrecy. And if agents' interests in setting up and growing busi-nesses are deemed important enough to be protected by rights (such as property rights over the required resources, contractual rights in respect of whom to hire and whom to sack, rights to be protected from fraudulent practices, etc.), then their interest in the relevant forms of secrecy should also be deemed important enough to be so protected. Note the conditional 'if agents' interests ...': there may be cases in which making proprietary information openly available to all and sundry would lead to better products and thus better promote human flourishing. (Think of openly available operating platforms and softwares, for example, such as Linux.) Still, even if trade secrecy is used mostly as a cloak to maximize profit for shareholders' benefit with little positive pay-off for most of us, it is hard to believe that maintaining competitive advantage never serves morally weighty interests.[9]

Consider, second, the fact that the economic and the political spheres are tightly interwoven. Information about privately owned or privately produced goods and services which would, if disclosed, undermine collective security and political agency can sometimes be treated as an economic secret worth protecting as a matter of right. With respect to collective security, suppose that our government acquires software from an IT company for managing our civilian critical infras-tructure and for protecting it from cyber-attacks. Suppose that if the software's code were disclosed to all and sundry, the IT company not only would find it

---

[9] I am grateful to Ross Bellaby for pressing me on this and supplying the example.

difficult to create patches and upgrades for its clients, but would also lose its competitive edge in general, thereby disincentivizing its board from continuing to invest in this area. As a result, our country's critical infrastructure would be under threat from cyber-warriors. We thus have a strong interest, on grounds of collective security, in this particular kind of information remaining secret—even though we do not have property rights in the business itself.

With respect to political agency, a state's ability to pursue its domestic and foreign policy agenda depends in part on the strengths of its economy and the revenues it can raise through taxation. To the extent that keeping some economic information secret enables businesses to survive and operate on the markets and thus to contribute to the health of our economy and thereby to our political agency, and on the assumption that we, citizens, have a right to exercise such agency, it is apt to say that we have a right to economic secrecy.

At this juncture, some readers will undoubtedly worry that my account yields both too broad and too thick a cloak of secrecy over the practices and activities of private companies. For on that conception, economic information the appropriation and disclosure of which would threaten our basic mode of life and our social, political, and economic values ought in principle to be regarded as secret. If so, and in the light of the ever-growing privatization of our critical infrastructure, any company whose weakening, let alone collapse, would jeopardize our collective security or political agency could claim protection from scrutiny. This, in turn, would open the door (as in fact it already seems to do) to the practice of shielding private companies from any kind of scrutiny simply on the grounds that they need protection from their competitors—at considerable cost, in fact, to individuals' well-being.[10] To illustrate the point with an example that is of particular relevance to the UK, we may all readily agree that information about the National Health Service the disclosure of which would destroy it (without countervailing benefits) should for that reason be regarded as a political secret—so central is health to our security. As it happens, privately owned companies are taking on a growing role in the delivery of health-care services in the UK—including companies, such as Virgin, for whom health-care is but one aspect of their activities. Is this to say that sensitive information about those companies in general, and not just their health-care arms, should be so protected as a means to ensure that they do not collapse? Were it so, Virgin in particular and similar private businesses in general would seem to be beyond the reach of political accountability.

The worry ultimately seems to be about the morality of privatization in general. I share it: notwithstanding my qualified endorsement of private property rights, I am doubtful that private companies—driven as they are by the imperative to maximize profits—are best placed to provide public goods. The point, though, is

[10] Bok, *Secrets*, 151–2.

that *if* we privatize, albeit wrongfully so, we must take steps to protect individuals from the harmful consequences of our decision, including secrecy measures. Economic information the disclosure of which *would*, by impairing a private corporation's competitive advantage, undermine the collective goods of political agency and security, can and ought to be regarded as secrets to which we, citizens, have a right. The question, then, is on what grounds, if any, economic espionage is morally justified.

4.3 Justifying Economic Espionage

States resort to economic espionage offensively and defensively.[11] Offensively used, it is a tool of both economic and geopolitical statecraft. States spy on foreign businesses in order to pass on the secret information they have thereby acquired to domestic businesses, with a view to helping them gain competitive advantage on open markets. They also use the information in their dealings with other states. For example, when negotiating a trade deal with Blue, Green might find it useful to know more about the strengths and weaknesses of Blue's economy than can be discovered from publicly available information. One way to do that is to appropriate information about the robustness of Blue's main businesses which those businesses are not willing to provide. Economic espionage is also a branch of 'standard' military-driven espionage: to the extent that Blue's military technology is in the hands of private firms and that Green wants to know more about Blue's military strengths and weaknesses than Blue is willing to disclose, Green will want to unearth both operational and proprietary information about those firms, as a means to guide its foreign policy *vis-à-vis* Blue and to consolidate its own position in their arms race.

Defensively, states use economic espionage as a tool to protect their citizens and businesses from the harms which, they believe, private firms occasion. For example, they use it as a means to help domestic firms fight corporate espionage at the hands of foreign competitors. They use it in their fight against transnational white-collar crimes such as fraud, bribery and corruption, as well as to combat global organized crime such as drug and people trafficking in those cases where ostensibly 'clean' firms are, in fact, dirty. They use it to protect their critical infrastructure (comprising both their military security infrastructure and essential civilian and dual use infrastructure) from such threats as may arise from foreign private firms. When states have entrusted the delivery of critical goods and services

---

[11] My empirical observations are drawn from the following works: J. J. Fialka, *War by Other Means— Economic Espionage in America* (W. W. Norton, 1997); Javers, *Broker, Trader, Lawyer, Spy*; Nasheri, *Economic Espionage and Industrial Spying*; Rustmann, *CIA Inc.*; P. Schweizer, *Friendly Spies* (Atlantic Monthly Press, 1993).

to foreign firms, they seek to asssess the extent of their vulnerability to the latter—particularly, though not exclusively, if those firms are linked to a putatively hostile foreign regime.

So much for what states actually do. My concern is with what they may and ought to do. As we saw at the close of s. 1.4.1, the main rationale for the existence of the state (as an alternative to anarchy), lies in its ability and willingness (via its officials) to provide for individuals' security and, more widely, their prospects for a flourishing life—put in deontic terms, to secure their fundamental moral rights and enable them to fulfil their fundamental moral duties. It is in fact a condition of a given state's legitimacy—of its officials' powers and rights to issue authoritative commands and to enforce those commands—that it should be able and willing to do just that. The question, then, is whether and when states may justifiably spy on foreign private businesses to bring about those ends.

In s. 4.2, I argued that business owners and employees, as well as consumers and residents, have a *pro tanto* right that some economic information about businesses should remain secret. To defend Green's decision to appropriate economic secrets about businesses registered and operating on Blue's territory or owned largely by residents of Blue, we must show either that the holders of the right to those particular secrets are liable to being spied on, or that, even though they are not liable, Green nevertheless has an overriding justification for so acting. (Whether Green is all-things-considered justified in engaging in economic espionage depends on whether its decision to do so is necessary, effective, and proportionate.)

Let me elaborate, starting with liability. Capitalism (I noted at the outset) is subject to moral norms. My property rights over the house I bought on the open market do not include a right to use it as a base for organizing armed robberies or as a brothel for victims of human trafficking. My property rights over ingredients which, taken separately, are wholly harmless and which can be bought perfectly legally, do not include a right to combine those ingredients to manufacture and sell to the highest bidder a weapon of mass destruction; nor do they include a right to keep the chemical formula I have invented for such a weapon secret. My property rights over my computer do not include a right to hack into my neighbour's computer-controlled gas and electricity supply to divert those resources to my house. Were I so to act, I would be derelict in my duty not to violate third parties' fundamental rights, and I would thus be liable to the appropriation of the relevant information about my property.

Furthermore, individuals whose security and democratic agency depend on having access to—albeit no property rights in respect of—those resources are also liable to losing secrecy about the relevant information if and when they deploy their agency to nefarious ends. Suppose that my son, who does not have property rights over my house, has turned the basement into a chemical lab and uses it to manufacture highly dangerous weapons. While he has a *pro tanto* right that information about what he gets up to while in my house remain unappropriated and undisclosed, he does not have a right to secrecy in respect of this particular activity.

Mutatis mutandis, those embarrassingly simple points apply to private businesses. Their owners and employees, as well as consumers and citizens who depend on them, do not have a right that the operational and proprietary information on which businesses rely remain secret if the information is used, either by those businesses themselves or by their 'host state', as a means to violate third parties' fundamental moral rights. The state, whose task it is to protect those fundamental rights, is morally justified in seeking to acquire such secrets—in so far as it can thus better discharge its functions.

The claim is wholly uncontroversial (I take it) in the following kind of case. Suppose that Green and Blue are at war, both kinetic and cyber. Corporation Weapons Inc. supplies Blue with military weapons and technology, while corporation InfoSys Inc. supplies its forces with IT resources. Suppose that Blue is the unjust aggressor. Green's firms are struggling to compete with Blue's, as a result of which Green is losing the war. Its leaders are morally justified in seeking to uncover relevant economic information about Weapons Inc. and InfoSys Inc, in the hope of undermining both firms by engaging in economic warfare and taking advantage of those firms' research and development activities.

More controversially, the claim also holds in peacetime. Suppose that Green has good reasons to believe that the large multinational, ostensibly private corporation which is entrusted with the maintenance of its civilian nuclear reactors—Energy Inc.—has very close links with the regime of hostile state Blue. Green has a justification for seeking to obtain detailed operational information about the corporation. Should such information not be forthcoming, and given that the health of its nuclear reactors is critical to Green's national security broadly understood, Green's leaders are justified in acquiring it against Blue's wishes, on the grounds that lack of forthcomingness might be indicative of Blue's nefarious designs on Green's energy sector.[12]

Some readers might object that I have chosen relatively easy cases, in which Green is under threat at the hands of another state in the context of a war or, in peacetime, in which its needs for energy, itself clearly part of its collective security, is at stake. Economic espionage in which neither feature obtains seems harder to justify, or so those readers might protest. Harder perhaps, but not impossible. Suppose that Energy Inc. is not subservient to Blue's leaders but that Green's authorities over time have become seriously concerned about its directors' and managers' ability and willingness to fulfil the terms of their contract, with serious implications (should those concerns be grounded) for Green's nuclear policy and,

---

[12] The United States now openly recognizes national security as an exception to the general prohibition on economic espionage. For a useful discussion of extant practice, see Lubin, 'The Liberty to Spy', 56–7.

thereby, its national security. In the face of Energy Inc.'s repeated obfuscating and dissembling responses to Green's concerns, the latter is morally justified in proceeding.

If I am right, resorting to economic espionage can be morally justified (subject to considerations of proportionality, necessity, and effectiveness) even if it does not target a business as a means to thwart another state. Moreover, it can be morally justified even if it targets a business whose activities threaten a state's national security understood more broadly as comprising, not just its military security or the security of its critical infrastructure (of which energy security is a paradigmatic example), but also the basic well-being of its population. Consider the following two examples. Global organized crime is widely regarded as a serious threat to collective security. It deprives states of billions of dollars in revenue every year and thus impairs their ability to discharge their functions. It takes the form of or is backed by threats of serious violence, and thus impairs its victims' individual security and, thereby, their well-being. Crucially (in the context of this book), it is enmeshed with transnational terrorist networks. Yet organized global crime does not operate in a vacuum: its proceeds are laundered through ostensibly legitimate firms, trusts, and corporations, thanks to *bona fide* lawyers, accountants, and consultancy firms.[13] The nexus of the criminal, the economic, and the political is a tightly woven fabric of contractual and non-contractual relationships. If political communities are morally justified in spying on criminal gangs as a means to thwart them, surely they are morally justified in spying on the businesses (be they legitimate or not) through which those gangs channel funds towards transnational terrorist activities.

The second example is this. Suppose that Green is locked in difficult negotiations with multinational pharmaceutical corporation Pharma Inc., from which it buys the medicine it then sells at heavily subsidized prices to its citizens. Pharma Inc. has a *de facto* monopoly over the manufacture of various life-saving drugs, of which it takes advantage to engage in predatory behaviour *vis-à-vis* Green. It knows full well that Green cannot afford not to buy those drugs and also that it cannot afford to pay the price demanded by Pharma Inc. without at the same time jeopardizing its ability to provide for other essential services. Pharma Inc. is derelict in its duties to Green's citizens. Its managers, employees, and shareholders are liable to the appropriation and disclosure of operational information about its pricing strategy. Under those circumstances, Green has a *pro tanto* justification (I believe) for stealing such information with a view to providing vital medical

---

[13] In 2016, the International Consortium of Investigative Journalists (ICIJ) published leaked confidential documents from the Panama firm Mossack Fonseca—documents which reveal the many ways in which criminal organizations use otherwise perfectly legal off-shore tax havens to hide and launder ill-gotten wealth and channel funds to terrorist organizations. The so-called *Panama Papers* can be found on the website of the ICIJ at https://www.icij.org/investigations/panama-papers (accessed on 17/08/2021).

treatment to its population; it might also be justified in stealing proprietary information about medical treatments in development with a view to facilitating the emergence of a domestic pharmaceutical sector over which it might have greater leverage.[14]

These are not the only cases in which agents—be they economic agents or the citizens whose well-being depends on their success—are liable to the loss of political secrecy. In more straightforwardly geopolitical cases, states resort to espionage as a means to check that other states comply with international agreements regarding (e.g.) ceasefire, disarmament, and nuclear proliferation. As we saw in s. 3.2, to the extent that those measure are morally justified and that there are good reasons to doubt that actors who are subject to them are compliant, the latter are liable to be spied upon. In a similar vein, states are morally justified in resorting to economic espionage as a means to monitor compliance with morally justified economic sanctions. It might seem odd, at first sight, to construe this as a case of *economic* espionage, since sanctions are used primarily as a tool of geopolitical statecraft. Yet, even though sanctions target a state's ability to buy and sell certain kinds of goods, products, and services, they operate against economic actors' ability to sell, and buy, those goods, products, and services to that state (or to its leaders).[15] To the extent that those actors, *qua* economic actors, do not have a right to transact with the target state, they no longer have a right to economic secrecy in respect of those transactions; to the extent that Green is morally justified in monitoring their compliance with the sanctions regime, it is morally justified in seeking to acquire the relevant information, by means of espionage if those actors refuse to cooperate.

So far, I have examined cases in which economic actors and the citizens or consumers who depend on their success are liable to the loss of economic secrecy. As I noted at the outset of this section, however, economic espionage might be justified even if its targets have retained their right to economic secrecy. For example, suppose that Green's services successfully hack into the Ministry's computer mainframe. They collect information about the cyber-attack which they suspect Blue to be planning, as well as secret information about InfoSys Inc.'s contracts with Blue as they pertain to the latter's major banks and hospitals. The

[14] In the summer of 2020, Britain's National cyber-Security Centre alleged that Russian state-sponsored hackers were mounting cyber-attacks against drug companies and research labs involved in developing a vaccine against COVID-19. (D. Sabbagh and A. Roth, 'Russian state-sponsored hackers target Covid-19 vaccine researchers,' *The Guardian* (16/07/2020).) Suppose that the allegations, though hotly denied by Russia, are true. This does not constitute a case of justified economic espionage by my lights. Although Russia, like the rest of the world, was/is facing a serious health crisis, it does not lack the resources to contribute to global efforts to develop a vaccine and is not at the mercy of extortionate practices on the part of those companies and labs.

[15] I develop this argument at length in C. Fabre, *Economic Statecraft—Human Rights, Sanctions and Conditionality* (Harvard University Press, 2018), chs. 2–3.

latter information is not relevant to the conflict between Green and Blue, but there is no way Green's cyber-specialists could avoid harvesting it. Green's specialists have inflicted a foreseen albeit unintended harm on InfoSys Inc. Its owners and employees are not liable to losing secrecy with regard to the firm's civilian contracts with Blue, nor for that matter are Blue's civilians. However, in just the same way as, subject to constraints of necessity, effectiveness, and proportionality, one may unintentionally albeit foreseeably harm an innocent bystander in the course of parrying a wrongful threat, so may Green act *vis-à-vis* InfoSys Inc. and Blue's civilians.

I have argued that on the aforementioned grounds and subject to the aforementioned conditions states are justified in resorting to economic espionage. They are also under a duty to do so. To reiterate, the rationale for the state, and the grounds for its legitimacy, is that it protects fundamental rights and enables individuals to fulfil their correlative duties better than would be the case in its absence. Its officials, acting on behalf of its citizens, are under a duty to protect individuals from rights violations at the hands of third parties. This includes a duty to acquire information about the wrongful threats posed by economic actors. Moreover, even if, for whatever reason, state officials are not in a given case under a duty to embark on a particular rights-protecting policy but are merely justified in doing so, they might still be under a duty to resort to economic espionage as a preliminary step. In so far as they are less likely to succeed at protecting rights if they act in ignorance of the relevant facts, they are under a duty to procure information about those facts; and to the extent that their policy might be unduly harmful to third parties such as economic actors, or to foreign consumers or citizens, they are under a duty to ensure, as much as possible, that they proceed on the basis of the relevant economic information.

Three final points, before I respond to some objections. First, the claim that Green must have a probable cause before spying on Blue (s. 3.4) applies here too.

Second, economic espionage is not justified as a means of pursuing an unjust foreign policy. States, and consequently their spies, who engage in it to such ends are not on a par, morally speaking, with states, and consequently their spies, who engage in it to rightful ends.

Third, economic espionage is not justified as a means to further the economic interests of one's residents and businesses at the expense of businesses (and, thereby, host states) which do not threaten third parties' fundamental rights. This implies, for example, that the time-honoured practice of procuring economic secrets solely for the sake of giving one's domestic firms a competitive advantage over foreign firms is not morally justified. The point applies even in cases in which economic espionage is a retaliatory response to the fact that the initial advantageous position of Blue's firms is due to Blue having conducted wrongful espionage activities on their behalf. For, generally, it does not follow from the claim that someone is unwarrantedly harming us in a particular way that we are justified in harming her in precisely this way.[16]

4.4 Objections

In this section, I examine some moral objections to economic espionage. A caveat: what follows is as good a reconstruction as I can give of those objections as they are sketched out in a largely empirical and not well-developed literature.

4.4.1 The Distributive Objection

A standard objection to economic espionage adverts to governments' difficulties in 'distributing' the information they have acquired. It has two strands. First, any decision by Green to help this or that domestic firm by passing on the economic secrets it has acquired through espionage would lay Green's leaders open to accusations of unwarranted favouritism, embroil them in corporate feuds, and weaken their authority.[17]

This is not particularly convincing as a wholesale rejection of economic espionage. It is compatible, for example, with spying on foreign firms solely for the protection of fundamental rights.

The second strand of the objection notes that firms operating on Green's territory and under its jurisdiction and whose activities are central to the health of its economy and the robustness of its civilian and military infrastructure might be wholly or partly owned either by foreign businesses with close links to their own state, or by foreign states themselves. By passing on sensitive information to a domestic subsidiary of a foreign-owned parent company, Green might unwittingly provide assistance to a putatively hostile power or direct economic competitor.[18]

This concern must be taken seriously. However, it is not specific to economic espionage. As we saw in s. 3.3, it is raised by intelligence-sharing in general. Suppose that Green decides to pass on critical military intelligence to its allies. It runs the risk that, if the latter have been penetrated by hostile intelligence agencies, the intelligence will be used to nefarious ends. In both this and the economic-espionage case, the party which passes on intelligence can never be certain that

---

[16] See also T. Pfaff, 'Bungee Jumping off the Moral High Ground', 97–9. Pfaff construes national security (which on his view is the only justification for espionage) much more narrowly than I do. For the claim that economic espionage is a justified way of levelling the playing field for domestic firms in the face of corrupt foreign practices, see Rustmann, *CIA Inc.*, 129.

[17] See, e.g., Fialka, *War by Other Means*, 8; Perry, *Partly Cloudy*, 154; Rustmann, *CIA Inc.*, 20.

[18] See, e.g., R. M. Fort, 'Economic Espionage', in R. Z. George and R. D. Kline (eds.), *Intelligence and the National Security Strategist* (Rowman & Littlefield, 2006), 241–2.

the latter will be used as it ought to be used. In just the same way as, in 'standard' intelligence-sharing cases, Green's government and intelligence agencies are under an obligation to pass on secret information on the basis of the best evidence at their disposal that it will not be used to unjust ends, so they must in economic-espionage cases. The obligation is not stringent enough to undermine the case for 'standard espionage'; nor is it stringent enough to undermine the case for economic espionage.

4.4.2 The Motivations Objection

Another objection to economic espionage is that intelligence officers are willing to risk their life for their country, but not for businesses.[19]

It is not entirely clear what the objection, so stated, is meant to show. It might mean that it is pointless for governments to embark on this particular course of action since they will not find willing agents to do it for them. Or it might mean that it is unfair of those governments to exploit their in-post agents' reluctance or inability to resign and thus to get them to do work which they find morally repugnant.

The objection relies on a questionable assumption with respect to intelligence officers' motivations. As a matter of fact, there is no evidence to suggest that all such officers in all contexts are reluctant to carry out this particular kind of work. But suppose for the sake of argument that the factual assumption is correct. On the first interpretation, the objection undermines the claim that economic espionage is *feasible*. If one takes the view that considerations of feasibility have no bearing on our moral obligations, then the objection fails to damage the claim that economic espionage is morally mandatory. If one takes the view that considerations of feasibility in general, and motivational considerations in particular, dictate the content of our moral obligations, then the objection does succeed at impugning the claim that economic espionage is (sometimes) morally mandatory; but it does not damage the claim that economic espionage is (sometimes) morally justified (since the fact that I cannot feasibly φ says nothing about my being justified in φ-ing.)[20]

---

[19] See, e.g., S. J. Rascoff, 'The Norm against Economic Espionage for the Benefit of Private Firms: Some Theoretical Reflections', *The University of Chicago Law Review* 83 (2016): 249–69; Perry, *Partly Cloudy*, 154.

[20] The literature on feasibility in general, and the relationship between motivations and obligations in particular, is vast. As a first cut, on the specific issue of motivation, see, e.g., D. Estlund, 'Human Nature and the Limits (if any) of Political Philosophy', *Philosophy & Public Affairs* 39 (2011): 207–37. For a thoughtful criticism of Estlund's view that motivations are largely irrelevant, see G. Elford, 'Pains of Perseverance: Agent-Centred Prerogatives, Burdens and the Limits of Human Motivation', *Ethical Theory and Moral Practice* 18 (2015): 501–14. See also Z. Stemplowska, 'Feasibility: Individual and Collective', *Social Philosophy and Policy* 33 (2016): 273–91.

On the second interpretation, the objection has bite only if intelligence officers' repugnance is well-grounded. If it is, their government is not justified in pressuring them so to work—though they themselves might have an excuse for giving in to pressure (for example, depending on the extent to which they act under duress). But if their reluctance is not well grounded, if, in other words, there is a *pro tanto* justification for resorting to economic espionage, the objection fails—in just the same way as it is not an objection to issuing a justified order to kill to a professional soldier that the latter finds such an act morally repugnant.

4.4.3 The Separate Spheres Objection

A third objection to economic espionage rests on the view that there is a sharp dividing line between the political and the economic spheres, such that espionage might be warranted against other states, but not against economic actors. The objection is hard to parse. It seems to take two forms. First, it is sometimes said that it is not in the interest of intelligence agencies to be captured by multinational corporations, albeit at the behest of their governments: more strongly put, the work of intelligence agencies ought not to be shaped by the pursuit of private economic interests.[21] Second, it might be thought that it is not the role of the state to help private businesses: if a business cannot gain and maintain competitive advantage over its rivals on its own, so be it.[22]

One can see the force of the first variant of the objection. Intelligence agencies must speak truth to power and, moreover, are morally required to do so for the sake of bringing about just ends, even at the expense of private economic interests. However, as we saw in ss. 4.2 and 4.3, the boundaries between the political and the economic, and thus between geopolitical-cum-military and economic espionage are blurred. To reiterate, to the extent that private businesses are central to a country's security widely construed and thus to the well-being of its population, there is a sense in which, even in a capitalist economy, the economic *is* political. By implication, in war, economic espionage aimed at shoring up a country's justified war effort is virtually indistinguishable from military-cum-geopolitical espionage; so is peacetime economic espionage aimed at protecting a country's civilian infrastructure and its citizens from wrongful threats.

The second variant of the objection relies on a minimalist understanding of the state's role in the economy. By that token, its proponents are committed to rejecting state subsidies. They might be willing to bite this particular bullet. But if one takes the view—as I do, as per s. 4.3—that a state may shore up businesses in fulfilment of its obligation to provide its citizens with prospects for a flourishing life, one can

---

[21] See, e.g., Rascoff, 'The Norm against Economic Espionage for the Benefit of Private Firms'.
[22] Fort, 'Economic Espionage', 240.

accept both state subsidies and more unusual forms of assistance in the form of access to secret economic intelligence.

Note in any event that, even against the normative background of a laissez-faire economy and a minimalist state, the objection only targets economic espionage for the sake of purely economic ends (which I myself reject.) It does not undermine economic espionage aimed at protecting the country's critical infrastructure; nor does it apply to economic espionage aimed at thwarting private businesses' garden-variety criminal activities: after all, even a minimalist state must provide for the security of its citizens.

Finally, across those two variants, the objection is not sensitive enough to the fact that some private businesses, notably multinational corporations, for many intents and purposes increasingly assume many of the functions of states. For consider. To bring about their ends, states issue commands which they regard as binding within their borders and employ coercive mechanisms to enforce those commands; they control economic exchanges both within and outside their borders by (*inter alia*) issuing currency, enforcing contracts, and adjudicating conflicts between economic agents. Businesses are similar to states in some of those respects. They hire private security guards to police their premises, and, in some cases, substitute their own criminal justice system for that of the state—as when retail businesses agree not to call the police when catching a shoplifter *in flagrante delicto* so long as he/she pays a fine on the spot. Managers issue wide-ranging directives to employees and resort to various coercive mechanisms to enforce those demands, such as withholding pay from their employees or firing them. In fact, in Western liberal democracies, employees are often subjected to far greater control at the hands of their bosses than citizens are subjected to at the hands of their governments. For example, in the United States, some firms prohibit their employees from using otherwise legal recreational drugs, have denied them bathroom breaks, dictate which topics of conversation they can broach during working hours, arrogate the right to sack them for their social-media activities outside such hours and prevent them from having consensual sexual relationships with fellow employees. Businesses also arbitrate disputes between consumers—the more so as the exponential growth of online transactions, with their rich potential for conflicts, makes it impossible for traditional courts to handle those disputes themselves. In the words of Elizabeth Anderson, employees and, to some extent, consumers, are thus subject to 'private government.'[23]

[23] Anderson, *Private Government*, esp. ch. 3. For an interesting account of the proliferation of private dispute resolution mechanisms in the digital age, see E. Katsh and O. Rabinovitch-Einy, *Digital Justice: Technology and the Internet of Disputes* (Oxford University Press, 2017). For a fascinating study of private criminal justice in the US retail sector, see J. Rappaport, 'Criminal Justice Inc.', *Columbia Law Review* 118 (2018): 2251–321. I am grateful to Frederick Wilmot-Smith for suggesting the latter two sources.

To the extent, thus, that private businesses willingly take on some of the accoutrements of the state and, more strongly still, aim to rival the state, they cannot claim immunity from state-sponsored espionage on the grounds that they are an altogether different kind of entity.

4.4.4 The 'Not Between Allies' Objection

A fourth objection to economic espionage targets such activities in so far as they are directed at the 'offending' state's allies. The objection is fuelled by concerns amongst American scholars and policy makers that French, German, Japanese, and Israeli governments—all allies of the United States—have all unashamedly (it seems) deployed their intelligence services against US firms.[24]

In responding to this objection, Pierre Marion, former director of French intelligence, argues that alliances protect military and diplomatic secrets, but not economic ones. In the economic realm, Marion claims, it is not morally inappropriate for allied states to construe one another as competitors and to regard businesses as fair game.[25]

Marion's response relies on two distinctions: that between the economic and the political realms, and that between allies and enemies. It fails for two reasons. First, once again, there is no clear-cut line of separation between the economic and the political realms. In the often-quoted words of Admiral Stansfield Turner, former CIA director, 'if this [the economy] isn't a national security matter, then what is?!'[26] While not all aspects of a country's economy are vital to its security, some are. Moreover, as I argued in ss. 3.2 and 3.3, whether an act of espionage is morally justified depends on the moral status of the ends which it seeks to further. Espionage in pursuit of unjust ends is morally wrong, irrespective of the fact that its targets are foreign economic actors rather than foreign states.

Second, espionage (of whatever kind) between allies is sometimes morally justified, for the simple reason that today's allies might be tomorrow's enemies. As we saw in s. 3.5, it is not the fact of the alliance itself that matters but, rather, whether or not a party to that alliance is warranted in inferring on the basis of the evidence at its disposal that its ally is planning to pursue unjust ends.

---

[24] See, e.g., Schweizer, *Friendly Spies*; Fialka, *War by Other Means*; D. L. Clarke, 'Israel's Economic Espionage in the United States', *Journal of Palestine Studies* 27 (1998): 20–35; S. Fink, *Sticky Fingers* (iUniverse, Inc., 2002). Not that the United States have shied away from similar activities: see, e.g., M. T. Clark, 'Economic Espionage: The Role of the United States Intelligence Community', *Journal of International Legal Studies* 3 (1997): 253–92, as well as Fink, *Sticky Fingers*, 52–4.

[25] Schweizer, *Friendly Spies*, 9 and ch. 5.

[26] Quoted in, *inter alia*, Fialka, *War by Other Means*, 7. For Turner's more considered view on this, see S. Turner, 'Intelligence for a New World Order', *Foreign Affairs* 70 (1991): 150–66. See also S. D. Porteous, 'Economic espionage: Issues arising from increased government involvement with the private sector', *Intelligence and National Security* 9 (1994): 735–52, 741.

If so, economic espionage between allies is sometimes warranted—though not on the grounds that it is economic rather than military-cum geopolitical; at the same time, military-cum-geopolitical espionage against allies is also sometimes warranted, the alliance notwithstanding.

4.5 Conclusion

To conclude, I have mounted a qualified defence of states' right to acquire economic secrets from foreign firms, for the sake of rightfully protecting the collective goods of security (broadly construed) and democratic agency.

As I suggested at the outset, there is much more to be said about economic espionage than I have been able to cover here—such as, *inter alia*, the privatization of intelligence acquisition, the ethics of business-on-business and business-on-state espionage, and the means by which secrets are acquired. The first two tasks must await another occasion. I now turn to the latter task.

5

Deception

5.1 Introduction

If the information which political communities need in order to thwart violations of fundamental rights were available through open sources, the task of justifying its acquisition would be relatively easy. If no one sought to appropriate secrets unwarrantedly, the task of justifying counter-intelligence activities would be unnecessary. Such is not the case: it is precisely because political communities hide much of such information from one another and at the same time seek to uncover one another's secrets that intelligence agencies, on orders from their leaders, deceive, manipulate, and sometimes blackmail or torture individuals in the course of their trade. Moreover, the information which they seek to acquire is rarely delivered to them on a plate. It needs to be uncovered piecemeal. A phone call, a troublesome email, a suspicious encounter, or an unexplained burst of spending may seem insignificant when considered on their own yet may yield crucial insights when properly combined and analysed. Hence the need for long and complex operations involving deception, manipulation, and sometimes coercion. Not only are those operations morally problematic on those grounds alone. In addition, they catch in their nets many individuals whose contribution to wrongful ventures might turn out to be negligible.

Of all the means by which political communities procure and protect secrets, torture has been the most extensively discussed in contemporary practical ethics. The broad consensus is that it is not morally permissible except, perhaps, in the most extreme and unlikely event that it should be necessary to prevent a ticking bomb from killing scores of civilians. I will not address torture in this book, first because I have nothing to add to an already extensive body of literature, but also, and more interestingly, because as we saw in s. 1.2, classical just-war theorists who discuss espionage are not particularly exercised by torture so much as by the fact that espionage is inherently deceitful. For example, on Kant's view, the spy is guilty of deception even when he merely collects intelligence through observation, and it is that which makes espionage an 'infernal art'. The problem also arises in counter-intelligence operations, which often involve deception. While there are reasons to resist Kant's vituperative denunciation, his concerns about the deception inherent in many intelligence activities are worth investigating.

Section 5.2 offers a brief account of deception and sketches out reasons why it is presumptively wrongful. Section 5.3 shows why and when deception in the service of espionage and counter-intelligence is morally permissible. Section 5.4 shows why and when it is morally mandatory. Section 5.5 responds to two objections. Section 5.6 explores some of the dilemmas which operatives face when conducting deception operations. I set aside until Chapter 7 (s. 7.6.4) the complicated issue of sexual deception.

Throughout the chapter, I refer to the agents whom Green's services use as a means to deceive Blue as Asset. I assume that Asset either belongs to Green (say he is a MI6 officer, or a British journalist who has agreed to feed information to MI6) or volunteers to work for Green, though does not belong to either Green or Blue. I thus set aside cases in which he is a member of Blue (say, a Russian civil servant or intelligence offficer working for MI6.) In other words, Asset is an infiltrator rather than a traitor. Treason raises distinctive issues which I tackle in Chapter 6.

Cases in which Asset is a member of neither Green nor Blue and offers his services to Green are few and far between. Some of the best-known and most influential intelligence agents of the Second World War fall in that category: Dusan Popov (aka Agent Tricycle), Juan Pujol Garcia (aka Agent Garbo), Wulf Schmidt (aka Agent Tate) and Lily Sergeyev (aka Agent Treasure) hailed respectively from Serbia, Spain, Denmark, and France. As members of the Double Cross system, they worked for the Allies and against Nazi Germany, yet were nationals of neither. Some of them had initially volunteered to work for Germany before switching sides. The main normative questions raised by cases such as these are the following: (a) may an individual offer her services to foreign power Blue without being explicitly authorized to do so by his/her government? (b) May she subsequently offer her services to Green, while pretending to Blue (with Green's assent and help) that she is still loyal? One's answer to the first question depends on one's views about the permissibility of private foreign enlistment in general. For what it is worth, I am inclined to think that explicit authorization by one's government is not a necessary condition for private foreign enlistment. One's answer to the second question depends on one's views on the limits of political loyalty. In Chapter 6, I shall make a limited case for treason. *A fortiori*, my arguments there apply to cases such as these, other things being equal.[1]

5.2 Concealing, Misleading, Lying, and Fabricating Evidence

Some agent, D, deceives another agent, L, when he knowingly causes or allows her to form or retain false beliefs about some facts. Deception can take many forms. *Inter alia*, D can deceive L by concealing information, *p*, which (D knows) L would

---

[1] For a wonderfully evocative portrait of those four agents, see B. McIntyre, *Double Cross: The True Story of The D-Day Spies* (Bloomsbury, 2012). My view on private foreign enlistment draws on my discussion of the requirement of legitimate authority in Fabre, *Cosmopolitan War*, ch. 4.

regard as relevant to her interaction with D. D can also deceive L to the effect that p by implying, falsely, that p. He can deceive her by lying to her outright, by forging evidence, or by double-bluffing.

On this account, D can be aptly described as deceiving or lying to L even if he is coerced into making a false statement to her. Others disagree.[2] It is worth noting though that if an individual cannot by definition be coerced into lying, double agents who are coerced by their community's enemies to feed false information to their superiors are not aptly described as lying to the latter. I find that claim deeply counter-intuitive.

Paradigmatic cases of deception in the present context are cases in which intelligence agencies insert one of their operatives into the enemy and instruct him to procure secrets by striking or exploiting relationships with the latter. For example, Soviet intelligence services used to deploy so-called 'illegals' in hostile countries—that is to say, agents who were given wholly fake identities and whose task was to procure sensitive information about their country of residence. It is known that the French overseas intelligence services also do so, and it would not be surprising if other services did as well.[3]

Deception is thought to be presumptively wrong for a range of reasons. It is wrong in so far as it is an abuse of trust; or it is wrong in so far as it gets the addressee to act as one wishes without her informed consent, thereby treating her only as a means to one's ends; or it is wrong in so far as it restricts the addressee's freedom justifiably to act as she wishes; or it is wrong in so far as it impairs our communicative relationships and makes it difficult if not impossible for us to relate to and cooperate with one another as moral and rational agents on a footing of equality—thereby undermining our prospects for a flourishing life.

Not all reasons apply to all the means by which agents deceive one another. Consider double-bluffing. D wants L to believe that p, which is false; he knows, however, that L does not trust him; L does not know that he knows that. D tells L that *not-p*, thus leading her to believe, falsely, that p. He clearly deceives her, but if he wrongs her (which is plausible), it cannot be because he abuses her trust since *ex hypothesi* she does not trust him.

---

[2] See K. Hawley, 'Coercion and Lies,' in E. Michaelson and A. Stokke (eds.), *Lying—Language, Knowledge, Ethics and Politics* (Oxford University Press, 2018).

[3] For particularly good empirical sources, see, e.g., J. T. Richelson, *A Century of Spies—Intelligence in the Twentieth Century* (Oxford University Press, 1995); Scott and Jackson, *Understanding Intelligence in the Twenty-First Century*; Andrew, *The Secret World*; Johnson, *The Oxford Handbook of National Security Intelligence*; Keegan, *Intelligence in War*. The Russian Intelligence Services have apparently followed in their predecessors' footsteps. In 2010, the FBI arrested ten of their illegals, the most famous of whom, born Anna Vasilyevna Kushchyenko, is better known under her married name Anna Chapman. She was sent back to Russian in a spy-prisoner swap between Russia and the US. (For an excellent account, see G. Corera, *Russians Among Us—Sleeper Cells and the Hunt for Putin's Agents* (Harper Collins, 2020).) Two recent TV series provide engrossing fictionalized accounts of Soviet and French illegals—respectively *The Americans* and *Le Bureau des Légendes*.

On all those acccounts, the longer the deception lasts and the closer the deceiver's relationship with those whom he deceives, the worse it is. On the majority of those accounts, other things being equal, fabricating evidence and lying outright are worse than misleading by implicature, and misleading by implicature is worse than concealing information. For example, some argue that the liar necessarily invites his interlocutor to trust him, whereas the person who misleads by implicature does not. Others hold that the liar constrains his interlocutor's autonomy to a much greater extent than the 'misleader' does: in misleading implicatures, the listener is given an opening to further question the deceiver and thereby to get to the truth of the matter. By contrast, the liar seeks to foreclose any such line of inquiry. Relatedly, it is also sometimes said that the liar takes fewer risks, precisely because by closing off further conversation when asserting that p, he is less likely to be found out than if he had merely implied that p.[4]

Let us assume then that deception is *pro tanto* wrong for any number of those reasons. And let us also suppose for the sake of argument that outright lying and fabrication are worse than other forms of deception, other things being equal. When we try and ascertain whether deception in the service of espionage and counter-intelligence operations is morally justified, we need to bear in mind that the deceptive acts are committed by individuals who operate in an institutional capacity, either on their own (as agents in the field exercising their initiative) or as part of a collective (as government officials who together decide whether to authorize or implement a particular operation.) As I noted in s. 2.2, whether a piece of information can be deemed to have been kept secret partly depends on the role and status, in relation to it, both of the individuals who remain silent and of those who are allowed access to it. The point applies to deception, whether it takes the form of lies, misleading statements, or fabricated evidence. Suppose that a private citizen of Green announces to the world at large via Facebook that his government does not negotiate with terrorists, even though he happens to know otherwise (as a result of, e.g., having overheard a conversation to that effect between his partner—a high-ranking officer of Green's intelligence services—and a senior Minister of Green's government.) He is lying. But he is not thereby engaged in a deceptive

---

[4] The contemporary literature on the phenomenology and wrongfulness of deception is huge. For two excellent and recent collections of essays which cover much of the terrain I briefly describe in this paragraph, see E. Michaelson and A. Stokke (eds.) *Lying—Language, Knowledge, Ethics and Politics* (Oxford University Press, 2018); J. Meibauder (ed.), *The Oxford Handbook of Lying* (Oxford University Press, 2019). For some classics in that literature, see (*inter alia*), S. Bok, *Lying—Moral Choice in Public and Private Life*, 2nd. ed. (Vintage, 1999); B. A. O. Williams, *Truth and Truthfulness: An Essay in Genealogy* (Princeton University Press, 2002); Carson, *Lying and Deception—Theory and Practice*; J. Saul, *Lying, Misleading, and What is Said—An Exploration in Philosophy of Language and Ethics* (Oxford University Press, 2012); S. V. Shiffrin, *Speech Matters: On Lying, Morality, and the Law* (Princeton University Press, 2014).

intelligence operation. Were the Minister herself to issue such a statement via her spokesman, she would be.[5]

In addition, to the extent that an agent deceives another only if he *knowingly* causes or allows her to form or retain a false belief, he is not deceitful if he is unwittingly used as a means to convey such a belief. Suppose that Green's services discover that one of their own agents has been passing on classified information about Green's foreign policy to Blue. Instead of arresting him, they use him as a conduit to pass on false information to Blue. They do not tell him as much, justifiably fearing that he would not be able to keep up the pretence. The agent himself does not deceive Blue: the operation's masterminds do.

Throughout this chapter, when I ask whether Green is justified in mounting a deception operation, or when I say that Green seeks to deceive Blue, I use the word 'Green' or 'Blue' as shortcuts to refer to their relevantly situated officials, field agents, etc. Unless otherwise stated, I do not distinguish between the Prime Minister or President, the heads of intelligence and security services, and their operatives in the field.

5.3 Permissible Deception

If deception is *pro tanto* wrong, the burden of proof lies with those who wish to lift the prohibition. Much of the philosophical literature on deception is a response to Kant's often-caricatured prohibition on lying. This section shows that the standard example of the Murderer-at-the-door is of limited value in the present context. With the help of variations on the standard example, it argues that deception as a means to acquire and protect secrets is morally permissible under certain conditions.

It is worth locating my argument in relation to the distinction, familiar in just-war theory and the laws of armed conflicts, between perfidy and ruse. Perfidy consists in deceitfully leading the other party to believe that one wants peace: pretending to surrender and falsely claiming that one is an unarmed civilian, only to exploit the other side's vulnerability, are paradigmatic examples. Ruse consists in deceiving the other party as to how and when one will attack: ambushes are a paradigmatic example. Perfidy is legally prohibited and tends to elicit greater moral condemnation than ruse, which is legally permitted. Deception in espionage and counter-intelligence operations involves both perfidious and ruse-like behaviour. In effect, I argue that under certain conditions, both kinds of deception operations are morally justified, indeed mandatory.[6]

---

[5] On group lies, see J. Lackey, 'Group Lies,' in Michaelson and Stokke (eds.), *Lying*.
[6] For a recent discussion of perfidy and ruse in the context of war—not of espionage—see A. Ripstein, *Rules for Wrongdoers—Law, Morality, War* (Oxford University Press, 2021), 42–52. Ripstein seems to

5.3.1 Kant Revisited

Here is the example in its canonical form:

Murderer-at-the-door A murderer turns up on my doorstep and asks me whether his intended victim is hiding in my house. I tell him, falsely, that she is not.

Kant is best known for the view that it is always wrong to lie to the murderer, although he also held the more nuanced and plausible view that the murderer has forfeited his claim not to be lied to and thus that I do not wrong him by lying to him. On the more nuanced view, I am not completely off the moral hook: though I do not wrong him, I violate a duty of humanity.[7]

Murderer-at-the-door is a case of protective deception in the service of defensive counter-intelligence: I lie to protect secret information which the murderer seeks to uncover, in order to stop him. The story of Rahab, who protected Joshua's spies from the king's pursuers, is a good early example (s. 1.2).

Compare with:

Murderer-at-large Murderer is planning an attack on someone who, he mistakenly believes, has betrayed him. Via his unwitting associates, I plant a false trail of evidence leading him to what he mistakenly thinks is the victim's house.

This is a classic case of protective deception in the service of offensive counter-intelligence: I deceive the murderer so as to protect secret information about the victim's whereabouts by using his own information-gathering network against him, thereby neutralizing his attack.

In those two scenarios, I thwart the murderer by sending him the wrong way. Contrast with:

---

endorse deception operations such as those mounted by the Allies in 1942–44, while rejecting false surrenders. I conjecture that he would reject as impermissible on grounds of perfidy some of the deception operations I describe in s. 5.3.2. My argument in this section is foreshadowed in a broader discussion of deception as a war tactic in C. Fabre, *Cosmopolitan War*, 268–76.

[7] I. Kant, 'Of Ethical Duties Towards Others, and Especially Truthfulness', in P. Heath and J. B. Schneewind (eds.), *Lectures on Ethics* (Cambridge University Press, 1997 [1755–85]). For discussions of Kant's views on lying in general, see, e.g., Carson, *Lying and Deception*, ch. 3; C. M. Korsgaard, 'The right to lie: Kant on dealing with evil,' *Philosophy & Public Affairs* 15 (1986): 325–49; A. W. Wood, *Kantian Ethics* (Cambridge University Press, 2008), ch. 14; D. Sussman, 'On the Supposed Duty of Truthfulness—Kant on Lying in Self-Defense', in C. Martin (ed.), *The Philosophy of Deception* (Oxford University Press, 2009); Shiffrin, *Speech Matters*, ch. 1. In his absolutist incarnation, Kant has an illustrious predecessor in St Augustine of Hippo. See Augustine, 'Against Lying' and 'On Lying' in R. J. Deferrari (ed.), *Augustine—Various Treatises* (The Catholic University of America Press, 2002).

Murderer-entrapped Same as in *Murderer-at-large* except that, this time, I lie in wait in the house, ready to kill Murderer.

Murderer-entrapped is another example of offensive counter-intelligence operations: I deceive the enemy as a means to place myself in a position to harm him. Compare now with:

Murderer-at-large* I do not know where Murderer is and whom he will attack next. I mill around his old neighbourhood and strike up conversations with his associates, from whom I hope to glean information, to track him down.

This is a classic case of espionage-related deception: I deceive in order to acquire information which the wrongdoer does not want me to have. I shall call this *acquisitive deception*.

There are many other variations on the canonical example, some of which I will rehearse presently. The lesson to draw from this short section is that the canonical case is helpful but of limited application here.

5.3.2 Deception in Espionage and Counter-intelligence: A First Cut

Here are some easy cases. Consider:

Infiltration₁ Green is locked in a conflict with Blue, a quasi-state organization intent on conquering swathes of territory via a mixture of conventional and terroristic means. Asset strikes up relationships with Blue's guerilla fighters, concealing his identity and true allegiances. He collects information about a possible attack on Green, which he passes on to Green's intelligence agencies. Green aims to eliminate those fighters before they can strike.

Asset engages in acquisitive deception, as I do in *Murderer-at-large**

Compare now deception in the service of protecting secrets—or, protective deception—as used in counter-intelligence operations. The history of the Allies' operations during WWII is rich in examples. *Operation Crossbow* nicely illustrates the effectiveness of deception to defensive ends along the lines of *Murderer-at-large*. By June 1944, Germany's long-range rockets (the V1 and V2) had become operational and were used to attack a number of strategic sites, in particular Central London. The Allies misled Germany's high command into shortening the rockets' range, as a result of which Central London was relatively untouched though at the expense of South London. They did so by, *inter alia*, using a double agent to feed the German High Command with false information about the campaign's success.

Operation Bodyguard, thanks to which the Allies deceived Germany's leadership as to the timing and location of their planned invasion of Western Europe, is the Allies' most significant and best-known operation of offensive counter-intelligence. Its masterminds employed a whole range of deceptive tactics. For example, its main component phase—*Operation Fortitude*—involved (*inter alia*) deploying fake invasion troops, complete with fake buildings, based in Scotland and the South of England, in the hope of leading the Germans to believe that the Allies would invade via Norway and Northern France. To confuse the Germans even further, the Double Cross system employed double agents who had been turned by or had volunteered with the British and fed false information back to Germany, in some cases through entirely fictitious networks.[8]

These cases are easy, because the individuals who are being deceived are liable to being killed anyway and Green knows that. On the plausible assumption that the right not to be killed is more stringent than the right not to be deceived, those agents *a fortiori* are liable to being deceived. Things are not always so easy, however, for two reasons.

First, in many cases, although the targets of the deception (be it protective or acquisitive) are *in fact* liable to being killed, Green does not know that. Consider:

Infiltration₂ Green's intelligence services have formed the reasonable belief that a new transnational terrorist network is gathering strength on Blue's territory. They do not know where exactly the network is operating; and while they suspect some prominent local figures to be involved, they do not have decisive evidence to that effect. They ask Asset to strike up relationships with those local figures and collect relevant information, by concealing his identity and true allegiances. Those locals' putative contributions to the network, if attested by the facts, would make them liable to being killed.

Even if, as a matter of fact, the prominent locals are liable to being killed and, by implication, liable to being deceived as means to stop their nefarious activities, Green, and Asset, are not epistemically licensed so to infer and, thus, are not subjectively justified in deceiving them unless they have independent reasons for believing that they are involved in the network. Now, in s. 3.4, I argued that knowingly giving reason for suspecting that one is engaged in the commission of a wrongdoing is a basis for liability to a loss of secrecy. By parity of reasoning, it is a

---

[8] On deceptions operations during WWII, see, e.g., M. Hastings, *The Secret War: Spies, Codes and Guerillas 1939–45* (William Collins, 2015); M. Howard, *Strategic Deception in the Second World War* (N. W. Norton, 1995); J. Levine, *Operation Fortitude* (HarperCollins, 2011); J. C. Masterman, *The Doublecross System, 1939–1945* (Pimlico, 1995); McIntyre, *Double Cross*. For a wonderful discussion of the ethical issues raised by *Operation Crossbow*, see S. Burri, 'Why Moral Theorizing Needs Real Cases: The Redirection of V-Weapons during the Second World War,' *Journal of Political Philosophy* 28 (2020): 247–69.

basis for liability to deception. If deception is wrong to the extent that it constrains the agent's freedom, it is wrong (at the bar of the freedom argument) only *vis-à-vis* those who do not give reasons for believing that they will abuse their freedom. If deception is wrong in so far as it constitutes an abuse of trust, it is wrong (at the bar of the trust argument) only *vis-à-vis* those who have shown themselves worthy of having their trust nurtured and respected. If deception is wrong to the extent that it makes it difficult, if not impossible, for us to relate to and cooperate with one another as moral and rational agents, it is wrong (at the bar of this argument) only *vis-à-vis* those who do not give us reasons for believing that they are unwilling so to cooperate. Whether Asset may justifiably deceive prominent locals in *Infiltration₂* depends on their conduct and on 'open source' evidence with Asset has been able to gather.[9]

Second, some of the individuals whom Asset deceives are not liable to killed. Consider:

Infiltration₃ Green has reasons to believe that Blue's leadership is in breach of Blue's treaty obligation not to enrich uranium. Should its suspicions turn out to be correct, it is planning to impose a raft of targeted economic and financial sanctions on high-ranking members of Blue's leadership and a number of their close associates. It inserts Asset into the relevant networks of influence, with a view to gathering evidence about both Blue's putative unranium enrichment programme and those individuals' financial assets. Failure to comply with the treaty would make the latter liable to those sanctions.

This is a case of acquisitive deception. Compare with a case of protective deception:

Unwitting Triple Agent Same as in *Infiltration₃* except that Green's services use Asset, who, they have discovered, has betrayed them for Blue, as an unwitting conduit to disinform Blue about Green's planned sanctions programme—thus turning Asset into a triple agent.

---

[9] For interesting accounts of the ethics of undercover policing along those lines, see Kleinig, *The Ethics of Policing*, ch. 7; Miller and Gordon, *Investigative Ethics*, ch. 11; C. Nathan, 'Liability to Deception and Manipulation: The Ethics of Undercover Policing', *Journal of Applied Philosophy* 34 (2017): 370–88. There are important differences between espionage and counter-intelligence in the service of foreign policy on the one hand, and police operations on the other hand, which have a bearing on such ethics. Most importantly, the police is meant to enforce the law of the land. When police officers deceive suspected criminals by, e.g., working undercover, they will often witness criminal offenses which they might not want to stop, notwithstanding their *raison d'être*, in order to catch the bigger fry. As we shall see in s. 5.6, intelligence officers and their assets also face severe dilemmas, but not ones centred around law enforcement.

I alluded to this case in s. 5.2, to make the different point that one deceives another person only if one knowingly causes her to form false beliefs. Here, Asset does not deceive Blue. He himself is deceived, alongside Blue's leaders. All directly contribute to Blue's wrongful ends. The degree to which individuals contribute to unjust ends makes a difference to the kind of harm one may deliberately impose on them. In this case, it seems plausible that Blue's leaders and Asset contribute to enough of an extent as to be liable to deception even though they are not liable to being killed.

Consider now the following two cases:

*Infiltration*₄ Green is fighting Blue, a transnational terrorist network operating from Blue's territory, and needs information about possible legitimate targets in that network. Asset mingles and strikes relationships with locals as a means to acquire information about such targets. Asset knows that those locals are not part of the terrorist network.

*Infiltration*₅ Same as in *Infiltration*₄ except that Asset feeds those locals with false information about Green's strategy regarding Blue—information which, he knows, will reach Blue's leadership.

One cannot appeal to the fact that those civilians are contributing to Blue's unjust ends in support of the claim that they may be so used. The question, then, is whether it is permissible to deceive someone who does not directly contribute to Blue's wrongful ends as a means to thwart rights violations. Suppose that in *Infiltration*₄, the locals have the information which Asset needs, yet refuse to provide it to him when (obliquely) asked. Or suppose that, in *Infiltration*₅, it is clear to Asset that they would refuse to mislead Blue's leadership willingly if asked to do so. In both cases, they refuse to help Green thwart Blue's rights violations. Suppose further that it is also clear that their refusal is grounded not in their fear of retaliation on Blue's part (assume that they would never be found out), but on the grounds that they do not particularly like Green and do not want to get involved. Under those circumstances, the locals are under a duty of rescue to Blue's victims to provide Asset with the assistance he needs. In s. 1.4.2, I argued that agents may sometimes justifiably harm another person as a means to get her to do what she is under a duty to do. Deception is a means by which Asset gets the locals to do what they are under a duty to do: we can think of it as an enforcement mechanism.

Not all such mechanisms are permissible. Asset may not torture those locals into supplying him with the relevant information or threaten to kill them if they refuse to participate in his protective-deceptive operation. Deception is different, as least in some of its forms. Suppose that Asset merely conceals who he is and eavesdrops on the locals' conversations. He is deceiving them, for he is allowing them to form false beliefs about his real identity. But he is not using them as a means to his and Green's ends: rather, he takes advantage of their carelessness. Intuitively, he is permitted to do so under the circumstances. Contrastingly, suppose that he lies to the locals outright about his real identity and allegiances, inserts himself in their private lives for months or years in order to invite their trust, and forms relationships with some of them. From his point of view, those relationships are purely instrumental. He is using those individuals as a means. Whether he may do so depends on the magnitude of their wrongdoing and the degree to which his deception harms them.

I take it that Asset is not justified in intentionally deceiving the locals if they neither directly contribute to Blue's wrongful ends nor are under a duty to help Asset thwart those ends. However, it is likely that, in the course of deceiving enemy wrongdoers, Asset will also unintentionally but foreseeably deceive the innocent. Consider:

> Infiltration$_6$ Green's services have identified a high-level Blue commander who, they have good reason to believe, is preparing an attack on Green's soil. They encourage Asset to insert himself in the commander's live-in entourage, including his innocent family members, with a view to spying on him, thereby also gathering information about his family.

The commander's relatives do not contribute to his unjust ends. Let us further assume that they do not have the option of leaving him.[10] Generally, one is sometimes justified in harming innocent civilians in pursuit of a just cause, as a foreseen but unintended side effect of otherwise-just missions (subject to the requirements of necessity, effectiveness, and proportionality.) By implication, Asset is sometimes justified in deceiving the commander's relatives as a foreseen but unintended side effect of the justified deception of responsible agents, thereby (justifiably) infringing their right not to be deceived (subject to the aforementioned requirements.)

So far, I have assumed that Green and Blue are on opposite sides of a conflict. Suppose that they are nominally allies. As we saw in s. 3.5, this does not make it wrong in itself for Green to spy on Blue. What matters is whether Green is epistemically licensed to infer from the best available evidence at its disposal that Blue might be planning to embark on an unjust foreign policy and whether, thus, it is subjectively justified in taking steps to ascertain whether its belief is true. Suppose

---

[10] As Jonathan Parry suggested to me, if they have that option but do not take it, thereby willingly exposing themselves to the risk of being deceived, perhaps they make themselves liable to being deceived, though one would need to know why they did not take the option. In any event, my point in the main text is that even if they lack that option, it may still be permissible to deceive them. For a defence of the relevantly similar view that under some circumstances, one makes oneself liable to defensive harm by not removing oneself from the scene of a confrontation, see Draper, *War and Individual Rights*, 150–9. The literature on using innocent civilians as shields is also of relevance here.

that Blue has given Green reasons for forming the belief that it is committing or planning serious rights violations, and that Green's belief is true. *Ex hypothesi*, Green is justified in obtaining those secrets: the question is by which means. Under those circumstances, officials within Blue who are responsible for giving such reasons to Green are liable to being deceived. Furthermore, to the extent that Green has a justification for engaging in deceptive tactics, it is all-things-considered permitted to do so, subject to considerations of necessity, effectiveness, and proportionality—whether the harm is caused intentionally to those who lack a claim against it, or uninentionally albeit foreseeably, as in *Infiltration*$_6$.

5.3.3 Deception in the Service of Unjust Ends

As we saw in s. 3.2, espionage and counter-intelligence are not morally justified means of pursuing unjust ends. In so far as Blue is spying on Green in the service of such ends, it is not justified in deceiving Green's members as a tool for intelligence-gathering to those ends. At the same time, as we also saw in s. 3.3, Blue owes it to its own members to try and ascertain whether it was morally mistaken in embarking on its (unjust) foreign policy in the first instance; it is also under a duty to Green's members to do the same in so far as it would thereby correct its mistaken decision to do so. Finally, it is under a second-best duty to try and minimize the commission by its own agents of violations of fundamental moral rights while they pursue those unjust ends.

Suppose, then, that Blue plants an asset in Green's services or directs its agents to infiltrate Green's civilian population. It imposes on the latter the *pro tanto* wrongful harms of deception. Even if it does so as a means to find out (in part) whether or not it is justified in continuing wrongfully to harm those individuals by conducting its chosen foreign policy, the fact remains that it does harm them by so doing, for it abuses their trust, restricts them in their rightful exercise of their freedom, and fails to engage with them on a footing of equality.

The foregoing points do not entail that Blue ought not to mount deception operations against Green. Recall one of the examples I used in s. 3.3: Blue is unjustifiably developing a new weapons programme, and Green is justifiably attempting to thwart it by mounting a cyber-attack on Blue, from a location which it seeks to keep secret. Suppose that Blue's military leadership have information to the effect that Green's cyber-weapons headquarters are located in a particular building. They also have contradictory information from another source that this building hosts Green's civilian IT mainframe. If Blue's spies report back that the building's computer mainframe is of purely civilian nature, Blue's military leadership, acting on broad orders from the government, will desist from bombing it, thereby sparing the lives and limbs of civilians who depend on it as well as of the workers who work there. If the spies report back that the building hosts

Green's cyber-command, Blue's military leadership will have it bombed, killing all inside. Suppose that Blue's intelligence services manage to place one of their own agents within Green's services. If that agent can ascertain where Green's civilian installations are and get Blue's air force not to bomb those sites, he will contribute to minimizing Blue's unjustifiable killings. This provides him, and his intelligence bosses, with a second-best—but only a second-best—justification to resort to deceptive tactics. Nevertheless, as we shall see in the next section, the fact that Asset and his bosses are only under a second-best justification so to act makes a difference to which kind of deceptive tactics they may justifiably employ.

For ease of exposition, in the remainder of this chapter I will speak of Green's deceptive operations, on the assumption that Green is pursuing just ends. *Mutatis mutandis*, however, my arguments apply to Blue's pursuit of such ends.

5.4 Mandatory Deception

Not only may Green's intelligence agencies, via Asset, sometimes justifiably engage in deception: under certain conditions they are under a duty to do so. This might seem obvious, yet the philosophical literature on the ethics of deception over-whelmingly focuses on the question of permissibility and neglects the question of mandatoriness.

There are two kinds of duties to deceive. First, an agent might be under a duty to deceive *in a particular way*, even if she is merely permitted, and not obliged, to deceive *simpliciter*. As I noted in s. 5.2, most people believe that other things being equal, it is better to conceal information than to engage in misleading implicature, and to engage in misleading implicature than to lie or forge evidence outright. One must use the least *pro tanto* wrongful options of all necessary and effective options. By implication, when other things are not equal, one may be morally required to lie rather than to conceal information. If lying is morally worse than other forms of deception in so far as it forecloses opportunities to get to the truth of the matter, then by that token it is the best of all deceptive options when those opportunities should be foreclosed. Pick any of the aforementioned cases and suppose that Asset has good reasons to believe that he would not be able to maintain his cover if he merely concealed his identity or engaged in misleading implicature. To the extent that his mission would fail, at possibly very high costs to Blue's victims, he is under a duty to lie outright.

Conversely, sometimes misleading by implicature is not as bad as lying. Suppose that *Blue's* intelligence agents could procure the information they need to further their unjust ends by employing misleading rather than mendacious tactics. This would increase the risk that *they* would be unmasked by Green's counter-intelligence services, relative to the mendacious tactic of, say, forging evidence outright. Hold constant the further risk that, were they to be unmasked, this would impair the ability of Blue's government to change their foreign policy in the direction of just ends. The fact that Blue's intelligence agencies have only a second-best justification to resort to deception in the first instance, by dint of the fact that their government is pursuing unjust ends, implies that they are under an obligation to expose themselves to greater risks than if their government were pursuing just ends and thus had a first-best justification for deceiving.

Second, an agent might be under a duty to deceive *simpliciter*. Here are two recent and interesting arguments to that effect, neither one of which is fully satisfactory. The first argument is set out by Tamar Schapiro in her illuminating article on Kant's moral rigorism. Schapiro argues that we owe it to one another to treat one another reciprocally as autonomous co-legislators in the Kingdom of Ends. By implication, we are under a duty not to manipulate one another since we would thereby impair one another's autonomy. We are also under a duty of honesty to one another, for when we address one another, we warrant ourselves to be truthful, and (again, in a spirit of reciprocity) rightfully demand as much from one another. When the murderer at the door asks me to tell him the truth about the whereabouts of his intended victim, he is inviting me to take part in an evil enterprise. In so doing, he shows that he is not committed to treating me as a co-legislator in the Kingdom of Ends. I am therefore under a duty to lie to him, so as to not be implicated in his betrayal of our moral relationship.[11]

Pace Kant, Schapiro concludes that we are under a duty to lie to the murderer, *at the bar of Kantian morality*. I agree. Even so, there is something missing from the picture—namely, the victim. For it seems odd to say, as I take Schapiro to do, that the reason why I must lie inheres in the murderer's betrayal of *my* moral relationship with *him*. Rather, it inheres in his betrayal of his moral relationship to the victim and, in the case at hand, in her right that he not kill her.

Compare with Alasdair McIntyre's defence of the duty to lie. McIntyre argues that some of our social and familial relationships, such as kinship or friendship, impose on us a particularly strong duty of care to one another. Indeed, we sometimes are under a duty to kill an attacker in defence of someone with whom we stand in this kind of relationship. Consider a Nazi official in the occupied Netherlands looking for Jewish children who, he rightly believes, are being sheltered by a Dutch woman. Suppose that the only way the woman can save the children is by killing him. Surely—McIntyre argues—she is under a duty to those children to do so, by dint of the fact that she has a duty of care to them to protect them. Suppose next that the Nazi merely asks her whether she is sheltering Jewish children. If she answers in the negative, he will leave. Given that she would be

[11] T. Schapiro, 'Kantian Rigorism and Mitigating Circumstances,' *Ethics* 117 (2006): 32–57, at 49–56.

under a duty to kill him were there no other option, she is under a duty to lie to him if she can thereby save the children's lives.[12]

McIntyre is on the right track, but his argument, as stated, does not go far enough, for two reasons. First, even if it applies to wars of political self-defence (at the considerable argumentative stretch of modelling political relationships on fairly close relationships), it does not apply to wars of humanitarian intervention, which are waged for the sake of distant strangers with whom we do not have a special relationship. Yet, as we saw in s. 1.4.1, we owe a duty of protection not just to those with whom we stand in a special relationship, but to all human beings wherever they reside in the world.

Second, McIntyre's argument does not apply to cases in which there is no duty to kill in defence of others. Yet, we owe a duty to deceive even those whom we are not under a duty to kill. Earlier I considered cases in which Asset deceives individuals who are not liable to be killed. In so far as we are under a duty to protect third parties from wrongful harm, we are under a duty to deceive wrongdoers as a means of discharging that duty, even if we are not, in the circumstances of the case, under a duty to kill those wrongdoers.

5.5 Some Objections

I have argued that deception in the service of acquiring and protecting political secrets as a means to conduct foreign policy does not wrong individuals who are planning to or actually commit serious rights violations, or who fail to fulfil their duty to stop such violations. I have also argued that deception is sometimes permissible even though it harms individuals who are not derelict in the aforementioned duties. This is so whether the deception takes the form of a lie, of fabricating evidence, of misleading by implicature, or of concealing relevant information.

Here are two possible objections The first objection draws on Seanna Shiffrin's rich and subtle Kantian argument in favour of lying to the Murderer-at-the-door, and against the kinds of deceptive tactics I defend here. There is much more to Shiffrin's account of the phenomenon and morality of lying than I can discuss here. Moreover, she focuses on lying, as distinct from deception. Still, with a bit of reconstruction, one can extract from her work a plausible and interesting line of argument against some forms of deception in espionage and counter intelligence operations.

---

[12] A. McIntyre, *Truthfulness, Lies, and Moral Philosophers: What Can We Learn from Mill and Kant* (Tanner Lectures on Human Values, 1994), 351–9.

On Shiffrin's view, whether an instance of lying is morally permissible depends on the content of what is being said. The murderer is asking you to tell him where his intended victim is. Were you to tell him the truth, you would provide him with what he needs in order to pursue his evil end *qua* evil end and become his accomplice. Shiffrin claims (and I agree) that you are morally justified in depriving him of such means by lying. Suppose now that the murderer desperately needs water before he can carry on. You have two options. On the one hand, you can mendaciously tell him that there is a well five minutes to the west—knowing that the time he will waste looking for it and his inability to quench his thirst will save his victim's life. On the other hand, you can tell him, truthfully, that the well is two minutes away to the east; you would enable him to get what he needs to pursue his end, but indirectly so—by enabling him to meet his basic need for water. In this case, you must tell the truth, for you must as far as possible preserve prospects for honest and sincere communication with the murderer. However grievous his wrongdoing, he remains worthy of respect and must be afforded prospects for redemption—prospects which your lie would undermine. While the imperative of affording him such prospects for redemption does not outweigh the imperative of not providing him with what he needs to further his unjust ends *qua* unjust ends, it does outweigh your understandable reason for not providing him with what he needs to further ends, such as quenching his thirst, which are not in themselves wrongful.[13]

With this account in hand, here is a possible Shiffrinean account of the ethics of deception operations. Her objection, which echoes Kant's concerns, focuses on the Murderer-at-the-door. In this standard case, the question is whether I may justifiably lie defensively so as to protect a secret about the victim—and thus, by extension, whether Green may justifiably engage in protective deception such as *Operation Crossbow*.[14] Shiffrin would endorse mendacious tactics in cases such as these.[15] She would also (I think) accept non-mendacious deceptive tactics in operations of defensive counterintelligence—but only so long as Green deprives Blue of what the latter needs to further its unjust ends *qua* unjust ends. However, she would reject both mendacious and non-mendacious tactics in non-standard

[13] The water-well example is Shiffrin's (see Shiffrin, *Speech Matters*, 34). I have made a couple of minor tweaks. Shiffrin relies on the familiar claim that there is a morally salient difference between supplying attackers with guns and supplying them with food. I criticize this claim in C. Fabre, 'Guns, Food, and Liability to Attack,' *Ethics* 120 (2009): 36–63. See also Draper, *War and Individual Rights*, 198–205; Frowe, *Defensive Killing*, 204–5. For a thoughtful discussion of Shiffrin's account with which I broadly agree, see K. Greasley, 'The Morality of Lying and the Murderer at the Door,' *Law and Philosophy* 38 (2019): 439–52.

[14] Minus the civilian deaths occasioned by the operation, which complicate cases such as *Murderer-the-door*. Those complications, important though they are for a full assessment of this and similar cases, are tangential to my point here.

[15] At any rate, she would not deem the use of those tactics wrongful *vis-à-vis* Blue's wrongdoers.

cases in which Green deceives Blue acquisitively as a means to procure its secrets or offensively as a means to protect its own. She would also object to defensive deceptive tactics aimed at depriving Blue of the all-purposes resources it needs to pursue both unjust and non-wrongful ends (analoguouly to water, in the Murderer case.). On Shiffrin's Kantian view, in so far as good faith between belligerents is necessary for peace, deceptive operations of that kind, which undermine it, are morally condemnable. The point applies to non-belligerent foreign policy: in so far as good faith between political communities is necessary for a *durable* peace, deceptive actions which undermine it are morally condemnable. In addition, by the objection's lights, deception operations are even more condemnable between allies.

I remain unconvinced. For a start, in wars of collective self-defence, the agents who carry out the deception are also those whose lives and livelihood are at stake. Suppose that you are the thirsty murderer's victim and do not have the means to defend yourself here and now. You can, however, pretend that you are not who you are, and, noticing his desperate need for water, send him the wrong way. It seems unreasonably demanding to insist that you must not lie other than to thwart his unjust ends *qua* unjust ends, even if lying would enable you to incapacitate him *tout court*. By parity of reasoning, in cases in which Asset has to decide whether to deceive Blue's members, failing which he himself would incur high risks of serious harm, he is not under a moral duty to allow himself to incur those costs. Moreover, when Green's leaders set up deception operations as a tool in the service of their just foreign-policy ends, they sometimes do so (if they have been democratically elected) on behalf and at the behest of Green's citizens. Green's citizens have delegated to their leaders the task of defending their own fundamental rights. To say that Green's intelligence services and their individual agents ought *not* to deceive is, in effect, to imply that those citizens ought to allow themselves to be wrongfully and grievously harmed by actors—Blue's leaders and forces—who *ex hypothesi* lack a justification for doing so.

There are further reasons to resist Shiffrin's objection. It is true that political communities and their leaders ought to nurture prospects for peace while at war and to maintain peace while not; and it is also true that wrongdoers remain worthy of respect. Shiffrin is entirely correct to insist that belligerents must not violate the rule that belligerents and combatants who show willingness to surrender or negotiate must be treated in good faith. Were she to broaden the point so as to encompass peacetime negotiations, she would also be correct. However, deception in the service of espionage or counter-intelligence operations need not destroy peace. France and Germany have done rather well, cooperation-wise, in the last sixty years, notwithstanding the fact that they were locked in three wars, two of them global, between 1870 and 1945; and espionage-related deception between allies, such as the NSA's operations against Germany which I will examine in s. 9.3, have not always undermined peace.

The second objection to espionage- and counter-intelligence-related deception takes as its starting point my own defence of espionage, and goes like this. As I argued in ss. 3.2 and 3.3, political communities are morally justified, indeed are under a duty, to engage in intelligence activities by dint of the general principle that we owe it to one another, as best we can, not to harm one another except on the basis of the relevant facts—put differently, except on the basis of what we believe to the best of our knowledge to be the *truth*. The task of intelligence agencies is precisely to help political leaders and citizens ascertain what the truth is with respect to their prospects for a just foreign policy. To deceive, however, is by definition to manipulate and falsify facts, and thus to eschew the truth, at least to some extent. The worry, then, is this. Intelligence agencies and their operatives, accustomed as they are to deceiving, might no longer be able to discern truth from falsehood and will lose themselves in the 'wilderness of mirrors'.[16] Political leaders and citizens, for their part, are likely to lose faith in the agencies on which they depend for the defence of their rights and the fulfilment of their duties in the realm of foreign policy.[17]

This second objection to deception is another variant of the charge, which we encountered in s. 3.2, that espionage operations are counter-productive. My response there applies here *mutatis mutandis*. Whether deception operations are morally justified depends in part on proportionality considerations. Admittedly, in order to know whether their deception operations meet the proportionality requirement, intelligence agencies might need to procure information which they do not have, and might be able to procure it only by deceptive means. We encountered this problem at the end of s. 5.3.2: it admits of the same answer here as it did then.

---

[16] The phrase 'wilderness of mirrors' is from T. S. Eliot's poem *Gerontion*. It was popularized as a description of the devastating impact of routine deception on counter-intelligence agents by James Jesus Angleton—head of the CIA's counter-intelligence services for the best part of the Cold War. Angleton, who had absolute faith in Kim Philby, was left devastated by the latter's betrayal and (it is often said) subsequently ran the Agency's counter-intelligence programmes to the ground by engaging in various witch-hunt campaigns against anyone (and there were many) whom he suspected, often wrongly, of spying for the USSR. See Weiner, *Legacy of Ashes*, 265–71 and 316–19; Omand, *How Spies Think*, ch. 6; D. C. Martin, *Wilderness of Mirrors* (Harper Collins, 1980).

[17] Compare with Shiffrin's objection to police officers lying to suspects about their legal rights or the strength of the evidence they have accumulated. Her objection is that it is the police's role not merely to uncover and stop crime but also explain to us, citizens and suspects, what our (legal) rights, duties, and liabilities are—particularly liability to punishment on the basis of the evidence gathered against suspects. By engaging in those sorts of lies, Shiffrin claims, the police subvert their epistemic role. (See Shiffrin, *Speech Matters*, 194–9.) The objection I address in the main text is slightly different. It is not the role of intelligence agencies to explain to leaders and citizens what their legal, let alone moral, obligations are. Rather, their role is to acquire and protect sensitive information, much of which is meant to remain secret. This claim does imply that they ought not to deceive their government, which needs to know the truth in order to make the relevant decisions: were they to deceive it, they would indeed subvert their function. But the claim does not imply that they ought not to deceive third parties as a means to acquire the truth.

5.6 Dilemmas of Deception

The resort to deception presents agents with severe dilemmas. I alluded to one kind of dilemma when describing *Operation Crossbow* in s. 5.3. In that case, as a result of the Allies' deceptive tactics, some individuals were killed by German forces, who would not have been killed otherwise. Another dilemma also confronted the British authorities during WWII: in order to hide from the Germans that their code-breakers had successfully broken the Enigma machine, they had to allow the German Navy to sink a number of Allied ships, at the cost of thousands of lives. In the first case, the British misdirected the Germans by supplying them with false information; in the second case, they protected their secret from the Germans by continuing to act as if nothing had changed. On the assumption (which I share) that *other things being equal*, harming is *pro tanto* harder to justify than allowing harm to happen, *Operation Crossbow* stood in greater need of justification than the measures taken to protect the Enigma secret.

Here is a different kind of dilemma, in which an agent causes harm to another person as a means to put himself in a position where he can deceive another party. Suppose that Asset needs to secure entry into Blue's military organization or terrorist cell. In order to do so, he has to deceive Blue's leaders. However, unless he stands a reasonable chance of obtaining Blue's secrets, he may not infiltrate himself into Blue's organization: deception is *pro tanto* wrong, and it is not enough, to justify committing it, that there should be a just cause for doing so. Therein lies the sting. The more trusted he is by Blue's leadership, the greater his chances of access and the higher the quality of the information he will get. But in order to be trusted by Blue's leaders and to reach a position where he will have access to the relevant secrets, he has to show willingness to participate in Blue's unjust ends. When those ends take the form of a war, a terrorist attack, or an arms deal, Asset must show willingness to contribute to wrongful deaths. The more willing and able he is so to participate, the more effective he will be at covertly thwarting Blue.

To illustrate:

> *Execution* Asset has been working for Green in Blue's terrorist cell for a few months. As final proof that he can be trusted with details of the cell's next campaign of suicide bombings on Green's territory, the cell leader asks him to shoot a Green captive in cold blood.

This is emphatically not an ivory-towerish case. For example, it was reported a few years ago that ISIS would test guerilla fighters in exactly this way six months or so after they had first joined. It is not far-fetched to assume that, were MI6 to plant one of its agents into that organization, he would face a very similar dilemma. In Britain's relatively recent past, albeit in the context of a conflict which many would regard as internal rather than transnational, the British intelligence services had a number of undercover officers within both IRA and Loyalist forces during the 1970s and 1980s, some of whom—it has been alleged—colluded in the assassination and torture of suspected traitors (to each cause) as a means of maintaining their cover.[18]

In one variant of *Execution*, modelled on Bernard Williams' famous case of Jim and the Indians, Asset has very good reasons for believing that the prisoner would die anyway. For example, the cell leader routinely executes prisoners.[19] I am tentatively inclined to think that Asset may do so himself—although I am also inclined (far less tentatively) to think that he is not under a duty to do so.

In another variant, by contrast, the prisoner would not die. For example, Asset knows that the cell leader normally keeps prisoners alive as bargaining chips to be used in potential negotiations with Green's leaders. In this case, I am strongly inclined to think that Asset may not execute the prisoner of war, albeit at the risk of failing to gain the cell leader's trust and of undermining his mission: one generally may not deliberately kill an innocent person who would not otherwise die imminently as a means to save others.

These are rough and ready intuitions, which need refining. In particular, we may wonder whether the costs Asset would incur were he to refuse to kill the prisoner make a difference. We might think, for example, that although he may not kill the prisoner as a means merely to save his mission, he may do so as a means to avoid blowing his cover altogether and thereby being killed by the leader himself. Duress may well provide Asset with a justification, and not merely an excuse, for killing the prisoner.[20]

I lack the space to do full justice to this question here. So suppose that I am wrong and that, contrary to what I have suggested, one may *never* deliberately kill an innocent person as a means of maintaining one's cover, even for the sake of averting mass casualties. The interesting question is whether, from the agent's point of view, Asset may infiltrate an organization in the knowledge that he will run a very high risk of having to commit such acts. The related question, from a leadership's point of view, is whether it may ask its agents to infiltrate terrorist networks, thereby exposing them to the considerable moral costs of being confronted by these kinds of dilemmas and by the risk of having to act in such a way as to make themselves liable to being killed. The answer, I believe, is that it should not use its agents in this way unless (at the very least) it has carried out a clear-eyed assessment of which exfiltration strategies it might put in place and of

[18] For a testimony about ISIS, see P. Cockburn, 'Life under Isis: Why I deserted the "Islamic State" rather than take part in executions, beheadings and rape—the story of a former jihadi', *The Independent* (16/03/2015). For the British case, see Omand and Phythian, *Principled Spying*, 114-7.

[19] J. Smart and B. A. O. Williams, *Utilitarianism: For and Against* (Cambridge University Press, 1973), 97-9.

[20] On duress as a justification for killing, see V. Tadros, 'Duress and Duty', in S. Bazargan and S. Rickless (eds.), *The Ethics of War* (Oxford University Press, 2017).

the agent's own ability to exfiltrate herself. The point applies, *mutatis mutandis*, to Asset's decision to accept the mission.

Consider one final case:

> *Incompetent Bomber* Asset is a low-level operative with limited bomb-making skills in a Blue terrorist network operating on Blue's territory. He is willing to supply information to Green about the cell in exchange for exfiltration into a safe country. Green's on-field officers help him give the impression to the terrorist leadership that he is much more skilled than he is, thanks to which his profile in the cell rises. As a result, Green is getting better information about the network's activities. However, once Asset is given more responsibilities, there is a heightened risk that his incompetence will cause more innocent civilians to die than would have been the case otherwise.

In this example, Green uses Asset as a witting means to its deception operations. Asset and his fellow cell-members are intervening agents in Green's intelligence operations and do not share sole responsibility for the ensuing deaths: Green does too, though not to the same extent as if it itself mounted an operation in the course of which the same number of civilians would be killed. Other things equal, it is harder to justify deception in *Incompetent Bomber* than in *Execution*: for in that case, unlike in *Execution*, Green enhances Asset's role in the cell in order to take advantage of his increased status as a killer.

5.7 Conclusion

I opened this chapter by observing that of the many ways in which spies procure and protect secrets, deception is what gives both espionage and counter-intelligence a bad name. Against such a view, I have defended the resort to deception as a means of procuring secret information about other foreign-policy actors and of defending one's own secrets against the latter's attempts to procure them.

Throughout, I have focused on cases in which the individual agents who participate in the relevant deception operations act on behalf of their political community. Their treachery is directed at foreign parties. However, more often than not, intelligence services recruit from within the enemy, for understandable reasons to do with, amongst other things, lack of relevant linguistic competence and local knowledge on the part of their own agents. Bluntly put, they recruit agents who are prepared to commit treason.

6

Treason

6.1 Introduction

Three out of the five kinds of spies listed by Sun Tzu in *The Art of War* are members of the enemy. As a contemporary writer on espionage notes, '[spying] is the art of betrayal. Almost inevitably, to gather secrets a spy must betray his country, or at least betray the trust placed in him by those who have given him access to the secrets.'[1] By that token, to run a spy in foreign territory is to incite, condone, and benefit from betrayal.

This is a live issue. The website for Britain's MI6 describes their work by means of a story involving a fictional but all too plausible businessman, Sami, who is willing to exploit his contacts within ISIS to pass on information to the British about the group's planned attacks. Sami's MI6 handler insists that Sami must stop as soon as he thinks that the risks are too high; at the same time, it is clear from the way the story unfolds that Sami might be engaged in the ongoing deception of individuals who regard him as one of their own. Going further back, the great intelligence battles of the Cold War were fought via traitors. Kim Philby, Oleg Penkovksy, Oleg Gordievsky, and Aldrich Ames are some of the best-known spies of that era. Philby was a member of the Cambridge Five spy ring. He was unmasked in the early 1960s and defected to Moscow, where he lived until his death in 1988. Penkovsky was a colonel with Soviet military intelligence and helped the US administration locate the rocket launch sites in Cuba and thus helped them defuse the missile crisis. He was arrested by the Soviets at the outset of the crisis, having been betrayed by a KGB mole within the NSA, and executed shortly thereafter. As the time of writing this, Gordievsky and Ames are still alive. Gordievsky, who ended his career as deputy head of the KGB station in London, worked for MI6 from the 1970s until he escaped from Moscow with MI6's help in 1985. He currently lives at an undisclosed location in England under the protection of the British Security Service. Ames, who was a CIA officer with particular expertise in Soviet counter-intelligence, was arrested in 1994 and is currently serving a life sentence in Indiana.[2]

---

[1] S. Grey, *The New Spymasters: Inside Espionage from the Cold War to Global Terror* (Penguin Books, 2016), 2.

[2] MI6's description of their work, complete with visuals and sound effects, can be found at https://www.sis.gov.uk (accessed on 17/08/2021). The literature on Philby's betrayal and, more generally, the so-called Cambridge Five, is huge. See, e.g., Grey, *The New Spymasters*; B. McIntyre, *A Spy Among Friends: Kim Philby and the Great Betrayal* (Bloomsbury, 2014), ch. 2; R. Davenport-Hines,

The 'treason war' is far from over. As recently as August 2020, a French intelligence officer was placed under investigation for passing on state secrets to Russia, while a former CIA employee was charged by the US authorities with a similar offence for China's benefit. In November 2020, a former officer with the Green Berets pleaded guilty in a US federal court to the charge of passing on classified information to Russia's intelligence services.[3]

Treason is one of the most serious criminal offences that there are. In the UK, a conviction for high treason carries a lifelong prison sentence, while breaching the Official Secrets Act carries a prison sentence of up to two years. In the US, a conviction for treasonous espionage carries between five years in jail and the death penalty. Had Gordievsky been captured, he would in all likelihood have been tortured and summarily executed.

Laws against treason are rooted in deep-seated moral revulsion about acts which, in the political realm, are paradigmatic examples of breaches of loyalty. The traitor deceives us, breaches promises—implicit or explicit—he has made to remain loyal, and leads us to doubt in the trustworthiness and dependability of our fellow citizens and public officials. As I noted in s. 2.2.2 when discussing the right to secrecy, to say that Blue's citizens have a right to secrecy against Green is to say, by implication, that they have a right against one another as well as against their officials that they not seek to help Green acquire Blue's secrets. The traitor seemingly breaches that duty. Moreover, when traitors engage in intelligence operations of the kind we encountered in Chapter 5, they are multiply treacherous. They deceive their fellow community members as to where their true allegiances lie; they deceitfully manipulate their colleagues and superiors into taking certain courses of action or making policy choices which they might not have taken otherwise; they often deceive their friends, partner, and children as to who they really are and what they do. In many cases, they do so over decades. It is often and precisely because the traitor is successful at personal betrayal that he is successful at treason.

Treason and its concomitant acts of personal betrayal present among the most serious ethical challenges to espionage and counter-intelligence operations. As I show in this chapter, however, they can be justified. Section 6.2 provides an account

---

Enemies Within: Communists, the Cambridge Spies and the Making of Modern Britain (William Collins, 2018). On Penkovksy, see G. Corera, *MI6: Life and Death in the British Secret Service* (Weidenfeld & Nicolson, 2011), ch. 4 (as well as chs. 2 and 5 for a good discussion of Philby's case.) On Ames, see, e.g., Weiner, *Legacy of Ashes*, 517–20. For a book-length account of Gordievsky's work and of his relationship with MI6, see B. McIntyre, *The Spy and the Traitor: The Greatest Espionage Story of the Cold War* (Penguin Books, 2019), as well as Gordievsky's autobiography. (O. Gordievsky, *Next Stop Execution* (Macmillan, 1995).)

[3] On the French case, see V. Mallet, 'French military officer held on suspicion of spying', *The Financial Times* (30/08/2020). On the CIA case, see J. E. Barnes, 'Ex-C.I.A. Officer Is Accused of Spying for China', *The New York Times* (17/08/2020). On the Green Berets case, see A. Goldman, 'Ex-Green Beret Admits He Betrayed U.S. While Spying for Russia', *The New York Times* (18/11/2020).

of the accusation of treason—of what a treasonous act consists in, and why it is presumptively wrongful. Sections 6.3–6.6 show that treason is sometimes morally permissible in principle, indeed mandatory—not merely between enemies but also between declared allies, and not merely at the behest of just foreign actors but also at the behest of unjust foreign actors. Section 6.7 tackles the complex question of traitors' acts of personal betrayal *vis-à-vis* their friends, relatives, and colleagues.

Two final preliminary remarks. First, for now (until Chapter 7), I set aside the issue of agents' motives—which range from commitment to an ideology, hatred of one's regime, financial greed, or simply the need to survive. Whether motives are relevant to the moral status of an act is too complex an issue to be tackled here. Accordingly, my claim that treason is sometimes morally justified holds subject to whether the traitor's motives are relevant to his act and, if they are, whether he acts from the right motives.[4]

Second, I set aside cases in which traitors plot to overthrow their leaders: neither Guy Fawkes, who attempted to kill King James I during the opening of Parliament in 1605, nor the members of the July 1944 plot against Hitler, are within my remit. Likewise, I do not attend to cases in which individuals join foreign forces and fight against their own community, such as (in recent years) Britons who enlisted with ISIS in the Middle East. I also set aside cases in which someone discloses political secrets to all and sundry with the aim of alerting public opinion to what they regard as morally objectionable practices. Daniel Ellsberg and the Pentagon Papers, and Edward Snowden and the NSA and GCHQ leaks, are beyond my remit. In keeping with the theme of the book, my focus is on what I call *informational* treason, as the act by which a (unauthorized) agent passes on his community's secrets to another community's intelligence services or government, and/or takes part in the latter's counter-intelligence deceptive operations against his own side.

6.2 Understanding Treason

Treason is a 'contested concept'. It is not always clear what and whom the alleged traitor is actually betraying: one person's traitor is more often than not another person's loyalist. Nevertheless, to describe someone as a traitor implies that he breaches presumptive obligations of loyalty to fellow members of his political community. This, in turn, carries the assumption that he stands in a particular relationship to those individuals. As Philby himself once put it, 'To betray, you must first belong. I never belonged.'[5] The question, then, is, what kind of relationship

---

[4] For an interesting set of case studies illustrating how complex and varied traitors' motives are, see E. Carlton, *Treason: Meanings and Motives* (Ashgate, 1998).

[5] M. Sayle, 'Conversations with Philby', *The Sunday Times* (17/12/1967). On the notion of contested concept, the *locus classicus* is W. B. Gallie, 'Essentially Contested Concepts', *Proceedings of the Aristotelian Society* 56 (1955): 167–98. On its application to betrayal, see A. Margalit, *On Betrayal* (Harvard

qualifies for treason and what obligations, as grounded in that relationship, the traitor presumptively breaches.

6.2.1 Treason, Nationality, and Membership

At first sight, we might think that the relationship of co-nationality (by which I mean purely formal citizenship) is a necessary and (together with the breach of relevant obligations) a sufficient condition for an agent to be aptly described as a traitor. My opening examples seemingly illustrate the claim that it is sufficient. Those agents were all nationals of the country whose secrets they divulged, and that alone, we might think, qualifies them as traitors. Furthermore, to see the force of the claim that nationality is a necessary condition, consider the case of Markus Wolf, the long-serving head of the GDR's foreign intelligence service—itself part of the infamous Stasi. After the reunification of Germany, Wolf was charged with and convicted of treason against the Federal German State. The Federal Constitutional Court subsequently overturned the verdict on the grounds that a national of a state duly acknowledged under international law (albeit defunct by the time of the trial) cannot be accused of treason against another state.[6]

Upon closer inspection, however, nationality is not a good basis for the charge of treason. On the one hand, it labels as traitors individuals who do not seem to act treasonously. Suppose that while travelling through Russia on an US passport, someone—call her Natasha—stumbles upon the abandoned briefcase of a Russian nuclear scientist and decides to pass on its content to the American Embassy. Unbeknownst to her, however, she is not American: she is in fact a Russian national. Yet, it would seem odd for the Russian authorities to regard her as a traitor. Not only does she have no substantive relationship to the Russian state and its citizens: she is not even aware that she is a Russian national. At the very least, we would need to add a knowledge requirement to the nationality condition. Even so, being a national of a particular country and aware of it is not enough. For suppose now that Natasha, who is in her fifties, knows that she is Russian, but has lived in the US since the age of five without ever coming back to Russia, and only has a formal connection, by dint of her citizenship, with the latter. Were she to stumble upon Russian secrets while residing in the US and pass on those secrets to (e.g.) the Pentagon, she would not be aptly regarded as a traitor to Russia either.

On the other hand, nationality does not account for cases in which the charge of treason seems apt. Consider the case of Klaus Fuchs. Fuchs, who was a German

University Press, 2017), 21–2. For a comprehensive sociological study of betrayal and treason which perfectly illustrates this point, see N. Ben-Yehuda, *Betrayals and Treason: Violations of Trust and Loyalty* (Westview Press, 2001).

⁶ M. Wolf and A. McElvoy, *Man Without a Face: The Autobiography of Communism's Greatest Spymaster* (Time Books, 1997), 373–9.

physicist and member of the German communist party, escaped to Britain from Nazi Germany in 1933 and worked on the Manhattan Project. Throughout the war and until 1949, he passed on details of the US and British nuclear programmes to the Soviet authorities, partly out of ideological commitment to communism, partly out of the conviction that so destructive a weapon could not be entrusted to one country alone but had to be shared in order to be neutralized. Fuchs was naturalized as a British subject in July 1942. If nationality is a necessary condition for treason, Fuchs was a traitor only after July 1942. This seems counter-intuitive: by then, he had been living in the United Kingdom for nine years; and he was doing exactly the same thing before and after that date.[7]

Or consider the case of William Joyce, aka Lord Haw-Haw—the last person to be executed for treason in the United Kingdom. Joyce was an American citizen of Irish descent who identified as British and who, thanks to his father's fraudulent application to the British authorities, was in possession of a British passport. Joyce joined the British Union of Fascists in the 1930s, fled to Germany in 1939, and was naturalized as German in 1940. There, he was hired by the German Ministry of Propaganda to work in the English-language section of the radio services, whence he issued virulently anti-British broadcasts until his capture by the Allies in 1944. His nationality was a key issue at his trial. At first, the prosecution argued that, as a British subject, he owed a duty of allegiance to the Crown which he had breached by working for Britain's enemy. The trial collapsed as soon as the defence team was able to prove that Joyce was not, in fact, a British subject. The prosecution returned to the breach with a new charge. As the holder of a British passport, albeit one fraudulently obtained, Joyce had enjoyed the protection of the British Crown; as such he was under a legal duty of allegiance to the latter, which he had violated by fleeing to and working for the enemy. The House of Lords ultimately found in favour of the Crown and Joyce was hanged in May 1946. On the prosecution's settled view, nationality was not a necessary condition for treason: enjoying the protection of the Crown (together with the other objective and subjective elements of the crime) was sufficient. Whether or not the prosecution was right on point of law, as a matter of morality it was right: intuitively, it seems that Joyce was a

---

[7] See, e.g., M. Rossiter, *The Spy Who Changed the World* (London: Headline Publishing, 2014) and, especially, F. Close, *Trinity—The Treachery and Pursuit of the Most Dangerous Spy in History* (Penguin Books, 2020). In 1950, with MI5 closing in on him, Fuchs confessed to the British authorities that he had passed on official secrets to the Soviets until 1949, and was sentenced to a 14-year jail term and stripped of his British citizenship. Upon his release from prison he emigrated to what was then East Germany, where he died in 1988. Fuchs' case is particularly interesting. Much of the technical information he passed on to the Soviets was his own work, which seems less bad than stealing the work of others. Moreeover, after the war and at a time when the United States would embargo any flow of information about their nuclear programme to their former allies, including Britain, Fuchs helped the latter develop its own nuclear programme—on one occasion, as he was about to leave Los Alamos, by passing on all the information he had acquired about US plans for a hydrogen bomb. Had they known what he was up to, the American authorities would have taken a very dim view of what, for all intents and purposes, was an act of espionage against them for the benefit of the British.

traitor, notwithstanding the fact that he was not British. There is no reason, morally speaking, to treat him any differently from John Amery, who was a British national and was hanged in December 1945, having pled guilty to similar offences.[8]

If nationality is both under- and over- inclusive, the question is what kind of relationship an agent must have with a political community in order to be aptly regarded as a traitor to it. In the light of Joyce's case, we might be tempted to concur with the House of Lords that enjoying the protection of the state, irrespective of one's nationality, is an apt basis for the charge of treason. We would be mistaken. For if merely enjoying the protection of the relevant authorities on whose territory one is located were enough, a tourist who enjoys such protection could aptly be regarded as a traitor. Yet this seems counter-intuitive. Whilte the tourist is under a moral obligation to obey the law of the land, his connection with the country he is visiting is so thin that his breach of the relevant obligations is not treasonous.[9]

Moreover, long-term protection does not seem to be enough either. Suppose that James is an African American citizen living in Mississipi in the 1950s. Although he enjoys consular protection while abroad by dint of holding a US passport, at home he is subject to mandatory segregation laws, is systematically discriminated against on the job and housing markets, and has to endure daily manifestations of racism by other American citizens. He is treated as a second-class citizen and does not enjoy what we may call *social membership* in the United States. Suppose that he stumbles upon a briefcase full of state secrets, and finds a way to pass it on to the Soviet Embassy in Washington. Assuming for the sake of argument that he would act wrongly, it is not clear that he would aptly be regarded as a traitor to the United States, in the light of the treatment which the latter's authorities, with the support (be it passive or active) of many of its citizens, mete out to him.[10] Contrast with Jake, also an American citizen, who in every possible way is treated as a first-class citizen. Were *he* to provide a foreign power with US state secrets, he clearly would be a much stronger candidate for the charge of treason. Compare, finally, with Carl, who is not an American citizen but who is a long-term resident in the US and enjoys the considerable economic and social benefits of such residence, minus those inherent in formal citizenship (of his volition, as he has decided not to apply for naturalization.) Pending further consideration, he too, I submit, would aptly be regarded as a traitor under those circumstances.

---

[8] For a good summary of Joyce's trial, see S. C. Biggs, 'Treason and the Trial of William Joyce,' *The University of Toronto Law Journal* 7 (1947): 162–95. For discussions of the case in the context of broader empirical accounts of treason, see M. Boveri, *Treason in the Twentieth Century* (Macdonald, 1961), ch. 15; R. West, *The Meaning of Treason*, 2nd. ed. (Macmillan/The Reprint Society, 1952), ch. 1.

[9] For a very interesting discussion of the ways the protection of the British Crown extends to foreigners, see J. Finnis, 'Nationality, Alienage and Constitutional Principle,' *Law Quarterly Review* 123 (2007): 417–45. I am grateful to Richard Ekins for the suggestion and for pressing me on the issue.

[10] As Ashwini Vasanthakumar suggested to me, the case of long-term undocumented immigrants who are unjustly denied the benefits of full citizenship is relevantly similar.

The examples of Jake and Carl, as contrasted with the example of James, suggest that social membership is a necessary condition for a relationship to be treason-qualifying. Carl and Jake enjoy it, whereas James does not. The 'social membership thesis' also reaches the correct conclusion in Klaus Fuchs' and William Joyce's cases. However, it needs refining. Return to Oleg Gordievsky. As a citizen of a totalitarian regime, his fundamental moral rights to the freedoms and resources needed for a flourishing life were not enforced in law. As a matter of fact, however, he was enjoying considerably more freedom and material comfort than ordinary Soviet citizens, by dint of his institutional position within the KGB—dominated freedom, in so far as it could be taken away from him at a moment's notice without due process, but freedom nonetheless. If not being treated as a social member is a necessary condition for being aptly labelled a traitor, then Gordievsky was not a traitor, which is intuitively implausible.

Gordievsky's case suggests that we should distinguish between *thick* and *thin* social membership. Someone enjoys thick social membership if and only if (a) her fundamental moral rights are enshrined in her community's legal system (such as to give her meaningful recourse should those rights be violated), and (b) those rights are not, as a matter of fact, routinely violated. Someone enjoys thin social membership if and only if her fundamental moral rights are not, in fact, routinely violated, whatever the law of her community might say. On the one hand, it seems apt to describe Gordievsky as a traitor—and, more generally, so to describe members of illiberal and/or undemocratic communities who nevertheless enjoy an array of *de facto* freedoms and benefits. On the other hand, it does not seem apt so to describe someone (like James) whose fundamental rights are routinely violated *de facto* and *de jure*. Taken together, those two points suggest that enjoying thin social membership is an appropriate basis for treason. *A fortiori*, so is thick social membership.[11]

However, although social membership is necessary for a relationship to be treason-qualifying, it is not sufficient. Consider Soviet 'illegals', who were inserted by the Soviets under fake identities (complete with fake passsports, fake jobs, etc.) in Western countries and lived there, sometimes for years. Two of the best-known illegals are William Fisher, also known as Rudolf Abel, and Konon Molody, also known as Gordon Lonsdale. Fisher was a British citizen by birth, but fled with his family to the USSR in the 1920s. By a long circuitous route, he joined the KGB and was trained to work and live as an illegal in the US—which he did for eight

---

[11] The claim that thick membership is not necessary makes space for the charge of treason in cases which the betrayed community is not a state. It can be a social and political community more broadly construed, which is centred around a political culture and is a source of various benefits, and which is not necessarily coextensive with national borders. Republicans in Northern Ireland, or the Pashtun in Afghanistan, come to mind. I am grateful to Emmanuela Cueva, Margaret Moore, and Andy Owen (to whom I owe the examples of Northern Ireland and the Pashtun) for pressing me on the notion of social membership.

years until his arrest in 1957. Molody was a Soviet citizen and lived undercover in the UK for years while working for the KGB. Both Fisher and Molody enjoyed all the benefits of long-term residence in the US and the UK respectively. If social membership is a sufficient condition for a wrongdoer to be charged with treason, those agents were guilty of treason to their country of residence. And yet, given that they were KGB agents all along and inserted into those countries with the explicit purpose of spying on them, it does not seem right to describe them as traitors. Indeed, as a matter of fact, they were charged with and convicted of espionage - not treason.[12] This strikes me as intuitively plausible. The relevant difference between illegals on the one hand, and individuals such as Jake and Carl on the other, is that the former have become members in order to act against the community and other members. Not only do they not think of themselves as full members of the community: it is essential to their work that they not identify with it. Put differently, they are not *bona fide* members. Jake and Carl, by contrast, are *bona fide* members. It is that, I suggest, which would mark them as traitors were they to pass on official secrets to third parties without being authorized to do so.[13]

Some readers might remain unconvinced. They might agree that illegals do not owe an obligation of loyalty to the regime against whom they have been sent to act by their own regime; but in so far as they have benefited from their social membership in that foreign community, albeit under false pretences, they are under some obligation of loyalty to that community's members. Put differently, *bona fide* social membership is a necessary condition for being charged with treason against the regime (and so illegals are not traitors in this sense); but it is not a necessary condition for being charged with treason against ordinary citizens (and so illegals are traitors in that sense.)

I see the force of the objection, particularly in those cases where although it makes sense to say that the illegals' regime, or state, is in conflict with the regime or state of the community on which they have to spy, it does not really make sense to say that both *citizenries* are in conflict with each other. (That said, if this is correct, the objection is not particularly strong in the case of Soviet

[12] On Molody's career as a Soviet illegal, Andrew and Mitrokhin, *The Mitrokhin Archive*, 532–37; Corera, *MI6*, 232–37. On Fisher's, see Weiner, *Enemies*, 204–7. Fisher was eventually swapped in 1962 with the US pilot Gary Powers.

[13] In his book on betrayal, Avishai Margalit argues that the traitor betrays the relationship of 'primal citizenship' in which he stands with fellow community members. At the heart of primal citizenship is 'the notion of a citizen as part of a political community, whose members imagine themselves as standing in thick relations to each other; relations on which their distinct collective identity supervenes.' (See Margalit, *On Betrayal*, 176 and ch. 5 in general.) Usually, a genuine legal citizen is a primal citizen: he is presumed by dint of his legal citizenship to share in the collective identity of the citizenry. Soviet illegals, on Margalit's account, were not primal citizens, hence were not traitors either. While Margalit and I reach the same conclusion with respect to this particular case, I do not endorse his argument, for two reasons. First, as I noted above, I do think that William Joyce was aptly described as a traitor even though he was not a citizen. Second, I reject the collective-identity argument for citizens' special obligations to one another.

illegals, given the wholesale mobilization of material and human resources by each side against the other during the Cold War.) Even so, there does seem to be an important difference between illegals and *bona fide* members, which might perhaps be captured in the following way. When Philby was unmasked, it was entirely appropriate for his colleagues and fellow citizens to say: 'But he is *one of us!*' When Fisher was unmasked, it would have been entirely appropriate for those whom he had deceived to say, instead: 'But I *thought* he was one of us!'

Suppose that I am wrong. If so, we are still left with the view that (to repeat) *bona fide* social membership is a necessary condition for charging wrongdoers with treason against their regime, but not for charging them with treason against ordinary citizens. Either way, it is social membership that matters: nationality or the fact that one enjoys the state's protection is irrelevant.

6.2.2 The Presumptive Wrongfulness of Treason

As I noted at the start of s. 6.2, to describe someone as a traitor implies that he breaches presumptive obligations of loyalty to fellow members of his political community. This presupposes that he stands in a particular relationship to the latter. That relationship, I have argued, is that of social membership. I now offer a hybrid, three-pronged argument in support of the claim that to commit treason is, presumptively, to commit a wrongdoing—such that the burden of proof lies on the shoulders of those who wish to defend it. This argument mirrors my earlier account (in s. 3.5) of the presumptive wrongfulness of spying on allies.

One may wonder what is distinctive about the claim that treason is presumptively wrongful. After all, one might think that the task of justifying it is tantamount to justifying the claim that individuals are under an obligation to obey the law of the state on whose territory they happen to be; or that it is tantamount to justifying the claim that an agent may not be complicitous in wrongful ends. If those points are true, there is nothing special about treason.

I do not think that this is quite right. As we saw above, even non-residents, such as tourists and travellers passing through, are under an obligation to obey the law, yet they are not aptly described as traitors when they breach it. Moreover, everyone is under a duty not to further wrongful ends. The traitor's breach is qualitatively different. Even if there is, generally, an obligation to obey the law which the traitor breaches, and/or a duty not to further wrongful ends which he also breaches, the charge of treason gives his dereliction a distinctive hue which needs explaining.[14]

---

[14] For an illuminating review of arguments against disobeying the law and their applicability—or not—to the crime of treason, see Y. Lee, 'Punishing Disloyalty? Treason, Espionage, and the Transgression of Political Boundaries,' *Law and Philosophy* 31 (2012): 299–342.

The first argument for the presumptive wrongfulness of treason (as distinct from the presumptive wrongfulness of disobedience to the law) appeals to trust. The traitor, it is said, impairs the political trust which other community members have in him *qua* fellow members—and therein lies his wrongful breach of loyalty. As a rough cut, some agent A displays political trust towards another agent B if she relies on B φ-ing in a political capacity, if she regards the fact of her reliance as providing B with a reason for φ-ing and if she expects B to be motivated to φ on the grounds, precisely, that A relies on him to φ. Now, suppose that Denis is a civil servant in Blue and in that capacity is entrusted by his superiors, who act on behalf of Blue's citizens, with official secrets. When Denis decides to pass on those secrets to Green, he breaches their trust in him *qua* public official. More importantly, he breaches his fellow citizens' trust: even though they have never met him and therefore do not trust *him*, Denis, not to pass on official secrets to Green, they trust whichever civil servants are in charge not to act in this way. Breaching that trust can constitute an act of treason.[15]

However, appeals to political trust do not exhaust accounts of its presumptive wrongfulness. If they did, treason would by definition be impossible in a political community in which there is general distrust between state officials, between state officials and citizens, and indeed between fellow citizens themselves. It would imply, for example, that Soviet citizens could not, by definition, be labelled as traitors to their community, such was the level of distrust within Soviet society. Yet, to repeat, it is apt to characterize Gordievsky as well as those of his fellow Soviet citizens who worked for foreign agencies as traitors. Appeals to trust have force, but are not enough.[16]

The presumptive wrongfulness of betrayal in personal relationships helps uncover a second argument for the presumptive wrongfulness of treason. Suppose that Carl does not trust Anna to keep his secret. Against his better judgement, he confides in her and asks her not to share what he has just told her with anyone else. In so doing, he makes it clear to her that he endorses the norm that one generally ought not to disclose that which one has explicitly been told in confidence. If she gives this undertaking and then goes on to disclose it all to Beth, she is betraying him. Even though he knew deep down that she would so act, she owes him an

---

[15] I draw on accounts of personal trust which can be found in, e.g., A. Baier, 'Trust and Antitrust', *Ethics* 96 (1986): 231–60; P. Pettit, 'The Cunning of Trust', *Philosophy & Public Affairs* 24 (1995): 202–25; K. Jones, 'Trust as an Affective Attitude', *Ethics* 107 (1996): 4–25; R. Hardin, *Trust and Trustworthiness* (Russell Sage Foundation, 2002); V. McGeer and P. Pettit, 'The Empowering Theory of Trust', in Paul Faulkner and Thomas Simpson (eds.), The *Philosophy of Trust* (Oxford University Press, 2017); M. Bennett, 'Demoralizing Trust', *Ethics* 131 (2021): 511–38. For a trust-based normative account of treason, see R. Ekins et al., *Aiding the Enemy: How and why to restore the law of treason* (Policy Exchange, 2018). For an empirical account, see Ben-Yehuda, *Betrayals and Treason*.

[16] On distrust in the Soviet Union, see G. Hosking, 'Trust and Distrust in the USSR: An Overview', *The Slavonic and East European Review* 91 (2013): 1–25. My criticism of the trust argument adds to Lee's criticism. See Lee, 'Punishing Disloyalty?', 328–9.

explanation and an apology. To be sure, she would also owe him an explanation and an apology even if she were a stranger to him and had merely come across sensitive information about him which, she ought to have assumed, he would want her to keep secret from third parties. But her explanation and apology, in this case, unlike the former case, would not need to take account of their pre-existing relationship, since there would be no such relationship to begin with.

Similar considerations apply to cases in which the parties have mutually understood and articulated expectations that they will not disclose sensitive intelligence to foreign powers. It is particularly apt when the agent has taken an oath to the effect that he would serve his country, or when he occupies a position such that, it is understood by all, he is bound by secrecy. Moreover, the point applies even in cases in which the traitor benefits rather than harms the vital interests of his fellow community members. Again, by analogy, even if Anna is benefiting Carl overall by disclosing his secret to Beth, she is still betraying him, and here too there is a sense in which she owes him an explanation and an apology. Likewise, Gordievsky provided the British and American governments with a raft of vital intelligence about the KGB's operations in Britain and, more importantly, about the mindset of Soviet leaders in the early 1980s, at a time of heightened tensions between the USSR and the US. Even if he benefited his fellow Soviet citizens overall by doing so (which seems plausible), there remains a sense in which he breached a presumptive obligation not to disclose their and their country's secrets in defiance of shared expectations of non-disclosure.

So far, we have two arguments in favour of the claim that treason is presumptively wrongful: the argument from political trust, and the argument from mutually understood expectations of confidentiality. The third argument goes like this. Return to the example of Jake, who provides a foreign power with US state secrets. Suppose that those secrets are of such a nature that, were he to pass them on to (e.g.) the Chinese authorities, he would expose some individuals to a serious risk of wrongful harm. He is under a presumptive duty not to do so—by dint of obligations which we all have to all other human beings, irrespective of any relationship which we may have with them or of what we have undertaken to do or not to do for them. In the original variant of the case, he is an American citizen who enjoys social membership in the United States. If he passes on those secrets to the Chinese, he would be aptly regarded as a traitor. To the extent that his act, *qua* treason, is presumptively wrongful, it cannot be *merely* by dint of the fact that he harms the vital interests of individuals who happen to be American. On the contrary, it must be by dint of his special relationship to the United States. For, otherwise, there would be no difference between his act and the act of *British* Jake who enjoys social membership in the United Kingdom and passes on exactly the same US secrets to the Chinese.[17]

---

[17] On which point I agree with Youngjae Lee. See Lee, 'Punishing Disloyalty?', 319.

The question, then, is what feature of that relationship grounds a presumptive duty not to pass on those secrets. As someone who enjoys social membership in the United States, Jake benefits from the ties that unite him to this particular political community. Yet, by passing on information to the Chinese authorities surreptitiously, he undermines the institutions which his fellow members support, thanks to which he can enjoy the benefits of membership, and on which they too are dependent. He accepts the benefits of membership while harming his fellow members: it is for this reason that his act of disclosure is presumptively wrongful.[18]

It might be objected that my defence of the presumptive wrongfulness of treason does not properly account for the intuition that, at the heart of treason—that which makes it wrong—is a breach of *loyalty*. For (the objection continues) it seems odd to say that individuals owe loyalty to their community because the latter confers benefits on them; and it seems even stranger to say that they owe loyalty to their fellow members because the latter contribute to the community's ability to provide them with benefits. Rather, they owe loyalty to their community because it is *their* community, period; they owe loyalty to their fellow members because the latter are *their* fellow members, period.[19]

Loyalty, on this view, is necessarily non-instrumental. Yet it need not be so. In institutional settings, it can take the form of commitment and willingness not to undermine institutions which do well by us and, thereby, not to harm our fellow members. Treason is presumptively wrong in so far as it consists in a breach of loyalty so construed. My defence thereof thus need not deny the importance of loyalty.

As should be clear, the charge of treason—as the commission of a presumptively wrongful act—is context-sensitive in so far it is shaped by shared understandings of what agents are meant to do in fulfilment of their duties to one another. Moreover, it holds irrespective of the agent's motives: whether Jake is motivated by hatred for his country, greed, or desire to improve the lot of his fellow members, what matters for the claim that he is presumed to have done wrong is what he has received from his community and/or what he is expected to do in return. Finally, on the account I have just given, acts of treason are presumptively worse than non-treasonous yet harmful acts, and some treasonous acts are presumptively worse than others.[20]

---

[18] The benefits argument I am sketching out here resembles Ekins et al.'s argument in their *Aiding the Enemy*. But it differs from theirs in the following respects. Unlike me and as noted in n. 16, they tie the receipt of benefits to political trust. In addition, they do not consider cases in which a community member does not benefit from his membership (and thus does not, on my view, have special duties to other community members). Finally, they assert that treason is always, and not merely presumptively, wrong. See Ekins et al., *Aiding the Enemy*. For a sceptical discussion of the appeal to benefits, see Lee, 'Punishing Disloyalty?', 319–22.

[19] Lee, 'Punishing Disloyalty?', 315–16.

[20] The claim that treasonous acts are worse, other things being equal, than non-treasonous acts is compatible with Goodin's view (which I defended in s. 1.4.1) that our duties to compatriots are derived from our general duties to human beings—that is to say, that our having those special duties is simply an efficient way of discharging those general duties. On this view, wrongfully harming a compatriot is

On the first count, other things being equal, it is presumptively worse of American Jake to pass on US secrets to the Chinese than it is of British Jake, to the extent that (to repeat) American Jake undermines the institutions thanks to which he benefits from social membership in the United States and on which his fellow Americans depend.

On the second count, suppose that Jake is an official—say, he is working for the CIA. His wrongdoing is worse, other things being equal, than if he were an ordinary citizen or even an employee working for an American company whose activities are critical to his country's infrastructure. My account accommodates this. Public officials are strongly expected by those whom they serve not to harm the latter's vital interests (even if, as a matter of fact, they are not trusted to do so); indeed, they will often have made an explicit commitment to do so (even if it should turn out that they honour their commitment in the breach rather than in the observance.) Admittedly, *qua* public officials, they are likely to be in a better position to form a justified belief that treason is warranted. Nevertheless, the fact that their official position is likely to make it easier for them to acquire a subjective justification for treason is compatible with the claim that, when things are equal (absent, then, the evidence), they are under a stronger presumptive duty not to commit treason than ordinary citizens.[21]

Furthermore, my account also accommodates the case of the unwitting triple agent (s. 5.3.2.) Suppose that Jake is a CIA employee and passes secret intelligence about the US to China. Unbeknownst to him, his CIA bosses are fully aware of what he is doing. Instead of handing him over to the FBI, they manipulate him into feeding to China intelligence which the US administration wants China to have. Jake does precisely what his country's leadership wants him to do. However, it is still apt to describe his act as treasonous and presumptively wrongful, in so far as he thinks that he is acting against the United States in defiance of the fact that he is understood to be under a role-based obligation not to breach secrecy.

6.3 Permissible Treason

Someone who wishes to disclose secret information about his political community's critical infrastructure without authorization needs to show that he has a justification for violating the trust his fellow members place in him, for defying

---

worse than wrongfully harming a distant stranger, but *only* contingently on the fact of that relationship and to the extent that in so doing I fail to discharge my general duties. Nevertheless, to the extent that we have such relationships, they demarcate those to whom we owe special duties, from those to whom we do not owe them.

[21] For the view that public officials are under more stringent moral duties than ordinary citizens, see J. Gardner, 'Criminals in Uniform', in R. A. Duff et al. (eds.), *The Constitution of the Criminal Law* (Oxford University Press, 2013). I am grateful to Ashwini Vasanthakumar for pressing me on this point.

shared expectations that he not so act, or for undermining the institutions thanks to which he enjoys the benefits of social membership and on which his fellow members also depend. He needs to show, in other words, that the presumption against treason is overridden by countervailing considerations. In this section and the next, I provide an account of those countervailing considerations. Unless otherwise stated, I focus on cases in which the traitor is a public official, since it is public officials, usually, who commit informational treason. But my arguments apply *mutatis mutandis* to ordinary individuals who happen to be in possession of sensitive information, or to company executives who sell their company's trade secrets to a foreign power in presumptive breach of their duty to their fellow members not to do so.

Let us assume that Blue's leadership is embarking on an unjust foreign policy: it authorizes, and its officials commit, violations of fundamental rights. At the very least, those individuals are *pro tanto* morally permitted not to take part in those wrongdoings in the first instance, and to extricate themselves from the unjust venture—for example, by resigning.[22]

The question at hand is whether they are morally permitted to go one step further and to act against Blue by passing on secrets about its policy to Green. Here is a simple analogy. Suppose that Albert becomes aware that his business partner Bob is planning unjustifiably to assault Gerald as part of their business venture. Not only is Albert morally permitted to get out of the business venture: he does not owe it to Bob not to thwart his unjust plans by warning Gerald of Bob's wrongful plans. By analogy, Asset does not owe it to Blue not to pass on to Green secret intelligence about Blue's *ex hypothesi* unjust foreign policy, thanks to which Green will be able to thwart Blue.

Suppose now that Gerald, who is aware of Bob's nefarious plan, has taken steps to protect information about his whereabouts and his preparedness for Bob's attack. Albert knows what those steps are. When Bob asks him whether (for example) Gerald has any inkling of what awaits him and whether he is armed, Albert lies. In s. 5.3.2, I argued that protective deception is *pro tanto* justified. The only difference between the cases I rehearsed there and this particular case is that Albert is an associate of Bob's. It is hard to see why this should make any moral difference to Albert's act of lying: one's presumptive duty not to act in defiance of mutually shared expectations of loyalty does not extend to a duty to allow the violation of an innocent person's fundamental rights. By analogy, Asset does not owe it to Blue not to help Green protect its secrets from Blue's attempts wrongfully to acquire them.

---

[22] I say *pro tanto*, for as C. A. J. Coady persuasively argues, it does not follow from the fact that one has initiated a wrongful course of action that one may, let alone must, desist here and now. The costs others would accrue if one were to desist must be taken into account as one considers how to extricate oneself. (Coady, 'Escaping from the Bomb'.)

The points made in the last two paragraphs hold even if Asset has explicitly undertaken to be loyal to Blue's leaders, for example by way of an oath. One can no more validly pledge loyalty to political actors who conduct an unjust policy than one can validly pledge to serve a Mafia boss who commits similar wrongdoings—even if one derives considerable benefit from belonging to either the Mafia or one's political community.[23]

Crucially, however, it does not follow from the claim that Asset does not wrong Blue by committing informational treason that he is morally permitted to do so all-things-considered. Before reaching the conclusion that he is, we must bear in mind the following considerations. First, Asset might have countervailing special obligations to third parties. Whether his act of treason is proportionate to the wrongs he seeks to thwart depends on the weight he may or ought to assign to their interests. Suppose that if Asset is unmasked as a traitor, his relatives will receive a ten-year sentence in a hard-labour camp, which they are unlikely to survive. Granted, Green is under a duty of care to protect both Asset and his dependents, for example by spiriting them out of Blue's territory at the first opportunity. Nevertheless, we can imagine cases in which a very high likelihood of discovery and collective punishment together with a very low likelihood of being afforded this kind of protection would combine to render Asset's act of treason, all-things-considered, impermissible.[24]

The second consideration pertains to what Green will or is likely to do with Asset's intelligence. Suppose that the intelligence is useless. Or suppose that it is useful but that Green will use it to wrongful ends, or not at all. For example, its services fail to realize how important it is. Or they do not trust Asset not to be a double agent—just as the Soviet authorities apparently never fully trusted Philby.[25] Or they lack the requisite analytic resources. Suppose further that Asset has very strong reasons to believe that such is the case. By disclosing secrets to Green, Asset might be aptly described as engaging in an overall harmless and honourable act of rebellion against Blue. At the same time, he might be more likely to expose third parties to pointless risks of harms. The difficulty is that he may not be in a position to form a grounded judgement as to the effectiveness and risks of his act of treason, precisely and in part because he is *ex hypothesi* an outsider in relation to Green. Treason is an act of treachery towards one's side, but it is also an act of faith in the other side.

---

[23] For the view that lying by means of promissory speech or in breach of an oath is morally wrong, even if it is done for the sake of saving innocent lives or, more generally, thwarting wrongful ends, see Grotius, *The Rights of War and Peace*, Bks III, ch. I, XVI, XVIII, and XIX.

[24] Green's duty of care to Asset to protect him from being unmasked is itself subject to moral constraints. Thus, Green's intelligence services are morally justified in dangling fake, non-existing traitors in front of Blue's counter-intelligence services, to divert their attention from Asset. But they may not lead Blue's services to yet another no longer useful traitor if the latter would be executed by Blue as a result.

[25] Andrew and Mitrokhin, *The Mitrokhin Archive*, 156–60.

As I averred in s. 1.4.2, one is fully justified in depriving some agent of that to which she has a presumptive right only if one has evidence that she is violating some other agent's fundamental rights or is wrongfully failing to protect that agent from rights violations, if one has formed a belief to that effect on the basis of that evidence, and if she is in fact acting in this way. By implication, Asset is fully justified in passing on information to Green's authorities only if the facts warrant doing so, and if he has formed the belief, anchored in the relevant evidence, that such are the facts. Contrastingly, if Asset lacks the relevant evidence, he is not fully justified in so acting—even if (for example) Green would make morally justified use of the information he would provide. Thus, while Gordievsky did have pretty good evidence that the British authorities would make morally justified use of the information he was able to provide them (based on Britain's relatively democratic traditions, commitment to the rule of law, etc.), Philby had no such evidence (on the contrary) that the Soviet authorities would do the same. Therein lies a morally crucial difference between their respective acts of treason.

Let me now address two important concerns one may have about my arguments thus far, drawn respectively from the works of David Estlund and the works of Youngjae Lee. I should say at the outset that Estlund and Lee might accept my central arguments: my discussion is not *ad hominem*. However, it is worth rehearsing those concerns, as they naturally arise from their works.

In his influential defence of a duty to obey unjust orders, Estlund argues that 'when authoritative commands arise out of an epistemic procedure of a certain kind there can be a duty to obey commands to carry out even some unjust policies or punishments.'[26] The procedures Estlund has in mind are democratic procedures, which issue in political justifications acceptable to all reasonable points of view. Those justifications ground authoritative commands. Estlund does not dispute that an agent who obeys an unjust order is guilty of wrongdoing. His point is that fair institutions are always vulnerable to making honest mistakes, and that under the aforementioned conditions, an agent is under a duty to do wrong and, by implication, is not at liberty to disobey.

In the context of informational treason, the argument applies to the officials of democratic states, who by dint of their institutional role are deemed to be under a special obligation not to divulge official secrets without authorization, and who (if Estlund is right) are not morally permitted so to act even if they have overwhelmingly strong reasons to believe that their silence protects serious rights violations. By contrast, the officials of non-democratic states are in principle at liberty to disobey unjust orders. Gordiesvky's treason does not fall foul of Estlund's argument. Moreover, the argument does not apply to officials who have been sacked, are retired or have resigned and thus are no longer part of a chain of

---

[26] D. Estlund, 'On Following Orders in an Unjust War,' *Journal of Political Philosophy* 15 (2007): 213–34, at 221.

authoritative command. For example, even if the Russian regime was meeting Estlund's procedural requirements in the 2000s (which is doubtful), the argument does not apply to Alexander Litvinenko, who worked as an FSB officer for a number of years, escaped to and settled in the UK, and allegedly informed on the Russian state for the benefit of MI6 before being murdered in 2006 by (it is widely alleged) Russian operatives. Nor does Estlund's argument apply to ordinary citizens or to the employees of critically important firms and corporations, for the same reason.[27]

Even once properly circumscribed, there are compelling reasons not to deploy Estlund's argument against informational treason. Granted, fair and democratic procedures through which authoritative commands are issued have a kind of legitimacy which the decision-making procedures of a criminal gang lack—even a gang with all the institutional accoutrements of a state. Nevertheless, even in a democratic country such as the United States, where Congress must authorize the resort to war, those constraints can all too easily be skirted. Moreover, it is worth noting that in neither France, India nor the UK (all fairly robust democracies, all in the top ten military powers) is the authorization of the legislature a necessary condition for going to war.[28] If anything, the point is stronger still when foreign policy short of war is at issue. Decisions to go to war are at least subject to some form of scrutiny, if not by the legislature, at least at the court of public opinion. Decisions to impose economic sanctions, enter into treaty negotiations, authorize arms sales, and order incremental troop deployments—far less so. Moreover, both the conduct of war and the pursuit of ends short of war are rich grounds for corruption and cover-ups, even in democratic regimes. The procedures by which those decisions are made are even less likely to meet Estlund's procedural requirements than decisions to go to war, and it is therefore much harder to object to informational treason in such cases. Admittedly, the lower down the intelligence cycle officials are, the less subjectively justified they are in committing treason, since the less confident they ought to be that they—rather than their superiors— are reaching the correct judgement. It remains true, however, that in the world as we know it, indeed even in the best or least bad parts of that world, opponents of informational treason will find little support in Estlund's argument.

A second objection to the claim that Asset is (under some circumstances) permitted to commit informational treason is drawn from Youngjae Lee's usurpation argument against treason. On Lee's view, the state cannot fulfil the valuable

---

[27] Litvinenko started his career as a KGB officer, and stayed on in the service's new incarnation as FSB after the break-up of the Soviet Union. His murder aroused worldwide condemnation. For a thorough account, see L. Harding, *A Very Expensive Poison* (Faber and Faber, 2017).

[28] In France, the government may deploy armed forces without the consent of the National Assembly and the Senate for up to four months. (Constitution Francaise, art. 35.) In India, the President may take the country to war as part of his/her emergency powers (Constitution of India, Part XVIII). In the UK, it is a convention, not a law, that the government should seek the consent of Parliament before declaring war.

functions which its members ask of it unless it is physically secure. It cannot enjoy physical security unless it, and it alone, has the power to make use of the required resources in general and to control the resort to violence in particular. Citizens who pass on state secrets to foreign actors or who disclose them to all and sundry usurp powers which are the state's alone and engage in 'foreign relations vigilantism'.[29] Although Lee focuses on treasonous disclosure, his arguments apply *a fortiori* to treasonous deceptive counter-intelligence.

Unlike Estlund's, Lee's argument applies to ordinary citizens as well as public officials, and to citizens and officials of non-democratic states as well as to those of democratic states. However, it stands or fails with arguments in favour of civil disobedience in general. There are good reasons for thinking that, at least in some cases, of which thwarting the rights violations which state officials commit in our name is one, disobedience—including active disobedience—is morally permissible. To the extent that active disobedience consists in appropriating resources or committing violent acts over which state officials normally have decisional powers and, thereby, consists in usurping those powers, the charge of usurpation alone does not undermine the permissibility of informational treason.

To this point, Lee, whose concern is with the moral foundations of the criminal law of treason, might respond that, even if treason as a form of civil disobedience is morally permissible, it still ought to be a criminal offence. For all I know, he might well be right. But my focus is on the morality of treason, not the morality of the criminal law thereof. Pending further objections to the contrary, thus, the case for informational treason stands.[30]

6.4 Mandatory Treason

I have argued that individuals are sometimes morally permitted to disclose secrets about their own political community to another political community, as a means to help the latter thwart the former's violations of fundamental rights—thereby committing treason. As I now argue, they are sometimes under a moral duty to do so.

Consider:

Passive Traitor Asset is a high-ranking officer in Blue's weapons development programme. He knows that if he absents himself from his desk on a specific day and at a specific time and leaves his computer logged on to his department's

---

[29] Lee, 'Punishing Disloyalty?', 341.

[30] For a recent and sustained argument in favour of civil disobedience, see K. Brownlee, *Conscience and Conviction—The Case for Civil Disobedience* (Oxford University Press, 2012). The claim that an act of civil disobedience can be deemed both morally permissible and justifiably subject to criminal sanctions is a staple of the relevant literature.

network, Officer Green and her team will manage to download secret information about the programme remotely.

Active Traitor Asset is a high-ranking officer in Blue's weapons development programme, and is in a position to download secret information and pass it on to Officer Green.

Doubly Active Traitor Asset is a high-ranking officer in Blue's weapons development programme and is in a position to pass on deliberately misleading information about Green's own operations to Blue's services, thereby deceiving the latter.

In s. 1.4.1, I posited that individuals owe to distant strangers a duty of protection from unwarranted harm. At the very least, this involves a duty to let them access what they need: if I stand between you and the resource without which you and others will die and which *ex hypothesi* you are morally justified in obtaining, I am under a duty to step aside to let you get it. That, in effect, is what Asset is asked to do in *Passive Traitor*. Furthermore, the duty of protection also can and often does involve actively helping people get what they need and are justified in obtaining: if you cannot get the life-saving resource to which you have a claim without my help, I am under a duty to give it to you. That, in effect, is what Asset is asked to do in *Active Traitor*. Finally, as we saw in s. 5.4, a duty to protect can and does include a duty to deceive: if you cannot get the life-saving resource to which you have a claim without my help, and if my lying to my superiors about (e.g.) your attempt to get it will maximize your chances of surviving, I am under a duty to help you get it and to lie to my superior. That, in effect, is what Asset is asked to do in *Doubly Active Traitor*. (Note that the duty to commit informational treason encompasses both a duty to pass on the needed intelligence to those who are under a wrongful threat of grievous harm, and a duty to pass on the needed intelligence to those victims' 'rescuers'.)

It might be thought that Asset's duty to commit treason is grounded in the fact that he occupies a position which gives him access to the relevant intelligence and thus puts him in a position to help Green. And, relatedly, it might also be thought that Asset is under a particularly stringent duty so to act if he chose to occupy such a position.[31]

It is true that individuals who freely take a particular course of action at time t_1 are sometimes under a duty to φ at time t_2, even though they would merely have been permitted (and not obliged) to φ had they taken a different course of action. For example, I am not under a duty to go to the beach. But if I go to the beach and notice a child at a serious risk of drowning, I am under a duty to try and rescue

---

[31] I am grateful for the suggestion to Kimberley Brownlee (who phrased it as tentatively as I have done here.)

her. Had I stayed at home and heard that there was a child in trouble at the beach, I would not have been under a duty to (e.g.) drive to the beach like a lunatic at serious risk to my own safety in order to get to the child.

However, individuals can be under a duty to help another person even if they have not chosen to put themselves in a position where they can help. Even if I am frogmarched to the beach at gunpoint, I am still under a duty to help the child. Furthermore, it is not always the case that agents are under a more stringent duty to help if they have willingly put themselves in a position to do so, than if they have not. Suppose that I am frogmarched to North Beach at gunpoint whereas you go to South Beach of your own accord. We are both faced with a child at risk of drowning. Other things being equal, the fact that I was coerced into going to the beach does not entail that my duty to the North Beach child to rescue her is less stringent than your duty to the South Beach child to rescue her.

If I am right, *anyone* who finds herself in possession of secret intelligence the disclosure of which would stymie violations of fundamental rights is under a duty to pass on that intelligence, thereby committing treason if she stands in a treason-qualifying relationship with the parties whose secret it is.

That said, the duty to commit treason is, like any duty, a *pro tanto* duty. The claim that treason can in principle be the means by which agents fulfil a general duty of assistance thus needs qualifying in the light of two considerations which, unfortunately, pull in opposite directions. On the one hand, there is a limit to the sacrifices we can reasonably expect putative Good Samaritans to incur for the sake of others. Treason is likely to be extremely costly to traitors—both physically and psychologically.[32] There might come a point where the magnitude of the costs a traitor would incur together with the likelihood that he would be found out and have to incur those costs exonerate him from a duty to betray. Where to set the threshold for unacceptable costs is impossibly hard to establish, in the same way as it is impossibly hard to reach fine-grained judgements as to how much by way of taxes a well-off individual may be expected to pay for the sake of the needy. I surmise, though, that a high risk of being executed, tortured, or sentenced to a lengthy prison term does constitute too high a cost.

On the other hand, the stronger individuals' degree of causal and moral respon-sibility for rights violations, the more grievous their wrongdoing should they fail to help, and the greater the costs they can be expected to shoulder when helping (including, in this context, the cost of being found out.) If I wilfully and unjustifiably put your life at risk, and if you can save yourself by killing me, I am

---

[32] In an article on secrecy, Daniel Ellsberg, the Pentagon Papers' whistleblower, makes the inter-esting point that officials who have made a promise to keep secrets as part of their job incur serious psychological costs if they break that promise. Keeping secrets becomes part of their identity, and disclosing those secrets is seen as a denial of who they are. See D. Ellsberg, 'Whistleblowing and National Secrecy,' *Social Research: An International Quarterly* 77 (2010): 773–804.

under a duty not to kill you in my own defence. By that token, if I can rescue you from my own lethal threat by divesting myself of a good without which I would die (for example, a protective vest), I am under a duty to do so.[33] But now suppose that Asset shares responsibility for the rights violations which Green is seeking to thwart, such that he is under a more stringent duty to commit informational treason than he would otherwise be, but not sufficiently responsible to be reasonably expected to incur the costs of lifelong imprisonment, let alone death, if he is unmasked. At the same time, it is quite likely that he will be exposed to those costs, at Blue's hands, precisely by dint of his high-ranking position. Asset's causal and moral responsibility for Blue's unjust policy renders his duty to commit treason *both* more and less stringent than if it would be if he were a menial official or an ordinary citizen. Of course, this will not always be the case. Asset might be high-ranking enough to enjoy high-level protection, thanks to which he might be able to get away with a moderately harsh punishment, particularly if his act of treason is or can be dressed up as relatively minor. We need to know the details of each case to ascertain whether a traitor is merely doing his duty or is acting in a supererogatory manner.

It might be objected that, were we to conclude that Asset is merely doing his duty, we would be both unduly harsh on him (in so far as he would be described as merely having done his duty and no more), and unduly critical of those similarly situated agents who, unlike him, remained loyal to their regime. Not so: to say that someone is under a duty to φ is compatible not only with the familiar claim that φ-ing is sufficiently costly that he does not deserve blame for not φ but also with the less familiar claim that he is deserving of praise for φ-ing, precisely for that reason.

---

[33] This claim might seem to be in tension with two separate claims. First, I said a few paragraphs ago that choosing to put oneself in a position where one can help does not (other things being equal) make a difference to the stringency of one's duty to help. But (I say here) if an agent has chosen to occupy a position which entails the commission of rights violations, and if being in that position *also* enables him to help victims, then he is under a stronger obligation to help than if he had not chosen to occupy this particular position. Reply: it is not the fact that the agent has chosen to put himself in a position where he can help which makes a difference to the stringency of his duty; rather, it is the fact that he has chosen to occupy a *rights-violating* position.

Second, and by that token, it might seem that the claim that officials who are responsible for rights violations are under a duty to incur greater costs, in committing treason, than non-responsible agents, is in tension with the claim (in s. 6.2.2) that officials are under a stronger duty *not* to commit treason than ordinary citizens. For now, compared to ordinary citizens, it seems that an agent's official position supports both the claim that he is under a more stringent duty to commit treason (in mitigation of his contribution, *qua* official, to rights violations), and the claim that he is under a more stringent duty *not* to commit it (on the grounds that he has explicitly undertaken to serve the relevant institutions). Reply: the latter claim applies other things being equal, and is compatible with the view that he is under a more stringent duty to betray when things are not equal. For example, an official who is partly responsible for rights violations is under a duty to act treasonably, whereas an ordinary citizen is not; or, if they are both under a duty to commit treason, he is under a more stringent duty to do so.

6.5 Treason and Unjust Ends

To recapitulate, treason is sometimes justified as a means to thwart a regime that is pursuing an unjust foreign policy. But now recall that, as we saw in s. 3.2, a regime which conducts such a policy is under a second-best obligation to ascertain whether its decision to continue with the policy is morally mistaken, and to use the information so obtained as a basis for changing course. Relevantly situated members of Green are under a moral obligation to betray Green as a means to help Blue's regime do precisely that. This might seem deeply counter-intuitive. Yet consider the following counterfactual example. In the months leading up to the bombings of Hiroshima and Nagasaki, the US administration repeatedly warned Japan's cabinet that Japan would face total destruction unless they surrendered unconditionally. But they did not tell the Japanese that they were developing an atomic bomb and were intending to use it to shock them into submission. Suppose that, had the Japanese authorities known about the bomb and its destructive power, they would have surrendered. Suppose further that a well-placed member of the US high command had known that, and had been in a position to feed information to the Japanese intelligence services about the Manhattan Project. I am inclined to think that he would have been justified in so doing, indeed obliged to do so, on two grounds. First, dropping atomic bombs on civilian populations is egregiously wrong, and the American administration therefore lacked a right not to be thwarted in this particular purpose. Second, if it had been the case that Japan would have surrendered upon being given the information, it would have been morally wrong on the part of the American administration itself not to issue the relevant warning. At that point, continuing with the war would *ex hypothesi* have been unnecessary, and the administration would not have had a right not to be thwarted in this way.[34]

The case is easy, because it involves thwarting some of the worst war crimes imaginable, namely, a imminent and systematic breach of the principle of non-combatant immunity via the use of weapons of mass destruction. In principle, however, there is no reason to exonerate members of Green of a duty to betray in cases involving lesser or fewer rights violations, subject to the aforementioned considerations of costs and to judgements as to the likelihood that the beneficiary of the treasonous act will use the information to rightful ends. Note, however, that the point holds only if Green's response to Blue's refusal to rescind its unjust policy is not morally justified. Return to the hypothetical case of the US and Japan in the closing stages of WWII. Suppose that the United States do not have nuclear

---

[34] For a sketch of the diplomatic steps leading up to the bombings, see G. L. Weinberg, *A World at Arms: A Global History of World War II* (Cambridge University Press, 1994), 882–93. The case is a counterfactual example, since it took two bombs for the Japanese cabinet finally to concede defeat. The mere disclosure of information before the first bombing would not have been enough to induce surrender.

capabilities, but are determined to carry on with the war by conventional means until they secure victory over Japan. Suppose also that the Japanese cabinet has formed the mistaken view that the American administration will seek peace terms within a certain time frame and before Japan is pushed to defeat, and knows that beyond that time frame, Japan will lose. Were they to know of the American administration's resolve, they would sue for peace now. Suppose further that the United States are morally entitled to continue with the war on the grounds that only thanks to a full military victory would they be able to secure just peace terms. They are not morally obliged to give the Japanese cabinet the classified information the latter would need in order to form the resolve to stop fighting. Consequently, individual members of Green ought not to disclose that information. Were they to do so, their act would be unjustifiably treasonous.

I have used a war case for illustrative purposes. *Mutatis mutandis*, everything I have said so far applies to non-war cases. Generally put, the stronger the likelihood that Green's leadership would get Blue's leadership to rescind its unjust foreign policy by disclosing hitherto secret information and that Green in turn would obtain what it is entitled to obtain, the stronger the case for a duty to commit treason were Green's leadership unwarrantedly to withhold the information.

6.6 Treason, Alliances, and Shared Goals

In s. 3.5, I argued that allies are sometimes justified in spying on one another. Suppose that Green and Blue are such allies and that Asset, who 'belongs' to Blue, offers to pass on political secrets to Green. At first sight, it might seem that he is not committing treason. On Philby's self-serving construal of his work as a double agent during WWII, given that Britain and the USSR were allies, he was simply working towards their shared goals. On my conception of treason, however, an act counts as treasonous just if the agent stands in the appropriate relationship with those whose secrets he is passing and acts in defiance of their directive not to disclose. On that definition, Philby was committing treason between 1941 and 1945. The fact that the UK and the USSR did share the goal of defeating Nazism is irrelevant. In any event, Philby's argument, if it works at all, applies only to those cases in which the information pertains to those shared goals. Yet, while Britain and the USSR did share the goal of defeating Nazi Germany, their post-war ends were certainly not compatible. There is evidence that Philby did try and frustrate the former for the sake of the latter.[35]

Suppose, then, that Green is *pro tanto* justified in seeking to obtain information which its ally Blue wishes to keep secret. The justification for treason which I

---

[35] On Philby's work during WWII, see P. Knightley, *The Master Spy: The Story of Kim Philby* (Knopf, 1989), especially ch. 8.

offered in ss. 6.3 and 6.4 applies to allies. For a start, the alliance might be one of pure expediency, where each party knows that the other will breach the agreement at the first opportunity. The 1939 pact of non-aggression between Germany and the USSR aptly illustrates the point. Richard Sorge, a German citizen who joined the Communist Party and volunteered to work as an undercover spy for Moscow following WWI, was justified in disclosing to Moscow what he knew of Germany's invasion plans in 1941.[36]

Moreover, an alliance might be robust at t_1 and yet disintegrate at t_5. As I noted in 3.5, what matters is not the fact of the alliance itself but whether Green is epistemically licensed in inferring from the evidence at its disposal that Blue might be planning to commit serious rights violations. If it is, then it is justified in trying to ascertain whether its belief is true by acquiring Blue's secrets. The fact that Asset's betrayal occurs in the context of a geopolitical alliance between Green and Blue does not in itself count against it.

This is not to deny that this fact makes a difference. As we saw in s. 6.3, the lower down the intelligence cycle Asset is, the less evidence Asset has to make the relevant judgement. The existence of an alliance between Green and Blue compounds the problem. For the closer the relationship between Blue and Green, the fewer and weaker the reasons Asset has to believe that Blue might in the future pose a credible and wrongful threat to Green's interests and the higher the evidentiary threshold which he must meet for his betrayal to be justified. However, the fact that the threshold is very high does not preclude the possibility that it can be met and that, when it is met, treason is (*pro tanto*) justified.

So far, I have assumed that Green and Blue stand on a footing of equality, that is to say, are both independent political communities. Now suppose that Blue belongs to a supra-national organization, and that this supranational organization (call it Supra) has a military force to which member states contribute both financially and by seconding military staff. Suppose further that Supra is conducting a large-scale military exercise (EXERCISE), so as to test its preparedness for a multi-front war with a non-member. Asset is a member of Blue's intelligence services and in the course of his work comes across sensitive information pertaining to Blue's side of EXERCISE, which he decides to disclose to Supra; or, he has been seconded to work for Supra and in the course of his work comes across sensitive information about Supra's side of EXERCISE, which he decides to disclose to Blue.

I have not encountered such cases in the contemporary empirical literature. Perhaps there have been some, which have remained secret. Even if there has not been a single such case, it is likely that, sooner or later, there will be one. The issue is not purely academic: it invites us to reflect anew on the ethics of overlapping and conflicting political and institutional loyalties.

---

[36] Sorge is widely regarded as one of the most successful spies of the twentieth century. See, e.g., Carlton, *Treason*, 177–83; Hastings, *The Secret War*, 110–14.

Let us suppose for the sake of argument that the sensitive information which falls into Asset's hands pertains to violations of fundamental rights, and that the disclosure of the information would enable its beneficiary to take the requisite protective steps—subject to countervailing considerations as described in s. 6.3. Let us suppose, in other words, that diclosure is *pro tanto* justified. The question is whether Asset would act *treasonously* (albeit justifiably) were he so to act.

In s. 6.2, I argued that the traitor is someone who enjoys *bona fide* social membership in a political community and who thus derives considerable benefits from that community, or who acts in defiance of explicit undertakings or mutually understood expectations that she will not violate the trust placed in her by fellow community members and/or harm their interests *qua* fellow members. To ascertain whether Asset would act treasonously, we need to distinguish between two cases. In the first case, Supra is *not* a kind of interstate organization in which individuals enjoy social membership. NATO is a textbook case of such an organization. To be sure, in so far as Blue is subject to NATO's directives *in relation to EXERCISE*, Asset's primary (presumptive) professional obligation is understood to be to NATO and not to Blue. Moroever, it is also plausible that Asset benefits from Blue's membership in NATO. However, whatever benefits he so derives are not granted to him directly by NATO. For this reason, even if he discloses sensitive information to Blue about EXERCISE without being authorized by NATO, it is not apt (on the social membership thesis) to describe him as a traitor to NATO. By implication, and precisely because he is a social member of Blue, if he discloses information about the latter, in relation to EXERCISE, to NATO, without being authorized to do so, he is acting treasonously.

In the second case, Supra *is* a kind of interstate organization in which individuals enjoy social membership. The European Union is a textbook example. Its individual members enjoy two kinds of citizenship, and thus typically two kinds of social membership: citizenship in one of the member states on the one hand, and EU citizenship on the other hand. While the latter is derivative of the former (in that one cannot be a EU citizen unless one is a German, Romanian, French, Irish, etc., citizen), it confers via EU law and its incorporation into domestic legislation a range of rights to its holders.[37] Suppose, then, that Blue belongs to the EU. Asset is a citizen—or social member—of Blue and (thereby) a citizen—or social member—of the EU. As it happens, the EU has a number of functional battle groups. So, suppose that Asset is seconded by Blue to work with the European Defence Agency, and in that capacity is tasked by the latter to work on EXERCISE. The question, you recall, is not whether he would act unjustifiably by passing on secret information about Blue to the EU and *vice versa* (I assume that he would

---

[37] For an accessible and recent account of what EU Citizenship is, see J. Shaw, 'EU Citizenship: Still a Fundamental Status?', in R. Bauböck (ed.), *Debating European Citizenship* (Springer International Publishing, 2019), 1–17.

be justified). Rather, the question is whether he would act *treasonously*, given that he benefits from membership in both. On my context-sensitive account of treason, whether he does depends on parties' mutual understandings of what their individual members are expected to do when facing dilemmas of that sort. It is not implausible to suppose that, in so far as Blue is subject to the EDA's directives and operational principles *in relation to EXERCISE*, Asset's primary (presumptive) obligation is understood to be to the EDA and not to Blue. If he discloses sensitive information to Blue about EXERCISE without being authorized by the EDA and in awareness that such authorization would not be forthcoming if asked for, he acts treasonously *vis-à-vis* the EU. By implication, and precisely because his presumptive obligation is understood (or, at any rate, should be so understood by his own goverment) to be to the EDA as far as joint exercises are concerned, if he discloses sensitive information about Blue (in relation to EXERCISE) *to the EDA* without being authorized to do so by Blue, he does not act treasonously vis-à-vis Blue.

6.7 Treason and Personal Betrayal

Traitors usually betray their friends, relatives, and colleagues. There is an important difference between (for example) Oleg Gordievsky and Hans Ferdinand Mayer. Mayer was a German scientist who, through his work for Siemens, had in-depth knowledge of Germany's military use of electronics. In November 1939, he approached the British Embassy in Oslo and gave them all the information at his disposal—never to be seen again. Contrastingly, Gordievsky committed multiple acts of deceptive betrayal against his colleagues over a number of years, as well as against his wife and daughters who (for understandable reasons) were not aware of his activities. The closing pages of his autobiography make painfully clear the toll which his decade-long collaboration with the British authorities and subsequent defection exacted on his relationship with his family.[38]

The question is whether personal deceptive betrayal makes unjustified treason morally worse, and whether it tips the balance against an otherwise justified act of treason. Unlike E. M. Forster, who famously hoped that he would have the courage to betray his country rather than his friend, the traitor betrays his friend *in order* the better to betray his country.[39]

Sometimes, traitors deliberately cultivate those relationships as a means to further their treasonous ends; sometimes, they are content to allow those rela-

---

[38] Gordievsky, *Next Stop Execution*. Mayer's information (known as the Oslo Report) was relayed to MI6, which did not take it seriously—though it turned out to be mostly accurate. See Hastings, *The Secret War*, 43–4; Keegan, *Intelligence in War*, 299–300.

[39] E. M. Forster, *Two Cheers for Democracy* (Penguin Books, 1951), 76.

tionships to develop in full awareness of the fact that they are living a lie. It might be thought that agents who in the course of their treasonous activities lie to their friends, relatives and colleagues *from the very beginning* about their true political allegiances and commitments, are not aptly described as betraying the relevant relationship, since there was no such relationship to begin with. But while in some cases the relationships that develop from those unpromising beginnings are purely and wholly sham, in other cases they are not: they evolve in a complex mix of deception, trust, affection, and shared worries about family and mutual friends. Accordingly, my account in what follows applies only to cases in which there is a relationship to betray.[40]

Consider unjustified treason first, of which I take Philby's to be a paradigmatic example. By all accounts, his colleagues in the intelligence community, and in particular MI6's Nicholas Elliot, who had been a friend as well as a colleague, felt deeply, woundedly betrayed by his decades-long treachery. What Philby did was markedly worse than if he had been a one-off traitor. That said, as Judith Shklar notes, victims of personal betrayal sometimes collude in their predicament, for example when they wilfully and unjustifiably ignore warning signs and are seduced by the traitor's charm or their shared social background. In her words, 'a careless, class-bound intelligence service, such as the British, is no different' from someone who is wilfully blind to his partner's infidelity.[41] She penned those words in the mid-1980s; had she done so in the late 1990s, she might have made a relevantly similar point about the CIA's shockingly incompetent failure to unmask Aldrich Ames. But we need to be careful here. The point is not that the traitor's colleagues can be blamed for their predicament just if they had the means to protect themselves from it. Rather, when the colleagues' unwillingness to stop the traitor stems from a morally objectionable form of loyalty, or morphs into negligence so reckless as to endanger innocent lives, those victims' case for occupying the moral high ground is somewhat shaky.

The traitor's betrayal of his intimates also makes unjustified treason worse, all things considered. In friendship and good familial relationships, the willingness to be truthful about the most important parts of our life and our character at the risk of making ourselves vulnerable to the other party's judgement, the trust that we have in others' such willingness and the awareness that they too so trust us are constitutive of the relationships. In professional relationships, by contrast, truthfulness and trust are valuable instrumentally, as conditions for colleagues

---

[40] I am grateful to Ashwini Vasanthakumar and Massimo Renzo for pressing me on this point. The complexities I try to capture in this paragraph are magnificently explored in the ten seasons of the series *The Americans* (even though the main characters, Philip and Elizabeth, are Soviet illegals and not American traitors.)

[41] J. Shklar, *Ordinary Vices* (Harvard University Press, 1984), 142. Elliot extracted a confession from Philby, a decade or so after Philby had left MI6. For a gripping account of the encounter between the two men, see McIntyre, *A Spy Among Friends*, chs. 17–18.

to achieve their joint ends. This is why, other things being equal, betraying one's intimates is worse than deceiving one's colleagues. True, the traitor's betrayal of his colleagues pertains to their joint professional enterprise and his own commitment to it (they think that he is a MI6 officer committed to fighting the Soviets alongside them, whereas he is anything but that.) By contrast, the traitor's betrayal of his close friends, spouse, or children need not pertain to what the latter believe is a joint enterprise of defeating the enemy.[42] Nevertheless, in deceiving them about his ideological commitments (or lack thereof), his professional activities, his hopes and fears about what the future holds, indeed his character, he destroys the very fabric of those relationships. Moreover, in some cases at least, he exposes them to the risk of suffering considerable hardship should his treachery be uncovered, yet without their being aware of it and thus without giving them a chance to exit the relationship if they can.

Suppose now that the traitor's act of treason *qua* treason is morally justified, in the sense that he does not wrong his fellow citizens. To the extent that his colleagues take part in the wrongful joint enterprise which he seeks to thwart by passing on information to Green, he does not wrong them by abusing their trust and using his standing with them as a means to procure the information. To quote from Gordievksy himself, in response to the charge of betrayal: 'the most criminal element of the criminal state was the KGB. It was a gang of bandits. To betray bandits was very good for the soul.'[43]

Matters are not so simple with the traitor's intimates. In fact, they are so complex that I can do no more than gesture at some of the dimensions of the traitor's dilemma—for it is a dilemma. As we saw in s. 6.3, whether his act of treason is, all things considered, permitted depends in part on the costs accruing to third parties, notably his family and friends, should he be found out. My concern here is with ways in which treason and its concomitant acts of personal betrayal undermine the traitor's personal relationships. The difficulty is this. The more unjust the regime (or the greater the traitor's involvment in its wrongdoings) and the more justified (*pro tanto*) his act of treason thus is, the more imperative it is for the traitor to protect his intimates by concealing from them what he does and the morally worse

---

[42] Sometimes it may do so. Suppose that Victor Laszlo, the leader of the resistance in the movie *Casablanca*, is in fact a Nazi undercover agent. His wife Ilsa might feel betrayed not just as his wife but as his wife-cum-companion in resistance activities, particularly in the light of her willingness to sacrifice her relationship with the love of her life to him and their joint work. In this paragraph, I draw on Dannenberg's account of lying and friendship. See J. Dannenberg, 'Lying Among Friends', in E. Michaelson and A. Stokke (eds.), *Lying—Language, Knowledge, Ethics and Politics* (Oxford University Press, 2018).

[43] Quoted in Corera, *MI6*, 28. Unsurprisingly, some of Gordievky's former colleagues take an extremely dim view of what he did—even if they themselves became dillusioned with the Soviet regime. A particularly apt example is that of Oleg Kalugin, once a rising star in the KGB. Kalugin, who looked after Kim Philby for a few years in Moscow, and who has become a staunch critic of both the Soviet regime and its successor, bluntly admits to despising Gordievsky and respecting Philby—out of patriotic love for his country. See Kalugin, *Spymaster*, 90 and ch. 5.

vis-à-vis them his betrayal is. If his intimates are themselves staunch supporters of Blue's *ex hypothesi* wrongful policies, the traitor's personal betrayal of their relationship might not be of great moral concern. But if they are not staunch supporters—if they are bystanders or even strong critics of the regime and its unjust policies—then some of the considerations which make an act of unjustified treason worse may well render an act of otherwise justified treason, if not all-things-considered impermissible, at least in some important sense wrongful at the same time. The closer the relationship, the more morally problematic the traitor's act is –particularly if the relationship is not one from which the traitor or his intimates can properly exit (think about his children, or his parents.)

These hand-waving points are unsatisfying as far as philosophical arguments go. Then again, they are a testimony to the complexity and richness of our personal relationships.

6.8 Conclusion

I have argued that passing on political secrets to the officials of a political community other than one's own (be it foe or friend) can be justified in principle, indeed mandatory, as a means to thwart grievous wrongdoings. The fact that, in so doing, one commits an act of treason against one's fellow community members does not render one's actions impermissible.

Suppose, then, that Asset would act justifiably in betraying Blue for Green's sake. By what means, if any, may Green get Asset so to act, bearing in mind that treason and betrayal are both inherently dangerous and, in the end, morally and psychologically costly? To this question, I now turn.

7

Recruitment

7.1 Introduction

Spies, double agents, and traitors are recruited and handled through a wide range of methods: money, flattery, ideological persuasion, downright threats—singly or in combination. In this chapter, I address some of the ethical difficulties which those practices raise. Section 7.2 describes several modes of recruitment. Sections 7.3–7.6 review in greater detail four problematic features of asset recruitment: the fact that assets often act for the wrong motives and that their handlers are complicitous in their moral dereliction; the fact that recruitment is often manipulative; the fact that it is often exploitative; the fact that it is often coercive.

Some preliminary points. First, by assets, I mean the following: members of Green who are recruited by its intelligence services to carry out *ad hoc* work; agents who belong to Blue and are recruited to work for Green (in other words, commit treason); and agents who are recruited by Blue or Green but who belong to neither, such as some of the key agents of the Double Cross system I mentioned in s. 5.1. I do not consider the recruitment of children (which, I take for granted, is morally impermissible). Nor do I consider the recruitment of individuals who wish to gain full-time employment with their country's intelligence services.

Second, I focus on the recruitment of human sources as distinct from the extraction of information by interrogational means. While there are similarities between the techniques used in both contexts, I am interested in the ways in which intelligence officers initiate and build long-term relationships with their agents in the field. The points I make below in favour of or against manipulative, exploitative, and coercive recruitment and handling apply, *mutatis mutandis*, to interrogation.[1]

---

[1] The ethics of interrogation in the context of intelligence activities overlaps with the ethics of interrogation in the context of policing. For a useful broad-brush account, see M. Skerker, 'Interrogation Ethics in the Context of Intelligence Collection,' in Goldman (ed.), *Ethics of Spying*. Here is a very troubling case of one-off exploitative interaction. In humanitarian interventions and post-conflict peacekeeping operations, the provision of essential services to local populations can sometimes assist with intelligence-gathering. One can imagine a deeply wounded guerrilla fighter who is led to believe that he will receive medical treatment from Green's on-field medics only if he passes on sensitive information about the guerrilla group to Green's military intelligence. (See M. L. Gross, *Military Medical Ethics and Just War* (Oxford University Press, 2021), ch. 10.) On children: what I take for granted is not, it seems, a foregone conclusion, even in a liberal democracy which professes to respect children's rights such as the UK. (See D. Gayle and I. Cobain, 'UK intelligence and police using child spies in covert operations,' *The Guardian* (19/07/2018).)

Third, my concern is with the recruitment and running over time of assets (henceforth, Asset) by their case officers (henceforth, Officer). Even though an agent may at first volunteer to work for Green, and gratis to boot, he is likely to require skilful handling by his case officer if he is to continue to provide reliable information. The officer's ability to persuade, flatter, cajole, and reassure him and his own receptiveness to it will (it is hoped) elicit and foster his trust and prove crucial to the success of the operation. Trust can go both ways, however: if both Officer and Asset work in the field, she too is vulnerable to him, since he could decide to betray her, or become careless and get her killed.

Fourth, unless otherwise specified, I assume throughout the chapter that Green is not recruiting Asset to further unjust ends—put differently, that it has a justification for enlisting him or her as a human source. My main concern is with the morality of the means by which it does so.

Finally, the recruitment of assets may expose bystanders to increased risks of harms. If, for example, it is known or rumoured that, in general, journalists are likely to be spies, journalists will incur a greater risk of being arrested for espionage by the authorities of the country in which they work even if there is no evidence to suggest that they are anything but what they say they are. Considerations such as these fall within the realm of proportionality.[2]

7.2 Some Cases

People become spies and traitors for a number of often overlapping reasons: material rewards, moral and political commitments, resentment and anger at their regime, a need for recognition, vulnerability to coercion. Here are some cases, which are fictionalized and stylized accounts of what we can glean from the empirical literature. For the sake of expository clarity, notably with the use of pronouns and possessive adjectives, I assume that Officer is a woman, and Asset a man. This does not reflect any view about women's supposedly innate manipulativeness and men's supposed susceptibility to being manipulated by women. Had I made the converse expository choice, I would no doubt have been vulnerable to the converse charge.[3]

---

[2] Thanks to Andy Owen for this point, which the case of Nazanin Zaghari-Ratcliffe illustrates.

[3] I will not overload this section with bibliographical references to specific historical examples. The cases I list below are referenced one way or another in the works I have cited so far in this book, in addition to those I will mention in this chapter. For an interesting take on agent recruitment and handling by a CIA officer, see R. Burkett, 'Rethinking an Old Approach: An Alternative Framework for Agent Recruitment: From Mice to RASCLS,' *Studies in Intelligence* 57 (2013): 7–17.

Committed Asset Asset is a high-ranking officer within Blue's military RD programme. He is resolutely opposed to Blue's foreign policy on moral grounds, even though he contributes to it by dint of his position. He approaches Green's intelligence services via Officer, who is the head of station in Green's embassy, and offers to provide Green with regular access to highly classified information.

Greedy Asset Asset is a middle-management employee within Weapons Inc., which is headquartered in, and sells military weapons and technology to, Blue. He lives beyond his means and approaches Green's intelligence services via Officer, head of station in Green's embassy. He offers to provide Green with regular access to highly sensitive operational information about Weapons Inc., in exchange for regular payments. By the time Blue's counter-intelligence services arrest him, he has received hundreds of thousands of dollars from Green.

Refugee Camp Asset is one of millions of displaced individuals who have been caught up in a war between Green and Blue and who now find themselves in a refugee camp. The camp has been infiltrated by militias loyal to Blue's regime. Asset is in a position to spy on those militias and to pass on information to Green's services. Officer tells Asset that if he cooperates with Green's services for a few months, they will get him and his family out and give all of them a chance at a new life in Green. Asset is under no illusion as to the fate that awaits him if he takes up the offer and if the militia men find out.

Journalist Asset works as a foreign correspondent for a highly respected newspaper in Green. Upon his promotion to the post of Correspondent in Blue, Officer approaches him on behalf of Green's intelligence services. Over the course of several weeks, she convinces him to give her some of the sensitive information he will uncover while in Blue instead of making it public via his newspaper. He is reluctant at first, but is flattered by her sincerely felt praise of his writings and her often-affirmed conviction that he is supremely skilled at drawing sources out.

Bitter Asset Asset is a mid-ranking civil servant in Blue's department of defence, who believes that his superiors have never truly recognized his talent and have inexcusably failed to promote him. Officer subtly plays on his bitterness and convinces him to pass on sensitive information about the resilience of Blue's military infrastructure to cyber-attacks—while at the same time stressing that he is doing the right thing.

False Flag Same as in *Bitter Agent*, except that Officer realizes that Asset is as hostile to Green as he is to his own regime. Officer pretends to work for Yellow, knowing that this is the only way to get Asset to betray Blue.

Conference Green's services regularly send agents to attend academic conferences to which Blue's top scientists are invited. At several of those events and under the guise of scientific exchanges, Officer poses as a scientist and gradually and subtly grooms her target—a high-level scientist from Blue with contacts in Blue's defence community, to defect for Green.

Immunity Asset—a top cyber-security specialist and a citizen of Green—has infiltrated Green's cyber-security programme on Blue's behalf. Green's counter-intelligence services unmask him and tell him that unless he is willing to work as a double agent against Blue, they will have him stand trial for treason, which carries a heavy prison sentence. Asset knows that if he agrees to the proposal and if Blue's services find out, they will in all likelihood kill him.

Sexual Blackmail Asset is a high-ranking official within Blue. Green's services blackmail him into passing on sensitive information about Green's military strategy by threatening to send compromising photos of his affair with another man. Homosexuality is a criminal offence in Blue.

Those methods raise a number of concerns. First, we might think that even if one is justified in betraying or deceiving one's community, one ought to do so only *for the right motives*—namely out of a commitment to thwarting's unjust foreign policy ends.

Second, we might worry that by playing on Asset's desire for flattery, need to convince himself that his motives are pure, resentment at his stalled career, or thirst for intellectual validation, Officer *manipulates* Asset.

Third, we might worry that by offering potential recruits what they badly need or want (money, a chance to escape from a murderous regime, or the opportunity to save their family) as the price to pay for providing sensitive information, intelligence agencies take advantage of those agents' predicament and lock them in an *exploitative* relationship.

Finally, we might worry that some of those techniques are *coercive*: a threat of lifelong imprisonment or of being exposed as a homosexual in a deeply homophobic society would leave Asset little choice but to comply with Officer's demands.

Those concerns often overlap. Coercion, exploitation, and manipulation often work because they play on their target's motivational temperament. A proposal might be coercively exploitative or, for that matter, exploitatively or coercively manipulative. I address those various concerns separately for the sake of analytical clarity, but my discussions thereof build upon one another.[4]

---

[4] For an illuminating discussion of the differences and connections between exploitation, manipulation, and coercion, see A. W. Wood, 'Coercion, Manipulation and Exploitation,' in C. Coons and M. Weber (eds.), *Manipulation—Theory and Practice* (Oxford University Press, 2014).

7.3 The Problem of Motives

Individuals who commit acts of espionage do so for a range of motives. Some act from moral and political commitments; others do so in the hope of gaining material rewards or out of resentment at their lack of career prospects, a sense of their own importance, hatred for their community, appetite for secrecy, or a combination of those. In the empirical literature, it is not uncommon to encounter a moral hierarchy of motives, with moral and political commitments ranked as the most noble, and financial incentives as the most ignoble. In the years following the unmasking of Kim Philby, a few of his critics would point out that he at least believed in the justice of the cause for which he had betrayed his colleagues, friends, and fellow citizens, and had served that cause since his student days, unfalteringly and without getting paid for it. So construed, his betrayal was not as wrong as if he had done it for money. Contrastingly, Aldrich Ames and Robert Hanssen, who also betrayed their country to the USSR but (it appears) purely out of financial motives, are ordinarily thought to have done something far worse—indeed, they elicit greater contempt, by and large, than Philby.

Those observations yield three questions: (1) whether an agent's motives make a difference to the permissibility, mandatoriness, or moral worth of his decision to spy for a foreign power; if so, (2) which motives, in the context at hand, count as right and wrong motives; and (3) whether it is wrong to entice an agent to spy when he would do so out of the wrong motives.

7.3.1 Motives and the Moral Status of Recruitment

On some views, the claim that an agent is acting permissibly or mandatorily is distinct from the claim that his act has moral worth—that it is morally good and that it invites praise. Consider a standard consequentialist position, to the effect that an act is permissible only if it brings about the best outcomes or conforms with a rule which is more likely to bring the best outcomes. Or consider the claim that an act is permissible only by dint of its features. Or, finally, consider the claim that although we cannot know for sure what an agent's motives are, we nevertheless make intuitively compelling judgements to the effect that her act is permissible. On all of those views, facts about the agent such as her motives or the fact that the act was particularly demanding on her do not help us determine whether the agent is doing the right thing. But they do help us determine whether her act—though permissible—also has moral worth. To illustrate, suppose that my son is in danger and that I can rescue him at no cost to myself. I do so not out of love for and commitment to him, but because I do not want to incur the reputational costs of appearing not to care for him. I do the right thing (saving his life). But (all three views can consistently say), my act of rescue lacks moral worth, or at any rate is certainly less worthy, other things being equal, than if I had saved him solely out of parental love.[5]

Contrastingly, on other views, the features of the act and the agent's motives both matter to the moral status of the act as permissible or not. On those views, to describe my act as 'saving my son' and to ask whether my act, so stated, is permissible, is to under-describe it. Rather, it must be described as 'saving my son out of concern for my reputation'. Once it is so described, we see that I act wrongly by rescuing him as I do. He has an especially strong claim against me, his mother, that when deciding what to do for him, I should do so in the light of the right considerations—in this instance, the mere fact that his survival depends on me who, as his mother, am under a stringent duty of care to him. When I act purely out of reputational concern, I wrong him.

7.3.2 Right and Wrong Motives

Settling the question of the relevance of motives to the (im)permissibility and moral worth of actions would take us far beyond the scope of this chapter. Instead, let us take it as a given that they are relevant to both in the following way: motives can add to the moral worth of a permissible act or render an impermissible act less unworthy than it would otherwise be; conversely, they can diminish the worth of a permissible act or render an impermissible act even more unworthy than it otherwise would be. In the remainder of this section, I argue that even if motives matter in that sense, moral and political commitments do not always redeem (even partially) a *prima facie* impermissible decision to spy for a foreign power or, on the contrary, confer moral worth on a *prima facie* permissible decision to do so—to a greater degree either way than other motives and notably financial motives.[6]

Suppose that Asset works for Green in the service of a grievously unjust policy, out of commitment to the cause. Whether his commitment has redemptive power surely depends on its content, and on the nature of the regime to whom Asset betrays his side. As I have noted, an important reason for attending to motives when evaluating actions is the thought that acting from a particular motive can itself be wrongful to the person *vis-à-vis* whom one acts. Some moral and political commitments clearly are of that kind—either because the ends which

---

[5] For discussions of what makes an act morally worthy, see, e.g., N. Arpaly, 'Moral Worth,' *The Journal of Philosophy* 99 (2002): 223–45; J. Markovits, 'Acting for the Right Reasons,' *Philosophical Review* 119 (2010): 201–42.

[6] A point of terminology: by '*prima facie* permissible/*prima facie* impermissible', I wish to capture the point that the act seems permissible/impermissible pending consideration of the agent's motives. Readers who believe that motives are irrelevant to (im)permissibility can instead frame my argument as follows: 'ideological commitments do not always increase the moral worth of an otherwise imper-missible decision to spy for a foreign power or on the contrary lessen the moral worth of an otherwise permissible decision to do so—to a greater degree either way than other motives and notably financial motives.'

they encapsulate are themselves wrongful, or because the means which they recommend to achieve those ends are wrongful, or both. Consider the ends first. In general, individuals who betrayed Britain or the United States to the Soviet Union tend to elicit greater sympathy, on account of their commitments, than those who betrayed them to Nazi Germany. For whatever else one might say about communism (a point to which I shall return presently), at least it advocates a society in which all human beings relate to one another as equals and in a spirit of goodwill and fraternity, rather than one built on racial supremacy. Considerations of that kind, I suspect, help explain some of the partially excusing comments one sometimes encounters in the literature on individuals who betrayed 'the West' for the sake of the USSR.

But now consider the means which, according to this ideology, one may or must employ in order to bring about the desired ends. To the extent that it is part and parcel of an ideology to take a stand on the legitimacy of those means, a moral and political commitment, *qua* such commitment, can redeem wrongful espionage only if those means are not grievously wrongful. When a commitment to grievously wrongful means in part motivates Asset to enable those wrongdoings, it simply cannot have redemptive power, even if the ends themselves are just and even if Asset is committed to those ends.

Furthermore, even if an ideology is silent on the issues of means, commitment to it is not in itself redeeming if it underpins support for a grossly abusive regime— irrespective of the fact that the ends which that regime pursues are construed as just ends. In that light, the fact that Philby was unquestionably committed to communism from his student days onwards and never wavered does very little if anything at all to redeem his many acts of betrayal—particularly when one bears in mind that he was at his most active at the height of Stalinism, including at a time when the true nature of that regime was not really in doubt.

Some readers who share my scepticism about the redemptive power of moral and political commitments per se might nevertheless insist that ideologically moti-vated impermissible espionage is not as wrong as espionage which is motivated by financial greed, other things being equal. I am not convinced. In fact, and this is particularly apposite in the case of agents, such as Philby, who sought to help the USSR out of commitment to communism, the willingness to support such grievous wrongdoings as those carried out by Stalin and (albeit to a lesser extent) his successors seems to make a mockery of communism itself. There is a particular kind of moral blindness in those who profess to believe in equality and fraternity and yet are willing to help a totalitarian regime in its pursuit of those values.

Consider now cases in which Asset agrees to spy for Green in the service of just ends and just means thereto, and suppose for now that he is merely justified, and not under a duty, to help Green by procuring information on Blue. We need to distinguish between three kinds of cases: Asset acts purely out of commitment to those ends; he acts out of commitment to those ends and is also motivated by the expectation of material gain, professional resentment, the thrill of secrecy and revenge; he acts purely out of non-ideological commitments. Some readers might be tempted to hold that Asset's act is morally better in the first case than in the second and *a fortiori* than in the third. I am sympathetic to that point. Asset's motives in the third case taint his decision to spy for Green, for he fails to give proper weight to those individuals whose fate partly depends on him and thereby wrongs them, as I wrong my son by rescuing him purely for reputational reasons, even if rescuing him is the right thing to do. I also take it, uncontroversially I hope, that Asset's decision to spy on Blue for Green is at its most worthy when Asset acts purely out of (morally justified) moral and political commitment to Green's ends.

Cases in which Asset acts from both moral and political commitments and what we may loosely call 'non-material motives' are more complex. Only some, but not all, such motives taint his actions. Imagine a North Korean defence official whose relatives were sent to a hard labour camp for daring to criticize the regime and did not survive. His career has been stymied by his superiors, who do not quite trust him. He decides to pass on sensitive information about the regime's nuclear policy to the United States, out of a commitment to thwart what he recognizes as the regime's grievously unjust foreign policy and bitterness at his lack of advancement. Even if there is a sense in which he is morally permitted to pass on secrets to the United States, all-things-considered what he does is less worthy than if he had acted purely out of moral and political commitment.

Compare and contrast with another North Korean official, who also opposes the regime on moral and political grounds but who is not so much bitter as enraged, and who wants to see the leadership humiliated by yet another diplomatic setback. Angry Asset's rage is amply justified, and the fact that it motivates him so to act does not render his act of betrayal unworthy.

Consider now cases in which Asset is motivated by the right kind of ideological commitments and the prospect of material gains. Recall *Greedy Asset*—in which Asset is a high-ranking intelligence agent within Blue who lives beyond his means. Suppose that he is also politically committed to fight against Blue. The financial rewards he is asking for provide some compensation for the risks which he is incurring; for example, Green would help him escape from Blue and settle in Green if he is about to be unmasked. Unless he demands more than what he can legitimately expect to be given, the fact that he will not commit to spy for Green unless he receives material compensation is no reason to regard his act as impermissible or unworthy, though it might be a reason to regard it as less worthy than if he were willing to betray Blue for free.

So far, I have assumed that Asset is not under a duty to work for Green. Let us relax that assumption. For example, his contribution to Blue's grievously wrongful policy is such that he is under a duty to approach Green's intelligence embassy. In this particular scenario, it is even more tempting to hold that his act of betrayal is morally the worse for being motivated by the lure of material gains. This would be too quick, however. For, generally, the claim that an agent is under a duty to do x does not imply that he must be willing to do it for free. As we saw in s. 6.4, the duty to betray is subject to a no-undue sacrifice proviso. The point I made in the last paragraph with respect to compensation holds here too.

7.3.3 Benefiting from Wrong Motives

Suppose that Asset is entirely motivated by money and that he has in his possession information about Blue's cyber-warfare programme. He tells Green's intelligence services that Blue is both ready and willing to deploy cyber-weapons against Green, and that he knows where and when Blue will act. The risks that Asset will be unmasked as a traitor to Blue are very low, yet he demands an extravagantly high sum of money and full relocation package in exchange for passing on that information. He is, in fact, extracting a bribe.

I take it that Assset's decision to spy for Green at the very least lacks moral worth. The question is whether Green is justified in paying him. I suspect that some readers would answer in the negative, on grounds similar to those often adduced against the recruitment of mercenaries. Mercenaries, it is often said, act wrongly precisely in so far as they are motivated to fight by the lure of money rather than commitment to the cause; to employ mercenaries is to collude in their wrongdoing and therefore wrongful. The same considerations might be thought to apply to Greedy Asset.

However, this objection to mercenarism does not undermine the claim that recruiting mercenaries is (sometimes) morally justified all-things-considered; by parity of reasoning, it does not undermine the claim that recruiting greedy agents is sometimes morally justified all-things-considered.[7] Suppose that Green has very good reasons to believe that Asset's intelligence is accurate; it has no other means of getting that intelligence; and obtaining the intelligence now will help in minimize casualties. Green would be justified in giving him the money, thereby enabling him to commit a morally unworthy act. If bribing Asset is the only or best way to access the information in time, to insist that Green should desist on the grounds that it ought not to collude in Asset's moral corruption is to confer undue weight on the preservation of both Asset's and Green's moral integrity relative to the protection of the fundamental rights of Blue's victims. More strongly still, Green is sometimes under a duty to the latter to pay Asset off, for example if it shares some responsibility for those victims' predicament or if it has supported Blue's regime in the past by supplying it with military expertise and equipment.

Moral and political commitments do not always positively affect the moral status of a decision to work for the enemy; conversely, the prospect of material

---

[7] See C. Fabre, 'In Defence of Mercenarism', *British Journal of Political Science* 40 (2010): 539–59.

and non-material gains does not always negatively colour the moral status of that decision either. In the remainder of this chapter, I explore ways in which intelligence agencies play on those motives to get assets to procure sensitive information about enemies and allies, often at great risk to their own lives and limbs.

7.4 The Problem of Manipulation

7.4.1 Manipulation

I am in some financial difficulties. I try to convince you to bail me out. I explain why I am short of funds, mention my previous successes as a businesswoman as evidence that I have the skills and experience to turn things around if you would only give me a loan, and present you with a detailed repayment schedule. I fail to persuade you: you tell me that you are not prepared to help, even though we both know that you have just inherited your wealthy parents' estate. I tearfully remind you of the several occasions in our long friendship when I provided you with emotional support. Those tears are not fake: I feel great affection for you— and even greater pity for myself. I exaggerate the extent of my difficulties and of the harm that would befall not just me but also my son, who is your godson, should I go bankrupt. I play down my own share of responsibility for my predicament. I know that you feel guilty about your inheritance and do not want to come across as stingy, so I point out that, were you to refuse to help me, your reputation in our circle of hard-up friends would suffer. I am not getting through to you at first, so I come back into the breach, day after day, until you finally give in. It would be unfair to say that I have coerced you into helping me, yet inaccurate to say that I have persuaded you to do so. Rather, I have manipulated you.

Manipulation lies somewhere between rational persuasion and coercion.[8] All three are means by which an agent, O, gets another agent, A, to do as O wishes. Sometimes, manipulation shades into coercion, as when O makes it prohibitively

---

[8] There is a small but growing literature on manipulation. See, e.g., C. Coons and M. Weber (eds.), *Manipulation—Theory and Practice* (Oxford University Press, 2014). Other important discussions can be found in the following: T. Scanlon, *What We Owe to Each Other* (Harvard University Press, 1998), pp. 298–99 and 317–22; A. Barnhill, 'What Is Manipulation?', in C. Coons and M. Webber (eds.), *Manipulation—Theory and Practice* (Oxford University Press, 2014); M. Baron, 'Manipulativeness', *Proceedings and Addresses of the American Philosophical Association* 77 (2003): 37–54; J. Blumenthal-Barby, 'A Framework for Assessing the Moral Status of "Manipulation"', in C. Coons and M. Webber (eds.), *Manipulation—Theory and Practice* (Oxford University Press, 2014); S. Buss, 'Valuing Autonomy and Respecting Persons: Manipulation, Seduction, and the Basis of Moral Constraints', *Ethics* 115 (2005): 195–235; M. Gorin, 'Do Manipulators Always Threaten Rationality?', *American Philosophical Quarterly* 51 (2014): 51–61; M. Gorin, 'Towards a Theory of Interpersonal Manipulation', in C. Coons and M. Webber (eds.), *Manipulation—Theory and Practice* (Oxford University Press, 2014); P. Greenspan, 'The Problem with Manipulation', *American Philosophical Quarterly* 40 (2003): 155–64; C. Mills, 'Politics and Manipulation', *Social Theory and Practice* 21 (1995): 97–112; R. Noggle, 'Manipulative Actions: A Conceptual and Moral Analysis', *American Philosophical Quarterly* 33 (1996): 43–55; J. Rudinow, 'Manipulation', *Ethics* 88 (1978): 338–47. My remarks in this section draw on that literature.

difficult, in fact sometimes impossible, for A not to do her bidding.[9] Manipulation can also shade into rational persuasion, as when O plays on A's emotions in order to get him to begin to see the force of a rational argument, at which point she properly engages with him as a deliberative agent. Nevertheless, one can manipulate without either coercing or engaging with the other person.

My opening *vignette* is a particularly thick example of a manipulative interaction. In order to get you to give me a loan, I use many of the techniques which manipulators standardly deploy. I deceive you by exaggerating the seriousness of my predicament and downplaying my part in it. I put pressure on you to accede to my request by refusing to let it go and depleting your stock of patience and willpower. I play on your feelings of friendship for me, guilt at your inherited wealth, and concern for your reputation. I seek to further my own ends without giving much thought to yours. Taken singly, none of those techniques is a necessary element of a manipulative act or relationship. One can manipulate merely by playing on the other party's emotions and desires (as I would do if I described my situation accurately yet guilt-tripped you into helping.) Perhaps surprisingly, one can also manipulate merely by engaging with the other party's deliberative faculties, and without playing on their psychological dispositions, so long as one gets her to do *x* by giving her reasons which she endorses but which, unbeknownst to her, do not track one's own—thanks to which she does do *x*.[10] Finally, although many accounts of manipulation stipulate that the manipulator seeks to further her own ends at her victim's expense, people often manipulate either paternalistically or as a means to further the ends of a third party.

Manipulation, in other words, is a 'plural' phenomenon. That being said, there are two conditions which must be met if O is to be aptly described as manipulating A. First, O must succeed at getting A to do what O wants, and A, moreover, must do it at least in part in response to O. Second, O must intend that A should do what she wants, and hope that A will so act in response to what O does or says to get her to do that: one cannot manipulate someone inadvertently.

So much, then, for the phenomenology of manipulation. What about its moral status? In common with deception and, as we shall see later on, with exploitation and coercion, manipulation is presumptively wrongful. When a manipulative act is deceptive, coercive, or, for that matter, exploitative, it is presumptively wrongful for the reasons which render deception, coercion, and exploitation presumptively wrongful. As we saw earlier, however, not all instances of manipulation are deceptive, coercive, or exploitative, and the presumptive wrongfulness of manipulation is thus not always parasitic on the presumptive wrongfulness of the latter three. On some views, in those non-parasitic, 'pure' cases, manipulation is presumptively wrongful because it impairs the autonomy, or freedom, of the manipulated person.

---

[9] For a good discussion, see Wood, 'Coercion, Manipulation and Exploitation'.
[10] Gorin, 'Do Manipulators Always Threaten Rationality?'

On other views, manipulation is presumptively wrongful because it manifests a lack of respect for its victim as a rational agent who is and thus ought to be treated as responsive to reasons, or whose deliberative capacities ought not to be undermined or subverted. On other views still, it is presumptively wrongful because it manifests an abuse of trust on the part of the manipulator—notably in close relationships, where the parties make themselves vulnerable to one another's capacity for using their intimate knowledge of one another to serve their own ends. These are all plausible arguments for the claim that manipulation is presumptively wrongful. In just the same way as manipulation is a plural phenomenon, it is presumptively wrongful for a number, and not just one, of those reasons. But it is also presumptively wrongful just if it manifests either one of those features.

Furthermore, manipulation is only presumptively wrongful: as we shall see, it can in principle be morally justified. Indeed, under certain conditions, there is a duty to manipulate. These are not avenues of enquiry which the philosophical literature has explored, so focused has it been on ascertaining why manipulation is wrongful.[11] Yet, in the particular context of recruiting and handling assets for espionage and counter-intelligence purposes, such exploration pays dividends. I first consider cases in which Officer manipulates Asset into supplying sensitive information without deceiving him, before turning to deceptive manipulation. Although I focus on the moral status of Officer's manipulative acts, it is important to remember that she and her colleagues are themselves vulnerable to being manipulated by their putative assets. Not only do they run the risk of being approached by a source who in fact is a plant from Blue's intelligence services: they also run the risk of being offered information which, they are told, will help them pursue their ends, whereas in fact, they are treated as 'useful idiots' in internecine local conflicts. This does not render their own manipulative acts justified, but it does serve as a reminder that relationships between handling officers and assets is not as asymmetrical, to the benefit of the former and the detriment of the latter, as one might think.

7.4.2 Non-deceptive Manipulation

In s. 7.2, I described the case of a greedy individual who approaches Green with an offer: he will spy on Blue for Green's intelligence services in exchange for considerable amounts of money. Suppose instead that Officer approaches Asset first and quickly realises that Asset is both greedy and resentful of the fact that he cannot afford a life of luxury on his current salary as a mid-level executive in Weapons Inc. Officer plays on Asset's feelings. When Asset mentions that he

---

[11] For a notable exception, see Baron, 'Manipulativeness.'

cannot afford a brand-new car and grumbles that he too should be able to go on luxury holidays twice a year instead of once every other year, she heartily agrees. After a few conversations of that kind, Officer makes her move: spy for us, and we will reward you handsomely. Compare *Greedy Asset* with *Journalist* and *Bitter Agent*. In all three cases, Officer takes advantage of Asset's temperament to get him to spy on Blue. In *Greedy Asset*, she plays on his greed and envy. In *Journalist*, she plays on his need to be flattered. In *Bitter Asset*, she plays on his feelings of bitterness. Is she acting wrongly, bearing in mind that she is justified in seeking to recruit him in the first instance?

Let us first stipulate that Asset is under a duty to spy for Green but would not do so if Officer were to appeal to rational persuasion alone. Under those circumstances, Officer's resort to manipulation is not morally reprehensible. In fact, to the extent that Green is under a duty to procure the information which Asset is in a position to pass on, manipulation is morally mandatory.

Cases in which Asset is merely permitted, and not obliged, to work for Green are more complex. They raise the interesting and neglected question of the connection (or lack thereof) between the moral nature of a motive on the one hand, and the moral status of the act of manipulation. As we saw in s. 7.3.2, some motives are more worthy, or less unworthy, than others. Consider *Journalist*. Admittedly, it would be better if Officer were able to persuade Asset to work for Green solely by means of rational persuasion. At the same time, most of us need to feel, at least some of the time, that we are valued and highly thought of. If Asset's need for flattery remains healthy, such that he is not so needy as to fully succumb to it, for example by taking on greater risks when working for Green than he would otherwise take were he to deliberate properly, her manipulative handling does not seem problematic.

Cases such as *Greedy Asset* and *Bitter Asset* should give us pause. Both greed and bitterness are destructive. Although this gives Officer a reason not to prey on, feed, and exacerbate those traits of character, the point is not dispositive, in the light of the ends Officer and Green pursue. Moreover, taking advantage of Asset's greed or bitterness is better, other things being equal, than playing on his understandable desire to be valued (or, at least, not as bad). To put the point generally, it seems worse, other things being equal, to take advantage of someone's morally neutral and, *a fortiori*, good dispositions than of some of his bad dispositions. Suppose that Asset, the journalist, not only needs to feel valued but also has an unusually strong sense of duty—to the point of being willing to incur serious risks to life and limb for the sake of doing what he believes is right. The correct way to react to his disposition is to respect and admire him for those traits, not to seize on their instrumental value. By contrast, a greedy or bitter Asset has no complaint—or at any rate, less of a complaint if those character traits are used against him.[12]

---

[12] I used to think otherwise. I am grateful to Massimo Renzo and Kieran Oberman for showing me that I was wrong.

7.4.3 Deceptive Manipulation

Other things being equal, deceptive manipulation is worse that non-deceptive manipulation. In the three cases I discussed in the previous section, Officer's manipulative tactics make it harder for Asset to refuse to work for Green than if she attempted to persuade him by rational means alone. But she does not make it as hard as she would if she were to misrepresent to him what she is getting him to do or what he might be getting in return for working for Green, and *a fortiori* if she were to lie to him outright.

As we saw in s. 5.2, deception is presumptively wrongful, on the grounds that it violates trust, constrains the agent's freedom, or treats him as a means only to one's ends. As we also saw, however, under certain conditions, deception is morally justified, indeed mandatory, as a means to acquire secret information possession of which helps thwart rights violations. In recruitment cases, deception works at one step removed: Officer is not using deception to elicit information from Asset but, rather, to induce him to get the information. If Asset is not under an independently justified duty to help Green, and if Officer can procure the information herself as easily and reliably as, and at no greater cost to herself than, Asset would if he were to do so, she owes it to Asset not to deceive him into doing it for her. If Asset *is* under a duty to help Green, the same considerations which justify the resort to deception as a means for Green's intelligence officers to acquire secret information about Blue also justify its manipulative use as a recruitment tool.

Suppose, however, that Asset is not under a duty to help Green. Either he contributes to Blue's unjust foreign policy, but the risks he would incur while working for Green are so high that he cannot legitimately be expected to incur them; or he is a mere bystander. Either way, he is merely permitted to help Green. Now, when I discussed *Infiltration₄* and *Infiltration₅* in s. 5.3.2, I argued that agents are not permitted opportunistically to deceive other parties as a means to procure the sensitive information which they need, when those parties are not under a duty to help. This seems to imply that Officer may not manipulate Asset by means of deception as a means to get him to work for Green. However, there is an important difference between those *Infiltration* cases and recruitment. In the former, those whom Green's intelligence officers opportunistically deceive are unwitting players in Green's plan to acquire information about Blue. In the latter, it is up to Asset to decide whether or not to pass on the information to Green. Granted, the more deceitful Officer is, the morally worse her recruitment tactics, because the less control Asset has over his decision to cooperate. Nevertheless, it is not implausible that, in some cases at least, the onus is on Asset to ascertain Officer's credentials and status. Recall *Conference*. Suppose that Officer does not explicitly say that she is a scientist working for Green. Asset assumes that she is: it does not occur to him that someone who is not a scientist would turn up at an academic conference. She deceives him opportunistically. At the same time, he seems rather naive in not at least considering the possibility that his late-night conversations with Officer about Blue's RD and military programmes might be a prelude to recruitment.[13]

That said, there are cases in which deceptive manipulation seems particularly problematic, such as *False Flag*. Officer knows that Asset is as hostile to Green as he is to Blue. She pretends to work for Yellow, knowing that this is the only way to get Asset to betray Blue.[14] False-flag recruitment takes different forms: Officer might lie to Asset outright, or deceive him by implicature, or fail to disabuse him. For example, suppose that she is an American intelligence agent embedded in a Canadian military unit. Asset, whose mother tongue is not English, who has never been to North America, and who has had very limited dealings with North Americans, cannot differentiate between a Canadian and an American accent. He infers, reasonably, that Officer is Canadian. Officer realizes in conversation that Asset would not contemplate working for the United States but might be persuaded to work for Canada. She does not disabuse him.

The key issue is how important it is that Asset should know whom he is working for. Asset's reasons for spying for what he thinks is Yellow but in fact is Green make a difference. Suppose that he does so out of deep-seated moral and political commitments: he wants to spy against Blue but only for Yellow (whose values as a political community he admires) and definitely not for Green (which he despises). If his commitments are not wrongful, it is wrong to deceive him about that: one's moral commitments are part of who we are, and that is particularly so in Asset's case. But it does not seem quite as wrong to deceive him if Asset's moral-ideological commitments take the form of mere opposition to Blue rather than commitment to Yellow specifically.

Suppose now that Asset is motivated mostly by the lure of financial gain, yet conditions his willingness to work on Green not being the beneficiary, or (which is slightly different) on Yellow being the beneficiary of his activities. Asset may well have very good reasons so to condition his offer. For example, Green's regime has supported Blue's regime in the past and thus put the latter in a position to commit such rights violations, of which Asset himself, or his family, has been a victim. Or Green has acquired a justified reputation for not being particularly competent at the intelligence business, or for not protecting its assets particularly well. And so on. In the light of Asset's reasons, it seems wrong of Officer to deceive him.

To recapitulate, manipulating someone into serving as a human source is sometimes morally justified, indeed mandatory. While some forms of manipu-

---

[13] See D. Golden, 'The Science of Spying—How the CIA Secretly Recruits Academics', *The Guardian* (10/10/2017).

[14] See, e.g., Omand and Phythian, *Principled Spying*, 80; Perry, *Partly Cloudy*, 141–2. Omand gives false flag a cautious endorsement as a means to recruit foreign nationals but rejects it as a means to recruit one's fellow citizens. I draw no such distinction, on the grounds (set out in s. 1.4.1) that national-cumpolitical borders are irrelevant to the conferral of fundamental rights and their correlative duties.

lation seem relatively benign, others are morally problematic and taint Officer's recruitment and running of her assets.

7.5 The Problem of Exploitation

7.5.1 Exploitation

In his interesting discussion (with David Omand) of some of the ethical issues raised by the recruitment and running of human sources, Mark Phythian claims that the relationship between a source and his handler is necessarily exploitative, as the handler uses the source as a means to her agency's ends.[15] *Pace* Phythian, however, using someone as a means is not enough to elicit the charge of exploitation. The voyeuristic photographer who takes pictures of a naked woman while she is asleep in her own home, for his sexual gratification and in the knowledge that she would not agree to this, is (wrongfully) using her as a means, but he is not exploiting her. To understand what is wrong with exploitation, we need to do more than merely invoke the prohibition on using as a means.[16]

Standardly, an agreement between two parties—say O and A—to the effect that A will do *x* in return for O doing *y* for him, is exploitative of A just if:

1. O stands to benefit from the agreement.[17]
2. O gets A to agree to her terms by seizing on a feature of A's or of his situation.
3. The outcome of the agreement, whereby O gets *x* and A gets *y*,
   (a) is harmful to A, or
   (b) results in an unequal distribution of gains between O and A such that O benefits to a greater degree than A, or
   (c) A getting *y* only if he does *x* subverts his will, even if the outcome neither is harmful nor constitutes an unequal distribution of gains, and even if A benefits overall.

An agreement can be exploitative without being wrongful to the exploited party. Imagine a culpable attacker who is locked in a ongoing shoot-out with his victim. His gun gets jammed. Unless he gets another gun, Victim will almost certainly kill him. Bystander has such a gun, and offers Attacker to sell it to him for £1M, which she knows is the sum total of Attacker's assets. Bystander clearly benefits from the

---

[15] Omand and Phythian, *Principled Spying*, 116ff.

[16] My remarks on the concept and phenomenon of exploitation in this section draw on an extensive literature. See, in particular: A. Reeve (ed.), *Modern Theories of Exploitation* (Sage, 1987); A. Wertheimer, *Exploitation* (Princeton University Press, 1996); J. Feinberg, *Harmless Wrongdoing— The Moral Limits of the Criminal Law—vol.4* (Oxford University Press, 1988), chs. 31–2.

[17] In what follows, when I say 'O', I mean not just Officer but Green, on whose behalf she acts.

transaction; she clearly takes advantage of Attacker's desperate situation; and there is a sense in which the transaction is harmful to Attacker, since were he to agree, he would survive but be destitute. I see no reason not to describe the agreement as exploitative. Yet in so far as Attacker lacks a claim that Bystander help him commit a wrongful killing, Bystander does not wrong him by doing so conditionally.

Still, it is presumptively wrong to harm another party or to take advantage of one of their features or of their situation to extract a greater benefit from them than they themselves would get. An agreement is *wrongfully* exploitative, thus, just if:

1. O benefits from the agreement;
2. O gets A to agree to her terms by seizing on a feature of A's or of his situation such that A would not agree otherwise;
3. The outcome of the agreement
   (a) is *wrongfully harmful* to A, or
   (b) results in an *unfair* distribution of gains between O and A such that O unfairly benefits to a greater degree than A, or
   (c) O *may legitimately be expected* to offer *y* to A without insisting on A doing *x*.

O wrongfully harms A or secures unfair terms from him when making A the offer in so far as she is derelict in her *prior*, independently justified duty not to harm him or not to secure unfair benefits at his expense.[18] Suppose that you stumble upon my encampment after a long trek in the desert, in desperate need of water. I have ample supplies of water and am under a duty of Good Samaritanism to you to help you quench your thirst. I offer to sell you a bottle for £1,000. If you refuse to pay, I will leave you to die. By threatening not to give you the water, I wrong you. By taking advantage of your predicament to get you to agree to divest yourself of £1,000, and thus to leave you with water but minus £1,000, when I could leave you with both £1,000 and the water which I am under a prior, independently justified duty to give to you, I wrongfully exploit you.

Mutatis mutandis, the point applies to cases in which I derive an unfair advantage from your predicament in the form of an unequal distribution of benefits. But it also applies to cases in which I do not bring about an unfair distribution of benefits between us. Suppose that I own something—*x*—which I want to get rid of and for which I have not been able to find a buyer. I know that you need *x* and can afford to buy it, though you would rather not buy it from me. I agree to sell you the water for a very modest amount, say £1, so long as you also buy *x*, which I offer at a price considerably lower than market price and one which, moreover, you

---

[18] Here I follow Thomas Christiano's account of wrongful exploitation. See T. Christiano, 'What is Wrongful Exploitation?', in D. Sobel, P. Vallentyne, and S. Wall (eds.), *Oxford Studies in Political Philosophy—vol. 1* (Oxford University Press, 2015). I defend those duties in s. 1.4.1.

can afford. The resulting distribution of gains is not unfair, nor are you harmed. Nevertheless, it seems that I wrongfully exploit you: after all, I could sell you the water for £1 unconditionally. By taking advantage of your need to buy x, though I know that you would rather not buy it from me, I wrongfully undermine your interest in deciding how and when you will procure x.[19]

7.5.2 Exploiting the Innocent

Consider the following scenarios. In *Refugee Camp*, Officer tells Asset that if he spies on Blue's militias for a few months, Green will offer him and his family asylum. In a variant of *Greedy Asset*—call it *Naive Asset*—Asset is a member of Blue, enjoys a relatively secure lifestyle in Blue, and by dint of his professional occupation has access to very sensitive information about Blue. However, he has no idea of what constitutes a fair payment for the work he agrees to carry out for Green, a fact of which Officer is well aware. By the time Asset is arrested by Blue's counter-intelligence services, he has received paltry sums of money yet has saved Green billions of dollars in research and development.

Refugee Camp and *Naive Asset* are paradigmatic cases of an exploitative agreement. In both cases, Officer's proposal improves Asset's situation relative to what it would have been absent the proposal. Howeuver, they differ in one important respect. In *Refugee Camp*, Asset's dire predicament and desperate need to get out mean that he has little choice but to accept an offer which, he also knows, is very risky. In effect, he is given a choice between two harmful options, even though Green could help him unconditionally. Green's proposal in *Refugee Camp* is a classic case of coercive exploitation. In *Naive Asset*, by contrast, Asset is not seeking to escape from such a predicament. Although he incurs a risk of severe harm if he is found out, his is a choice between two acceptable options (not working for Green and enjoying his secure lifestyle, vs earning more money in exchange for working for Green). In this case, Green's proposal is a classic case of non-coercive exploitation. A useful way to frame the difference between the two cases is by considering the baseline against which Asset's situation is to be compared. If the baseline is the counterfactual of the proposal not being made, then the two cases are not interestingly different. But there is another relevant baseline, to wit, the counterfactual of Green giving Asset resources without asking for anything in return. In *Refugee Camp*, Asset would escape his overall awful predicament; in *Naive Asset*, he would be better off still than he is above the harmfulness threshold.

Ex hypothesi, Asset is not contributing to Blue's unjust ends. On my account of wrongful exploitation, Green wrongfully exploits him if it is derelict in its prior

---

[19] I owe the point and the example to Massimo Renzo.

and independently justified duty of assistance to him. Suppose that Green is under an unconditional duty to Asset to help him secure prospects for a flourishing life. For example, Green is directly responsible for Asset's dire predicament, and (let us assume) is under an unconditional reparative duty to offer him asylum. Or suppose that Asset has already provided rafts of information to Green, as a result of which he is at a much higher risk of being exposed. In so far as Green is under an independently justified unconditional obligation to offer Asset asylum, it wrongfully takes advantage of his predicament to get him to agree to risk further severe harm merely to get what he is owed anyway. The worse his predicament is and the less able therefore he is to resist Green's demand, the worse Green's wrongdoing.

Suppose now that Green is not under a prior, independent duty to help Asset. Even so, Officer's offer can be exploitative. For example, in cases such as *Naive Asset*, Officer's offer is not harmful to Asset, but Green nevertheless derives unfair gains from Asset's complete ignorance of the value of the information he provides them. Green may not be under a duty to benefit him, but if it chooses to do so, it ought to do so in the right way.

It might be thought that cases such as *Refugee Camp*, though easy to imagine, are few and far between. Instead, it might be thought that even though Green is under a duty to offer asylum to a certain number of refugees, it is not under such a duty to any specific refugee. I agree, but this does not make a difference to the moral status of its decision to condition its offer of asylum on Asset spying on the militias at great risk to himself. Needs is a just basis for an allocative decision. Willingness to do something which one is not under such a duty to do, when the reason why that is so is that it carries high risks of serious harm, is not.

I have assumed that Green's duty is unconditional. But perhaps Green, though under a duty to help Asset, may justifiably subject its performance of its duty to certain conditions. This is not as mysterious a suggestion as it might seem. As I argue elsewhere in the context of the ethics of aid conditionality, your need for cash might place me under a duty to make it available to you, but conditional on you paying me back. My duty to help you is grounded in your need; the reason why I may justifiably impose such a condition on you is that merely giving you the cash is too much to ask of me, while loaning it to you is not.[20] By parity of reasoning, it is possible in principle for Green not to be under a duty to Asset to help without asking for anything in return, yet at the same time to be under a duty to help him, albeit conditionally so. If so, the question is that of which conditions it may or may not impose, by way of espionage activities, on those individuals, in return for its help.

[20] See C. Fabre, *Economic Statecraft*, 13–14.

The same question arises in cases in which Green is not under a duty to help *tout court*, so let me turn to those cases instead. Suppose, then, that Green is not under a duty to grant asylum to anyone, or to give more help to refugees than it is already giving. Even so, it does not follow that Green may justifiably offer Asset the incentive of asylum to spy on the militias. For it may be that, *if* Green is willing to offer asylum, it should do it unconditionally. In particular, we should worry about the degree to which Asset is truly and freely consenting to the agreement, even though the agreement benefits him overall and the distribution of gains between him and Green is not unfair. His predicament is dire precisely because he is damned in the short term yet potentially safe in the long run if he spies for Green (given the fate that will befall him if he is exposed, and the rewards he would get if he is successful), and safer in the short term yet damned in the long term if he does not (for precisely the converse reasons). Moreover, we should also worry about the degree to which the agreement overall is harmful or deepens inequalities between Green and Asset. It is harmful to Asset if, in fact, Asset would be better off not transacting but is led by the wretchedness of his predicament to minimize the risks he is running. The same worry arises when the agreement, though not harmful to Asset, nevertheless leaves him considerably worse off than Green, as in *Naive Asset*.

7.5.3 Exploiting the Guilty

So far, I have assumed that Asset is innocent of Blue's rights violations. But now suppose that he is contributing to those unjust ends. Does this make a difference to the moral status of Green's offer?

Let us first suppose that, notwithstanding Asset's contribution to Blue's unjust foreign policy ends, he is not under a duty to work for Green. For example, even if he shares responsibility for Blue's actions, the sacrifices he would have to incur exceed that which may justifiably be asked of him. Or there may be reasons to doubt that he freely chose to work for Blue, which weakens his degree of responsibility for his contribution to their rights violations and thus weakens his duty to help. (For example, Blue is akin to ISIS, and recruited Asset as a child soldier.)

Given that Asset is not under a duty to spy on Blue for Green, Green wrongfully takes advantage of his predicament, for reasons similar to those adduced in s. 7.5.2 against the exploitation of the innocent. Take the real-life case of Victor Tolkachev. Tolkachev, who was an engineer at a Soviet military research institute, contacted the CIA chief of station in Moscow in 1978 and, out of hatred for the Soviet regime, gave thousands of pages of documents relating to Soviet aviation technology to the United States. It is estimated that by the time he was arrested and executed by the Soviets in 1986 (having been betrayed by a disgruntled former CIA employee), he had provided the United States with information worth billions of dollars. The payments he received in return were paltry by comparison. There is no evidence that he would have asked for more money had he been aware of the value of his work, but there is evidence that the CIA itself was not at all keen to apprise him of it.[21] Notwithstanding his membership in the military of a grievously unjust regime, Tolkachev was not under a duty to do as much as he did for the United States (on grounds of excessive burdens as articulated in s. 6.4.) If what he received was not commensurate with the supererogatory work he did, and if the reason why that was so was that the CIA took advantage of his ignorance, then he was wrongfully exploited by the latter.

In principle, we can imagine cases in which Asset is under an unconditional duty to help Green by spying on Blue, by dint of his contribution to their unjust policy. For example, Asset is a top-ranking member of Blue's intelligence services who wishes to retire in Green and seeks to parlay his knowledge of Blue's secret-service apparatus into a bargaining advantage. Or recall *Naive Asset*, in which Asset (let us now assume) does share responsibility for Blue's unjust ends, and in which the distribution of gains between Green and Asset is vastly unequal, to the latter's detriment. To the extent that Green would benefit from the agreement, that it gets Asset to do its duty by offering him the incentive of asylum, and that the agreement is harmful to Asset (in the sense that he uncurs a non-trivial risk of serious harm by spying on his Blue), the agreement can aptly be described as exploitative. But in so far as Green is not, *ex hypothesi*, under an independently justified duty to Asset to help him by offering him asylum, it does not wrongfully exploit him by conditioning its offer to his willingness to be recruited.

Note that the key point is that Asset is contributing to Blue's unjust ends, *not* that he is responsible for the fact that he has placed himself in a situation where he is vulnerable to exploitation. But even if he is responsible for putting himself in that situation, this fact alone does not suffice to provide Green with a justification for exploiting him. To see this, return to *Refugee Camp* and suppose that Asset had the (morally acceptable) opportunity to flee to a safer zone but did not do so. It is unduly harsh, I think, to hold that someone's responsibility for their predicament exonerates third parties from a duty to rescue them from harm—however grievous the harm. If so, Green remains under a duty to provide him with some assistance and would wrongfully exploit him if it conditioned the performance of its duty to his acceptance of harmful or unfair terms. Moreover, given that it is precisely because Asset chose to stay in the camp that he is in a position to help Green, it would seem wrong of the latter to regard his responsibility for his predicament as a reason not to help him.

---

[21] See D. E. Hoffman, *The Billion Dollar Spy: A True Story of Cold War Espionage and Betrayal* (Doubleday, 2015), esp. 117.

7.6 The Problem of Coercion

7.6.1 Coercion

In s. 7.5, we examined a range of exploitative proposals, some of which, as in *Refugee Camp*, are coercive and not merely exploitative. In this section, we turn to cases in which Officer seeks to get Asset to work for Green by issuing a threat of harm. In those earlier cases, Asset is made better off by Officer's intervention in his practical deliberation while in these cases, Officer's intervention makes him worse off than he would be if he were left alone. For example, in *Immunity*, Asset is given a choice between standing trial and being sentenced to a lengthy jail term or going free and working for Green.[22]

Some agent, O, coerces another, A, into φ-*ing* just if O wants A to φ, intentionally acts in such a way as to make it prohibitively difficult or impossible for A not to φ, and succeeds in getting A to φ. Although an offer can be coercive (if it is one which A cannot refuse), typically O coerces A by threatening severe harm if he does not comply with her demands. Moreover, O can be aptly described as coercing A into φ-ing whether or not she is entitled to make it impossible or prohibitively difficult for A not to do her bidding. While coercing another person is presumptively wrongful (in so far as it impinges on their freedom), it need not be always wrong. In particular, subject to the requirements of necessity, effectiveness, and proportionality, one may justifiably coerce someone as a means to prevent him from violating another party's fundamental rights, to deter him from violating those rights, or (in cases of coercive offers) to induce him to respect those rights.

My brief account of coercion sets sufficient conditions for an act to be coercive. The only condition which I commit myself to viewing as necessary is the intentionality condition: one cannot coerce someone inadvertently. I remain agnostic for my purposes here on the following two questions: whether one can be described as coercing another person when one applies brute physical force; whether A is coerced into φ-ing only if he does φ solely in order to avoid being subjected to what O indicated would happen if he does not comply.[23]

---

[22] Here is an example which in some respects resembles *Immunity*, and which should be of particular historical interest to some readers. The philosopher Stuart Hampshire, who worked for British intelligence at the end of the Second World War, would sometimes tell the following story. A German prisoner of war whom Hampshire was interrogating agreed to answer his questions on condition of being handed over to the British authorities instead of the French Resistance. Hampshire refused to make him that promise on the grounds that he lacked the requisite authority. The prisoner decided not to cooperate, was turned over to the French and executed. (See T. Nagel, 'Types of Intuition', *London Review of Books* (03/06/2021).) I am grateful to Jan Goldman for reminding me of this case.

[23] Robert Nozick's 1969 seminal paper on coercion revived discussions of the issue in analytical philosophy. (R. Nozick, "Coercion," in S. Morgenbesser, P. Suppes, and M. White (eds.), *Philosophy, Science, and Method: Essays in Honor of Ernest Nagel* (St Martin's Press, 1969).) Subsequent important works include: A. Wertheimer, *Coercion* (Princeton University Press, 1987); M. Gorr, 'Toward a

With those points in hand, whether Officer is permitted to recruit Asset by threatening to harm him depends, first, on whether Asset is under a duty to help Green, such that Officer's threat is aptly construed as a means to enforce that duty; second, on whether the harm with which Officer threatens him is disproportionate or necessary; third, on whether coercion is effective. On that last point, professional intelligence officers often claim that, even if assets can be coerced into beginning to work as a human source, they will usually prove reliable over time only if their handlers are able to use non-coercive methods such as flattery, ideological persuasion, and empathy.[24] This seems wholly plausible. If so, it follows that it is morally impermissible to resort to the coercive techniques I describe in the following sections. However, as a matter of fact, coercion does play a part in recruitment, and it is worth investigating it independently of the effectiveness condition. In what follows, I assume for the sake of argument that the condition is met.

7.6.2 Threats of Punishment

In *Immunity*, it matters whether the punishment which Asset would suffer is just. If it is, and if Asset is under a duty to help Green, Officer's recourse to coercion is *pro tanto* justified. But if the punishment were unjust (if, for example, the sentence itself were unduly harsh relative to Asset's wrongdoing, and/or Yellow's jails are rife with physical and sexual violence), Officer may not so act.

Cases such as *Immunity* are relatively straightforward. In the remainder of the chapter, I investigate another coercive recruitment technique, to wit, blackmail.

7.6.3 Informational Blackmail

Blackmail was and probably still is one of the ways in which intelligence agencies procure information about both enemies and allies—by getting enemy agents to betray their side. I say 'was', for Western agencies claim not to resort to those means; I say 'probably still is' because in the light of what we know of the practices of a number of intelligence agencies, it would be naive to think that, even if we take Western agencies' words at face value, no other agency engages in blackmail.[25]

Theory of Coercion,' *Canadian Journal of Philosophy* 16 (1986): 383–405; M. Gunderson, 'Threats and Coercion,' *Canadian Journal of Philosophy* 9 (1979): 247–59; V. Haksar, 'Coercive Proposals—Rawls and Gandhi,' *Political Theory* 4 (1976): 65–79; C. Ryan, 'The Normative Concept of Coercion,' *Mind* 89 (1980): 481–98.

[24] See, e.g., Perry, *Partly Cloudy*, ch. 8. Recall Sun Tzu's injunction to rulers that they treat their spies generously (s. 1.2).

[25] On blackmail as a recruitment tool in the Soviet Bloc and Russia, see, e.g., Wolf and McElvoy, *Man Without a Face*; V. Cherkashin and G. Feiffer, *Spy Handler—Memoirs of a KGB Officer* (Basic Books, 2005).

Here are some common objections to blackmail in general. The blackmailer exploits the blackmailee's vulnerability; he engages in an unproductive transaction; in the case of informational blackmail, he unjustifiably violates his victim's privacy; he seeks to appropriate money which is not rightfully his; and (partly for those reasons) he treats his victim as a means only to his ends; he coerces his victim in a way that manifests morally objectionable disregard for her interests. As has often been noted, however, it seems hard to explain what is wrong with blackmail in cases in which the blackmailer is morally entitled on the one hand to disclose the information in question and on the other hand to ask for money. In such cases, the claim that blackmail is wrong appears paradoxical, since it rests on the thought that two moral rights can make a wrong. I am not primarily concerned with the paradox. Rather, I aim to show that, under certain conditions, blackmail may be used as a recruitment tool.[26]

Blackmail can take many forms, ranging from threats to disclose information to threats of harming the victim or her loved ones. The latter cases are straightforwardly coercive acts—similar to *Immunity*, and I will say no more about them. Instead, I focus on informational blackmail, to wit, a threat of harmful disclosure unless the other party complies with one's demands.[27]

Blackmail is morally impermissible if the blackmailer is under an independently justified duty to disclose the information anyway, or if the blackmailer is under a duty not to threaten disclosure (whether or not he may act on the threat).

Consider first the duty to disclose. Suppose that Blue and Yellow are at war. Green's intelligence services discover that Asset, a high-ranking member of Blue's cyber-defence unit, has been recruited by Yellow and is passing on to the latter rafts of information about Blue's strategies for defending its critical civilian infrastructure from cyber-attacks. Were Yellow to act on that information, for example by

---

[26] For important accounts of blackmail, see G. Williams, 'Blackmail,' *Criminal Law Review*, 1954, 79–92; R. Nozick, *Anarchy, State, and Utopia* (Basic Books, 1974), 84ff.; J. G. Murphy, 'Blackmail: A Preliminary Inquiry,' *The Monist* 63 (1980): 156–71; E. Mack, 'In Defense of Blackmail,' *Philosophical Studies* 41 (1982): 273–84; J. Lindgren, 'Unraveling the Paradox of Blackmail,' *Columbia Law Review* 84 (1984): 670–716; Feinberg, *Harmless Wrongdoing*, 238–76; H. Evans, 'Why Blackmail Should Be Banned,' *Philosophy* 65 (1990): 89–94; M. Gorr, 'Liberalism and the Paradox of Blackmail,' *Philosophy & Public Affairs* 21 (1992): 43–66; M. Clark, 'There Is No Paradox of Blackmail,' *Analysis* 54 (1994): 54–61; S. Smilansky, 'May We Stop Worrying about Blackmail?,' *Analysis* 55 (1995): 116–20; M. N. Berman, 'Blackmail,' in J. Deigh and D. Dolinko (eds.), *The Oxford Handbook of Philosophy of Criminal Law* (Oxford University Press, 2011); J. R. Shaw, 'The Morality of Blackmail,' *Philosophy & Public Affairs* 40 (2012): 165–96. On the permissibility of blackmail in the context of espionage, see also Bellaby, *The Ethics of Intelligence*, 137–42.

[27] A definitional point: it is common in the literature to define blackmail as a threat to do something one is otherwise permitted to do anyway (such as disclosing personal information about the blackmailee), in return for the addressee's compliance with one's demands. By contrast, a threat to do something one is not permitted to do in return for the addressee's compliance is extortion, not blackmail. This is in line with the criminal law of blackmail and extortion in a number of jurisdictions. Intuitively, however, it seems apt to use the word 'blackmail' for both kinds of cases, at least when the threat is a threat of informational disclosure. Readers who disagree with me can replace 'blackmail' with 'extortion', as nothing (justificatory) hangs on this definitional move.

disrupting Blue's water supply networks, it would violate the fundamental rights of dozens of thousands of innocent civilians within Blue. Green, who would also like to recruit Asset, threatens to reveal to Blue the fact that he is a double agent working for Yellow unless he agrees to give them secret information about Blue's military cyber-capabilities. If Green does not disclose, it secures information from Asset which would in the longer run contribute to furthering its just foreign policy ends. If it does disclose, however, it saves Blue's civilians from grievous harms at the hands of Yellow here and now. In this and relevantly similar cases, I am inclined to think that Green must disclose to Blue what Asset is up to.[28] If so, it may not blackmail him as a means to recruit him, since by blackmailing him, it offers to keep silent, in breach of its duty of disclosure to Blue, as reward for complying with its demand that he work for them.

Suppose that, contrary to what I have just said, Green is permitted both to withhold from Blue information about Asset's espionage activities, and to disclose those activities to Blue. Whether Green may blackmail Asset depends on (a) whether Asset is under an independently justified duty (and is not merely permitted) to accede to Green's request for help; (b) and, when Asset is under that duty, the nature of the threat Green is making.

Suppose that Asset is *not* under a duty to help further Green's foreign-policy ends, for example, because he would be at such high risk of severe harm were he unmasked by Blue's counter-intelligence that he could not reasonably be expected to put himself in such a situation. Even if Green is permitted to disclose information about Asset that the latter would rather be kept secret, or on the contrary to keep silent, it does not follow that it may extract from Asset services which he is not under a duty to provide as the price for its silence. To see this, suppose that Asset is guilty of tax evasion, would be tried in an open court if charged, and would incur a just sentence if convicted. Green is in a position to denounce him to Blue and is at liberty to do so, but let us also suppose that it may choose to keep the information secret. (For example, Blue's authorities have consistently failed to help Green's authorities fight financial crime, such that Green is not under a duty to help Blue this time, particularly in the light of the fact that Blue's foreign policy vis-à-vis Green is unjust.) Even though Asset lacks a claim that information about his crime not be made public, given that the risks he would run by helping Green are in excess of what he may reasonably be expected to incur, Green may not use the threat of disclosure to compel him to do so.

Suppose, next, that Asset is under a duty to work for Green. Green is morally permitted to get Asset to do his duty via the threat of disclosure, subject to considerations of proportionality and necessity. I do not find that conclusion

---

[28] The fact that Green has to choose between protecting its own members and protecting Blue's innocent civilians is irrelevant, it seems to me, to its decision: once again, respect for fundamental moral rights does not depend on national-cum-political borders.

particularly controversial. By analogy, suppose that some agent, Andrew, culpably sets fire to a building with the aim of killing his business associate who, he knows, is working late. If you believe that Andrew is under a duty to go in and rescue his associate (as I am tempted to think) then you may readily accept that blackmailing him into going in is morally permissible. The point applies, *mutatis mutandis*, to intelligence recruitment.

Consider, finally, the point about the nature of the threat Green is issuing to Asset. I noted in the last paragraph that the threat of disclosure is subject to considerations of necessity and proportionality, even when Asset is under a duty to work for Green. Suppose, first, that Green would not wrong Asset by disclosing the information. If so, Green may permissibly threaten to do so. Return to the tax evasion case. If the punishment which Asset would incur for tax evasion is just, Asset lacks a claim that the information be kept secret. If, moreover, Green has not acquired the information by wrongful means, and the harms accruing to third parties as a result of Green's disclosure are not disproportionate, Green is morally permitted to disclose Asset's wrongdoing. If so, then *a fortiori* it may threaten to do so.

So far, so good. Now, suppose that Green is under a duty not to disclose the information which Asset would much rather be kept secret. The question is whether Green's authorities may nevertheless threaten to disclose as a means to get Asset to work for them. Remember *Sexual Blackmail*, where Asset, a high-ranking officer in Blue's army, is married but has a string of homosexual encounters. When Asset refuses to spy for Green, Officer threatens to launch a smear campaign against him, centred around his sexuality: Asset's career and marriage would be over, and as homosexuality is a criminal offence in Blue, he would very likely be thrown in jail.

This is a classic example of blackmail operations as carried out by intelligence agencies from the former Soviet bloc, though other intelligence agencies have sometimes been alleged to use similar tactics. I take it as uncontroversial that Green is under a duty not to disclose Asset's homosexuality, in the light of the grievously unjust harms that would accrue to him as a result. But it does not follow that it may not threaten to do so. Whether one is permitted to issue a threat depends on whether the harms accruing from the threat itself are proportionate and necessary. Accordingly, Green is permitted to threaten Asset with the disclosure of sensitive information (even though it is not permitted actually to disclose that information), if the disclosure furthers a just end and if the threat thereof would not breach those constraints.[29]

So far I have stipulated that the information which Green threatens to disclose is information about some prior act of Asset's. Yet as soon as Asset starts working

[29] For a good discussion of the harms caused by threats of blackmail, see R. W. Bellaby, *The Ethics of Intelligence* (Routledge, 2014), 138.

for Green, Green is in possession of a vital and dangerous piece of information about Asset, namely the fact, precisely, that he is working for its services against Blue—indeed, when he is a citizen of Blue's, that he is committing treason. This inescapable feature of Asset's relationship with Green might be thought to ground the following objection. Even if Green does not explicitly blackmail Asset into *continuing* to pass on secret information about Blue by threatening to expose him to Blue's counter-intelligence services, their relationship unfolds in the shadow of ongoing, implicit blackmail. So construed, Asset's predicament is relevantly similar to a slave at the mercy of his master's goodwill. Even if blackmail is morally justified as a one-off recruitment tool, its ongoing use, albeit implicit, is not.[30]

In reply: first, as I noted above, even if under the circumstances Green is not permitted to disclose Asset's role to Blue, it might be permitted to threaten to do so. Second, it is worth remembering that although Asset is vulnerable to Green, Green is also vulnerable to Asset. Intelligence services are always worried that the individual who agrees to betray his side for them, whether under threat or not, is in fact a plant and will feed them disinformation or, worse, draw his handlers into an ambush. Even if he is not a plant, it is always open to Asset subsequently to confess to Blue's counter-intelligence services that he has been turned by Green, and to offer to be turned back against the latter. Of course, Asset runs the risk of being executed by Blue instead. Even so, it is likely that Blue, before executing him, will extract from him as much information about Green as it can—information which Green's services will unavoidably have disclosed to Asset while handling him. To reiterate, the relationship between assets and their handlers is not as asymmetrically favourable to the latter as we might think.

To recapitulate, Green is morally permitted to blackmail Asset with the disclosure of information which Asset would rather be kept secret unless Asset complies with his demands if and only if: (a) Green is not under a duty to disclose the information anyway, (b) Green is permitted to threaten disclosure, (c) Asset is under a duty to comply with the demand, and (d) the threat itself of disclosure (as a means to enforce Asset's duty) meets the standard constraints on the imposition of harm.

7.6.4 Entrapment

I have said nothing so far about the conditions under which Green acquired the damaging information thanks to which it blackmails Asset. We can imagine cases in which Green's services have placed Asset under surveillance, either by infiltrating an agent into his network (as described in s. 5.3) or by means of long-

---

[30] I am grateful to Massimo Renzo for raising this problem.

range observation (to be rehearsed in s. 8.3.) If they are lucky, they will catch Asset in the act.

Suppose now that they entrap Asset into committing an act the disclosure of which would be severely detrimental to him. Assume for the sake of argument that, pending assessment of the moral status of Green's act of entrapment, Green is morally justified in blackmailing Asset. Intuitively, it is harder to justify blackmail in entrapment cases than in cases in which Green is not part of the causal nexus leading to Asset committing that act. Harder, but, I tentatively suggest, not impossible.[31]

Philosophical discussions of entrapment tend to focus on so-called legal entrapment, whereby law enforcement agencies deliberately induce someone to commit a crime with a view to prosecuting him for it. Much of the debate pertains to the fact that in many jurisdictions, the fact that someone has been entrapped by the police is a defence against a criminal prosecution. My concern is with putative justifications for entrapment to blackmailing ends, not for punitive purposes. Consequently, many of the standard objections to legal entrapment, which advert to claims about punishment, do not apply to blackmail-entrapment.[32]

Green entraps Asset, I shall assume, when it resorts to deception as a means to induce or persuade him to commit an act the disclosure of which would be severely detrimental to him. For example, the act is a criminal offence; or the act, though not a criminal offence, is morally wrong and is regarded as such by Asset's relatives, friends, colleagues, etc.; or, though neither a criminal offence nor morally wrong, it is and would be regarded as seriously embarrassing to Asset. The question is whether Green wrongs Asset by procuring the relevant information in this particular way, such that its subsequent act of blackmail, even if it is all-things-considered, justified, is morally tainted. (I take it for granted that entrapment which causes grievous harm to third parties who are not under an independently justified duty to incur such harm is morally wrong, even if it does not wrong the target himself.)

Sexual entrapment is a classic recruitment tool. It was routinely used by (amongst others) Soviet-era intelligence services and apparently continues to be used by their successors.[33] Consider:

[31] I am grateful to Jonathan Parry for overcoming, by rational persuasion alone, my initial reluctance to discuss entrapment.

[32] Important works on entrapment include: A. Altman and S. Lee, 'Legal Entrapment,' *Philosophy & Public Affairs* 12 (1983): 51–69; G. Dworkin, 'The Serpent Beguiled Me and I Did Eat: Entrapment and the Creation of Crime,' *Law and Philosophy* 4 (1985): 17–39; D. J. Hill, S. K. McLeod, and A. Tanyi, 'The Concept of Entrapment,' *Criminal Law and Philosophy* 12 (2018): 539–54; H. L. Ho, 'State entrapment,' *Legal Studies* 31 (2011): 71–95; P. M. Hughes, 'What Is Wrong with Entrapment?,' *Southern Journal of Philosophy* 42 (2004): 45–60; H. Kim, 'Entrapment, Culpability, and Legitimacy,' *Law and Philosophy* 39 (2020): 67–91; R. L. Lippke, 'A Limited Defense of What Some Will Regard as Entrapment,' *Legal Theory* 23 (2017): 283–306.

[33] Markus Wolf, the former head of the GDR's foreign intelligence service, is open and unapologetic about this in his memoirs. (Wolf and McElvoy, *Man Without a Face*.) See also see M. Weiss, 'The Hero

Sexual Blackmail* Asset is a high-ranking official within Blue and is married to a woman with whom he has children. Green's services have placed him under surveillance and form the suspicion that he is a closet homosexual. They set up a fake identity for one of their own male agents, who entices Asset into a sexual relationship. Two weeks into that relationship, Green's services reveal to Asset his lover's real identity, produce compromising evidence, and threaten to reveal his affair to Blue's counter-intelligence services unless Asset agrees to work for them.

Whether sexual entrapment is morally justified partly turns on what counts as valid consent to sexual relations. On one possible view, the fact that Asset would not have consented to having sex with Green's agent if he had known the latter's real identity does not invalidate his consent to having sex with him. On another, far more restrictive view of valid consent, there are certain kinds of information the concealment of which invalidates consent. Something as fundamental as the fact that the male agent works for the intelligence agency of a country which is hostile to Asset's own country is a paradigmatic example of this kind of information.

On the more permissive view, Green's services are not inducing Asset to have sex to which he does not consent. Nevertheless, the permissive view is compatible with the claim that it is seriously wrong to deceive someone into having sex (though not wrong such as to invalidate consent.) It is thus open to proponents of the permissive view to condemn sexual entrapment.

On the restrictive view, by contrast, Asset does not validly consent to having sex with this particular individual. His lover can be aptly described as raping him, and Green's services as being complicitous in his rape. If the restrictive view of consent is correct, whether Green's services are justified in so entrapping Asset depends on whether it can ever be permissible to rape another person. I lack the space to adjudicate this particular debate here. Let me simply note, for the record and without ambiguity, that I endorse the restrictive view and the view that rape is never permissible. Sexual entrapment in general and for blackmailing purposes in particular is morally wrong *vis-à-vis* its target.[34]

Let us bracket those cases aside, and consider non-sexual entrapment, as in:

Who Betrayed His Country,' *The Atlantic* (26/06/2019). The 'hero' in Weiss' story is an Estonian soldier of Russian origin who fell victim to an operation of sexual entrapment at the hands of Russia's services in the mid-2000s. He passed on intelligence about Estonia's military capabilities and Estonia's allies (notably the US and the UK) to the Russian authorities for almost ten years, was caught by Estonia's Internal Security Service and is currently serving a lengthy jail sentence. Sexual deception has been a tactic of law enforcement agencies as well, for intelligence-gathering purposes rather than blackmailing purposes. For example, in the 1980s, the British police infiltrated undercover officers into animal rights and green activist movements and encouraged those officers to have sexual relationships with female activists—only for the officers abruptly to disappear, often wrecking the lives of those women and of the children whom they had fathered. For a recent summary of the 'Spy Cops' scandal, see P. Lewis and R. Evans, 'Secrets and Lies: Untangling the UK Spy Cops Scandal,' *The Guardian* (28/10/2020).

[34] By implication, sexual deception as a means not to recruit but merely to gather information is morally wrong as well.

Greedy Asset* Asset is a middle-management employee within Weapons Inc., which is headquartered in Blue and which sells military weapons and technology to the latter. Green's services know from routine surveillance that he lives beyond his means. They plant Officer into Weapons Inc. with the task of luring Asset into committing tax fraud. Once Asset has transferred funds to an offshore bank account, Officer discloses her real identity to Asset and threatens to denounce him to Blue's authorities.

The fact that Asset (let us suppose) would not have consented to embezzling larger funds had he known of Officer's true identity does not account for what, on some views, is morally troubling about this case. In a recent article, Jeffrey Howard mounts one of the best philosophical arguments to date against entrapment.[35] Howard correctly argues that we must disentangle the moral status of an act of entrapment from the moral status of its (usually) punitive ends. Even if punishment in a given case is morally justified, Howard argues, it is morally wrong to induce another agent to commit a wrongdoing. By extension (Howard would readily agree), even if blackmail is morally justified, it is morally wrong to induce its target into committing a wrongdoing so as to hold sway over him. Here is why. To respect another person as a moral agent is to respect his moral powers, of which there are two. One such power is the ability to frame, revise, and pursue a conception of the good. The other is the ability to reach judgements about right and wrong and to act on the basis of those judgements. To respect the latter is, first, to recognize that it exists; second, to expect of that agent that he will so act and to support him in his successful exercise of that ability. There are limits, of course, to what we are morally obliged to do so to support him. For example, an African American man who takes a stroll through a predominantly white neighbourhood in the knowledge that his mere presence might provoke local white supremacists to attack him is not wrongfully failing to respect the latter's moral power. This is because he has an independently justified right to freedom of movement. By contrast, one does not have the independently justified right to incite someone to commit tax fraud. Thus, in so far as an agent who acts wrongly does not successfully exercise her moral power, to induce her so to act, by acting in a way one does not have an independently justified right to do, is to subvert her moral power wrongfully and thus to fail to respect her as a moral agent.

Let us grant Howard the claims that an agent who acts wrongfully does not successfully exercise his moral power and that we owe it to one another to support one another in our successful exercise of that power. Even so, Howard's condemnation of entrapment warrants two critical responses in the context of this

[35] J. W. Howard, "Moral Subversion and Structural Entrapment," *Journal of Political Philosophy* 24 (2016): 24–46, at 28–37.

chapter. (I suspect that Howard would reject the first response; but he need not reject the second.)

First, suppose that Asset is strongly predisposed to commit the act into which Green seeks to entrap him. Suppose that Greedy Asset has already committed small-scale, undetectable tax fraud on multiple occasions, is aware that he does not have the skills to do so on a larger scale, and is waiting for precisely the kind of technical help which Officer offers him. Howard believes that even if an individual is predisposed to commit a particular kind of wrongdoing anyway, to increase the probability that he will do so is to fail to respect him as a moral agent and thus to wrong him. I disagree. True, Officer has increased the likelihood that Asset would commit this *token*-act of tax fraud. However, she does not plant the idea of committing this *type*-act in his mind, nor does she stoke temperamental dispositions which he did not already have. It is not clear in what way she fails to support him in his successful exercise of his moral power. Even if she does fail, she does not wrong him. For to say that she wrongs him is to imply that he has a grievance against her for inducing him to commit large-scale tax fraud. But given that he is predisposed to do exactly that, he lacks a grievance and she therefore does not wrong him.

Second, in the cases at hand here, *ex hypothesi*, Asset is under a duty to help Green (which is why Green is permitted to threaten him with disclosure.) Even if Officer entraps Asset into committing a wrongful act, and even if Asset was not predisposed so to act before Officer came on the scene, she does so as a means to get him to do that which he is under a duty to do anyway. Granted, it would be better if Asset came to that realization himself: indeed, by Howard's lights, this would count as a successful exercise of his moral power. Ideally, then, and other things being equal, Officer should try means other than entrapment, such as some of the less manipulative techniques described earlier on. However, if she fails to persuade Asset to cooperate, she is justified in entrapping him, subject to considerations of proportionality.

The last clause is crucial. Consider a scenario which draws on landmark entrapment cases in US jurisprudence:

> *Addiction* Asset is a mid-ranking civil servant in Blue's department of defence. He is also a recovering drug addict who, despite a long history of relapses, has managed to remain drug-free for a year. Officer entraps him into buying drugs—a criminal offence in Blue—whereupon she discloses her role in Green's intelligence services and threatens to denounce him to Blue's law-enforcement agencies unless he passes on sensitive information about the resilience of Blue's military infrastructure to cyber-attacks.

Even if Asset is under a duty to commit treason, and *even if* Officer had independently come by the information that Asset had relapsed and been morally justified in blackmailing him, she may not entrap him into a potentially catastrophic relapse: the harm he would thereby suffer is disproportionate to his contribution to Blue's unjust policy.

Entrapment is morally troubling and philosophically fascinating. There is more to say about it than I can do here. In quick summary, subject to standard constraints on harm imposition, the considerations which support Green blackmailing Asset into passing on sensitive information about Blue also support some limited forms of entrapment.

7.7 Conclusion

Manipulation, exploitation, coercion, in deference to or profiting from greed, envy, bitterness, anger . . . The picture I have painted in this chapter of some of the relationships between human sources and their recruiters and handlers seems to give credence to the view that espionage and counter-intelligence are dirty business. Often dirty, to be sure; yet, not necessarily to be condemned for it.

This chapter concludes my account of the ethics of dealing with human sources. In the next two chapters, I turn to the technological side of espionage and counter-intelligence, and to mass surveillance.

8

Technology

8.1 Introduction

So far, I have focused on what the empirical literature on espionage calls HUMINT, or intelligence which is obtained from or by an asset in the field. In this chapter, I address forms of espionage and counter-intelligence which do not require direct interaction between an asset and her handler but which proceed via technological means, or TECHINT.

There is a bewildering array of TECHINTs. Broadly speaking, there are three kinds of TECHINTs. First, SIGINT is the interception of the target's signals. It comprises COMINT—as when Green intercepts a communication such as a phone call or text message from its target, and ELINT—as when Green intercepts electronic signals emitted by the target. Second, OBSINT consists in observing a target. It includes IMINT, which is the collection of images via cameras or satellite, and MASINT, which is the collection of information via measurements and signature traces from targets' technical features. Third, CYBINT consists in collecting information in cyber-space.[1]

To illustrate: Green's intelligence agencies intercept and decrypt an email from a high-ranking official in Blue's regime (COMINT). They pinpoint the location from which the email was sent (ELINT). Analysis of the content and location of the email leads them to believe that Blue is developing nuclear weapons, in violation of its legal obligations under an international treaty. Thanks to satellite images, Green's intelligence agencies spot a structure which looks like a military nuclear development facility (IMINT). Notwithstanding Blue's assurances that the facility is not used for anything other than the production of non-nuclear missiles, Green's agencies also discover, thanks to especially placed sensors, the presence of radioactive material in the vicinity of the site (MASINT); they also successfully hack into the main server of Blue's ministry of defence and exfiltrate data about Blue's uranium enrichment programme (CYBINT). At no point did Green rely on having an agent in the field to provide the required information.

---

[1] For a useful list of various kinds of intelligence sources, see D. Omand, *Securing the State*, 29–30; Gill and Phythian, *Intelligence in an Insecure World*, ch. 4. The acronym OBSINT is of my own coinage (as far as I am aware: I have not encountered it yet). I needed an umbrella term for imagery and measurement intelligence.

My aim is to investigate whether there are deep moral differences between resorting to human sources on the one hand, and intercepting signals and conducting remote observation and detection on the other hand, *vis-à-vis* the targets and collateral victims of intelligence activities. I deny that there are. Section 8.2 brings out the issues at stake by rehearsing some historical examples. Section 8.3 offers a contrastive moral assessment of HUMINT and TECHINT. Section 8.4 considers whether cyber-intelligence, to wit, the use of computers to target other computers, raises distinct moral issues.

Two caveats. First, many intelligence operations combine both human and non-human resources. My focus on the latter is not meant to downplay the importance of the former—on the contrary: technical operations often require human agents, either as conduits (unwitting or not) of malware or as additional sources thanks to whom technical data can be better interpreted. Second, I leave until the next chapter the issue of mass surveillance, whereby Green's authorities surveil entire populations as a means to find out whether there is probable cause to mount a targeted operation on specific individuals.

8.2 Mapping the Terrain

I opened this book with Moses, whose spies had to go to Canaan to gather the information he needed. In that respect, Moses' spies are similar to Francis Gary Powers, who flew a U2 spy plane on a reconnaissance mission into the USSR's airspace in 1960 (only to be shot down and captured by the Soviets.)[2] In another respect, however, Moses' spies are light years away from the US pilots of a reconnaissance squadron who remotely operate spy drones in Afghanistan airspace from their US base thousands of miles away. In this latter example, while the means by which the observation takes place (namely, the drone) may be located in the target's airspace, its controllers are not. Further away still from Moses, geosatellite intelligence enables observation to take place wholly from outside the target's territory, airspace, and territorial waters.

Observation is only one dimension of espionage: another is the interception of putatively secret communications. To give but a few examples, Francis Walsingham, Elizabeth I's intelligence chief and the founder of one of the most effective intelligence services of the age, brought down Mary, Queen of Scots by having her letters intercepted and decoded. A century later and across the Channel, Louis XIII's chief Minister, Cardinal Richelieu, set up an office (the famous *cabinet noir*) entirely devoted to the routine interception and deciphering of all diplomatic correspondence in transit on French-controlled territory. The Sun King, Louis

---

[2] Powers was subsequently swapped for William Fisher, aka Rudolf Abel, one of the best-known Soviet illegals (s. 6.2.1.) The switch is recounted in Stephen Spielberg's 2015 movie *The Bridge of Spies*.

XIV, made extensive use of Richelieu's system. Closer to us in time, Britain's *first* operational act at the outbreak of the First World War was to dispatch HMS *Alert* to dredge and cut Germany's submarine telegraph cables. As a result, the German High Command had to rely on radio communications, which the Allies were able to intercept: this was the whole point of the operation. Three years later, the German High Command decided to step up their campaign of unrestricted submarine warfare in the Atlantic. The German Foreign Secretary Arthur Zimmermann sent an encrypted cable—the so-called Zimmermann telegram—to the President of Mexico, offering an alliance with the latter (involving the return to Mexico of Arizona, New Mexico, and Texas) should the United States enter the war against Germany and lose. The British intercepted and decrypted the cable, but were reluctant to pass it on to the United States right away: although they surmised that this would help sway American public opinion in favour of entering the war, they did not want the Germans to infer that their code had been broken. They eventually transmitted the telegram to the US administration, which made it public in March 2017. The telegram and its disclosure were a crucial step towards the United States' entry into the war. Better known still, at least in Britain, are the WWII feats of the cryptanalysts of Bletchley Park, who not only broke the code of the German Enigma machine, thereby giving Britain and its allies a decisive advantage at sea, but also decoded communications between Hitler and his top commanders. Finally, in some of the most explosive phases of the NSA wiretapping scandal, documents leaked by Edward Snowden revealed that the Agency had tapped the mobile phones of over 100 staff members in the German Chancellery, including the mobile of Chancellor Merkel herself. Snowden also revealed that GCHQ had tapped the phones of the negotiating teams at the G20 forum in London in 2009.

These cases are the bread and butter of the collective perceptions of espionage. They are also fairly 'old school': they tell of interceptions of military, political, and diplomatic secrets, on land, in air, in space, and at sea. Yet, as we saw in Chapter 4, political leaders have always been interested in their allies' and enemies' economic secrets. Their intelligence agencies employ the same means as deployed in military, diplomatic, and political intelligence. Moreover, espionage now takes place in what strategists call the fifth dimension of war and national security: cyber-space. The sea change occurred at the end of the Cold War, when the world's main powers realized that they could harness computers not just to decrypt secret communications but also to hack into computer networks. Cyber-espionage has essentially two aims: to discover—through one's computers—military, political, diplomatic, and economic information about the target; to map out how the target's cyber-infrastructure handles its military, political, diplomatic, and economic institutions, policies, and processes. In the first case, Green's intelligence agencies hack into Blue's computer networks in order to find out (e.g.) Blue's bidding strategy for an order of new unmanned aerial vehicles. In the second case, they hack into Blue's computer networks in order to learn about (e.g.) the ways in which they control its existing UAVs.[3]

Faced with those various methods, intelligence agencies have developed a number of protective mechanisms. First, they resort to encryption. Second, they hide their secrets in plain sight. To illustrate with a counter-example, it seems that the Soviets were alerted to the importance of the research carried out by American physicists on nuclear fission during WWII partly because the US government suddenly decided to classify it: as a result, academic journals suddenly dried up—a fact which did not go unnoticed by the Soviets. It might have been better to continue to allow those scientists to publish their findings. In a related vein, it might sometimes be better to disclose accurate but pointless facts in order the better to hide valuable information. Instead of protecting secrets with a 'bodyguard of lies', as Churchill promised Stalin to do with information about *Operation Overlord*, we might sometimes want to protect them with a 'bodyguard of truths'.[4] Third, intelligence agencies engage in deceptive technical operations. For example, they bait Blue into hacking into their own computer networks by dangling seemingly important lines of code (so-called honeypots): they divert Blue's computers from the information Blue is after and in the process also map out Blue's cyber-espionage capabilities.[5] Fourth, they disrupt their target's endeavour at the source by hacking into its networks to modify their codes.

This brief excursion into the more technical side of intelligence activities yields the following lines of normative inquiry. First, does resorting to technical rather than human means make a difference to the moral status of the operation—and, if so, does the choice of specific technical means make a difference? Second, which moral limits are there, if any, on the selection of those targets?

---

[3] In this and the previous paragraphs, I have drawn on the following sources: Andrew, *The Secret World*, chs. 10 and 13; H. Sebag-Montefiore, *Enigma: The Battle for the Code* (London: Weidenfeld & Nicolson, 2000); Omand, *How Spies Think*, ch. 7; B. Tuchman, *The Zimmermann Telegram* (Penguin Books, 1958); Greenwald, *No Place to Hide*; Harding, *The Snowden Files*. For a fascinating account and history of TECHINT since the beginning of the twentieth century, see Corera, *Intercept*. The other four dimensions of war and national security, and thus espionage and counter-intelligence, are land, sea, air, and space.

[4] On the US/Soviet example, and for the general point which it illustrates, see J. E. Sims, 'The future of counter-intelligence: the twenty-first century challenge', in I. Duyvesteyn et al. (eds.), *The Future of Intelligence—Challenges in the 21st century* (Routledge, 2015); Close, *Trinity*, 107–8. Churchill's exact words to Stain at the 1943 Teheran conference, as recorded in his memoirs, were that 'truth is so precious that she should always be attended by a bodyguard of lies.' See W. Churchill, *The Second World War, vol. 5—Closing the Ring*, 5th ed. (Penguin Classics, 2005), 338.

[5] M. N. Schmitt (ed.), *Tallinn Manual 2.0 on the International Law Applicable to Cyber Operations* (Cambridge University Press, 2017), 173–4; E. Gartzke and J. R. Lindsay, 'Weaving Tangled Webs: Offense, Defense, and Deception in Cyberspace,' *Security Studies* 24 (2015): 316–48.

8.3 Of Machines and Humans

8.3.1 Eyes and Ears vs Lenses and Bugs

In s. 5.3.2, I canvassed the following hypothetical case:

Infiltration₁ Green is locked in a conflict with Blue, a quasi-state organization intent on conquering swathes of territory via a mixture of conventional and terroristic means. Asset strikes up relationships with Blue's guerilla fighters, concealing his identity and true allegiances. He collects information about a possible attack on Green, which he passes on to Green's intelligence agencies. Green aims to eliminate those fighters before they can strike.

I argued that Asset is morally permitted—indeed, under certain conditions, under a duty, so to act. Compare *Infiltration₁* with:

Eavesdropping Asset loiters around local markets, places of worship, and cafés, and eavesdrops on conversations between suspected guerrilla fighters.

Tail Asset discreetly tails suspected guerrilla fighters from one place to the next, and makes a record of where they go, whom they meet, and so on.

In neither case, let us suppose, is Asset known to the fighters. In the next chapter (s. 9.3.2), I shall argue that to the extent that eavesdropping and tailing constitute violations of privacy, they are presumptively wrong. Even so, the presumption can be lifted. If targets are liable to being killed, then *a fortiori* they are liable to being observed and eavesdropped on in the course of planning for their wrongful ends. Even if they are not liable to being killed, their contribution to Blue's wrongful ends may well be such that they are nevertheless liable to being observed and eavesdropped on.

Now suppose that Green can extract the same information by placing insect-like robots in the guerrilla fighters' houses. Or suppose that the guerrilla fighters communicate via mobile phones and email and that Green's agencies are able to intercept their communications.[6] Green is morally permitted so to act: there does not seem to be a morally salient difference between eyes and lenses or between ears and bugs. By parity of reasoning, resorting to TECHINT in counter-intelligence operations is also *pro tanto* justified. Remember *Operation Fortitude*, thanks to which the Allies deceived the Germans that the 1944 invasion of France would take place

---

[6] On spy robots, see P. Lin and S. Ford, 'I, Spy Robot: The Ethics of Robots in National Security Intelligence,' in J. Galliot and W. Reed (eds.), *Ethics and the Future of Spying* (Routledge, 2016). For a wonderful history of eavesdropping, see J. L. Locke, *Eavesdropping—An Intimate History* (Oxford University Press, 2010).

near Calais (s. 5.3.2). By building fake garrisons and landing barges and by massing troops in Scotland and the south-east of England, and thanks to misleading radio traffic, it turned the enemy's own technical resources (aerial reconnaissance and radio interception) against it. If using human agents and their fictitious networks to communicate misleading information to their German handlers was morally justified, so was luring German reconnaissance planes into taking misleading photographs of fake preparations, and so was tricking German radio operators and cryptanalysts into intercepting and deciphering bogus communications.

In fact, it seems that Green is justified in privileging TECHINT, indeed can be under a duty to do so. Lenses and bugs will not have been manipulated, exploited, or coerced into performing this task. Green does not need to worry about their motives, the risks they would incur if discovered, and the harms they would accrue as a result of engaging in the long-term deception of fellow human beings. At the bar of the necessity requirement (s. 1.4.2), one is morally justified in exposing someone to a given harm H only if one has formed the belief, in the light of the best available evidence, that there is no lesser morally weighted harm h the imposition of which would bring about one's morally justified ends. The requirement is usually framed as a constraint on the direct imposition of harm on one's targets. But it also constrains one's decision to expose one's agents to harm at the hands of those targets. Green, in other words, has a duty of care to its assets to expose them to the least morally weighted harm.

In other respects, however, TECHINT raises some difficulties which should give us pause. First, it is not always effective. The features of machines which lead us to prefer them to humans—their predictability, their imperviousness to emotions, and so on—often instil misplaced confidence in their ability to get the job done. For example, it is sometimes alleged that once Bin Laden discovered that his phone communications were intercepted, he resorted to more traditional forms of spycraft such as using couriers, at which point the NSA went blind. Had intelligence agencies been willing to invest in cultivating human sources within Al Qaeda, they might have been better prepared for 9/11. Moreover, even if we can intercept communications, the harvest (such as fragments of phrases, or code words) is often piecemeal and not easily intelligible. Finally, the more sophisticated TECHINT is, the more information it hoovers up, and the harder it is for analysts to overcome informational overload.[7]

---

[7] On the Bin Laden case and more generally on the weaknesses of signals intelligence as a means to thwart international terrorism, see M. Aid, 'All Glory is Fleeting: Sigint and the Fight Against International Terrorism,' in W. K. Wark (ed.) *Twenty-First Century Intelligence* (Routledge, 2005). For a more sceptical take on the Bin Laden case, see B. Gellman, *Dark Mirror: Edward Snowden and the Surveillance State* (Bodley Head, 2020), 273–4. The problems inherent in absorbing large quantities of information are thought to be particularly acute for China, which is one reason why, according to some commentators, it is less powerful a 'cyber-actor' than is often supposed in the West. See J. R. Lindsay, 'The Impact of China on Cybersecurity: Fiction and Friction,' *International Security* 39 (2014): 7–47.

Effectiveness is a constraint on harm imposition. Diverting resources towards a particular end and, in so doing, depriving third parties of benefits to which they have a *pro tanto* right, when one has strong reasons to believe that one will not succeed, is wrongful. TECHINT is costly. It requires financial resources and technological know-how which could be deployed elsewhere: while some of the technological means by which intelligence agencies collect information have dual, civilian-cum-security purposes, not all do. To divert such resources to ineffective means, thereby allowing third parties to incur the costs of (e.g.) a less effective health-care system, is wrongful *vis-à-vis* those individuals.

Second, in many cases, it is essential to the success of a TECHINT operation that its target should have no awareness that she is under observation or that her communications are intercepted. (Not in all cases, though: in WWI, the German leadership would have known that their communications would be intercepted by the Allies.) This is also true of *Infiltration₁*: the success of Asset's operation depends on the guerrilla fighters' having no inkling that he is not who he claims to be. Nevertheless, there is an important difference between arms-length espionage and cases such as these. In *Infiltration₁*, Asset's targets know that he is there. They can decide whether to engage with him or not; they have control over what they tell him, whom they introduce him to, whether they take phone calls in front of him, and so on. In the TECHINT case under scrutiny, by contrast, they will not see the spy drones hovering at high altitude; they might hear wasps in the kitchen but have no idea that those insects are spy robots. As we saw in s. 1.4.1, that of which we are not aware can nevertheless harm us, and the resort to those means of collecting information thus stands in need of justification. To be clear: I do not claim that TECHINT always fares worse, along that dimension, than HUMINT. Rather, the use of surveillance technology of which the target is not aware is worse, along that dimension and other things being equal, than the infiltration of an agent of whose presence, even if not his identity, the target is aware.[8]

Ex hypothesi, the guerrilla fighters have given Green's agencies probable cause to investigate them. Even if they are harmed by TECHINT, they are liable to such harm. However, if Green can collect the information it needs in less harmful ways, it is under a *pro tanto* duty to do so: necessity dictates against TECHINT and in favour of an operation such as *Infiltration₁*. (It will not help differentiate however between arms-length TECHINT and arms-length HUMINT such as *Eavesdropping* and *Tail*.) Whether Green is under an all-things-considered duty to do so depends on the relative severity, for those fighters, of the harm of intrusion

---

[8] On the wrongfulness of surreptitious voyeurism in general, see, e.g., D. Nathan, 'Just Looking: Voyeurism and the Grounds of Privacy,' *Public Affairs Quarterly* 4 (1990): 365–86, as well as Stanley Benn's influential paper on privacy. (S. Benn, 'Privacy, Freedom and Respect for Persons,' in J. R. Pennock and J. W. Chapman (eds.), *Privacy–Nomos XIII* (Atherton Press, 1971).) For the view, which I reject here, that surreptitious voyeurism which is not acted upon does not harm us, see T. Doyle, 'Privacy and Perfect Voyeurism,' *Ethics and Information Technology* 11 (2009): 181–9.

relative to the harm of being deceived, as well as on the weight Green ought to assign to the protection of its own agents relative to the weight it ought to assign to the fighters' interest in not being observed or deceived.

Whether Green ought to resort to TECHINT rather than HUMINT, or indeed to a combination of both, must be decided on a case-by-case basis. This seems blindingly obvious. Yet, recurrent complaints to the effect that intelligence agencies have privileged one over the other suggest that the truth of this particular matter is perhaps not as securely grasped as the charge of obviousness implies. In any event, philosophically speaking, bringing into view the range of considerations which ought to be balanced against one another is not a meaningless task.

8.3.2 State Officials, Diplomats, Spies, and Company Executives

In this section, I evaluate the ethics of TECHINT in the light of the kind of agents which those operations routinely target. As we saw in Chapter 5 and earlier in this chapter, some agents are liable to being deceived and/or placed under surveillance by dint of their contribution to their political community's unjust foreign policy. Intelligence agencies routinely place state officials, including heads of state, heads of governments, diplomats, and the executives of major companies under surveillance; they also routinely intercept their communications. Those practices are controversial. Edward Snowden's revelation that the NSA and GCHQ had tapped into Chancellor Merkel's phone and had intercepted the communications of G20 negotiators were thought to be a low point for those intelligence agencies. The decision by the then-Australian government to spy on Timorese officials during their 2004 negotiations over access to oil and minerals in the Timor Sea, which was discussed in s. 2.4, is less known outside Australia but no less controversial for it.

As a matter of law, diplomats, diplomatic correspondences and archives, and the premises of diplomatic missions, are deemed inviolable by the 1961 Vienna Convention on Diplomatic Relations and the 1963 Vienna Convention on Consular Relations. Embassies, consulates, and the homes of diplomatic staff may not be entered into and searched without the consent of the sending state; nor can the diplomatic bag be opened and diplomats' communications intercepted by the receiving states and third-party states. The Vienna Conventions apply to diplomatic premises and staff the principles of territorial integrity and national self-determination which are at the heart of public international law: the premises of the American Embassy in London are as inviolable as if they were situated in Seattle; the American Ambassador to the United Kingdom, who represents the United States, is as inviolable as if she were based in Washington DC.

Setting the law aside, the question is whether merely by dint of occupying a particular role and outside the immediately life-threatening context of a military conflict, an agent is a legitimate target of TECHINT operations. (I frame the question in terms of TECHINT, rather than HUMINT, simply because intelligence agencies nowadays tend to (e.g.) intercept diplomats' communications electronically rather than turn their lovers into double agents.) On the contractarian view of espionage, the answer to that question is unequivocally 'yes'. By taking on the function of a minister or diplomat, or by becoming a spy, one has entered 'the game', a crucial and widely accepted move of which is mutual espionage. By extension, the contractarian view straightforwardly applies to TECHINT in the service of economic espionage: if you are in charge of negotiating a major contract for the sale of military technology, it is well understood by all relevant parties, yourself included, that you are fair game with respect to your professional activities and to those areas of your private life which might impinge on those activities.[9]

However, as I argued in s. 1.3.2, contractarian accounts of the ethics of espionage and counter-intelligence ask the wrong question. The question is not whether a particular practice is or hypothetically would be accepted by all: the question is whether it is morally permissible irrespective of those shared understandings. Moreover, as I stressed in s. 3.4 when dealing with the problem of infinite regress raised by the fact that espionage is a response to the problem of uncertainty, Green must have probable cause. The mere fact that an individual occupies a role in Blue's administration or in a private company which is an essential part of Blue's infrastructure does not on its own give Green such a cause. Green must have evidence-based reasons to believe that the individual is acting in such a way as to be liable to being subject to observation and interception tactics.

State officials are responsible for the conduct of their community's foreign and national security policy, including its intelligence activities in the service of such policy. Whether there is probable cause to target them depends on three factors: the broader geopolitical and geo-economic context in which the proposed intelligence operation is taking place; what Green may reasonably infer from the nature of the office held by the official; the official's ostensible conduct in cases where the office she holds does not in itself suggest that she makes a significant contribution to her country's foreign and national security policy.

Suppose that Blue has unwarrantedly invaded Green. In a war context, it is wholly unproblematic to place Blue's leaders under surveillance. In fact, not doing so would be a grave dereliction of duty. Or suppose that Green and Blue are nominally allies in a joint war against Yellow, but that there is a long history of prior enmity between them. Again, Green's intelligence agencies have probable cause, as provided by the context, to spy on Blue's leaders.

To do so in peacetime, however, and *a fortiori* in the context of friendly diplomatic relations, is much more problematic. Hitler in 1942 under the gaze and

---

[9] See, e.g., Macnish, *The Ethics of Surveillance*, 85; Pfaff, 'Bungee Jumping off the Moral High Ground', 81–4; Skerker, 'The Rights of Foreign Intelligence Targets'.

ears of the Allies: clearly yes; Merkel in the 2000s under the gaze and ears of the United States: probably not.

In between war and peace lies a vast and gray area of diplomatic tensions, disputes over borders and trade, and intense economic and industrial competitiveness. Suppose that Green and Blue are locked into a low-level, attritional conflict which falls short of war but which threatens to escalate. Subject to moral constraints on espionage (in particular, that it should serve just ends), Green's intelligence agencies have a justification for intercepting President Blue's communications—and, indeed, vice versa. Or return to the example I gave in the introduction to this chapter to illustrate different forms of TECHINT: Green, let us suppose, has acquired imagery and measurement intelligence via satellites and sensors that Blue is in breach of its morally justified international legal obligations not to develop nuclear weapons; at the same time, Blue's officials are obstructing attempts by weapons inspectors to monitor compliance. Again, under those circumstances, it is hard to object to the interception of President Blue's communications.[10]

Government ministers are one thing. State officials are another. In one of the largest known cyber-espionage operations ever mounted against a government, cyber-units from China's PLA (it is alleged) hacked into the servers of the US Office of Personnel Management and appropriated the personal details of *twenty million* government employees. It is not clear what the Chinese authorities (assuming that they were behind the attack) will want to do with such information. But it is hard to think of any plausible justification for the operation: being a state official (or government employee) does not make one liable to have one's personal information targeted by a foreign government. One's conduct, in that capacity, is relevant. To illustrate, Green cannot reasonably infer from the mere fact that a civil servant works at the Ministry for Rural Affairs that she plays a significant role in Blue's national security policy. Suppose, however, that she is known to attend high-level meetings in which Blue attempts to assess Green's resilience to variations in the price of essential foodstuff. Green might reasonably infer that she is making a significant contribution to Blue's foreign policy in that particular dimension. Even so, this does not in itself provide Green with a justification for intercepting her email. To repeat, context matters: if the context is one of fractious trade negotiations between Green and Blue in which Blue has the upper hand, against a long-term past background of harmfully exploitative conduct on Blue's part against Green, Green might well have a justification for treating her as a legitimate target of an intelligence operation. Otherwise, it does not.[11]

---

[10] For another brief argument along similar lines, see Bellaby, *The Ethics of Intelligence*, 86.
[11] For a contemporaneous report of the OPM hack, see J. Hirschfel Davis, 'Hacking of Government Computers Exposed 21.5 Million People,' *The New York Times* (09/07/2015).

Diplomats and private company executives are another matter. Neither, it might perhaps be argued, are in charge of Blue's foreign and national security policy: the former merely represent Blue, while the latter merely help provide essential services. The grounds upon which TECHINT is justified as a means to acquire information from foreign state officials do not—it seems—apply here.

Not so fast. Consider diplomats first. They often take an active part in their government's foreign policy, particularly when they engage in clandestine diplomacy. In that respect, they are no different from relevantly situated state officials. Second, even when they do not conduct their community's foreign and national security policy, they know about it.[12] With that fact in hand, one can justify intercepting their communications or bugging their premises as follows. Again, assume that the context is one of war, or serious tensions short of war, between Blue and Green. Suppose further that it is entirely reasonable of Green to assume that Blue's diplomats in Green have information to the effect that Blue's regime is about to embark on an unjust policy against it. First, under some circumstances, as I argued in s. 6.4 through the case of *Active Traitor*, they are under a duty to pass on that information to Green—in other words, to commit treason. If so, they are liable to visual and auditory observation: Green would not wrong them if it were to tap their phones or bug their residence.

Second, suppose that Blue's diplomats are not under a duty to betray their country's secrets, on the grounds that they would thereby expose themselves and their family to unduly high risks of unduly severe punishment were they discovered. It does not follow that they are not legitimate targets for surveillance. To say that I am under a duty to give you x is to say the following: I am under a duty to incur the loss of x, and/or I am under a duty to take such steps as are necessary to ensure that you get x, and/or I am under a duty to incur some costs attendant on x being retrieved from me. To object that giving you x is too costly is to say, either that the loss of x is too onerous a burden, or that the steps that I ought to take to ensure that you get x are too demanding, or that the costs I would incur from the process of your retrieving x from me are too high, or a combination of some or all of these. The claim that Blue's diplomats are not under a duty, on grounds of demandingness, to take such steps as to ensure that Green gets the needed information is compatible with the claim that they are under a duty to accept the loss (which is theirs as well as, jointly, his fellow officials and citizens) of that secret. It is also compatible with the claim that the costs of being placed under surveillance and having their communications intercepted by Green are not so onerous that they ought not to incur them.

---

[12] Macnish also thinks that the fact that diplomats have information about their government's (unjust) policy makes them legitimate targets; but as far as I can see, he does not provide a justification for that claim. Macnish, *The Ethics of Surveillance*, 85. As an aside, diplomacy and espionage have long been intimately connected: diplomats have served as spies, and *vice versa*. For an interesting overview of political leaders' use of spies as diplomats, see J. A. Gentry, 'Diplomatic Spying: How Useful Is It?,' *International Journal of Intelligence and CounterIntelligence* 34 (2021): 432–62.

Consider next company executives who work for firms which are interwoven in or part of Blue's critical infrastructure. They do not set or conduct national-security or foreign policy in the way and to the extent that Blue's government ministers do. Nevertheless, they often help shape it, and make decisions about the means through which it is implemented and thus contribute to it. In s. 4.3, I argued that business employees do not have a right that the operational and proprietary information on which businesses rely remain secret if the information is used, either by those businesses themselves or by their 'host-state' Blue, as a means to violate the fundamental rights of Green's members (or, for that matter, the rights of third parties whom Green justifiably helps protect). If Green has strong evidence that a company executive in Blue contributes to an unjust policy or fails to disclose such information as might enable Green's leaders to thwart rights violations, it may justifiably target him in a SIGINT operation. There is no reason to treat them differently from Blue's state officials.

8.4 Cyber-intelligence

So far, I have considered cases in which the TECHINT operation targets human beings, irrespective of the specific means by which it does so. The last thirty years or so have witnessed exponential growth in cyber-espionage and counter-intelligence (for short, cyber-intelligence)—concomitant with the exponential growth and reach of computers and networks thereof on all continents and across all facets of our individual and collective lives.[13] Just as we must ascertain whether there are salient moral differences between HUMINT and TECHINT, we must ascertain whether there are salient moral differences between so-called kinetic TECHINT and TECHINT in cyber-space—or CYBINT.

Defining cyber-space is notoriously difficult. It is best thought of as 'the realm of computer networks (and the users behind them) in which information is stored, shared and communicated online.'[14] It comprises logical, physical, and human elements. Its logical components are data (or information) and the softwares and protocols which process it while at rest and handle it in transit. Its physical

---

[13] In July 2021, an international consortium of media outlets revealed that the Israeli cybersecurity company NSO had developed a software—Pegasus—capable of surreptitiously and remotely turning any iPhone or Android phone into a surveillance device. Detecting an infection is almost impossible. To date, NSO has sold Pegasus to a number of governments which (according to the company) were contractually bound to use it solely to legitimate ends such as fighting crime and thwarting terrorist activities. However, a massive data leak suggested that some of NSO's clients are also using it to spy on their political opponents, human rights activists, investigative journalists, and foreign state officials. France's National Agency for the Security of Information Systems (ANSSI) was the first national authority to confirm, in August 2021, that traces of a Pegasus infection had been found on phones belonging to journalists. For detailed information about Pegasus, see *The Guardian*'s dedicated web resources at https://www.theguardian.com/news/series/pegasus-project (accessed on 06/08/2021).

[14] P. W. Singer and A. Friedman, *Cybersecurity and Cyberwar* (Oxford University Press, 2014), 13.

components are the computers, cables, handheld devices, and routers on which the data is stored and through which it transits. Its human elements are the users of those networks.

To ascertain whether resorting to CYBINT is morally justified, we must bear in mind two constitutive features of cyber-space. First, when we send emails or call up websites, we send data over the Internet—which is the global network of our planet's billions of computers, servers, and handheld devices. The data—an email, a request for a website—does not travel whole: it is disaggregated into multiple data packets, each of which travels through the fastest available route before they are all reassembled together into that email or that request. The fastest route is not the geographically shorter one. Before writing this paragraph, I traced the route taken by my request to access my University's website from my home in Oxford. The data packets into which it split as it left my computer went to the United States, various points in the United Kingdom, the Netherlands, and Sweden, before it came back on to my screen as the University's web page. It took my website request milliseconds to travel thousands of miles. It takes me ten minutes to cycle the two miles between my home and my office.

Second, personal data, data related to our critical civilian infrastructure, and data related to our military capabilities by and large travel through the same highways in cyber-space. It is possible to isolate a computer or network from the Internet and from other networks through the use of air gaps. However, transferring data from another computer to an air-gapped computer must be done manually, for example via a USB stick. Air gaps are cumbersome, which is why there are relatively few air-gapped systems: most of the data travels via the Internet, which is a perfect and pervasive example of a multiple-use facility.

8.4.1 Cyber-espionage

Now, compare the following real and hypothetical cases:[15]

Colossus In 1944, the scientists and engineers of Bletchley Park construct a machine, which they call Colossus, thanks to which they manage to decrypt

---

[15] The hypothetical examples of cyber-operations in this section are drawn from reports regularly compiled by, *inter alia*, the UK's National Cyber-Security Center and the US's National Counterintelligence and Security Center, the *Tallinn Manual 2.0*, and descriptions of major cyber-espionage operations in T. Rid, *Cyber War Will Not Take Place* (Oxford University Press, 2013), ch. 5. Those operations include China's alleged operations against the US DOD, Pentagon and defence industry; China's alleged operation, termed *Shady Rat*, against a number of Western and Asian countries' national and international Olympic committees; an operation, termed *Flame*, allegedly conducted by the US and Israel against Iran; an attack, again allegedly carried out by the US, termed *Gauss*, against Lebanon-based banks suspected of holding Hezbollah's accounts. On Colossus, see Corera, *Intercept*, 30–7.

intercepts of communications between Germany's highest-ranked generals and Hitler himself.

Colossus was arguably the world's first multipurpose computer. It worked on messages which had been intercepted by other means and which were fed into it. Contrast with:

Hacking₁ Blue has attacked Green without just cause. Green's agencies hack into the computer mainframes of Blue's Ministry of Defence and Weapons Inc., one of Blue's major private defence companies, thanks to which they intercept₁ communications about Blue's new missile-launching system.

Suppose for the sake of argument that Green acts permissibly in *Colossus*. At first sight, it seems that it acts permissibly in *Hacking₁*. True, in *Colossus*, it does not interfere with the physical infrastructure of Blue's communications, whereas in *Hacking₁*, it does. Could this make a difference, such that *Colossus* is morally permitted whereas *Hacking₁* is not?

I doubt it. Consider:

Bug Same as in *Hacking₁* except that Green's intelligence services plant a bug in the car of Blue's chief of Defence Staff, thereby garnering valuable information about Blue's new missile-launching system.

I struggle to conceive of a plausible argument to the effect that Green acts impermissibly in *Bug*. *Prima facie*, there is little difference between *Bug* and *Hacking₁*, and it seems, therefore, that Green acts permissibly in the latter case.

Could it be, though, that *not* interfering with the other side's physical communication infrastructure is morally preferable, other things being equal? Here is an argument to that effect.

At the bar of the necessity requirement, we ought to inflict the least amount of morally weighted harm that is necessary to achieve our justified ends. In *Colossus*, the British inflicted on the Germans the harm of breaching the secrecy of their communications. In *Bug* and *Hacking₁*, Green inflicts on Blue a similar harm, *as well as* the harm of not having control over their physical infrastructure (a car, Internet routers, and computers). Normally, Blue's interest in exercising such control would be protected by two kinds of rights: property rights as held by Blue's citizens if the computers, routers, etc., are public assets or by private corporations operating in Blue; sovereignty rights as held by Blue's citizens to make laws in respect of who may use and have access to that physical infrastructure. Even if Blue is liable to the harms attendant on not exercising such control, Green ought to opt not to impair it if it can achieve the same ends by less invasive means. Or so it might be thought.

It is not clear that the argument works. For—it might be objected—we have rights to control not merely the physical means by or in which we communicate, but also those communications themselves, of which we are after all the authors.[16] This includes, above all, the right to control who can hear such communications. If so, appealing to the moral desirability of not lessening Blue's control over its physical infrastructure does not support opting for non-invasive over invasive means of intelligence collection—for *Colosssus* over *Hacking₁* and, for that matter, *Bug*: control is lost in all three cases.

In any event, things are not equal. To the extent that Green is faced with an adversary which communicates in cyber-space, it has a very strong justification for collecting information in that space. Green cannot afford not to know how that system operates, before it operates. If the protection of fundamental rights provides Green with a just cause for spying on Blue, if the information it requires is located in cyber-space (whether in its physical or logical components) and if acquiring that information in cyber-space via cyber-means is the only way it can do so, this gives it a *pro tanto* justification for doing so.

I say *pro tanto*, rather than 'all-things-considered'. For the cyber-means by which it does so are relevant. So is the collateral damage it carries the risk of.

On the first count, there are different ways in which one can hack into another party's computer network.[17] *Hacking₁* is under-described. In its simplest and least problematic variant, Green's cyber-spies hack into Blue's mainframe from behind their desks. Contrast with:

> *Hacking₂* Green has identified a high-ranking official in Blue's MOD who, it has reason to believe, has access via his laptop to the air-gapped part of Blue's mainframe it is interested in. It successfully plants an infected USB stick into his briefcase. The next time the official plugs the USB stick into his laptop, the virus will insert itself into the mainframe and provide Green with the back door it needs.

In effect, Green is turning the official into a unwitting double agent. This case is relevantly analogous to the case of officials who, I argued in s. 8.3.2, are sometimes under a duty to pass on official secrets to the other side yet fail to fulfil it.

But now consider:

---

[16] Bellaby, *The Ethics of Intelligence*, 76–7. The objection I am tentatively mooting here draws on some of the same considerations as justify intellectual property rights (see s. 4.2).

[17] One could also make it easier to hack in the first instance. For example, a government could insist that exports of encryption softwares be subject to licence, and ensure that a condition of such licence is that the software should have an inbuilt vulnerability or back door. This is not specific to cyber-espionage, though it is particularly salient in this context. The risk, of course, is that everyone, and not just those who wish to make wrongful use of encryption, will be vulnerable. For an interesting account of the British government's policy on such exports in the 1970s and 1980s, see Corera, *Intercept*, ch. 6. For discussion in the current context, see, e.g., D. Anderson, *A Question of Trust–Report of the Investigatory Power Review* (Her Majesty's Government, 2015), 61–3.

Hacking₃ Green hacks into and harnesses the combined power of millions of badly protected computers and mobile devices owned by ordinary, unsuspecting individuals, all over the world, in order to break through Blue's cyber-defences.

Those networks of 'zombie computers', or botnets, are a staple of cyber-crime. They are used to hack into banks' networks, harvest consumers' credentials, take down commercial rivals' websites, and steal vast amounts of confidential information regarding (e.g.) countries' and international corporations' defence-related sensitive information.[18]

At first sight, it seems wrong to press millions of unsuspecting computer users into the service of one's espionage ends, however justified the latter are. Upon closer inspection, however, suppose that some of those computers belong to Blue's citizens, without whose contribution Blue's regime would not be able to conduct its unjust foreign policy. Depending on the magnitude and nature of their contribution, they are liable to the imposition of proportionate harm as a means to thwart the threat which their regime poses. Even if they are not liable to being killed (on the grounds that this would be a disproportionate response to their contribution), they might be liable to having their personal computing devices used without their knowledge.

Suppose now that most of the computers do not belong to agents who contribute to Blue's unjust policy. Some belong to Blue's citizens who are not contributors; others to citizens from other countries: Green for example, but also Yellow, White, etc. Green's citizens are under a duty to one another to contribute to the defence of their rights. Moreover, as we saw in s. 1.4.1, all individuals wherever they are in the world are under duties (subject to costs) to help secure one another's fundamental rights. Blue's citizens who do not contribute to their regime's policy are under a duty to help the victims of that policy fight for their rights. Citizens of Yellow and White might also be under a duty to provide assistance to Green—even if their political community is not a signatory of a defensive alliance with Green, and *a fortiori* if it is.

There are many ways in which those individuals can discharge their duty to provide assistance. Having their computer resources used as part of a botnet in pursuit of just ends is one such way. It would be better, of course, if they could be called upon to do so openly and transparently. Since for Green to do so would be entirely self-defeating, it may do so surreptitiously as a second-best means to get those individuals to do what they are under a duty to do. By analogy, suppose that, as Joel Feinberg famously suggested, you are lost in a blizzard and will die unless you find refuge in my cabin, in my absence. You are morally justified in

---

[18] See, e.g., Corera, *Intercept*, ch. 10. One of the documents leaked by Snowden suggests that China and the United States are using botnets for espionage purposes. (See https://edwardsnowden.com/2015/01/19/defiantwarrior-and-the-nsas-use-of-bots/ (accessed on 17/08/2021).)

breaking in. Suppose that you cannot inform me in advance of what you are about to do and cannot tell me about it afterwards: I will never know that my cabin has been broken into. Even though it would be better if I knew, that fact alone cannot make the difference between life and death. You are still justified in breaking in. The point applies to cyber-cases.[19]

Consider now the problem of collateral damage. A cyber-attack can cause damage (whether collateral or deliberate) to the physical and logical components of a computer network. Physical damage includes hardware failure, as when a computer will no longer switch on or when an entire network will be overloaded to the point of not functioning. Logical damage includes, *inter alia*, the corruption or deletion of data (such as banking or medical records), or the corruption or deletion of lines of code which are critical to the smooth running of the operating system or software. As a result, computer users and those who do not use but depend on computers may well incur harm: if my banking or medical records have been wiped out, I will very likely suffer financial and health-related hardship. Now, computer users such as you and I use the same cyber-infrastructure as our governments and private corporations, and air gaps are not hacker-proof. As a result, inserting a virus into the computer of one engineer in Weapons Inc. might lead to thousands of civilian computers being infected not just within the borders of the country in which Weapons Inc. operates, but throughout the world as well. Mounting an attack on a government mainframe by exploiting a software vulnerability might cause a loss in network connectivity affecting millions of users. Exploiting a back door into a target's network in order to map out traffic might at the same time hoover up information on the Internet activities of individuals who are unrelated to the cyber-operation. Moreover, once a piece of malware spreads beyond its intended target, it can be appropriated and used by cyber-criminals, thereby inflicting further harm. The attacker must still take such harm into account when deciding whether to attack: as we saw in s. 3.3, intervening and non-intervening agents share responsibility for those harms.[20]

Admittedly, the examples I have just given have their analogues in both kinetic warfare and old-style TECHINT. On the first count, military strategists have to decide whether or not to attack a dual-purpose infrastructure such as a power plant; and military conflicts are breeding grounds for small- and large-scale criminality (the black-market arms trade, the sexual exploitation of vulnerable refugees, the drug trade, etc.) On the second count, placing a diplomat under close video and audio surveillance will capture not just her job-related comings

---

[19] J. Feinberg, 'Voluntary Euthanasia and the Inalienable Right to Life,' *Philosophy & Public Affairs* 7 (1978): 93–123.

[20] On cyber-collateral damage, see S. Romanovsky and Z. Goldman, 'Understanding Cyber Collateral Damage,' *Journal of National Security Law and Policy* 9 (2017): 233–58; B. Valeriano, B. Jensen, and R. C. Maness, *Cyber Strategy—The Evolving Character of Power and Coercion* (Oxford University Press, 2018), 172.

and goings and conversations but also her private interactions with her friends and family, indeed, the comings and goings of passers-by in the streets near her embassy.

However, the fact that the problem is not unique to cyber-operations does not render it any less acute. Whether or not Green is morally justified all-things-considered in launching an operation of cyber-espionage is subject to the requirement that the collateral damage it will thereby inflict not be disproportionate. The point straightforwardly draws on the ethics of defensive harming in general. The problem in this context, however, is that it is especially difficult to ascertain how a computer virus will behave, and in particular how fast it will replicate and how much damage it will do. The same considerations which support the resort to cyber-espionage—namely the pervasiveness, power, and speed of computers—are also and precisely what makes it morally problematic. As we shall now see, cyber-counter-intelligence operations face the same difficulty. I shall sketch a response which applies to both cases at the close of the next section.

8.4.2 Cyber-counter-intelligence

Political communities and their leaders are not idle in the face the threat of cyber-espionage. Consider:

> *Countermeasures* Green's cyber-security centre, which is part of its intelligence apparatus, helps Green's government departments as well as firms essential to its critical infrastructure protect themselves from cyber-attacks. Counter-measures include, for example, installing firewalls and directing malware into seemingly interesting but in fact worthless parts of its networks, whence it turns the malware into a cyber-spy against Blue's own networks.

This simple example belies the three main problems which counter-intelligence operations must solve. First: identifying the nature of the threat. Suppose that Green's cyber-security and counter-intelligence experts spot some unusual traffic around particular routers or some heavier-than-usual activity with one of their firewalls. Their first task is to determine whether the network is under attack. For all they know, it might not be: the packets which are being rerouted or which are attempting to breach the firewall might have been corrupted by a badly designed application thousands of miles away, with no noxious intention on the part of its programmers.

Suppose now that they have established hostile intent. Next, they need to ascertain whether they are vulnerable to cyber-espionage or to cyber-sabotage. These are distinct problems. In cyber-espionage, one seeks to acquire information; in cyber-sabotage, one seeks to damage or render inoperative the target's infrastructure. One of the most famous examples of cyber-sabotage was carried out (it is alleged) by Israel and the United States in the late 2000s against Iran's nuclear enrichment facility at Narantz. A piece of malware, called Stuxnet, was inserted via a USB stick into the computer of one of Iran's nuclear engineers or of a foreign expert on a visit to the facility. From that computer, Stuxnet was able to move into Narantz's air-gapped network and to take control of the centrifuge system, causing it some damage over a period of months. Another well-known example is the denial of Internet services which Estonia—one of the most densely wired society in the world—suffered for a few weeks in 2007, allegedly at the hands of pro-Russia hacktivists.[21]

The Narantz operation and the Estonia case take us into the territory of cyber-warfare, which is not my concern in this book. My focus is on cyber-intelligence. However, both cyber-war and cyber-intelligence start with an attack on the target's networks, and it is not always clear which is which. Moreover, even if to the best of their knowledge Green's cyber-defence and counter-intelligence specialists are confident that Green is subject to cyber-espionage rather than cyber-sabotage, they might equally reasonably assume that Blue's cyber-spies have managed to create a code which could be used for an operation of cyber-sabotage at some later date.

Second: attribution. Recall that data travels in packets over thousands of miles and through different countries. Each packet contains information about the source and destination of the data. However, sophisticated cyber-specialists can disguise the origin of an attack relatively easily by using a virtual private network or hijacking a botnet. Even if Green's specialists see that an operation against Green's critical infrastructure emanates from within Yellow's territory, they have to remain alive to the possibility that the attack in fact cames from within Blue. Even if they correctly determine that the attack comes from within Blue, they might not be able to ascertain *who* launched it. It could be Blue's agencies. But it could also be a gang of cyber-criminals who steal sensitive materials to sell it on, a gang of disaffected hackers, a botnet or an agent which has hijacked a botnet.[22]

Granted, the attribution problem is not unique to cyber-operations. Just as intelligence agencies sometimes recruit assets under a false flag (s. 7.4.3), so they sometimes conduct intelligence cyber-operations. Moreover, in some cases, the operation is so sophisticated, is of such nature, or takes place in such a context, that it can be reasonably attributed to a party which is known to have the capacity to mount it, the power to authorize or condone it, and the motive for conducting it or for allowing it to happen. Some recent cyber-espionage operations against

---

[21] See, e.g., Corera, *Intercept*, 74–83. On cyber-sabotage, see, e.g., Rid, *Cyber War Will Not Take Place*, ch. 4. It appears that Israel mounted a similar attack in April 2021. (M. Chulov, 'Israel Appears to Confirm It Carried Out Cyberattack on Iran Nuclear Facility', *The Guardian* (11/04/2021).)

[22] On the problems of identification and attribution, see, in particular, S. W. Brenner, *Cyber Threats: The Emerging Fault Lines of the Nation State* (Oxford University Press, 2009), chs. 4 and 5; Rid, *Cyber War Will Not Take Place*, ch. 7; Singer and Friedman, *Cybersecurity and Cyberwar*, 72–6, 148–9. On hijacking botnets, see Valeriano, Jensen, and Maness, *Cyber Strategy*, 196.

the US defence industries have been reliably attributed to one of China's cyber-battalions in Shanghai.[23] Nevertheless, the problem is more acute in the case of cyber-operations than in other kinds of espionage operations.

Third: speed. A party which notices unusual cyber-activity around or in its networks will not have the time to identify whether it is the target of an attack, whether the attack is an act of cyber-war or an act of espionage, and who is behind it. As a result, it will struggle to minimize the damage it will occasion. Speed compounds the problems of identification and attribution. Once again, the problem is not unique to cyber-espionage. The difficulties raised by the threat of an attack which one will not be able to thwart, and the resulting temptation of attacking pre-emptively, are well known: nuclear missiles in particular can travel across continents in a matter of minutes. But, once again, it is particularly acute in this realm: milliseconds are not minutes. While a large scale cyber-attack will not kill hundreds of thousands of people in a manner of minutes, a large-scale attack on the entire civilian and military infrastructure of a country will severely harm scores of people over weeks or months. Hence the importance of identifying as quickly as one can whether one is subject to cyber-espionage or cyber-war, and at whose hands—yet in a time frame which makes the task extraordinarily difficult.[24]

Faced with those three problems, Green has several options. It can build robust cyber-defensive counter-intelligence capacities. It can mount offensive counter-intelligence operations (for example, and as already suggested, by turning the attacker against itself). It can destroy putatively hostile parties' physical cyber-infrastructure by kinetic means (such as cutting off cables—though this would inevitably cause collateral damage to innocent civilians whose Internet traffic runs alongside those cables). It can mount a preventive cyber-war. It can mount a combination of all of these.

Since my concern is with cyber-intelligence operations, I leave aside both kinetic responses and the resort to a preventive cyber-war. I also assume that one is pre-sumptively justified in resorting to purely defensive cyber-counterintelligence—the equivalent of locking up sensitive official documents in a safe. This leaves us with two interesting questions. First, given that the vulnerability of Green's critical infrastructure to cyber-espionage is in part a function of the vulnerability of the networks and computers used by ordinary computer users, are the latter under an enforceable moral obligation to protect their own equipment? I believe so. We are under duties to take reasonable steps to ensure that our possessions are not used by

---

[23] M. S. Schmidt and D. E. Sanger, '5 in China Army Face U.S. Charges of Cyberattacks,' *The New York Times* (19/05/2014).

[24] One some views of cyber-war, we are facing a cyber-Armageddon at the hands of a combination of terrorist groups, international criminal organizations, and states cyber-battalions. On other views, the prospects of a large-scale cyber-war are nil. For a review of this debate, see G. R. Lucas, *Ethics and Cyber Warfare—The Quest for Responsibility in the Age of Digital Warfare* (Oxford University Press, 2017), esp. ch. 1. Lucas concludes—and I am inclined to agree—that the sceptical view relies on an overly narrow conception of war.

third parties for the commission of wrongdoings. If I cannot be bothered to lock up my car even though I know that, given where I live, there is a strong chance that it might be stolen by a gang of joyriders whose driving antics have already put people at risk, I act wrongly *vis-à-vis* the latter. The same goes with my computer. In this case, the means by which my moral obligation can be enforced are rather simple. As George Lucas argues in his recent book on cyber-warfare, one could make it legally mandatory for Internet service providers to bar a computer from accessing the Internet unless it is equipped with protective software (something which could be done automatically), just as drivers may not drive unless they have a licence and their car meets basic safety requirements.[25] Admittedly, in the computer case, the suggestion is that a computer should actually be denied access to the Internet. In the driving case, I can physically drive my car even if it is unsafe or if I do not have a licence: the means by which my moral obligation is enforced take the form of *ex post* punishment if I am found out. But this difference between the two cases is entirely contingent on the state of our technology and on governments' willingness to use it: imagine a system whereby we cannot unlock a car unless we produce (via a barcode) a valid driving licence. The two cases are analogous in the crucial relevant respect: highways, be they made of concrete or of data travelling on fibre-optic cables, are not free for all zones.

Second, may Green resort to offensive cyber-measures? The most offensive of such measures consists in directing malware into seemingly interesting but in fact worthless parts of its networks, whence it turns the malware into a cyber-spy against the network which, one thinks, is at the origin of the attack. Once inside that network, Green can map it out and feed false information into it. The NSA has mounted a number of operations of that kind in the last few years, notably against China's PLA cyber-arm, as has Georgia against its powerful neighbour Russia.[26]

Singer and Friedman contrast this tactic with what they term 'past intelligence programs', and claim that 'it's the difference between reading the enemy's radio signal and being able to seize control of the radio itself.'[27] However, the contrast between 'old style' and cyber-operations is overdrawn. The history of espionage and counter-intelligence is replete with tales of seizing control and disrupting the enemy's communications at the source. That, in fact, was a crucial aspect of the Double Cross system: some of the German spies captured in Britain were turned by MI5 and coerced into sending back false reports to their masters. The difference between this kind of operation and 'turning' the other side's computer networks

---

[25] Lucas, *Ethics and Cyber Warfare*, 138–9. The claim that I am under a duty to protect my computer from being used by wrongdoers in a botnet is compatible with the aforementioned claim that third parties may break through my firewall and use my computer to morally justified ends.

[26] On the US 'hack back' operations against China, see Valeriano, Jensen, and Maness, *Cyber Strategy*, ch. 7. On the case of Georgia, see Rid, *Cyber War Will Not Take Place*, ch. 7. On deception and cyber-counter-intelligence in general, see, e.g., Gartzke and Lindsay, 'Weaving Tangled Webs.'

[27] Singer and Friedman, *Cybersecurity and Cyberwar*, 128–9.

is that, in the former case, the operation took place on British soil. In the cyber-case, by contrast, and assuming that Green has identified Blue as the author of the attack, it is taking the fight into Blue. It is invading its cyber-space in both its virtual and physical dimensions: virtually by modifying its codes, physically by having its malware travel alongside fibre-optic cables into Blue's territory and infect its computer networks. With that point in hand, some might be tempted to object to Green's act in this case, while condoning the turning of German radio operators on British territory, by appealing to Blue's putative ownership rights over both and/or sovereignty rights over its share (as it were) of cyber-space. This will not do, however, for the same reasons as deployed earlier in the context of cyber-espionage: if Blue's agents are responsible for the attack to which Green is subject, then they are liable to the invasion of their cyber-space rights. Subject to considerations of necessity, effectiveness, and proportionality, Green may justifiably proceed.

Suppose now that Green operates under conditions of fivefold uncertainty: it does not know whether it is facing an attack (as opposed to malfunctioning cyber-activity); if so, whether the attack is an act of cyber-espionage or cyber-war; if the former, who is responsible for it; nor can it predict what kind of damage it will inflict on its targets; nor, finally, is it in a position to assign probabilities to those various options. May it justifiably proceed with offensive countermeasures? It might seem tempting to say 'no'. The less one knows, one might hold, the more cautious one should be. For it is morally preferable, one might insist, to run the risk of unwarrantedly making oneself vulnerable to wrongful harm by doing nothing, over running the risk of unwarrantedly causing a wrongful harm to an innocent party. Given that, in this scenario, Green does not know, it ought merely to defend itself from what might or might not be a hostile operation (by installing firewalls), and not go on the offensive.

This putative argument against offensive cyber-counter-intelligence might also be deployed against cyber-espionage, in the light of the difficulty of ascertaining what and how much collateral damage the latter might cause. There are reasons to reject it in both contexts, however. Even if Green does not know of this particular incident what it consists of exactly, it may, in fact must, work on the assumption that third parties have attempted in the past, are attempting now, and will attempt in the future to mount an operation of cyber-espionage against its critical infrastructure, both civilian and military: such is the reality of the world, here and now, in which it (indeed, all of us) operate, and it would be irresponsible to ignore it.[28] Moreover, even if it is true that the more harm one might wrongfully inflict, the more cautious one ought to be, it is also true that other things being equal, the less time one has to assess whether one is under threat, the less cautious

[28] The Center for Strategic and International Studies, one of the world's most highly respected think tanks, keeps an up-to-date and sobering list of significant cyber-incidents at https://www.csis.org/programs/technology-policy-program/significant-cyber-incidents (accessed on 17/08/2021).

one *may* justifiably be. This, of course, is subject to the magnitude of the threat one has reason to believe one might be facing and to the degree to which one's response is proportionate: the fact that I only have a split second to determine whether Blogg is about to punch me on the nose or to wave his hand in the direction of my face does not provide me with a justification for cutting off his arm. It does, however, provide me with a justification for ducking, even though Blogg will hit the wall and damage one of his fingers as a result. And if I had more time and could shout a warning instead of ducking, that is what I ought to do. But the narrower one's window of opportunity, the greater the range of morally weighted harms one may inflict as a necessary step to thwarting what one believes might be a serious attack on (in this instance) one's ability to procure the information one needs to conduct a morally justified national security and foreign policy.

Under conditions of uncertainty and time constraints as described so far, and bearing in mind the magnitude of the risks of harms which Green believes, to the very best of its imperfect knowledge, it would not merely inflict but incur, Green is subjectively justified in attempting to infiltrate the network from where the unusual activity seems to be originating, in order to ascertain whether or not it is under attack, and from whom. Put differently, *investigative* cyber-counter-intelligence (or counter-espionage, as some scholars call it) is morally justified in the light of the best available evidence. In fact, it is morally mandatory as a condition for further and morally justified *destructive* action such as manipulating that network so that it feeds back misleading information to its controllers.

Admittedly, Green might not be objectively justified in so acting: it may be that the evidence at its disposal is false. Moreover, even if Green is objectively as well as subjectively justified in so acting, it might occasion considerable harm to the network's users or those who are dependent on it. Then again, the possibly wrongful harms and risks thereof which a given investigative CYBINT operation will occasion might be relatively small, to each sufferer, relative to the harms Green's members would incur if they are under attack. Suppose that Green exposes thousands of computer users or computer-dependent individuals to risks of wrongful harms. Those risks might not be significant enough to be justifiably aggregated and weighted against the aggregated risks of being exposed to an unjustified operation of cyber-espionage and/or an unjust policy. Even though (*ex hypothesi*), Green does not know how serious those risks of harms are, this alone does not prohibit it from seeking to investigate. By analogy, if I have some reason to believe that my child might be at risk of harm, and if I can ascertain whether that is so by driving to the place where I think he might be, I am justified in so doing—even though there is a chance that he might be fine and a risk that I might through no fault of my own lose control of my car and cause a pedestrian serious harm. Of course, it behoves me to maintain my car and drive carefully. These, in fact, condition my being justified to drive to where I think my child is. By analogy, Green must take the relevant precautions, failing which its investigative cyber-operation would not be justified. Subject to those precautions and under the aforementioned conditions, it might be.

8.5 Conclusion

To briefly conclude, there are no deep and morally salient differences between the human and the kinetic technology of espionage and counter-intelligence operations, with respect to the targets and collateral victims of those operations. The three often-noted challenges raised by cyber-operations—identification, attribution, and speed—are more acute than they are in 'old style' operations. But they are not so acute as to warrant prohibiting their use or to call for different normative principles.

9
Mass Surveillance

9.1 Introduction

So far in this book, I have considered the ethics of espionage and counter-intelligence operations against agents about whom there are reasons to believe—by dint of their role, the context within which they fulfil that role, and their conduct—that they might be engaged in an unjust foreign policy. In this final chapter, I address the ethics of placing large groups of people under surveillance for the purposes of ascertaining who, amongst them, is planning to take part in rights violations at the behest or on behalf of foreign actors.

That intelligence agencies have long collected information about ordinary people is not news. But as Edward Snowden explosively leaked to the world in 2013, they do so to an unprecedented extent nowadays, thanks to the Internet and the power of computers. The word 'mass' in 'mass surveillance' denotes both the sheer number of individuals—in effect, virtually all of us at any one time—on whom intelligence agencies can spy upon and the sheer amount and range of information about those individuals which they can collect and analyse.

Whether the collection of bulk data helps thwart terrorist attacks has proved one of the most contentious issues in the debate between Snowden and his critics. To the extent that mass surveillance is harmful, *if* it is ineffective, it is morally unjustified. I do not know where the truth of the matter lies. Instead, then, and for the sake of argument, I grant proponents of mass surveillance the empirical premise on which they rest their case. My aim is to investigate whether effective mass surveillance—effective, that is, at thwarting violations of fundamental rights in the context of foreign policy writ large—is morally justified.

The chapter proceeds as follows. Section 9.2 reviews contemporary mass surveillance practices as described by Edward Snowden and mounts the best possible case in their favour. Of all the objections levelled against mass surveillance, two stand out: the claim that it violates the right to privacy, and the claim that it is parasitic on and entrenches unfair inequalities. Section 9.3 argues that the privacy objection is not as decisive as it seems. Section 9.4 argues that the fairness objection, though contingent on extant practices, is very powerful. In the world as it is, I conclude, mass surveillance is morally wrong.

Two caveats. First, my aim is not to provide an account of the ethics of surveillance in general. Although some of my arguments apply to its use in other contexts, notably domestic law enforcement, not all do.

Second, I do not tackle the resort to mass surveillance as a means to conduct information warfare. There is little doubt that some of the practices I examine here, such as the mining and analysis of openly available data, are used by some governments to direct tailored fake news or political propaganda on Twitter and Facebook to susceptible users. While the ethics of information warfare is worth exploring in its own right, it is not my concern here.[1]

9.2 A Putative Defence of Mass Surveillance

Of the many surveillance programmes which the NSA and GCHQ singly and together have mounted, the following are the best-known. Under the terms of TEMPORA, GCHQ could intercept all digital traffic landing in the UK such as emails, VOIP communications, and instant messages, and store the data for up to three days and the meta-data for up to thirty days. Under the terms of PRISM, the NSA collected user data from nine major US Internet companies. Unencrypted Google and Yahoo traffic was hoovered up by both the NSA and GCHQ, while DISHFIRE gave the former access to billions of text messages a day. Under the terms of CO-TRAVELLER, the NSA would track the movements of anyone whose path would cross that of known intelligence targets. The NSA and GCHQ are not the only intelligence agencies to operate such programmes. The German Federal Intelligence Service (BND) is alleged to have collaborated with the NSA— an allegation which was particularly explosive given sensitivities in Germany about state surveillance.[2]

Not all of those programmes are or were designed to collect data in bulk. Some— for example PRISM—were used to gather data on specific targets. Nevertheless, intelligence agencies can collect our emails and text messages, the phone calls we place over the Internet, and our social media posts. They can get a detailed picture of who we are and what we do by collecting two kinds of data: data which we ourselves put out there in the public and widely accessible domain (by going out on to the streets and roads under the gaze of CCTV cameras, by posting publicly on Twitter, Instagram, and Facebook); and data which we willingly disclose on the assumption (we think) that it will be used only by its intended recipients (as when we log on to Amazon, the Inland Revenue, or our bank.) The former is open

---

[1] On private data mining and the Brexit campaign, see C. Cadwalladr, 'The Great British Brexit Robbery: How Our Democracy Was Hijacked,' *The Observer* (07/05/2017) and M. Evans, 'Exclusive: How a Tiny Canadian IT Company Helped Swing the Brexit Vote for Leave,' *The Daily Telegraph* (24/02/2017). For a hair-raising discussion of information warfare as a means to undermine democratic institutions, see Omand, *How Spies Think*, ch. 10.

[2] The documents relating to those programmes are available from the Edward Snowden's document repository at https://edwardsnowden.com (accessed on 17/08/2021). For a brief description of those programmes, on which I draw here, see D. Anderson, *A Question of Trust*, 330–3. On Snowden's story, see G. Greenwald, *No Place to Hide;* Harding, *The Snowden Files;* Gellman, *Dark Mirror.*

source intelligence (OSINT), while the latter is protected information intelligence (PROTINT). Agencies can get such data while at rest by accessing our computers, our phones, and the servers of social media and online companies, and while in transit by tapping into the fibre-optic cables along which it travels. They can access data not merely about what we do and say, but about our bodily characteristics, thanks to images collected by cameras and analysed via facial recognition software, or to the eyeprints and fingerprints we use to log on to our electronic devices (what we may perhaps call BIOINT, or biometrics intelligence).[3]

Although the existence of the aforementioned programmes was kept secret until Snowden's disclosures, there are many commercially developed and open-source softwares application which intelligence agencies have since been alleged to use to monitor entire populations. For example, the platform Hadoop enables its users to harness computer networks for the storage and processing of huge amounts of data, while the programme Geofeedia enables its users to collect all the social media posts of all the users from a particular geographical area (a neighbourhood, a city, etc.) for a given period. Although, as a quick Google search shows, the site for Geofeedia gives no information at all on the product, it is listed on various product comparison websites, and has been allegedly banned by Facebook and Twitter from accessing user accounts (though there is some opacity on the degree to which those two companies have really severed those links.)[4]

Collecting data, whether directly or by requesting that third parties share it, is one thing. Keeping it so that it may be accessed at any point in the future is another. So is processing and analysing it—at which point it becomes information. There are two main ways of doing so. One can enter a search term, for example, 'how many Toyota cars were bought in 2020'. Or one can ask a computer to correlate various bits of data with a view to drawing inferences and making

---

[3] The acronym PROTINT was coined by David Omand. (See D. Omand, 'The Future of Intelligence: What are the Threats, the Challenges and the Opportunities?', in I. Duyvesteyn et al. (eds.), *The Future of Intelligence—Challenges in the 21st century* (Routledge, 2015).) For a general overview of contemporary mass surveillance, see D. Lyon, *Surveillance after Snowden* (Polity Press, 2015). For a wonderfully lively and at times terrifying account of the degree to which private corporations collect and trade in our personal data, see C. Veliz, *Privacy is Power—Why and How You should Take Back Control of Your Data* (Bantam Press, 2020). On social media and intelligence collection, see D. Omand, J. Bartlett, and C. Miller, 'Introducing Social Media Intelligence (SOCMINT),' *Intelligence and National Security* 27 (2012): 801–23 and K. Lim, 'Big Data and Strategic Intelligence,' *Intelligence and National Security* 31 (2016): 619–35. In this chapter and unless otherwise specified, I use the phrase 'personal information' to refer to both OSINT and PROTINT. Regarding BIOINT, law enforcement agencies have long been able to store and share fingerprints and DNA profiles. But nowadays, you no longer have to have been involved, however tangentially, in a criminal investigation in order for your fingerprints to be recorded and stored: all it takes is for you to log on to your mobile phone via fingerprint recognition, which exposes your mobile phone manufacturer to a request by the government to make your fingerprint data available.

[4] See https://hadoop.apache.org (accessed on 17/08/2021); https://geofeedia.com (accessed on 17/08/2021). On intelligence agencies' use of Geofeedia and Hadoop, see D. Van Puyvelde, S. Coulthart, and M. S. Hossain, 'Beyond the Buzzword: Big Data and National Security Decision-Making,' *International Affairs* 93 (2017): 1397–416.

probabilistic predictions about its subjects. For example, one can ask about the car-buying patterns of individuals from a particular age group and income bracket. In the intelligence context, in the first case, one asks who owns the car bearing a specified number plate which was caught on CCTV cameras being driven at speed away from the scene of a terrorist attack. In the second case, one seeks to ascertain whether individuals with a given set of characteristics are likely to travel to countries known for sheltering terrorist groups. At a greater level of granularity, one can ask which individuals with those characteristics are likely to travel there based on previous travelling and consumption patterns. To make those more complex judgements, intelligence analysts rely on their systems' ability to mine and process large data sets thanks to algorithmic tools.[5]

At the time of writing, the existence of some of the programmes at the heart of Snowden's allegations, such as PRISM, has been acknowledged by US officials, not least G. W. Bush himself. The US, the UK, and Germany have since passed laws purporting to regulate the surveillance of their own citizens.[6] Perhaps Snowden has grossly exaggerated what intelligence agencies have the capacity to do and their willingness to do it. If so, what follows can be construed as an answer to the question: '*would* it be morally permissible for intelligence agencies to develop and deploy mass surveillance capacities along the aforementioned lines?' Alternatively, perhaps Snowden is right that we now live under the gaze of a computerized version of Bentham's Panopticon. If so, what follows can be construed as an answer to the question: '*is* it morally permissible for intelligence agencies so to act'?

Here is a simple answer to both questions. The earlier we can detect a threat in general, and to fundamental moral rights in particular, the better. It enhances our chances of parrying the threat; and if the threat materializes, it gives us more time to prepare for it and to minimize its impact. More strongly still, it seems that we are under a duty to try and detect threats as early as possible. We owe that

[5] For particularly clear descriptions of how data mining works, see, e.g., K. J. Strandburg, 'Monitoring, Datafication, and Consent: Legal Approaches to Privacy in the Big Data Context,' in J. Lane et al. (eds.), *Privacy, Big Data and the Public Good—Frameworks for Engagement* (Cambridge University Press, 2014); J. Millar, 'Core Privacy: A Problem for Predictive Data Mining,' in I. Kerr, V. Steeves, and C. Lucock (eds.), *Lessons from the Identity Trail: Anonymity, Privacy and Identity in a Networked Society* (Oxford University Press, 2009); W. J. Lahneman, 'IC Data Mining in the Post-Snowden Era,' *International Journal of Intelligence and CounterIntelligence* 29 (2016): 700–23; Van Puyvelde, Coulthart, and Hossain, 'Beyond the Buzzword.' For an intricate account of the way in which new data about agents emerges and coalesces into a virtual identity, see A. Henschke, *Ethics in an Age of Surveillance—Personal Information and Virtual Identities* (Cambridge University Press, 2017), esp. ch. 5.

[6] On Bush's comments about PRISM, see L. Johnson, 'George W. Bush Defends PRISM: "I Put That Program In Place To Protect The Country"', *The Huffington Post* (01/07/2013). PRISM was discontinued in 2015, but the NSA continues to collect vast amounts of data from telecommunications companies. (See C. Savage, 'N.S.A. Triples Collection of Data From U.S. Phone Companies,' *The New York Times* (04/05/2018).) On 3 September 2020, the Ninth Circuit Court of Appeal found that the bulk collection of US citizens' phone records was illegal. This followed a similar 2021 judgment by the European Court of Human Rights against GCHQ. (See, respectively, R. Satter, 'NSA Surveillance Exposed by Snowden Was Illegal, Court Rules Seven Years on,' *Reuters* (03/09/2020). H. Siddique, 'GCHQ's Mass Data Interception Violated Right to Privacy, Court Rules,' *The Guardian* (25/05/2021).

duty to putative victims, of course. But we also owe it to individuals who would normally be tasked with thwarting and/or mitigating such threats (police officers at home, soldiers abroad, paramedics attending bomb sites, etc.): it is an instantiation of our general duty of care not to expose them unnecessarily to the concomitant costs of their acts of rescue. Furthermore, and more controversially, we also owe a duty of care to some of the individuals who are causally though not (fully) morally responsible for their acts and to whom, therefore, we are under a particular duty of care. Think, for example, of vulnerable teenagers who have been radicalized and who would benefit from early intervention before they actually blow themselves and scores of people up.

Proponents of mass surveillance need not deny that much of the data which intelligence agencies collect about us is initially gathered by multinational private corporations whose ends (relentless drive for profits, shameless consumer and political manipulation, etc.) are morally questionable. In response, they stress that the fact that information was collected in the service of wrongful ends does not entail that, once available, it may not be used even to just ends; moreover, the harms accruing from private corporations' data-mining practices must be weighed against the goods brought about by mass surveillance. Unless one is prepared to give up on mass surveillance altogether, the aforementioned considerations, suitably constrained by proportionality, do weigh in the balance.

Indeed, these are considerations of precisely the kind which, as we saw in ss. 3.2 and 3.3, support the permission and duty to spy. Yet, as we also saw there, there has to be a probable cause for doing so. Given that the overwhelming majority of citizens do not give rise to such a cause, it is hard to see how one can justify mass surveillance along those lines. At this juncture, however, proponents of mass surveillance will very likely argue that the probable cause requirement is too strong. It is all very well to say that intelligence agencies must have evidence-based reasons for believing that someone is engaged in the planning and commission of serious wrongdoing in order justifiably to place him under surveillance. But more often than not, they simply do not have the evidence they need, just because many of the threats which we face originate with groups whose membership is fluid and spans international borders. While intelligence agencies may not know yet who those groups and their members are, they have ample and well-grounded evidence for believing that some group, somewhere, is planning an attack on civilian targets. For all they know, that group, whichever and wherever it is, is planning its operation from abroad, yet they have no human sources *in situ* and no information that would enable them to identify targets for the kind of TECHINT operations I described in Chapter 8. Or the group is relying on homegrown agents, yet no concerned parent has alerted the authorities to the growing radicalization of their son or daughter.

In s. 3.4, I argued that if one does not have grounds for believing that a party has embarked on or is planning to conduct an unjust policy, one must act on the assumption that they are not liable to being spied upon. As I also noted, however, this does not imply that one ought to do nothing at all to gather relevant intelligence. In particular, one may procure openly available sources of information such as eyewitness reports and satellite images of troop movements. By parity of reasoning (the proponents of mass surveillance are likely to argue), intelligence agencies may at the very least procure relevantly similar sources of information about civilian populations in general, such as images available in the public domain and collected via CCTV camera, and social media posts. Once filtered and properly analysed, such information can tell us whether there *is* probable cause to investigate further. If there is, more data, for example in the form of emails, geospatial location, and purchasing history, must already be available for further analysis. This provides some justification for the collection and retention of PROTINT, which one did not intend to be visible and audible to all and sundry. But only when the analysis of open sources has given intelligence agencies probable cause may they justifiably retrieve already-collected non-open information about specific individuals for analysis.

Such is the case for mass surveillance which one can extract from public discourse, intelligence agencies, and government officials.[7] In the next two sections, I evaluate the main two objections which are levelled against it: the objection from privacy, and the objection from fairness.

9.3 The Privacy Objection

9.3.1 Defining Privacy

Privacy has resisted consensual definitions. On so-called reductionist views such as endorsed by Judith Jarvis Thomson's, violations of what we call the right to privacy are nothing more than violations of other rights. If I rummage through your rucksack to find out what you routinely carry around, I violate your property right over your rucksack. If I listen to your phone conversations, I violate your right not to be listened to, which is itself derivative of your right over your person. One need not appeal to the notion of privacy and of a right thereof to account for the wrongdoing I commit against you.[8]

---

[7] For some case studies, in which intelligence agencies such as GCHQ foiled terrorist plots thanks to bulk data collection, see Anderson, *A Question of Trust*, 336–7. The defence of mass surveillance which I present here is one which David Omand would endorse. See Omand and Phythian, *Principled Spying*, ch. 5. See also Skerker, 'The Rights of Foreign Intelligence Targets,' though Skerker's argument is less permissive of intelligence agencies than Omand's. In particular, while Omand grants those agencies latitude with respect to what they can do to foreigners which he denies them at home, Skerker is equally restrictive (on which point I agree with him.)

[8] J. J. Thomson, 'The Right to Privacy,' *Philosophy & Public Affairs* 4 (1975): 295–314.

If Thomson's reductionist thesis is true, it spares us from the philosophical labour of establishing what privacy actually consists in. When intelligence agencies commit what we are tempted to call privacy violations, all we need to do in order to ascertain whether they acted wrongly is to identify which rights over things and persons, if any, they have violated.

Unfortunately, we cannot have it so easy. *Pace* reductionism, the claim that the wrong done by privacy invasions can be explained by rights other than the right to privacy is compatible with the claim that there is a right to privacy from which those other rights derive. As T. M. Scanlon puts it, the rights which Thomson has in mind protect an interest in 'having a zone of privacy in which we can carry out our activities without the necessity of being continually alert for possible observers, listeners, etc.'[9] Privacy and the right thereto provide support for the view that (e.g.) I have a right against you that you not open my safe to look at its content without my permission. The latter right, far from making the right to privacy redundant, in fact derives from it.

I am sympathetic to anti-reductionism about privacy. The challenge consists in providing an account of what privacy is, and thus of what harm is done to agents when it is invaded. On what one may call essentialist approaches, there is a set of invariant singly necessary and jointly sufficient conditions under which agents can be deemed to enjoy privacy. There are two notable exceptions to essentialism: Daniel Solove's family resemblance approach, and Helen Nissenbaum's contextualist approach.

Solove argues that extant conceptions of privacy are either too broad (in that they consider as private that which in fact is not), or too narrow (in that they exclude from the scope of what is private that which in fact is.) Instead, we should adopt both Wittgenstein's notion of family resemblance and John Dewey's pragmatic approach to philosophical inquiry, and look for privacy in certain context-specific practices and situations. We are in the presence of privacy (as it were) when we have identified ways of disrupting those practices which resemble each other. For example, the practice of preserving one's anonymity as an author is disrupted when one's identity is disclosed without one's consent; the practice of having sex in the seclusion of one's home is disrupted by surveillance. Those two practices are sufficiently similar that we can in both cases say that they belong to the family of private practices.[10]

The weakness of this approach is that we cannot know what belongs or not to the family (and thus which practices and which kinds of disruption to rule in or out) unless we already know what privacy is, which is precisely what we are trying

---

[9] T. Scanlon, 'Thomson on Privacy,' *Philosophy & Public Affairs* 4 (1975): 315–22, 317. See also J. H. Reiman, 'Privacy, Intimacy, and Personhood,' *Philosophy & Public Affairs* 6 (1976): 26–44.

[10] D. J. Solove, 'Privacy and Power: Computer Databases and Metaphors for Information Privacy,' *Stanford Law Review* 53 (2001): 1393–462; D. J. Solove, *Understanding Privacy* (Harvard University Press, 2008).

to establish. Unpromising as the essentialist quest for a definition of privacy might be, at least it has the merit of not being structurally question-begging.[11]

Another important non-essentialist approach has been developed by Helen Nissenbaum, whose work on the impact of new technologies on privacy is one of the most influential and sophisticated to date. Nissenbaum is sympathetic to Solove's appeal to context. In her view, we cannot make much progress when evaluating whether an act or practice violates privacy if we try to define the latter in the abstract. Rather, we must be sensitive to the fact that we collect personal information from, and share it with, a huge variety of actors in a broad range of contexts such as personal relationships, when we are at work, when we shop online, or when we interact with government agencies. Unlike Solove, however, Nissenbaum eschews the notion of family resemblance and instead draws attention to the different norms which shape our informational practices. For example, the norms which regulate the collection and dissemination of information between doctors and patients differ from those which govern informational relationships between police officers and suspects, or between parents and children. Informational norms are rooted in and can be assessed at the bar of the deeper goals and values which we cherish. In her own words, 'a practice under investigation is judged a violation of contextual integrity if it runs afoul of context-relative informational norms, which are specified in terms of contexts, actors, attributes and transmission principles.'[12] Given that violating contextual integrity is *prima facie* wrong, a diagnosis to the effect that a practice violates contextual integrity has both descriptive and normative valence.

As Nissenbaum concedes, the main challenge to her account lies in the tension between its innate convervatism and the fact that today's contextual norms are yesterday's unacceptable privacy violations. Either we foreclose the possibility that a practice which violates established norms might nevertheless be morally justified, which seems an unacceptable concession to 'the tyranny of the normal', or we accept that possibility, in which case the judgement that a practice violates contextual integrity carries no normative weight. The path lies somewhere in between, Nissenbaum tells us. To ascertain whether a practice is morally justified, we must decide whether (to paraphrase her), it supports, achieves, or promotes 'relevant contextual values'.[13]

The difficulty, of course, is that those values themselves change, and that appealing to context will therefore not help us judge whether they are morally

[11] For a good critique of Solove's approach, see C. Veliz, *The Ethics of Privacy* (Oxford University Press, forthcoming).
[12] H. Nissenbaum, *Privacy in Context—Technology, Policy and the Integrity of Social Life* (Stanford University Press, 2010), 181 and, more generally, ch. 7.
[13] Nissenbaum, ib. 164 and ch. 8 generally. See also L. Austin, 'Privacy and the Question of Technology,' *Law and Philosophy* 22 (2003): 119–66 for a good discussion of the problem, based on Nissenbaum's earlier work.

justified. Nissenbaum acknowledges the difficulty and pins her colours to the mast of Michael Walzer's theory of social meanings. That theory, and the principles of distributive justice which it underpins, are too much at odds with the meta-ethical foundations of this book to be of use here. That said, the fact that our informational practices are shaped by contextual norms is beyond doubt. The claim that a careful normative assessment of those practices must be sensitive to the context in which they occur is also plausible. We can accept both, however, yet endorse an essentialist approach to privacy.

Essentialist approaches to privacy broadly divide as follows: privacy as being left alone; privacy as control over how one appears to others or over information about oneself; privacy as the extent to which others have unwanted access to us or to information about us; privacy as absence of interference with important decisions about our life or, more widely, with what constitutes us as persons; privacy as a state of affairs in which others do not have undocumented knowledge about us.[14]

None of those approaches are satisfactory. Many of Solove's and Nissenbaum's criticisms are well-taken, as are many of the criticisms which proponents of essentialist approaches level against one another. Nevertheless, they are on the right track, methodologically speaking. Given that my concern is with the collection and dissemination of information, I restrict myself to informational privacy—as distinct from decisional privacy as the ability to make important decisions about one's life. With that in mind, I suggest the following: X enjoys informational privacy *vis-à-vis* some third party Y at time *t just if* Y either does not have access to information about X at *t*, or has access to it but does not avail herself of it at *t*. Such information includes information that is sensitive, intimate, and personal, typically about her health, her sexual life, her most personal relationships, her moral and political commitments, and her daily movements, hobbies, shopping habits, and occasional encounters. Suppose that X sends Y a letter in which she discloses information of that kind about herself. Y never opens that letter. He has access to the information (all he needs to do is open the letter), but still, so long as he does not read it, X enjoys informational privacy in respect of it and *vis-à-vis* him.[15]

Four features of this account matter in the present context. First, privacy is closely related to, but nevertheless different from, secrecy. Unlike secrecy, privacy need not be informational: it can be sensorial or spatial. Moreover, while any piece of information, no matter how trivial, can be kept and treated as a secret,

---

[14] See, in the order in which those views are listed: S. D. Warren and L. D. Brandeis, 'The Right to Privacy', *Harvard Law Review* 4 (1890): 193–220; A. Marmor, 'What Is the Right to Privacy?', *Philosophy & Public Affairs* 43 (2015): 3–26, J. Rachels, 'Why Privacy is Important', *Philosophy & Public Affairs* 4 (1975): 323–33, A. Westin, *Privacy and Freedom* (Atheneum, 1967), and Bok, *Secrets*, 10-4; R. Gavison, 'Privacy and the Limits of Law', *The Yale Law Journal* 89 (1980): 421–71 and Veliz, *The Ethics of Privacy*; Reiman, 'Privacy, Intimacy, and Personhood'; W. A. Parent, 'A New Definition of Privacy for the Law', *Law and Philosophy* 2 (1983): 305–38.

[15] Here, I follow Carissa Veliz's account of privacy.

only some kinds of information (as outlined earlier) are candidates for privacy. Second, we can enjoy informational privacy while in public places and lose it while in the confines of our home. Third, we do not lose privacy if the information that is accessed fundamentally mischaracterizes us—whether we disclose the information ourselves or whether it is collected and shared, without our consent, by someone else.[16] Suppose that Blogg, who has been unemployed for a while, tells Smith that he is a high-flier in a well-known international corporation. He asks Smith not to disclose that information to their neighbour. Smith cannot resist the allure of a good gossip and promptly tells the neighbour. Although he has breached Blogg's trust, he has not impaired his privacy. Nor would he have done so if he had spied on Blogg and formed the same mistaken belief. I say 'fundamentally': if Blogg, who works for Google, tells Smith that he works for Apple, I would be inclined to say that Smith does impair his privacy, albeit in a relatively minor way. In this case, the information is fairly trivial, as it relates only to which specific firm Blogg works for in a given sector. In the first case, by contrast, the information pertains to whether Blogg has a job at all or not, and thus to a central component of Blogg's life: it is in that sense that it fundamentally mischaracterizes him. Finally, whether we have control over the acquisition and disclosure of the relevant information is irrelevant to our enjoying privacy. I may be desperate to bare it all, and to all and sundry, but if I am unable to do so as a result of not having access to social media, or if I bare it all on social media but no one else has access to that particular medium, I still enjoy privacy in respect of that information. Conversely, I lose privacy just if I bare it all and if people read the posts.

9.3.2 The Objection

Mass surveillance, it is objected, is a violation of the right to privacy. To say that X has such a right against Y is to say (on the aforementioned account of privacy) that X's interest in the relevant information remaining inaccessible or unaccessed is important enough to hold Y under a duty not to try and access it or, if the information is accessible to Y, not to avail himself of it, without X's consent.

So construed, the right to privacy does not seem to do justice to privacy worries about mass surveillance. For the worry is not just that third parties have access to information about us: the worry is that they (in this context, state officials) are able at any time to access that information without our consent, indeed without

---

[16] The view I moot here is controversial. On this view, someone who *always* forms profoundly mischaracterizing beliefs about others on the basis of information which he has procured and mistakenly believes to be true does not cause them to lose privacy. My take is that he attempts to invade their privacy, but fails. (I thank C. Veliz, who strongly disagrees with me on this point, for the example.)

our knowledge. Put differently, the worry is that, although the information may remain unaccessed by dint of the fact that officials do not go and look for it, it remains *accessible*. In the language of Philip Pettit's conception of freedom as non-domination, we may well enjoy privacy yet be dominated in respect of it. Privacy is valuable, for reasons I sketch below, but so is control over whether or not we will retain or lose it. Suppose that X's daughter sends Y a letter in which she discloses personal information about X without X's consent. X has an interest in deciding whether or not Y should open that letter, which is important enough to hold third parties under a duty not to act against his wishes. On a Pettitean construal of the right to privacy, thus, it is a right that the relevant information should remain unaccessed or 'unprocessed' unless we decide otherwise—for short, that it should be inaccessible to third parties.[17]

The value of privacy—the reason why it is deemed important enough to be protected by a right—is standardly held to reside in its contribution to individual and collective goods. If we know that we are observed, we are likely to find it harder to frame, revise, and pursue a conception of the good with which we identify without fear of the unsolicited and judgemental gaze of others. We are also likely to find it harder to sustain familial and social relationships with spontaneity and integrity. To be afforded the privacy we demand, moreover, is to be treated with respect, as ends in ourselves rather than as instruments for the satisfaction of third parties' appetite for information. This is precisely the kind of consideration which motivates the thought (which we encountered in s. 8.3.1) that covert surveillance of which the target is not and never will be aware can be wrongful.

The value of privacy also resides in its contribution to the collective goods of national security and democratic agency. Regarding the former, some of the information we disclose, wittingly or not, might be relevant to it, as when military personnel upload their running routes on applications such as Strava, thereby disclosing the supposedly secret location of military bases.[18] Regarding the latter,

---

[17] See Pettit, *Republicanism*. For a sophisticated application of Pettit's framework to privacy, see Veliz, *The Ethics of Privacy*. Two points. First, applying Pettit's language to privacy does not commit me to endorsing his republican conception of freedom. Second, the consent proviso does not reintroduce through the back door the view that control is central to privacy itself. Analogously, I enjoy good physical health just if my body functions as it should, whether or not I have any control over the fact that it does. To say that I have *a right to good health* is to say that other parties are under a duty not to act in such a way as to make me ill or a duty to give me what I need so that I overcome my illness, unless I consent to being made ill or to waive medical treatment. Whether I have a right to good health is a separate question from the question of whether I am in good health.

Incidentally, my account of privacy and the right thereto differs from K. Macnish's. While we both agree that control (as distinct from access) is not necessary for privacy, he seems to think that it follows that it is not necessary for the right thereto either. This leads him to reject mass surveillance not on the grounds that it violates privacy but on the grounds that it violates other interests such as, precisely, one's interest in controlling access to the information. I argue that it violates the right to privacy itself. See K. Macnish, 'Government Surveillance and Why Defining Privacy Matters in a Post-Snowden World,' *Journal of Applied Philosophy* 35 (2018): 417–32.

[18] Veliz, *Privacy Is Power*, 86.

in s. 2.4, I argued that members of a political community have a right that information the unauthorized appropriation or disclosure of which would threaten (*inter alia*) the collective good of political agency be treated as a political secret. By implication, they also have a right that information about themselves be so regarded in so far as, once obtained and analysed, it can be used to undermine their political agency—for example, by making them vulnerable to threats of being harmed on account of their political views, or by making them the targets of relentless and blinkering political propaganda.[19]

Of the millions of individuals who are placed under surveillance, the overwhelming majority are not planning to commit violations of fundamental rights. Consequently, they retain their rights to the freedoms and resources they need in order to be autonomous and to exercise their democratic agency and, more deeply, a right to be treated with respect. By implication, they retain their right to privacy. This is why tailing and eavesdropping on people is presumptively wrongful. Pending argument to the contrary, then, mass surveillance violates their right.

9.3.3 Unintended Effects and Intentional Disclosure

In this section, I reject two arguments against the privacy objection.

The Argument from Unintended Effects
The first argument against the privacy objection appeals to the distinction between intended and unintended harmful effects. True, the argument concedes, millions of individuals who are not complicit in or are not aware of plans to attack us or third parties lose some degree of privacy through mass surveillance. However, the harm they thereby incur is an unintended, albeit foreseen, effect of bulk data collection and interception. Just as it is sometimes morally permissible to kill innocent civilians as a foreseen though unintended side effect of bombing a munitions factory, it is sometimes morally permissible to subject innocent

---

[19] On the views mooted in this paragraph, privacy is instrumentally valuable to political agency. On other views, it has intrinsic political value, as constitutive of democratic equality, as a requirement of public justification, or as constitutive of the political condition of republican freedom. See, respectively, A. Lever, 'Privacy and Democracy: What the Secret Ballot Reveals,' *Law, Culture and the Humanities* 11 (2015): 164–83; D. Mokrosinska, 'Privacy and Autonomy: On Some Misconceptions Concerning the Political Dimensions of Privacy,' *Law and Philosophy* 37 (2018): 117–43; A. Roberts, 'A Republican Account of the Value of Privacy,' *European Journal of Political Theory* 14 (2015): 320–44. I find the instrumental view more compelling, but my arguments at the end of this section about the wrongfulness of mass surveillance in relation to privacy do not hinge on rejecting the view that privacy has intrinsic value. For an extensive discussion of the deleterious effects of data mining on democracy, see Veliz, *Privacy Is Power*, esp. 87–92.

civilians to the aforementioned harms as a side effect of surveilling those who are liable to surveillance.[20]

The argument does not succeed. In fact, it is a good example of how *not* to apply just war theory to the context of espionage.[21] To see this, contrast mass surveillance with *Infiltration₆*, which we first encountered in s. 5.3.2:

> *Infiltration₆* Green's services have identified a high-level Blue commander who, they have good reasons to believe, is preparing an attack on Green's soil. They encourage Asset to insert himself in the commander's live-in entourage, including his innocent family members, with a view to spying on him, thereby also gathering information about his family.

There I argued that Asset is justified in deceiving the commander's relatives as a foreseen but unintended side effect of his just mission. The argument from unintended effects holds that the situation of the civilians in mass surveillance is relevantly analogous to that of the commander's relatives: they are all innocent, and if it were possible, intelligence agencies in the former case and Asset in the latter case would avoid harming them if they could. Those two specific points are correct. However, there is a salient difference between the two cases. In *Infiltration₆*, there are good reasons to believe that one agent—the commander—is engaged in the commission of wrongdoings while the others are not: Asset is not acquiring information about his relatives as a means to elicit information about his designs. (At any rate, we can construct the case in this way, by stipulating that the commander does not share any of his designs with his family). In the case of mass surveillance, by contrast, Green's intelligence agencies do not know who is engaged in the commission of wrongdoing, and the only way to get that piece of information is to subject everyone to surveillance. It is simply not the case that the privacy loss and concomitant harms incurred by innocent civilians are merely a foreseen but unintended side effect of mass surveillance. On the contrary, they are deliberately imposed: that, in fact, is *the whole point*.[22]

---

[20] See, e.g., Macnish, *The Ethics of Surveillance*, 64 and 95. Macnish merely moots the argument. Though he expresses some doubts, those are rooted in worries about proportionality—whereas I deny that the doctrine of double effects applies to this case at all.

[21] See also Miller, 'Rethinking the Just Intelligence Theory of National Security Intelligence Collection and Analysis', 218.

[22] K. V. Rønn and K. Lippert-Rasmussen, 'Out of Proportion? On Surveillance and the Proportionality Requirement', *Ethical Theory and Moral Practice* 23 (2020): 181–99. Note: my claim applies to *mass* surveillance and to cases in which Green's intelligence agencies have reasons to believe that a particular individual is posing a threat and decide to place every single one of his acquaintances, relatives, friends, etc., under surveillance. The argument from unintended effects applies to targeted surveillance practices in which Green's intelligence agency place a suspect under surveillance and unavoidably, at the same time, gather information about his acquaintances.

The argument from intentional disclosure

The second argument goes like this. Granted—it concedes—the deliberate collection, dissemination, and aggregation of personal information which individuals who are not engaged in the commission of rights violations clearly do not wish to make available to all and sundry is a violation of their right to privacy. But individuals who make information about themselves public, for example by posting on Facebook, have in effect consented to its appropriation by third parties, and thus have no privacy complaint.[23]

This is too quick. The fact that I intentionally disclose a piece of personal information *p* does not release third parties from all and any of their privacy-related duties towards me.[24] Suppose I tell you that I am planning to travel to Greece. Furnished with that piece of information, together with other bits of information you have gathered from our conversations over the last few months, you could, if you thought long and hard about it, work out that I am planning to take part in banned humanitarian rescue operations in the Mediterranean. At the same time, you also have good reason to believe that I would not want you to know this, let alone disclose it to others. You are under a privacy-related duty not to aggregate all that I have disclosed and not to exercise your analytical and deductive powers to draw inferences about what I might get up to; you are also under a duty not to disseminate those inferences to third parties.

Suppose now that I send you an email about my travelling plans, intending that you should read it. I know that your partner will also receive it as you share your account with her. The fact that I foresee that your partner will receive the email and that she is aware of that does not license her to infer that she may read it. Analogously, consider Thomson's well-known example of the couple who have a blazing row at home and who can be heard from the street.[25] Suppose (unlike in the original example) that they are aware that the window is open but cannot be bothered to close it. It seems to me that we remain under a duty not to make a point of deliberately listening to them—and, indeed, would also be under a duty not to do so if they were arguing on the street. If this is correct, then *a fortiori*, my foreseeing that *p* will be made available for collection and dissemination as a result of my act of disclosure does not release third parties from duties not to

---

[23] See, e.g., David Omand's argument in Omand and Phythian, *Principled Spying*, ch. 5. There is a related version of that argument, which does not apply to mass surveillance but, rather, to the practice of bugging the cars, houses, and offices of diplomats who are suspected of being spies. 'If you choose to play that game', the argument goes, 'you must accept that you will be bugged, so whatever you say to your husband, friends, colleagues, is fair game'. As I reject the construal of espionage as a game whose rules are understood and accepted by its players (ss. 1.3.2 and 8.3.2), so I reject that argument.

[24] See in particular B. Rumbold and J. Wilson, 'Privacy Rights and Public Information,' *Journal of Political Philosophy* 27 (2019): 3–25; H. Nissenbaum, 'Protecting Privacy in an Information Age: The Problem of Privacy in Public,' *Law and Philosophy* 17 (1998): 559–96. The example which follows in the main text is mine.

[25] See Thomson, 'The Right to Privacy,' 296.

collect, disseminate, and aggregate. The point is particularly strong in those cases in which I do not have a choice as to whether to disclose, or in which, though I do have a choice, I have a positive justification for disclosing. Suppose that I have a positive justification for disclosing to you, my best friend, that I am off to Greece, as you need to know of my whereabouts should something happen, in my absence, to my Alzheimer-ridden mother. If you have good reason to assume that I would not want you to know *why* I am off to Greece, you are still under a privacy-related duty to me not to make the requisite deductive and analytical efforts even if you also know that I foresee that you are able to piece the truth together. By parity of reasoning, it does not follow from the fact that I am willing to disclose some of my shopping and travelling habits that I am willing to have intelligence agencies aggregate those bits of information with a view to forming a complete profile of me. This does not establish that they may not justifiably do so. But it does show that appealing to the fact of intentional disclosure does not protect mass surveillance from the privacy objection.

In individual, one-to-one cases such as these, the thesis I am defending here might seem overly demanding: for it seemingly implies that we are under a moral duty never to draw inferences about others on the basis of information they have willingly disclosed.[26] Now, I agree that it would be too demanding to expect of ourselves that we exercise sufficient control over our cognitive activities as to have no unbidden thoughts of that kind, or as to not notice, interpret, and remember patterns of behaviour. However, it is not too demanding to expect of ourselves not to *apply ourselves* to the task of working out what others get up to. In any case, the aforementioned thesis no longer seems so demanding when applied to the collection of big data by large organizations—and so, in this context, by intelligence agencies in collaboration with large private corporations—with the ability to infer detailed information about us on the basis of OSINT: all it takes is for them not to set up the relevant programmes, period.

If it is to succeed as a move to reject the privacy objection to mass surveillance, the argument from intentional disclosure must show that by intentionally disclosing information about themselves to all and sundry, individuals have waived their right that third parties not appropriate, disseminate, and aggregate it. I have argued that, *if* one accepts in the first instance that there is such a right, the argument fails.

9.3.4 Privacy and the Duty to Protect

Let us take stock. At the close of s. 9.3.2, I averred that the millions of agents whose personal information is collected, shared, and analysed by intelligence agencies

---

[26] Rumbold and Wilson, 'Privacy Rights and Public Information.'

are not engaged in the commission of rights violations, and thus are not liable to the invasion of their privacy by means of mass surveillance. Pending argument to the contrary, I said, mass surveillance violates their right. Two such arguments, the argument from unintended effects and the argument from intentional disclosure, have been found wanting. As things stand, the privacy objection remains on the table. In the remainder of this section, I argue that it is partly vulnerable to a third argument—to wit, the argument from duty.

Mass surveillance is meant to address the problem of deep uncertainty, namely that although there are strong reasons to believe that some third parties are at risk of serious rights violations, there is often no way of ascertaining when, where, and by whom, other than (it is claimed) by collecting and mining bulk data about all of us. Now, in s. 1.4.2, I argued that contribution to rights violations is not the only basis for losing one's presumptive right not to be harmed. It is also sometimes permissible deliberately to harm someone as a way for an actor to enforce his duty to protect third parties from wrongful harm—subject, of course, to considerations of necessity, effectiveness, and proportionality. (Hence my claim, in s. 8.4.1, that is is sometimes permissible to press computer users into service via botnets.) Even if we incur a privacy-related harm when our personal information is collected and mined in ways which we did not intend, it is a harm which we are sometimes under a duty to incur for the sake of protecting putative victims.

I shall qualify this claim presently. Note, first, that there are two ways of construing the duty. Suppose that Green (our government) is collecting and mining personal information about all of us in order to forestall the violation of *our* fundamental rights. Our duty to incur the aforementioned privacy-related harms can be construed as a duty to do our share for the sake of collective security. Alternatively, suppose that Blue is collecting and mining information on us (members of Green), on the grounds that it justifiably believes that the wrongful attack to which its citizens shall be subject is likely to originate from some group amongst us. Our duty can be construed as an instantiation of our general duty to protect those in need.

It might be objected that the bulk collection and mining of personal information is a disproportionate response. Dozens of millions of individuals incur a privacy-related loss, yet the number of people who die at the hands of terrorists (terrorism being the ostensible main justification for mass surveillance) has stood at roughly 21,000 world-wide per year on average.[27]

---

[27] I rely on figures supplied by the Oxford Martin School in collaboration with the charity Global Change Data Lab. (See https://ourworldindata.org/terrorism (accessed on 17/08/2021). The National Consortium for the Study of Terrorism and Responses to Terrorism has interesting data on terrorism-related deaths. For example, between 1995 and 2016, US fatalities worldwide stand at 3,658 (see https://www.start.umd.edu/ (accessed on 17/08/2021). For accounts of the principle of proportionality in the context of mass surveillance, see Macnish, 'Government Surveillance and Why Defining Privacy Matters in a Post-Snowden World'; Rønn and Lippert-Rasmussen, 'Out of Proportion?'

Whether we may harm the former for the sake of the latter depends on whether we may aggregate the lesser harms incurred by the very many and deem them to outweigh the more serious harms incurred by the few. On strict anti-aggregation views, we may not do so, however great the number of those who incur the lesser harm. On strict pro-aggregation views, we must do so, however grievous the harm incurred by the few and minor the harms incurred by the many. Neither view seems plausible.[28] A more plausible view holds that aggregation is sometimes permissible, depending on the relative size of each group, the magnitude of the harms incurred by each, and the seriousness of those harms relative to each other. The latter consideration is particularly important. Even if it is permissible to spare millions from a mild cold at the cost of allowing a few to suffer a medium cold, it is not permissible to do so at the cost of even only a few people dying. On this more plausible view (proponents of the objection might insist), the privacy harms incurred by individuals subject to mass surveillance surely are serious enough that, when they are incurred by millions, they can be deemed to outweigh the admittedly more serious harms (to life and limb) incurred by the far fewer victims of terrorist attacks.

If the limited-aggregation objection succeeds, the duty argument fails and (once again) mass surveillance falls foul of the privacy objection. Now, as it is standardly construed, the limited aggregation objection pits two wholly different groups of individuals against each other. However, in some cases, mass surveillance is targeted at a large group of individuals, all of whom are at risk of an attack, but only some of whom will actually be subject to it. In such cases, the limited-aggregation objection holds that the lesser privacy-related harms incurred by all of us outweigh the more serious harm to life and limb incurred by a subset of all of us, albeit a subset which for all we know may include any one of us.

Setting that complication aside, I agree that limited aggregation is permissible under the aforementioned conditions. I also agree that mass surveillance is vulnerable to the privacy objection combined with the limited aggregation objection. However, as I now suggest, this is so *only in some respects*. Suppose that Green's intelligence agencies collect and mine the publicly available personal information of all of their citizens, with a view to forestalling the operations of transnational terrorist networks on Green's territory. At time t_1, their computers hoover up accessible-to-all social media posts, CCTV camera images, Google Earth sight-

---

[28] For scepticism about both strict anti- and pro-aggregation views in general and for attempts to develop constraints on permissible aggregation, see, e.g., V. Tadros, 'Localized Restricted Aggregation,' in D. Sobel, P. Vallentyne, and S. Wall (eds.), *Oxford Studies in Political Philosophy—vol. 5* (2019); A. Voorhoeve, 'How Should We Aggregate Competing Claims?', *Ethics* 125 (2014): 64–87. For another defence of the Duty View, see Skerker, 'The Rights of Foreign Intelligence Targets'. There are two differences between Skerker's approach and mine. He embraces the Rawlsian contractarian approach to espionage which I rejected in s. 1.3.2; and he does not address the problem of aggregation. We both agree, however, that the duty to protect individuals from rights violations is owed irrespective of borders and can take the form of being subject to some degree of privacy invasion.

ings, and freely available publications (aka OSINT). Their softwares application look for certain word patterns and triangulate their findings appropriately. When those findings generate the same suspicion as would give probable cause to trigger a more invasive investigation if obtained other than by bulk collection, the system sends a warning about the subject—call him Blogg—to their human analysts. At t_2, the analysts consider the findings and decide whether or not to mount a more invasive investigation by looking into information which Blogg disclosed only to some people or companies on the assumption that it would not be accessed by anyone other than its intended recipients (aka PROTINT).

The privacy objection holds that Green's intelligence agencies are violating Blogg's right to privacy. This is true only if Blogg incurs a privacy loss. The first question, then, is whether Blogg loses privacy between t_1 and t_2. Now, when we think of privacy being lost, we tend to assume that we lose it *vis-à-vis* another human being, that is to say, an agent who is capable not only of purposefully watching and listening but of forming moral judgements in respect of the information thereby provided. This strikes me as correct. Suppose that a modern-day Robinson finds himself on an island which was vacated thirty years ago because of global warming and on which there still are functioning albeit long-forgotten CCTV cameras. No one, anywhere in the world, is or ever will be aware of the existence of the cameras, and what they record about Robinson will therefore never be seen by anyone. Robinson would not have enjoyed more privacy if he had shipwrecked himself on a CCTV-free island. One cannot lose privacy *vis-à-vis* a machine, any more than one can lose it *vis-à-vis* one's watchful dog.[29]

This implies that if a government were to set up a surveillance programme entirely based on computerized processes at time t_1, with no involvement on the part of any moral and rational agent from that point onwards, we would not be able to deem its decision wrongful by appealing to the fact that it would result in mass privacy loss. To be sure, we might deem it wrongful by appealing, *inter alia*, to the value of individuals' relationship to state authorities being mediated by moral and rational agents. Moreover, if the government takes this decision without our consent or that of our democratically elected representatives, we might deem it wrongful on democratic grounds. But these concerns, serious though they are, are not privacy-related.

If so, up to the point at which the warning has been sent, Blogg has not lost his privacy *vis-à-vis* Green's intelligence agencies, since he has not been read about, looked at, and listened to by an intelligence (human) agent. In more general terms, the computerized bulk collection and mining of OSINT does not *in itself* fall foul of the privacy-cum-limited-aggregation argument. If, as is routinely said, human

[29] See also Skerker, 'Moral Concerns with Cyberespionage,' 262; Veliz, *The Ethics of Privacy*.

intelligence analysts consider only a tiny fraction of the data which they collect, this is not a trivial finding.[30]

The next question, then, is whether the mere fact of a human agent looking at the data and the use of more invasive practices such as the mining of PROTINT undermine Blogg's privacy. On the first count, if the data compiled by Green's computers about Blogg on the basis of his freely available personal information fundamentally mischaracterizes him, the fact that a human agent is processing it and drawing further inferences from it does not, in itself, cause Blogg to lose privacy: as we saw in s. 9.3.1, one can lose one's informational privacy only in respect of information which is not fundamentally mischaracterizing. On the second count, so long as the collection and mining of PROTINT is done solely by computers without human involvement, Blogg does not suffer a privacy loss either and his right to privacy, therefore, is not violated.

Thus, Blogg suffers a privacy loss as a result of mass surveillance only if a human agent avails herself of bits of information about him which do not fundamentally mischaracterize him. Suppose now that Green's analyst procures some of Blogg's PROTINT or that she directs a computer to mine and analyse his OSINT and then deploys her analytical and deductive powers in such as way as to form an accurate profile of Blogg which he would not want her to access. Blogg does not have control over whether or she acts in those ways. The question is whether she violates his right to privacy. Well, not necessarily. For as per the duty view constrained by the limited-aggregation view, whether Blogg suffers a *wrongful* privacy loss depends on the magnitude of the harm he incurs, the magnitude of the harm which placing him under surveillance forestalls, and the magnitude of both harms relative to each other.

One final worry about the duty view. Outside the United States, the most controversial of Snowden's revelations pertained to the United States' mass surveillance of non-US citizens, notably the populations of their putative allies such the United Kingdom and Germany: it is one thing (the worry goes) for a government to spy on its own citizens, it is quite another for it to spy on foreigners in general, and on those with whom it has formed an alliance in particular. Even if the former is morally justified, the latter is not.

In reply: I am not persuaded. Consider first the claim that a government may not spy on foreign populations with whom it does not have an alliance. That claim might be grounded (in its proponents' minds) in the thought that the reach of a government does not legitimately extend beyond its borders. If so, this is mistaken: a government may justifiably prosecute a foreigner for a crime committed against one of its nationals even if the crime was committed on the territory of another state; it may also impose economic sanctions on foreign companies as a means

---

[30] See, e.g., Lim, 'Big Data and Strategic Intelligence,' 632; N. Couch and B. Robins, *Big Data for Defence and Security* (Royal United Services Institute, 2013).

to thwart rights violations. I cannot provide a full defence of the justifiability of extraterritorial harm imposition here, but the underlying principle is this. As I averred in s. 1.4.1, all individuals, wherever they reside in the world, owe it to another to secure for another the freedoms and resources necessary for a flourishing life. On this view, members of Yellow are under *pro tanto* duties to help members of Green thwart threats to their fundamental rights, and Green's government has a *pro tanto* justification for enforcing their duty if their own government will not do it.[31]

That being said, it does not follow that Green's government must distribute those protective costs evenly between its citizens and Yellow's members. In particular, other things being equal, the fact that (*ex hypothesi*) Green is under threat implies that its citizens are under a greater obligation to take on the burden of thwarting the threat than, e.g., Yellow's citizens. Put in general terms, *ex ante* and other things being equal, beneficiaries of a particular course of action are under a duty to shoulder more of its costs than third parties. With that general point in hand, what matters is not, per se, the fact that Green's citizens stand in a particular political relationship *vis-à-vis* one another from which Yellow's citizens are excluded: what matters is the fact that they jointly are under threat. If Blue is planning a wrongful attack on both Green and Yellow, both citizenries are under duties to one another to help thwart it, irrespective of the presence or absence of a political relationship.

Consider next the claim that a government may not resort to the mass surveillance of a foreign population with whom it has an alliance. As we saw in s. 3.5, the mere fact of an alliance does not in itself warrant the claim that spying on one's allies is never justified. Moreover, some alliances are defensive alliances and thus impose on their members duties of assistance to one another which they would not have otherwise. In sum, the duty view applies across borders.

9.4 The Fairness Objection

On the duty view, some aspects of mass surveillance practices do not fall foul of the privacy objection, while others do. Another objection to mass surveillance holds that the algorithmic processes on which it relies are parasitic on existing unfair inequalities; as a result, decisions made on the basis of those processes (for example, whether to subject a particular individual to a more invasive investigation) worsen those inequalities.

In what follows, I first identify why and how algorithmic decision-making errs in general, and errs in ways which give rise to the objection in particular. I do so with the following, rough and ready understanding of unfair inequalities, as

---

[31] I offer an account of extraterritorial punishment in Fabre, *Cosmopolitan Peace* ch. 7, and of the extra-territorial dimension of economic sanctions in Fabre, *Economic Statecraft*, ch. 3.

unequal treatment based on features of persons which are irrelevant from a moral point of view. I then evaluate the objection in the light of recent works on wrongful discrimination and racial profiling.

9.4.1 Algorithmic Unfairness

The amount and range of data which we generate in our daily lives and the speed at which we do so are staggering. I have already given a flavour of range and speed. To give you an idea of the amount, Twitter users together send around *200 billion* tweets a year—a tally which is dwarfed by the 200 or so billions of emails which we all send and receive *every day*.[32] Those mind-boggling numbers are set to increase year on year. Add in posts from all social media, images collected from dozens of millions of CCTV cameras around the world, and the metadata collected from billions of mobile phones, and it becomes clear that such data cannot be collected, stored, and processed other than by computers, data servers, and algorithms. Unfortunately, and contrary to what we might like to think, these are not always reliable ways to ascertain the who, why, when, and how of serious threats. For all too often, the data which algorithms are asked to process and the design of those algorithms are rooted in and worsen existing unfair inequalities between social groups and members thereof.

To see this, suppose that Green's intelligence agencies have been monitoring electronic and social media chatter from a number of individuals suspected or known to belong to transnational terrorist groups. Their system alerts them to social media posts coming from one such individual—call him X—mentioning the words 'brothers', 'blood of the enemies', and the name of Green's capital city. Green wants to know who X's contacts are and where they are located; whether he and his contacts have travelled by the same means at the same time, where to and where from; what financial transactions if any they might have made; where, when and for how long they have met. To do that, they widen the net so that each person with whom X has been in contact (whether by phone or by doing something as simple as entering the same shop at the same time or exchanging a few words) is subject to the same data searches. As their informational trove expands, they seek to identify behavioural patterns which, based on previous cases, yield descriptive and predictive probabilistic judgements as to the likelihood that this or that individual might belong to a terrorist cell or that this cluster of individuals might be preparing an attack.[33]

---

[32] The website *Internet Live Stats* keeps a live tally of tweets and emails at https://www.internetlivestats.com (accessed on 17/08/2021).

[33] I am drawing on a publicly available document in which GCHQ describes the ways in which its analysts work. To be clear, I am not implying that GCHQ analysts are guilty of bias. (See GCHQ, How does an analyst catch a terrorist?, technical report (2019), available at https://www.gchq.gov.

The problem is that algorithms are only as good as the data which they process and on which they are trained. When the data is incomplete, corrupted, or false, errors can lead to mistaken ascriptions of responsibility and thus to the wrongful imposition of harm in the form of more invasive surveillance or defensive harm. Answering even as simple a question as 'Whom did X meet on such and such day?' can be fraught with moral difficulties. Suppose that facial recognition software identifies someone, Y, as having met with X shortly after a particularly intense burst of Twitter activity on X's account. Whether the analysts are warranted in forming the judgement that X and Y met depends on the accuracy of the algorithm and on the amount and range of images on the basis of which the algorithm reaches (and trained itself to reach) its conclusion. This, in turn, is likely to be parasitic on various patterns of unfair inequalities. Suppose that the software collects photos from driving licences and trains itself to match faces with images by using those photos. Suppose further that Y has been identified as a citizen of Green and of Somalian descent. Finally, suppose that (as is the case in the United Kingdom) citizens of African descent have the lowest rate of car ownership of all ethnic groups, and that this can be traceable to unfair inequalities in wealth. The algorithm will have far fewer driving-licence photos with black faces than with Caucasian faces and will be less well trained to recognize those faces accurately. As a result, it will throw up more false positives for individuals of African descent than for individuals of European descent. The former are more likely to be wrongly identified as being Y than the latter.[34]

uk/information/how-does-analyst-catch-terrorist (accessed on 17/08/2021).) In the remainder of this section, I rely on the following sources: F. Kraemer, K. van Overveld and M. Peterson, 'Is There an Ethics of Algorithms?', *Ethics and Information Technology* 13 (2011): 251–60; J. Lerman, 'Big Data and Its Exclusions', *Stanford Law Review Online* 6 (2013); K. Spielmann, 'I Got Algorithm: Can There Be a Nate Silver in Intelligence?', *International Journal of Intelligence and CounterIntelligence* 29 (2016): 525–44: Van Puyvelde, Coulthart, and Hossain, 'Beyond the Buzzword'; C. O'Neill, Weapons of Maths Destruction (Penguin Books, 2016); J. Kleinberg et al., *Discrimination in the Age of Algorithms* (National Bureau of Economic Research, 2019) (available at https://www.nber.org/papers/w25548 (accessed on 17/08/2021)); S. Corbett-Davies and S. Goel, 'The Measure and Mismeasure of Fairness: A Critical Review of Fair Machine Learning', *Cornell University arXiv* (14/08/2018), On the specific question of how best to measure algorithmic fairness, see D. Hellman, 'Measuring Algorithmic Fairness', *Virginia Law Review* 106 (2020): 811–66.

[34] Relevant statistics (which cover the periods 2002–06 and 2014–18) are available from the British Government at https://www.ethnicity-facts-figures.service.gov.uk/culture-and-community/transport/car-or-van-ownership/latest (accessed on https://www.nber.org/papers/w25548). The charge of undue race-based bias in law enforcement has been levelled mostly in the US. According to a recent report on facial-recognition programmes and policing in England and Wales, there is no evidence of such bias in those regions. (See A. Babuta and M. Oswald, *Data Analytics and Algorithms in Policing in England and Wales: Towards A New Policy Framework* (Royal United Services Institute, 2020).) Here is a twist. Suppose that the trait on which the algorithm predicts behaviour is unequally shared between, e.g., citizens of European and African descent. Suppose further that the only way to equalize the risk that citizens of those groups will be mistakenly identified as potential terrorists is to lower the evidentiary threshold for subjecting the former to more invasive investigation, relative to the latter. This, however, is unfair to citizens of European descent who, as a result, incur a higher risk than previously of being mistakenly identified as potential terrorists. There is a sense, thus, in which one cannot remedy algorithmic unfairness without resorting to another kind of unfairness. In reply: first,

A similar problem arises when answering questions such as what is the degree to which X's behaviour fits both his usual behavioural patterns and that of individuals with similar demographics, and the likelihood that X's behaviour is predictive of a threat. One important issue is that of what algorithms have been trained to identify as a normal pattern and deviations therefrom, and what probabilistic inferences they have been trained to draw from such information. For example, according to a 2017 survey conducted by the Pew Research Center, patterns of gun ownership in the US correlate with political affiliation (Republicans and Independent vs Democrats), patterns of 'habitat' (rural vs urban), gender (male vs female), and ethnicity (white vs non-whites). A white American male who owns several guns, lives in the rural South, and identifies as a staunch anti-federal state Republican fits what may be called a normal pattern of gun ownership in that country. A youngish American of Middle Eastern descent who lives in New York and does not record a party political affiliation does not. Suppose that the algorithm has been trained to identify attacks on civilians by young men of Middle Eastern descent as terroristic attacks while attacks by white supremacists are simply recorded as 'mass shootings'. It is easy to see why a red flag might be issued if a thirty-year-old New Yorker who was born in Morocco suddenly buys guns, hires a truck, and posts anti-West, pro-ISIL messages on Instagram, but not if a long-term white resident of Colorado buys a bunch of assault weapons, hires a truck, and posts violent anti-federal and racist messages on Twitter. Given that some of the deadliest terrorist attacks of the last two decades in Western democracies have been carried out by individuals claiming alt-right allegiances, this should give us pause.[35]

Let us assume for the sake of argument that the data and algorithms on which Green's analysts rely are accurate and do not reflect unfair inequalities. Still, intelligence analysts have to make a judgement call as to how to interpret the information they are given. Suppose that X and Y are in contact and that the analysts are able to get not just the metadata of their interactions (how often and where they meet, how they communicate, etc.), but their content too. Suppose further that the pattern of their phone calls takes the following form: X phones Y on a regular basis and gives numbers in the format 'three elevens and two thirteens'. Green's analysts discover that a number of other individuals whose social media posts fit patterns of radicalization also place calls of that kind to Y's number. Y, every time, replies 'OK'. It is tempting for Green's analysts to assume that those

there might be a better alternative, in the form of improving the quality of the data on which we rely; second, even if there is no better alternative, we can at least say that we ought to act in such a way as to avoid *worsening* existing unfair inequalities between citizens of African and those of European descent. I am grateful to Lippert-Rasmussen for pressing me on this. For an intricate discussion of the issue in the context of algorithmic sentencing, see Hellman, 'Measuring Algorithmic Fairness'.

[35] Recall in particular Anders Breivik's killing of sixty-nine young socialist activists in Norway (2011) and Brenton Harrison's killing of forty Muslims in Christchurch NZ (2019). The Pew Center study is available at https://www.pewsocialtrends.org/2017/06/22/the-demographics-of-gun-ownership (accessed on 17/08/2021).

numbers represent orders for weapons, and for Green's authorities to order a strike on the location which has been linked to Y's phone. As it happens, the location is a kebab restaurant and the numbers are food orders.[36]

Analysts make mistakes. The risk is that, even if it is true that individuals fitting X's and Y's characteristics are more likely than not to be shopping for weapons, analysts will discount the possibility that, in this instance, the content of the communications might be innocuous. If they discount that possibility out of racial and religious biases against individuals such as X and Y, their mistake takes the form of an unfair bias which is parasitic on and worsens existing unfair inequalities in the ways members of the relevant social groups are treated. The point applies to comparative assessments of the threat posed by transnational Islamist radicalism on the one hand, and white extremism on the other. Indeed, intelligence chiefs in the UK and the United States have recently warned of the growing threat posed by far-right extremism, not just domestically but transnationally as well, and of the comparative lack of attention which it has garnered from governments and citizens. It is not unrealistic to suppose that the tendency to underemphasize this threat is in part rooted in racist and religious prejudices. To be sure, the risk is not unique to the interpretative challenges posed by algorithmic decision-making: it also arises with more 'standard' forms of data collection and analysis, including non-automated collection such as observation. But the risk is compounded by widespread and undue confidence in computers ('maths don't lie', 'machines are morally neutral', etc.)[37]

The objection is particularly potent against the duty view. It is all very well to say that we are under a (cross-border) duty to share the burden of protecting ourselves and third parties by having some of our personal information collected, stored, and analysed: the problem is that the burden is likely to fall disproportionately on those who are already unfairly disadvantaged.[38]

9.4.2 Profiling

To recapitulate, there is algorithmic unfairness when the data and algorithms on which intelligence analysts rely reflect existing unfair inequalities, or when analysts interpret correct and 'non-reflective' data in ways which are themselves biased. In our current geopolitical context, a man who identifies as Muslim and is of Middle Eastern or South Asian origin is far more likely to be targeted than a middle-aged American white Catholic woman.

---

[36] I thank Andy Owen for this example.

[37] The Center for Strategic and International Studies recently published a report on the growing threat posed by far-right movements in the US (see https://www.csis.org/analysis/escalating-terrorism-problem-united-states (accessed on 17/08/2021)).

[38] See, e.g., Henschke, *Ethics in an Age of Surveillance*, 248.

In this section, I argue that to the extent that mass surveillance practices are unfair in those ways, then we ought to eschew them—unless we succeed in developing machine-learning techniques which avoid negligent and prejudicial discriminatory treatment.[39]

Discrimination can take different forms. Direct discrimination consists in imposing a harm or disadvantage on a particular person on the basis of a characteristic of his (say, he is from Pakistan). Quite often, it stems from negative prejudices. Thus, an intelligence analyst who interprets the predictive statistical inference of an algorithm in the light of such a judgement ('this person is from Pakistan and Pakistanis are sympathetic to anti-Western terrorism') is guilty of direct discrimination against the relevant individuals. Indirect discrimination, by contrast, occurs when laws and policies have a harmful or disadvantageous impact on individuals who belong to certain groups, and when the reason why that is so can be traced back to past direct discrimination. In the present context, it occurs when the harms of mass surveillance fall on groups in ways which are parasitic on patterns of direct discrimination against those agents. The use of facial-recognition software which relies on driving-licence photos and thus throws up more false positives for members of ethnic minorities is vulnerable to the charge of indirect discrimination if the reason why those individuals are less likely to have access to a car is that they and/or their ancestors have been directly discriminated against, as a result of which they are less wealthy than members of the ethnic majority.

The distinction between direct and indirect discrimination cuts across the distinction between statistical and non-statistical discrimination. Discrimination which is informed purely by negative prejudices is non-statistical. By contrast, statistical discrimination, be it direct or not, is informed by the belief that the trait on the basis of which the harm or disadvantage is imposed is statistically relevant. An analyst who believes that it is statistically relevant that X is of Somalian origin engages in (direct) statistical discrimination.

Inequalities which are traceable to prejudices based on ethnic or religious affiliation, country of origin, gender, and age, are morally wrong—though there

---

[39] Not all unfair treatment and resulting inequalities amount to discrimination; and not all discrimination amounts to unfair treatment defined as treatment based on irrelevant characteristics—though discrimination necessarily involves unequal treatment. See K. Lippert-Rasmussen, *Born Free and Equal? A Philosophical Inquiry into the Nature of Discrimination* (Oxford University Press, 2013), especially chs. 2–3. In the next two paragraphs, I broadly follow Lippert-Rasmussen's categorization of various forms of discrimination. The philosophical literature on discrimination in its various manifestations is vast. In addition to Lippert-Rasmussen's important book, I draw throughout this section on the following works: L. Alexander, 'What Makes Wrongful Discrimination Wrong? Biases, Preferences, Stereotypes, and Proxies', *University of Pennsylvania Law Review* 141 (1992): 149–219; S. Moreau, *Faces of Inequality: A Theory of Wrongful Discrimination* (Oxford University Press, 2020); B. Eidelson, *Discrimination and Disrespect* (Oxford University Press, 2015); P. S. Shin, 'Treatment as an Individual and the Priority of Persons Over Groups in Antidiscrimination Law', *Duke Journal of Constitutional Law & Public Policy* 12 (2016): 107–34; R. J. Arneson, 'What is Wrongful Discrimination?', *San Diego Law Review* 43 (2006): 775–808.

is no consensus as to why discrimination in general, and discrimination based on prejudices in particular, are wrongful. The following views have been put forward in the relevant literature: discrimination is wrongful to the extent that it harms its victims; that the discriminator entertains prejudices against its victims; that it amounts to treating people on the basis of features which they have not chosen (a fairly common interpretation of the phrase 'irrelevant from a moral point of view'); that it creates unfair inequalities both within and outside groups. For example, it creates unfair inequalities between innocent white individuals and innocent Pakistanis who are more likely than the former to be wrongly identified as terrorists; it also creates unfair inequalities between innocent Pakistanis and guilty Pakistanis, who are equally likely on the basis of facial features alone to be flagged up but who are treated unequally in the sense that the former, unlike the latter, are treated in ways to which they are not liable.

A full account of the wrongfulness of discrimination is beyond the scope of this chapter. Still, I have argued throughout that we owe it to our fellow human beings to treat them on the basis of beliefs grounded in the best available evidence about what they have done: this, in fact, is precisely what grounds the duty to spy. But by that token, it is also precisely what grounds the duty not to subject them to invasions of privacy, and *a fortiori* to the imposition of yet further harms, on the basis of evidentially suspect beliefs. (One implication of this view is that differential treatment based on prejudice is morally objectionable even when the person who is harmed or disadvantaged is objectively liable to such treatment.)

So far, so simple. Suppose now that the belief on the basis of which X is targeted is true. It is true, as a matter of fact, that the majority of perpetrators of terrorist attacks or attempted attacks in Europe and the United States since 9/11 have been young men professing a commitment to some versions of Islam and of Middle Eastern or South Asian origin. (It is also true that the majority of victims of such attacks *in* the Middle East and South Asia are Muslims—a crucial point to which I shall return.) Why not draw inferences about X who, let us continue to assume, is Pakistani, on the basis of that fact? To put the point differently, why not take the view that the mere fact that X has certain demographic characteristics gives Green's services probable cause for investigating him further?

In the cases which preoccupy us here, some agent, X, is deliberately subjected to unwarranted harm on the basis of the epistemically warranted belief that individuals who share the relevant characteristic are more likely than individuals who do not share it to engage in certain kinds of rights violations. At this juncture, there are three options. We can hold that profiling on the basis of non-spurious statistical inference is never subjectively justified and thus never fully justified. This seems a non-starter, for some discriminatory practices involving profiling do seem warranted: for example, barring children from driving while allowing adults to do so, and diverting law-enforcement resources towards policing a football match rather than a garden show.[40] Alternatively, we can hold that profiling is always subjectively justified (and, so long as the evidence is true to the facts of the matter, fully justified). Yet, intuitively, there is a difference between directing police resources in the way just suggested and having intelligence agencies' computers systematically red-flag airline passengers of Middle-Eastern or South Asian origin for additional investigation. A third option, then, consists in discerning when profiling is subjectively (and thus fully) justified and when it is not.

Profiling raises moral concerns in so far as it is tied to practices and patterns of behaviour which are themselves unjust, in two ways. First, and most obviously, it gives rise to moral concerns when its use is parasitic on and worsens existing patterns of injustice.[41] At the risk of pointing out the obvious, pulling passengers who look Arab aside at airports to carry out additional identity checks in full view of other passengers risks further deepening the widespread prejudicial belief that all Arabs are would-be terrorists. In fact, even if it is merely known, and not seen, that airport policy, on the advice of intelligence services, is to conduct such checks on passengers of certain ethnic backgrounds and nationality, individuals who have those characteristics are likely to be further stigmatized in general.

Those factual claims seem plausible. If they are correct, we have strong reasons to resist profiling. Indeed, there are strong reasons to resist it even if we were never aware of it.[42] Let us imagine that additional checks are carried out on individuals of a certain ethnic or nationality profile without anyone being aware that this is standard policy. This is not as far-fetched as it sounds. Before Snowden's revelations, we did not know how comprehensive mass surveillance programmes were, how they worked, and how they were used. It is entirely possible then that in the years preceding Snowden, a number of individuals have been subject to profiling-based investigations on grounds of national security, without anyone being any the wiser about it. But if, as I have argued, one can be wrongfully harmed by what one does not experience, one can be wrongfully harmed by such practices.

Second, profiling gives rise to moral concerns when the reason why the statistical inferences on which it rests are accurate tracks injustice. While the causes of

---

[40] This last example is Lippert-Rasmussen's. See Lippert-Rasmussen, *Born Free and Equal?*, 81. For the pervasiveness of profiling and, more generally, of social policy based on statistical generalizations, see in particular F. Schauer, *Profiles, Probabilities and Stereotypes* (Harvard University Press, 2006).

[41] See, e.g., Lippert-Rasmussen, *Born Free and Equal?*, ch. 11; K. Lippert-Rasmussen, 'Algorithmic Discrimination and Compounding Injustice', (Copenhagen Workshop on Algorithmic Fairness, November 2020.), Schauer, *Profiles, Probabilities and Stereotypes*, ch. 7; Eidelson, *Discrimination and Disrespect*, ch. 6; A. Mogensen, 'Racial Profiling and Cumulative Injustice', *Philosophy and Phenomenological Research* 98 (2019): 452–77. In this section, I evaluate the claim that profiling can constitute a violation of a moral duty. There is another and, on some views, related concern, namely that it can constitute an epistemic failure. For recent discussions, see, e.g., S. Moss, *Probabilistic Knowledge* (Oxford University Press, 2018); R. J. Bolinger, 'The Rational Impermissibility of Accepting (Some) Racial Generalizations', *Synthese* 197 (2020): 2415–31; E. Begby, *Prejudice—A Study in Non-Ideal Pyschology* (Oxford University Press, 2021). As Begby powerfully argues, the problem with so-called algorithmic unfairness is not that it is algorithmic: it is that it is parasitic on injustice.

[42] *Pace* Eidelson, *Discrimination and Disrespect*, 215–18.

terrorism are complex and multifaceted, it seems plausible that it has been fuelled in part by foreign and domestic policies conducted by a number of governments over the last thirty years—ranging from support for Israel's occupation of the West Bank, to the 2003 invasion and subsequent occupation of Iraq, and to discriminatory policies against first- to third-generation immigrants from African and Middle-Eastern countries. To be clear: my point is *not* that those terrorist attacks were morally justified. Emphatically, they were not. My point, rather, is that they can in part be explained in this way. If this is true, and to the extent moreover that those policies were and are profoundly unjust, the fact that individuals who come from communities which have been subject to those policies are more likely to pose this kind of threat is in part made true by the commission of those injustices as well as by ongoing failures to rectify them. If so, it is objectionable on the part of those governments and their citizenries to impose on *innocent* members of those communities a greater share of the cost of protecting us all from threats on our security.

It might be objected that (as I noted a few paragraphs ago) members of those communities are themselves more likely to be the victims of those attacks than members of the majority. To the extent that they are greater *ex ante* beneficiaries of efforts at thwarting those attacks, it is not unfair (the objection states) that they should be asked to shoulder a greater share of the relevant burdens.[43]

In reply: it may well be true that if, for example, the United States and their allies apply profiling techniques to the trove of information they get from mass surveillance programmes as a means to thwart terrorist attacks *in the Middle East*, they will thereby benefit local populations in the Middle East. However, the factual premise on which the objection rests is likely to be false in those cases in which profiling is used to thwart attacks on Western targets. Moreover, even when the factual premise is true, the objection fails to take into account the fact that the policies which partly explain why profiling is not statistically spurious and which give rise to the need for it also partly explain why members of those communities are more likely to be the victims of terrorist attacks. To impose on them a greater share of the protective burdens is, in effect, to victimize them twice.

---

[43] For this kind of argument in the context of law enforcement, M. Risse and R. Zeckhauser, 'Racial Profiling', *Philosophy & Public Affairs* 32(2004): 131–70. Risse and Zeckhauser are *not* defending racial profiling as it currently operates in US law enforcement: on the contrary, they condemn it as grievously unjust on the grounds that it is parasitic on and compounds racism. Their claim is that racial profiling can be justified in principle in a non-racist society. For a powerful criticism, see A. Lever, 'Why Racial Profiling Is Hard to Justify: A Response to Risse and Zeckhauser', *Philosophy & Public Affairs* 33 (2005): 94–110, as well as Lippert-Rasmussen, *Born Free and Equal?*, ch. 11.

9.5 Conclusion

In this chapter, I have defended the following views. First, not all aspects of mass surveillance issue in a loss of privacy. When they do, they can under some conditions be justified as the bar of duties to protect one another from rights violations. If and when those conditions are not met, the privacy objection stands. Second, concerns that mass surveillance practices exhibit and entrench existing unfair inequalities ought to be taken seriously. Admittedly, those concerns stand or fall with the quality of the data and algorithms on which those practices rest. However, the fact that they are contingent in this way does not make mass surveillance any less morally problematic here and now.

Epilogue

In conclusion, let me briefly rehearse the main theses I have defended in this book and sketch out further lines of inquiry.

Espionage consists in acquiring secrets about other political communities which we have reason to believe they would rather keep from us. Counter-intelligence consists in defending our own secrets from them. A normative account of the ethics of spying writ large must begin with a defence of secrecy. Accordingly, I argued that individuals have a right to secrecy in respect of sensitive political, military, strategic, and economic information about their community, to the extent that secrets protect their security, democratic agency, and economic rights. However, the right to secrecy, as any other right, is only a *pro tanto* right. As we saw, espionage and counter-intelligence activities are morally justified as a means, but only as a means, to thwart violations of fundamental rights or risks thereof, subject to meeting the requirements of necessity, effectiveness, and proportionality. The point applies not just to espionage and counter-intelligence in the service of political, military, and security-related ends; it also extends, more controversially, to the economic realm. In the course of defending those claims, I argued that deception, treason, manipulation, exploitation, blackmail, eavesdropping, and computer hacking as means to acquire and protect secrets are sometimes justified. Mass surveillance, on the other hand, is not.

In contrast with the dirty-hands approach, thus, I argued that the spies whom, John Le Carré tells us, we will always need and whom he describes as 'a procession of vain fools', do not always dirty their hands. In contrast with the contractarian approach, I maintained that the moral norms at issue here are not the rules of a game or the code of a professional practice which parties do or would hypothetically endorse either because they benefit from their equal application or because they see one another as standing on a footing of equality irrespective of the ends which they pursue. Rather, those norms hold irrespective of whether political leaders and their citizens as a matter of fact share or would hypothetically accept them.

My account of the ethics of espionage and counter-intelligence differs from extant contemporary approaches in another important way. Those approaches, in common with the ethics of defensive harm, deception, coercion, and manipulation, focus on the permissibility of intelligence activities. With Sun Tzu and Hobbes but for different reasons, I argued that more often than we might think, those activities are morally mandatory. This stronger and more controversial claim is grounded in an account of the duties of assistance which individuals owe to one another irrespective of borders. On the face of it, that account itself is not particularly controversial. Its constitutive principles are a cornerstone of international human-rights discourse. It does, however, have fairly controversial implications for the acquisition and protection of secrets in the context of foreign policy writ large.

In some respects my defence of intelligence activities is quite permissive, by dint of the domains over which it applies and the means which it allows. In other respects, it is quite demanding, along two dimensions: those activities are justified only in response to violations of fundamental moral rights, and those means are, under certain conditions, not merely permitted but mandatory as well.

These two points taken together raise at least two concerns, neither one of which I have properly tackled here, and both of which are thus unfinished business. First, although I have mentioned some of the worries which state secrecy elicits for democratic accountability, I have been silent on another difficulty raised by my account. In the name of national security, some liberal-democratic jurisdictions, such as the United Kingdom and the United States, routinely hold criminal trials behind closed doors and deny defendants access to the full details of the charges they are facing—in violation of basic principles of natural justice. They also routinely deny plaintiffs who seek redress against alleged official abuses and courts judgments the material needed to make their case. More controversially still, American administrations have refused to release their own interpretation of national security legislation. As a result, the liberty-infringing practices in which they engage on the basis of such interpretation cannot be properly challenged. In the United Kingdom, there are similar worries about the expansion of secret trials. Secrecy in the name of security, thus, presents a threat to the integrity of the justice system.

Second, although I have repeatedly argued that the means by which intelligence officers and their assets procure and protect secrets are (under certain circumstances) justified *vis-à-vis* those whom they target or who are caught into the net, I have not discussed the fact that they may have a deeply corrupting effects on those agents themselves. Keeping secrets can breed insularity, arrogance, and a dismissive attitude to those who are not in the know. Lying, deceiving, manipulating, exploiting, coercing, and betraying can have a deeply corrosive impact on individuals' moral integrity and can cause them long-term psychological harm. Of course, there is a sense in which we *want* those individuals to be troubled by what they are doing, in the same way as we want soldiers not to be indifferent to the fact that they kill, even if they do so to just ends and even though, in some cases, we hold them under a duty so to act. There is growing awareness of the moral and psychological injuries which soldiers incur. So there should be with respect to individuals engaged in intelligence activities.

A complete account of the ethics of intelligence operations would address those risks to the stability of democratic institutions and the well-being of their actors. It would also pursue questions to which I have only briefly alluded at various points. I have focused on the acquisition and protection of secret information in the context of foreign policy writ large. As I noted in the Introduction, however, the boundaries between conducting a foreign policy and enforcing the law, and between the public and the private, are increasingly porous. Thus, although there are differences between the ethics of espionage and the ethics of policing, it would pay to investigate what they have in common. Moreover, although there are (obviously) profound differences between political agents with the authority to enforce directives over some territorial jurisdiction, and private actors such as corporations and, for that matter, individuals acting in a private capacity, it would pay to investigate whether my defence of intelligence activities extend to, *inter alia*, corporate espionage, investigative journalism, and whistle-blowing.

The ethics of espionage and counter-intelligence might seem a somewhat narrow object of inquiry. Yet, as I hope to have shown, it enables us to think afresh about a range of issues in moral and political philosophy. That, to my mind at least, is a large part of its enduring appeal.

Bibliography

Aid, M. 'All Glory is Fleeting: Sigint and the Fight Against International Terrorism'. In W. K. Wark (ed.), *Twenty-First Century Intelligence*. Routledge, 2005.

Alban, J. R. and Allmand, C. T. 'Spies and Spying in the Fourteenth Century'. In C. T. Allmand (ed.). *War, Literature, and Politics in the Late Middle Ages*. Liverpool University Press, 1976.

Aldrich, R. J. 'Transatlantic Intelligence and Security Cooperation'. *International Affairs* 80 (2004): 731–53.

Aldrich, R. J. *GCHQ: The Uncensored History of Britain's Most Secret Agency*. Harper Press, 2011.

Alexander, L. 'What Makes Wrongful Discrimination Wrong? Biases, Preferences, Stereotypes, and Proxies'. *University of Pennsylvania Law Review* 141 (1992): 149–219.

Alford, S. *The Watchers—A Secret History of the Reign of Elizabeth*. Penguin Books, 2013.

Altman, A. and Lee, S. 'Legal Entrapment'. *Philosophy & Public Affairs* 12 (1983): 51–69.

Anderson, D. *A Question of Trust—Report of the Investigatory Power Review*. Technical report. Her Majesty's Government, 2015.

Anderson, E. *Private Government: How Employers Rule Our Lives (and Why We Don't Talk about It)*. Princeton University Press, 2017.

Andrew, C. *The Defence of the Realm: The Authorized History of MI5*. Penguin Books, 2012.

Andrew, C. *The Secret World: A History of Intelligence*. Allen Lane, 2018.

Andrew, C., Aldrich, R.J., and Wark, W. K. (eds.). *Secret Intelligence—A Reader*. Routledge, 2009.

Andrew, C. and Mitrokhin, V. *The Mitrokhin Archive: The KGB in Europe and the West*. Penguin Books, 1999.

Andrew, C. and Mitrokhin, V. *The Mitrokhin Archive II: The KGB and the World*. Penguin Books, 2005.

Anscombe, G. E. M. 'Modern Moral Philosophy'. *Philosophy* 33 (1958): 1–19.

Arneson, R. J. 'What Is Wrongful Discrimination?'. *San Diego Law Review* 43 (2006): 775–808.

Arpaly, N. 'Moral Worth'. *The Journal of Philosophy* 99 (2002): 223–45.

Augustine. 'Against Lying'. In R. J. Deferrari (ed.), *Augustine—Various Treatises*. The Catholic University of America Press, 2002 [AD 420].

Augustine. 'On Lying'. In R. J. Deferrari (ed.), *Augustine—Various Treatises*. The Catholic University of America Press, 2002 [AD 395].

Austin, L. 'Privacy and the Question of Technology'. *Law and Philosophy* 22 (2003): 119–66.

Babuta, A. and Oswald, M. *Data Analytics and Algorithms in Policing in England and Wales: Towards A New Policy Framework*. Royal United Services Institute, 2020.

Baier, A. 'Trust and Antitrust'. *Ethics* 96 (1986): 231–60.

Baker, C. D. 'Tolerance of International Espionage: A Functional Approach'. *American University International Law Review* 19 (2004): 1091–1113.

Bar-Joseph, U. and McDermott, R. *Intelligence Success and Failure—The Human Factor*. Oxford University Press, 2017.

Barnes, J. E. 'Ex-C.I.A. Officer Is Accused of Spying for China'. *The New York Times* (17/08/2020).

Barnhill, A. 'What Is Manipulation?'. In C. Coons and M. Weber (eds.), *Manipulation—Theory and Practice*. Oxford University Press, 2014.

Baron, M. 'Manipulativeness'. *Proceedings and Addresses of the American Philosophical Association* 77 (2003): 37–54.

Bazargan, S. 'The Permissibility of Aiding and Abetting Unjust Wars'. *Journal of Moral Philosophy* 8 (2011): 513–29.

Begby, E. *Prejudice—A Study in Non-Ideal Pyschology*. Oxford University Press, 2021.

Bellaby, R. W. *The Ethics of Intelligence*. Routledge, 2014.

Bellaby, R. W. 'The Ethics of Whistleblowing: Creating a New Limit on Intelligence Activity'. *Journal of International Political Theory* 14 (2018): 60–84.

Bellaby, R. W. 'Too Many Secrets? When Should the Intelligence Community be Allowed to Keep Secrets?'. *Polity* 51 (2019): 62–94.

Benbaji, Y. and Statman, D. *War by Agreement*. Oxford University Press, 2019.

Benn, S. 'Privacy, Freedom and Respect for Persons'. In J. R. Pennock and J. W. Chapman (eds.), *Privacy—Nomos XIII*. Atherton Press, 1971.

Bennett, M. 'Demoralizing Trust'. *Ethics* 131 (2021): 511–38.

Ben-Yehuda, N. *Betrayals and Treason: Violations of Trust and Loyalty*. Westview Press, 2001.

Berman, M. N. 'Blackmail'. In J. Deigh and D. Dolinko (eds.), *The Oxford Handbook of Philosophy of Criminal Lawy*. Oxford University Press, 2011.

Betts, R. K. 'Analysis, War, and Decisions: Why Intelligence Failures are Inevitable'. *World Politics* 31 (1978): 61–89.

Betts, R. K. 'Surprise Despite Warning'. In C. Andrew, R. J. Aldrich, and W. K. Wark (eds.), *Secret Intelligence—A Reader*. Routledge, 2009.

Biggs, S. C. 'Treason and the Trial of William Joyce'. *The University of Toronto Law Journal* 7 (1947): 162–95.

Bing, C. and Taylor, M. 'Exclusive: China-backed Hackers "Targeted COVID-19 Vaccine Firm Moderna"'. *Reuters* (30/07/2020).

Blumenthal-Barby, J. 'A Framework for Assessing the Moral Status of "Manipulation"'. In C. Coons and M. Weber (eds.), *Manipulation—Theory and Practice*. Oxford University Press, 2014.

Bok, S. *Secrets: On the Ethics of Concealment and Revelation*. 2nd. ed. Vintage Books, 1989.

Bok, S. *Lying—Moral Choice in Public and Private Life*. 2nd. ed. Vintage, 1999.

Bolinger, R. J. 'The Rational Impermissibility of Accepting (Some) Racial Generalizations'. *Synthese* 197 (2020): 2415–431.

Boveri, M. *Treason in the Twentieth Century*. Macdonald, 1961.

Brenner, S. W. *Cyber Threats: The Emerging Fault Lines of the Nation State*. Oxford University Press, 2009.

Brock, G. *Global Justice: A Cosmopolitan Account*. Oxford University Press, 2009.

Brownlee, K. *Conscience and Conviction—The Case for Civil Disobedience*. Oxford University Press, 2012.

Buchanan, A. *Institutionalizing the Just War*. Oxford University Press, 2017.

Burkett, R. 'Rethinking an Old Approach: An Alternative Framework for Agent Recruit ment: From Mice to RASCLS'. *Studies in Intelligence* 57 (2013): 7–17.

Burri, S. 'Why Moral Theorizing Needs Real Cases: The Redirection of V-Weapons during the Second World War'. *Journal of Political Philosophy* 28 (2020): 247–69.

Buss, S. 'Valuing Autonomy and Respecting Persons: Manipulation, Seduction, and the Basis of Moral Constraints'. *Ethics* 115 (2005): 195–235.

Buuren, J. van. 'Analyzing International Intelligence Cooperation: Institutions or Intelligence Assemblages?'. In I. Duyvesteyn et al. (eds.), *The Future of Intelligence—Challenges in the 21st century*. Routledge, 2015.

Cadwalladr, C. 'The Great British Brexit Robbery: How Our Democracy Was Hijacked'. *The Observer* (07/05/2017).

Caney, S. *Justice Beyond Borders: A Global Political Theory*. Oxford University Press, 2005.

Carlton, E. *Treason: Meanings and Motives*. Ashgate, 1998.

Carnegie, A. and Carson, A. *Secrets in Global Governance—Disclosure Dilemmas and the Challenge of International Cooperation in World Politics*. Cambridge University Press, 2020.

Carson, T. L. *Lying and Deception—Theory and Practice*. Oxford University Press, 2010.

Cassam, Q. *Vices of the Mind*. Oxford University Press, 2019.

Champion, B. 'A Review of Selected Cases of Industrial Espionage and Economic Spying, 1568–1945'. *Intelligence and National Security* 13 (1998): 123–43.

Cherkashin, V. and Feiffer, G. *Spy Handler—Memoirs of a KGB Officer*. Basic Books, 2005.

Chesterman, S. '"The Spy Who Came in From the Cold War"—Intelligence and International Law'. *Michigan Journal of International Law* 27 (2006): 1077–130.

Chesterman, S. *Shared Secrets: Intelligence and Collective Security—Lowy Institute Paper 10*. Lowy Institute, 2006.

Christiano, T. 'What is Wrongful Exploitation?'. In D. Sobel, P. Vallentyne, and S. Wall (eds.), *Oxford Studies in Political Philosophy—vol. 1*. Oxford University Press, 2015.

Chulov, M. 'Israel Appears to Confirm It Carried Out Cyberattack on Iran Nuclear Facility'. *The Guardian* (11/04/2021).

Churchill, W. *The Second World War, vol. 5—Closing the Ring*. Fifth ed. Penguin Classics, 2005.

Clark, M. 'There Is No Paradox of Blackmail'. *Analysis* 54 (1994): 54–61.

Clark, M. T. 'Economic Espionage: The Role of the United States Intelligence Community'. *Journal of International Legal Studies* 3 (1997): 253–92.

Clarke, D. L. 'Israel's Economic Espionage in the United States'. *Journal of Palestine Studies* 27 (1998): 20–35.

Clausewitz, C. von. *On War*. Edited by M. Howard and P. Paret. International Finance Section, Dept. of Economics, Princeton University, 1984 [1832].

Close, F. *Trinity—The Treachery and Pursuit of the Most Dangerous Spy in History*. Penguin Books, 2020.

Clough, C. 'Quid Pro Quo: The Challenges of International Strategic Intelligence Cooperation'. *International Journal of Intelligence and CounterIntelligence* 17 (2004): 601–13.

Coady, C. A. J. 'Escaping from the Bomb: Immoral Deterrence and the Problem of Extrication'. In H. Shue (ed.), *Nuclear Deterrence and Moral Restraint*. Cambridge University Press, 1989.

Coady, C. A. J. 'The Problem of Dirty Hands'. In E. N. Zalta (ed.), *Stanford Encyclopedia of Philosophy*. Fall 2018.

Cockburn, P. 'Life under Isis: Why I Deserted the "Islamic State" rather than Take Part in Executions, Beheadings and Rape—The Story of a Former Jihadi'. *The Independent* (16/03/2015).

Cole, D. *Just War and the Ethics of Espionage*. Routledge, 2015.

Coons, C. and Weber, M. (eds.). *Manipulation—Theory and Practice*. Oxford University Press, 2014.

Cooper, J. *The Queen's Agent*. Faber and Faber, 2011.

Corbett-Davies, S. and Goel, S. 'The Measure and Mismeasure of Fairness: A Critical Review of Fair Machine Learning'. *Cornell University arXiv* (14/08/2018).

Corera, G. *MI6: Life and Death in the British Secret Service*. Weidenfeld & Nicolson, 2011.

Corera, G . *Intercept: The Secret History of Computers and Spies*. Weidenfeld & Nicolson, 2015.

Corera, G. *Russians Among Us - Sleeper Cells and the Hunt for Putin's Agents*. Harper Collins, 2020.

Couch, N. and Robins, B. *Big Data for Defence and Security*. Royal United Services Institute, 2013.

Cunningham, A. P. 'The Moral Importance of Dirty Hands'. *Journal of Value Inquiry* 26 (1992): 239–50.

Dannenberg, J. 'Lying Among Friends'. In E. Michaelson and A. Stokke (eds.), *Lying—Language, Knowledge, Ethics and Politics*. Oxford University Press, 2018.

Davenport-Hines, R. *Enemies Within: Communists, the Cambridge Spies and the Making of Modern Britain*. William Collins, 2018.

De Vattel, E. *Le droit des gens ou, Principes de la loi naturelle, appliqués à la conduite et aux affaires des nations et des souverains*. Carnegie Institute, 1916 [1758].

Dobos, N. *Ethics, Security, and the War-Machine—The True Cost of the Military*. Oxford University Press, 2020.

Dochartaigh, N. O. 'Together in the middle: Back-channel negotiation in the Irish peace process'. *Journal of Peace Research* 48 (2011): 767–80.

Dorn, A. W. 'United Nations Peacekeeping Intelligence'. In L. K. Johnson (ed.), *Oxford Handbook of National Security Intelligence*. Oxford University Press, 2010.

Dover, R., Goodman, M. S., and Hillebrand, C. (eds.). *Routledge Companion to Intelligence Studies*. Routledge, 2014.

Downing, T. *1983—The World at the Brink*. Abacus, 2018.

Doyle, T. 'Privacy and Perfect Voyeurism'. *Ethics and Information Technology* 11 (2009): 181–9.

Draper, K. *War and Individual Rights: The Foundations of Just War Theory*. Oxford University Press, 2016.

Duyvesteyn, I. et al. (eds.). *The Future of Intelligence—Challenges in the 21st century*. Routledge, 2015.

Dworkin, G. 'The Serpent Beguiled Me and I Did Eat: Entrapment and the Creation of Crime'. *Law and Philosophy* 4 (1985): 17–39.

Eidelson, B. *Discrimination and Disrespect*. Oxford University Press, 2015.

Ekins, R. et al. *Aiding the Enemy: How and Why to Restore the Law of Treason*. Policy Exchange, 2018.

Elford, G. 'Pains of Perseverance: Agent-Centred Prerogatives, Burdens and the Limits of Human Motivation'. *Ethical Theory and Moral Practice* 18 (2015): 501–14.

Ellsberg, D. 'Whistleblowing and National Secrecy'. *Social Research: An International Quarterly* 77 (2010): 773–804.

Erskine, T. '"As Rays of Light to the Human Soul"? Moral Agents and Intelligence Gathering'. In L. Scott and P. Jackson (eds.), *Understanding Intelligence in the Twenty-First Century—Journey in the Shadows*. Routledge, 2004.

Estlund, D. 'On Following Orders in an Unjust War'. *Journal of Political Philosophy* 15 (2007): 213–34.

Estlund, D. 'Human Nature and the Limits (if any) of Political Philosophy'. *Philosophy & Public Affairs* 39 (2011): 207–37.

Evans, H. 'Why Blackmail Should Be Banned'. *Philosophy* 65 (1990): 89–94.

Fabre, C. 'Guns, Food, and Liability to Attack'. *Ethics* 120 (2009): 36–63.

Fabre, C. 'In Defence of Mercenarism'. *British Journal of Political Science* 40 (2010): 539– 59.

Fabre, C. *Cosmopolitan War*. Oxford University Press, 2012.

Fabre, C. *Cosmopolitan Peace*. Oxford University Press, 2016.

Fabre, C. *Economic Statecraft—Human Rights, Sanctions and Conditionality*. Harvard University Press, 2018.

Fägersten, B. 'European Intelligence Cooperation'. In I. Duyvesteyn et al. (eds.), *The Future of Intelligence—Challenges in the 21st century*. Routledge, 2015.

Fatić, A. 'The Epistemology of Intelligence Ethics'. In *Ethics and the Future of Spying*, edited by J. Galliott and W. Reed. Routledge, 2016.

Feinberg, J. 'Voluntary Euthanasia and the Inalienable Right to Life'. *Philosophy & Public Affairs* 7 (1978): 93–123.

Feinberg, J. *Harmless Wrongdoing—The Moral Limits of the Criminal Law—vol.4*. Oxford University Press, 1988.

Ferrill, A. 'Roman Military Intelligence'. In K. Neilson and B. J. C. McKercher (eds.), *Go Spy the Land—Military Intelligence in History*. Praeger, 1992.

Fialka, J. J. *War by Other Means—Economic Espionage in America*. W. W. Norton, 1997.

Fink, S. *Sticky Fingers*. iUniverse, Inc., 2002.

Finnis, J. 'Nationality, Alienage and Constitutional Principle'. *Law Quarterly Review* 123 (2007): 417–45.

Firth, J. M. and Quong, J. 'Necessity, Moral Liability, and Defensive Harm'. *Law and Philosophy* 31 (2012): 673–701.

Forster, E. M. *Two Cheers for Democracy*. Penguin Books, 1951.

Fort, R. M. 'Economic Espionage'. In R. Z. George and R. D. Kline (eds.), *Intelligence and the National Security Strategist*. Rowman & Littlefield, 2006.

Foster, P. and Evans, M. 'Exclusive: How a Tiny Canadian IT Company Helped Swing the Brexit Vote for Leave'. *The Daily Telegraph* (24/02/2017).

Frowe, H. 'A Practical Account of Self-Defence'. *Law and Philosophy* 29 (2010): 245–72.

Frowe, H. *Defensive Killing*. Oxford University Press, 2014.

Frowe, H. *The Ethics of War and Peace*. 2nd. ed. Routledge, 2016.

Gallie, W. B. 'Essentially Contested Concepts'. *Proceedings of the Aristotelian Society* 56 (1955): 167–98.

Gardner, J. 'Criminals in Uniform'. In R. A. Duff et al. (eds.), *The Constitution of the Criminal Law*. Oxford University Press, 2013.

Gartzke, E. and Lindsay, J. R. 'Weaving Tangled Webs: Offense, Defense, and Deception in Cyberspace'. *Security Studies* 24 (2015): 316–48.

Gavison, R. 'Privacy and the Limits of Law'. *The Yale Law Journal* 89 (1980): 421–71.

Gayle, D. and Cobain, I. 'UK Intelligence and Police Using Child Spies in Covert Operations'. *The Guardian* (19/07/2018).

GCHQ. *How does an Analyst Catch a Terrorist?*. Technical Report. 2019.

Gellman, B. *Dark Mirror: Edward Snowden and the Surveillance State*. Bodley Head, 2020.

Gendron, A. 'Just War, Just Intelligence: An Ethical Framework for Foreign Espionage'. *International Journal of Intelligence and CounterIntelligence* 18 (2005): 398–434.

Gentili, A. *De Jure Belli Libri Tres*. Edited by J. Rolfe. Clarendon Press, 1933 [1588–89].

Gentili, A. *De Legationibus Libri Tres*. Oxford University Press, 1924 [1585].

Gentry, J. A. 'Diplomatic Spying: How Useful Is It?'. *International Journal of Intelligence and Counterintelligence* 34 (2021): 432–62.

Gill, P. and Phythian, M. *Intelligence in an Insecure World*. Polity Press, 2012.

Golden, D. 'The Science of Spying—How the CIA Secretly Recruits Academics'. *The Guardian* (10/10/2017).

Goldman, A. 'Ex-Green Beret Admits He Betrayed U.S. While Spying for Russia'. *The New York Times* (18/11/2020).

Goldman, J. (ed.), *Ethics of Spying: A Reader for the Intelligence Professional*. Vol. 1. Scarecrow Press, 2005.

Goldman, J. (ed.), *Ethics of Spying: A Reader for the Intelligence Professional*. Vol. 2. Scarecrow Press, 2010.

Goodin, R. E. 'What Is So Special about Our Fellow Countrymen?'. *Ethics* 98 (1988): 663–86.

Gordievsky, O. *Next Stop Execution*. Macmillan, 1995.

Gorin, M. 'Do Manipulators Always Threaten Rationality?'. *American Philosophical Quarterly* 51 (2014): 51–61.

Gorin, M. 'Towards a Theory of Interpersonal Manipulation'. In C. Coons and M. Weber (eds.), *Manipulation—Theory and Practice*. Oxford University Press, 2014.

Gorr, M. 'Toward a Theory of Coercion'. *Canadian Journal of Philosophy* 16 (1986): 383–405.

Gorr, M. 'Liberalism and the Paradox of Blackmail'. *Philosophy & Public Affairs* 21 (1992): 43–66.

Greasley, K. 'The Morality of Lying and the Murderer at the Door'. *Law and Philosophy* 38 (2019): 439–52.

Greenspan, P. 'The Problem with Manipulation'. *American Philosophical Quarterly* 40 (2003): 155–64.

Greenwald, G. *No Place to Hide—Edward Snowden, the NSA and the Surveillance State*. Penguin Books, 2014.

Grey, S. *The New Spymasters: Inside Espionage from the Cold War to Global Terror*. Penguin Books, 2016.

Gross, M. L. *Military Medical Ethics and Just War*. Oxford University Press, 2021.

Grotius, H. *The Rights of War and Peace*. Edited by R. Tuck. Liberty Fund, 2005 [1625].

Gunderson, M. 'Threats and Coercion'. *Canadian Journal of Philosophy* 9 (1979): 247–59.

Gutmann, A. and Thompson, D. *Democracy and Disagreement*. Harvard University Press, 1996.

Haksar, V. 'Coercive Proposals—Rawls and Gandhi'. *Political Theory* 4 (1976): 65–79.

Hansson, S. O. 'Decision Making Under Great Uncertainty'. *Philosophy of the Social Sciences* 26 (1996): 369–86.

Haque, A. A. *Law and Morality at War*. Oxford University Press, 2017.

Harber, J. R. 'Unconventional Spies: The Counterintelligence Threat from Non-State Actors'. *International Journal of Intelligence and CounterIntelligence* 22 (2009): 221–36.

Hardin, R. *Trust and Trustworthiness*. Russell Sage Foundation, 2002.

Harding, L. *The Snowden Files*. Faber and Faber, 2014.

Harding, L. *A Very Expensive Poison*. Faber and Faber, 2017.

Hart, H. L. A. 'Are There Any Natural Rights?'. *The Philosophical Review* 64 (1955): 175–91.

Haslam, J. *Near and Distant Neighbors—A New History of Soviet Intelligence*. Oxford University Press, 2015.

Hastings, M. *The Secret War: Spies, Codes and Guerillas 1939–45*. William Collins, 2015.

Hawley, K. 'Coercion and Lies'. In E. Michaelson and A. Stokke (eds.), *Lying—Language, Knowledge, Ethics and Politics*. Oxford University Press, 2018.

Hellman, D. 'Measuring Algorithmic Fairness'. *Virginia Law Review* 106 (2020): 811–66.

Henschke, A. *Ethics in an Age of Surveillance—Personal Information and Virtual Identities*. Cambridge University Press, 2017.

Hill, D. J., McLeod, S. K. and Tanyi, A. 'The Concept of Entrapment'. *Criminal Law and Philosophy* 12 (2018): 539–54.

Hirschfel Davis, J. 'Hacking of Government Computers Exposed 21.5 Million People'. *The New York Times* (09/07/2015).

Ho, H. L. 'State Entrapment'. *Legal Studies* 31 (2011): 71–95.

Hobbes, T. *On the Citizen*. Edited by R. Tuck and M. Silverstone. Cambridge University Press, 1998 [1642].

Hoffman, D. E. *The Billion Dollar Spy: A True Story of Cold War Espionage and Betrayal*. Doubleday, 2015.

Hohfeld, W. N. *Fundamental Conceptions as Applied in Judicial Reasoning*. Yale University Press, 1919.

Hollis, M. 'Dirty Hands'. *British Journal of Political Science* 12 (1982): 385–98.

Hosking, G. 'Trust and Distrust in the USSR: An Overview'. *The Slavonic and East European Review* 91 (2013): 1–25.

Howard, J. W. 'Moral Subversion and Structural Entrapment'. *Journal of Political Philosophy* 24 (2016): 24–46.

Howard, M. *Strategic Deception in the Second World War*. N. W. Norton, 1995.

Huggler, J. 'German Intelligence Accused of "Spying on USA"'. *The Daily Telegraph* (22/06/2017).

Hughes, P. M. 'What Is Wrong with Entrapment?'. *Southern Journal of Philosophy* 42 (2004): 45–60.

Hunt, L. W. *The Retrieval of Liberalism in Policing*. Oxford University Press, 2018.

Iordanou, I. *Venice's Secret Service—Organizing Intelligence in the Renaissance*. Oxford University Press, 2019.

Jackson, P. 'On Uncertainty and the Limits of Intelligence'. In L. K. Johnson (ed.), *The Oxford Handbook of National Security Intelligence*. Oxford University Press, 2010.

Javers, E. *Broker, Trader, Lawyer, Spy: The Secret World of Corporate Espionage*. Harper-Collins, 2010.

Jeffery, K. *MI6—The History of The Secret Intelligence Service 1909-1949*. Bloomsbury Publishing, 2010.

Johnson, Loch K. (ed.). *The Oxford Handbook of National Security Intelligence*. Oxford University Press, 2010.

Johnson, Luke 'George W. Bush Defends PRISM: "I Put That Program In Place To Protect The Country"'. *The Huffington Post* (01/07/2013).

Johnson, W. R. *Thwarting Enemies at Home and Abroad*. Georgetown University Press, 2009.

Jones, C. *Global Justice—Defending Cosmopolitanism*. Oxford University Press, 1999.

Jones, K. 'Trust as an Affective Attitude'. *Ethics* 107 (1996): 4–25.

Jones, S. and M. Arnold. 'UK Spymasters Raise Suspicions over Kaspersky Software's Russia Links'. *The Financial Times* (12/11/2017).

Kalugin, O. *Spymaster*. Smith Gryphon Ltd, 1994.

Kamm, F. M. 'Failures of Just War Theory: Terror, Harm, and Justice'. *Ethics* 114 (2004): 650–92.

Kamm, F. M. *The Moral Target: Aiming at Right Conduct in War and Other Conflicts*. Oxford University Press, 2012.

Kant, I. 'Perpetual Peace: A Philosophical Sketch'. In H. Reiss (ed.), *Kant—Political Writings*. Cambridge University Press, 1991 [1795].

Kant, I. 'Metaphysics of Morals'. In H. Reiss (ed.), *Kant—Political Writings*. Cambridge University Press, 1991 [1797].

Kant, I. 'Of Ethical Duties Towards Others, and Especially Truthfulness'. In P. Heath and J. B. Schneewind (eds.), *Lectures on Ethics*. Cambridge University Press, 1997 [1755–85].

Katsh, E. and O. Rabinovitch-Einy. *Digital Justice: Technology and the Internet of Disputes*. Oxford University Press, 2017.

Keegan, J. *Intelligence in War—Knowledge of the Enemy from Napoleon to Al-Qaeda*. Pimlico, 2004.

Kim, H. 'Entrapment, Culpability, and Legitimacy'. *Law and Philosophy* 39 (2020): 67–91.

Kleinberg, J., et al. *Discrimination in the Age of Algorithms*. National Bureau of Economic Research, 2019.

Kleinig, J. *The Ethics of Policing*. Cambridge University Press, 1996.

Knaus, C. 'Witness K and the "Outrageous" Spy Scandal That Failed to Shame Australia'. *The Guardian* (09/08/2019).

Knightley, P. *The Second Oldest Profession: Spies and Spying in the Twentieth Century*. Penguin Books, 1988.

Knightley, P. *The Master Spy: The Story of Kim Philby*. Knopf, 1989.

Korsgaard, C. M. 'The Right to Lie: Kant on Dealing with Evil'. *Philosophy & Public Affairs* 15 (1986): 325–49.

Kraemer, F., van Overveld, K. and Peterson, M. 'Is There an Ethics of Algorithms?'. *Ethics and Information Technology* 13 (2011): 251–60.

Kumar, R. 'Risking and Wronging'. *Philosophy & Public Affairs* 43 (2015): 27–51.

Kutz, C. 'Secret Law and the Value of Publicity'. *Ratio Juris* 22 (2009): 197–217.

Lackey, J. 'Group Lies'. In E. Michaelson and A. Stokke (eds.), *Lying—Language, Knowledge, Ethics and Politics*. Oxford University Press, 2018.

Lahneman, W. J. 'IC Data Mining in the Post-Snowden Era'. *International Journal of Intelligence and CounterIntelligence* 29 (2016): 700–23.

Lango, J. W. 'Intelligence about Noncombatants: The Ethics of Intelligence and the Just War Principle of Noncombatant Immunity'. *International Journal of Intelligence Ethics* 2 (2011): 50–76.

Lazar, S. *Sparing Civilians*. Oxford University Press, 2015.

Lazar, S. 'Deontological Decision Theory and Agent-Centered Options'. *Ethics* 127 (2017): 579–609.

Lazar, S. 'In Dubious Battle: Uncertainty and the Ethics of Killing'. *Philosophical Studies* 175 (2018): 859–83.

Lazar, S. 'Risky Killing—How Risks Worsen Violations of Objective Rights'. *Journal of Moral Philosophy* 16 (2019): 1–26.

Le Carré, J. *The Secret Pilgrim*. Penguin Books, 2011.

Le Carré, J. *The Spy Who Came in from the Cold*. New ed. Penguin Classics, 2014.

Lee, Y. 'Punishing Disloyalty? Treason, Espionage, and the Transgression of Political Boundaries'. *Law and Philosophy* 31 (2012): 299–342.

Lefevre, S. 'The Difficulties and Dilemmas of International Intelligence Cooperation'. *International Journal of Intelligence and CounterIntelligence* 16 (2003): 527–42.

Lerman, J. 'Big Data and Its Exclusions'. *Stanford Law Review Online* 6 (2013).

Lever, A. 'Why Racial Profiling Is Hard to Justify: A Response to Risse and Zeckhauser'. *Philosophy & Public Affairs* 33 (2005): 94–110.

Lever, A. (ed.). *New Frontiers in the Philosophy of Intellectual Property*. Cambridge University Press, 2012.

Lever, A. 'Privacy and Democracy: What the Secret Ballot Reveals'. *Law, Culture and the Humanities* 11 (2015): 164–83.

Levine, J. *Operation Fortitude*. HarperCollins, 2011.

Lewis, P. and Evans, R. 'Secrets and Lies: Untangling the UK "Spy Cops' Scandal". *The Guardian* (28/10/2020).

Lim, K. 'Big Data and Strategic Intelligence'. *Intelligence and National Security* 31 (2016): 619–35.

Lin, P. and Ford, S. 'I, Spy Robot: The Ethics of Robots in National Security Intelligence'. In Jai Galliot (ed.), *Ethics and the Future of Spying*. Routledge, 2016.

Lindgren, J. 'Unraveling the Paradox of Blackmail'. *Columbia Law Review* 84 (1984): 670–716.

Lindsay, J. R. 'The Impact of China on Cybersecurity: Fiction and Friction'. *International Security* 39 (2014): 7–47.

Lippert-Rasmussen, K. *Born Free and Equal? A Philosophical Inquiry into the Nature of Discrimination*. Oxford University Press, 2013.

Lippert-Rasmussen, K. 'Algorithmic Discrimination and Compounding Injustice' (Copenhagen Workshop on Algorithmic Fairness, November 2020.)

Lippke, R. L. 'A Limited Defense of What Some Will Regard as Entrapment'. *Legal Theory* 23 (2017): 283–306.

Locke, J. L. *Eavesdropping—An Intimate History*. Oxford University Press, 2010.

Luban, D. 'The Publicity Principle'. In R. E. Goodin (ed.), *The Theory of Institutional Design*. Cambridge University Press, 1996.

Lubin, A. 'The Liberty to Spy'. *Harvard International Law Journal* 61 (2020): 185–243.

Lucas, G. R. *Ethics and Cyber Warfare—The Quest for Responsibility in the Age of Digital Warfare*. Oxford University Press, 2017.

Lyon, D. *Surveillance after Snowden*. Polity Press, 2015.

Machiavelli, N. *The Art of War*. Edited by C. Lynch. Chicago University Press, 2003 [1521].

Mack, E. 'In Defense of Blackmail'. *Philosophical Studies* 41 (1982): 273–84.

Macnish, K. *The Ethics of Surveillance: An Introduction*. Routledge, 2017.

Macnish, K. 'Government Surveillance and Why Defining Privacy Matters in a Post-Snowden World'. *Journal of Applied Philosophy* 35 (2018): 417–32.

Mahon, J. E. 'Secrets v. Lies: Is There an Asymmetry?'. In E. Michaelson and A. Stokke (eds.), *Lying—Language, Knowledge, Ethics, and Politics*. Oxford University Press, 2018.

Mallet, V. 'French Military Officer Held on Suspicion of Spying'. *The Financial Times* (30/08/2020).

Margalit, A. *On Betrayal*. Harvard University Press, 2017.

Markovits, J. 'Acting for the Right Reasons'. *Philosophical Review* 119 (2010): 201–42.

Marmor, A. 'What Is the Right to Privacy?'. *Philosophy & Public Affairs* 43 (2015): 3–26.

Martin, D. C. *Wilderness of Mirrors*. HarperCollins, 1980.

Masterman, J. C. *The Double-Cross System, 1939–1945*. Pimlico, 1995.

Mavrodes, G. I. 'Conventions and the Morality of War'. *Philosophy & Public Affairs* 4 (1975): 117–31.

McCarthy, D. 'Rights, Explanation, and Risks'. *Ethics* 107 (1997): 205–25.

McGeer, V. and Pettit, P. 'The Empowering Theory of Trust'. In Paul Faulkner and Thomas Simpson (eds.), *The Philosophy of Trust*. Oxford University Press, 2017.

McIntyre, A. *Truthfulness, Lies, and Moral Philosophers: What Can We Learn from Mill and Kant*. Tanner Lectures on Human Values, 1994.

McIntyre, B. *Double Cross: The True Story of The D-Day Spies*. Bloomsbury, 2012.

McIntyre, B. *A Spy Among Friends: Kim Philby and the Great Betrayal*. Bloomsbury, 2014.

McIntyre, B. *The Spy and the Traitor: The Greatest Espionage Story of the Cold War*. Penguin Books, 2019.

McMahan, J. *Killing in War*. Oxford University Press, 2009.

McMahan, J. 'The Morality of Military Occupation'. *Loyola International and Comparative Law Review* 31 (2009): 101–23.

McMahan, J. 'Who Is Morally Liable to be Killed in War'. *Analysis* 71 (2011): 544–59.

Meibauer, J. (ed.). *The Oxford Handbook of Lying*. Oxford University Press, 2019.

Michaelson, E. and Stokke, A. (eds.). *Lying—Language, Knowledge, Ethics, and Politics*. Oxford University Press, 2018.

Millar, J. 'Core Privacy: A Problem for Predictive Data Mining'. In I. Kerr, V. Steeves, and C. Lucock (eds.), *Lessons from the Identity Trail: Anonymity, Privacy and Identity in a Networked Society*. Oxford University Press, 2009.

Miller, R. W. 'Beneficence, Duty and Distance'. *Philosophy & Public Affairs* 32 (2004): 357–83.

Miller, S. *The Moral Foundations of Social Institutions—A Philosophical Study*. Cambridge University Press, 2010.

Miller, S. 'Rethinking the Just Intelligence Theory of National Security Intelligence Collection and Analysis: The Principles of Discrimination, Necessity, Proportionality and Reciprocity'. *Social Epistemology* 35 (2021): 211–31.

Miller, S. and Gordon, I. A. *Investigative Ethics: Ethics for Police Detectives and Criminal Investigators*. Wiley-Blackwell, 2014.

Mills, C. 'Politics and Manipulation'. *Social Theory and Practice* 21 (1995): 97–112.

Mogensen, A. 'Racial Profiling And Cumulative Injustice'. *Philosophy and Phenomenological Research* 98 (2019): 452–77.

Mokrosinska, D. 'Privacy and Autonomy: On Some Misconceptions Concerning the Political Dimensions of Privacy'. *Law and Philosophy* 37 (2018): 117–43.

Mokrosinska, D. 'Why States Have No Right to Privacy, But May Be Entitled to Secrecy: A Non-consequentialist Defense of State Secrecy'. *Critical Review of International Social and Political Philosophy* 23 (2020): 415–44.

Montesquieu. *The Spirit of the Laws*. Edited by A. M. Cohler. Cambridge University Press, 1989 [1748].

Moss, S. *Probabilistic Knowledge*. Oxford University Press, 2018.

Moreau, S. *Faces of Inequality: A Theory of Wrongful Discrimination*. Oxford University Press, 2020.

Murphy, J. G. 'Blackmail: A Preliminary Inquiry'. *The Monist* 63 (1980): 156–71.

Musco, S. 'Intelligence Gathering and the Relationship Between Rulers and Spies: Some Lessons from Eminent and Lesser-known Classics'. *Intelligence and National Security* 31 (2016): 1025–39.

Nagel, T. 'War and Massacre'. *Philosophy & Public Affairs* 1 (1972): 123–44.

Nagel, T. 'Types of Intuition'. *London Review of Books* (03/06/2021).

Nasheri, H. *Economic Espionage and Industrial Spying*. Cambridge University Press, 2005.

Nathan, C. 'Liability to Deception and Manipulation: The Ethics of Undercover Policing'. *Journal of Applied Philosophy* 34 (2017): 370–88.

Nathan, D. 'Just Looking: Voyeurism and the Grounds of Privacy'. *Public Affairs Quarterly* 4 (1990): 365–86.

Naticchia, C. 'Transparency and Executive Authority'. In C. Finkelstein and M. Skerker (eds.), *Sovereignty and the New Executive Authority*. Oxford University Press, 2019.

Navarro Bonilla, D. '"Secret Intelligences" in European Military, Political and Diplomatic Theory: An Essential Factor in the Defense of the Modern State (Sixteenth and Seventeenth Centuries)'. *Intelligence and National Security* 27 (2012): 283–301.

Nielsen, K. 'There Is No Dilemma of Dirty Hands'. In I. Primoratz (ed.), *Politics and Morality*. Palgrave Macmillan, 2006.

Nissenbaum, H. 'Protecting Privacy in an Information Age: The Problem of Privacy in Public'. *Law and Philosophy* 17 (1998): 559–96.

Nissenbaum, H. *Privacy in Context—Technology, Policy and the Integrity of Social Life.* Stanford University Press, 2010.

Noggle, R. 'Manipulative Actions: A Conceptual and Moral Analysis'. *American Philosophical Quarterly* 33 (1996): 43–55.

Nozick, R. 'Coercion'. In S. Morgenbesser, P. Suppes, and M. White (eds.), *Philosophy, Science, and Method: Essays in Honor of Ernest Nagel.* St Martin's Press, 1969.

Nozick, R. *Anarchy, State, and Utopia.* Basic Books, 1974.

Nussbaum, M. C. *Creating Capabilities—The Human Development Approach.* Harvard University Press, 2011.

O'Kane, E. 'Talking to the Enemy? The Role of the Back-Channel in the Development of the Northern Ireland Peace Process'. *Contemporary British History* 29 (2015): 401–20.

O'Neill, C. *Weapons of Maths Destruction.* Penguin Books, 2016.

Oberdiek, J. *Imposing Risk—A Normative Framework.* Oxford University Press, 2017.

Olson, J. M. *Fair Play: The Moral Dilemmas of Spying.* Potomac Books, 2006.

Oltermann, P. and Ackerman, S. 'Germany Asks Top US Intelligence Official to Leave Country over Spy Row'. *The Guardian* (10/07/2014).

Omand, D. 'Ethical Guidelines in Using Secret Intelligence for Public Security'. *Cambridge Review of International Affairs* 19 (2006): 613–28.

Omand, D. *Securing the State.* Hurst & Co., 2010.

Omand, D. 'The Future of Intelligence: What Are the Threats, the Challenges and the Opportunities?'. In I. Duyvesteyn et al. (eds.), *The Future of Intelligence—Challenges in the 21st century* Routledge, 2015.

Omand, D. *How Spies Think—Ten Lessons in Intelligence.* Penguin Books, 2019.

Omand, D., Bartlett, J. and Miller, C. 'Introducing Social Media Intelligence (SOCMINT)'. *Intelligence and National Security* 27 (2012): 801–23.

Omand, D. and Phythian, M. *Principled Spying—The Ethics of Secret Intelligence.* Oxford University Press, 2018.

Parent, W. A. 'A New Definition of Privacy for the Law'. *Law and Philosophy* 2 (1983): 305–38.

Parfit, D. *On What Matters—vol. 1.* Oxford University Press, 2011.

Parry, J. and Viehoff, D. 'Instrumental Authority and Its Challenges: The Case of the Laws of War'. *Ethics* 129 (2019): 548–75.

Perry, D. *Partly Cloudy—Ethics in War, Espionage, Covert Action, and Interrogation.* 2nd. Rowman & Littlefield, 2016.

Pettit, P. 'The Cunning of Trust'. *Philosophy & Public Affairs* 24 (1995): 202–25.

Pettit, P. *Republicanism—A Theory of Freedom and Government.* Oxford University Press, 1999.

Pfaff, T. 'Bungee Jumping off the Moral High Ground: Ethics of Espionage in the Modern Age'. In J. Goldman (ed.), *Ethics of Spying: A Reader for the Intelligence Professional* vol. 1. Scarecrow Press, 2005.

Pfaff, T. and J. R. Tiel. 'The Ethics of Espionage'. *Journal of Military Ethics* 3 (2004): 1–15.

Plouffe, W. C. J. 'Just War Theory as a Basis for Just Intelligence Theory: Necessary Evil or Sub-Rosa Colored Self-Deception'. *International Journal of Intelligence Ethics* 2 (2011): 77–116.

Pogge, T. and Moellendorf, D. (eds.). *Global Justice: Seminal Essays—Global Responsibilities I.* Paragon House, 2008.

Porteous, S. D. 'Economic Espionage: Issues Arising from Increased Government Involvement with the Private Sector'. *Intelligence and National Security* 9 (1994): 735–52.

Pozen, D. E. 'Deep Secrecy'. *Stanford Law Review* 62 (2010): 257–339.

Prunckun, H. *Counterintelligence—Theory and Practice*. Rowman & Littlefield, 2012.

Quinlan, M. 'Just Intelligence: Prolegomena to an Ethical Theory'. *Intelligence and National Security* 22 (2007): 1–13.

Quong, J. *The Morality of Defensive Force*. Oxford University Press, 2020.

Rachels, J. 'Why Privacy Is Important'. *Philosophy & Public Affairs* 4 (1975): 323–33.

Rappaport, J. 'Criminal Justice Inc.' *Columbia Law Review* 118 (2018): 2251–321.

Rascoff, S. J. 'The Norm against Economic Espionage for the Benefit of Private Firms: Some Theoretical Reflections'. *The University of Chicago Law Review* 83 (2016): 249–69.

Raz, J. *The Morality of Freedom*. Clarendon Press, 1986.

Reeve, A. *Modern Theories of Exploitation*. Sage, 1987.

Reiman, J. H. 'Privacy, Intimacy, and Personhood'. *Philosophy & Public Affairs* 6 (1976): 26–44.

Richelson, J. T. *A Century of Spies—Intelligence in the Twentieth Century*. Oxford University Press, 1995.

Rid, T. *Cyber War Will Not Take Place*. Oxford University Press, 2013.

Ripstein, A. 'Three Duties to Rescue: Moral, Civil, and Criminal'. *Law and Philosophy* 19 (2000): 751–79.

Ripstein, A. *Rules for Wrongdoers—Law, Morality, War*. Oxford University Press, 2021.

Rishikoff, H. 'Economic and Industrial Espionage: Who Is Eating America's Lunch and How to Stop it?'. In J. E. Sims and G. L. Burton (eds.), *Vaults, Mirrors, and Masks: Rediscovering U.S. Counterintelligence*. Georgetown University Press, 2009.

Risse, M. and Zeckhauser, R. 'Racial Profiling'. *Philosophy & Public Affairs* 32 (2004): 131–70.

Roberts, A. 'A Republican Account of the Value of Privacy'. *European Journal of Political Theory* 14 (2015): 320–44.

Rodin, D. *War and Self-Defense*. Clarendon Press, 2002.

Romanovsky, S. and Goldman, Z. 'Understanding Cyber Collateral Damage'. *Journal of National Security Law and Policy* 9 (2017): 233–58.

Rønn, K. V. and Lippert-Rasmussen, K. 'Out of Proportion? On Surveillance and the Proportionality Requirement'. *Ethical Theory and Moral Practice* 23 (2020): 181–99.

Rose, S. *For all the Tea in China*. Hutchinson, 2009.

Rosen, G. 'Culpability and Ignorance'. *Proceedings of the Aristotelian Society* 103 (2003): 61–84.

Ross, A. and Ball, J. 'GCHQ Documents Raise Fresh Questions over UK Complicity in US Drone Strikes'. *The Guardian* (24/06/2015).

Rossiter, M. *The Spy Who Changed the World*. Headline Publishing, 2014.

Rothenberg, G. 'Military Intelligence Gathering in the Second Half of the Eighteenth Century—1740-1792'. In K. Neilson and B. J. C. McKercher (eds.), *Go Spy the Land—Military Intelligence in History*. Praeger, 1992.

Rudinow, J. 'Manipulation'. *Ethics* 88 (1978): 338–47.

Rumbold, B. and Wilson, J. 'Privacy Rights and Public Information'. *Journal of Political Philosophy* 27 (2019): 3–25.

Rustmann, F. W. J. *CIA Inc.—Espionage and the Craft of Business Intelligence*. Brassey's Inc., 2002.

Ryan, C. 'The Normative Concept of Coercion'. *Mind* 89 (1980): 481–98.

Sabbagh, D. and Roth, A. 'Russian State-sponsored Hackers Target Covid-19 Vaccine Researchers'. *The Guardian* (16/07/2020).

Sagar, R. *Secrets and Leaks: The Dilemmas of State Secrecy*. Princeton University Press, 2013.

Satter, R. 'NSA Surveillance Exposed by Snowden Was Illegal, Court Rules Seven Years on'. *Reuters* (03/09/2020).

Saul, J. *Lying, Misleading, and What is Said—An Exploration in Philosophy of Language and Ethics*. Oxford University Press, 2012.

Savage, C. 'N.S.A. Triples Collection of Data From U.S. Phone Companies'. *The New York Times* (04/05/2018).

Sayle, M. 'Conversations with Philby'. *The Sunday Times* (17/12/1967).

Scanlon, T. 'Thomson on Privacy'. *Philosophy & Public Affairs* 4 (1975): 315–22.

Scanlon, T. *What We Owe to Each Other*. Harvard University Press, 1998.

Schapiro, T. 'Kantian Rigorism and Mitigating Circumstances'. *Ethics* 117 (2006): 32–57.

Schauer, F. *Profiles, Probabilities and Stereotypes*. Harvard University Press, 2006.

Schmidt, M. S. and D. E. Sanger. '5 in China Army Face U.S. Charges of Cyberattacks'. *The New York Times* (19/05/2014).

Schmitt, M. N. (ed.). *Tallinn Manual 2.0 on the International Law Applicable to Cyber Operations*. Cambridge University Press, 2017.

Schweizer, P. *Friendly Spies*. Atlantic Monthly Press, 1993.

Scott, L. and P. Jackson (eds.). *Understanding Intelligence in the Twenty-First Century—Journey in the Shadows*. Routledge, 2004.

Sebag-Montefiore, H. *Enigma: The Battle for the Code*. Weidenfeld & Nicolson, 2000.

Shaw, James R. 'The Morality of Blackmail'. *Philosophy & Public Affairs* 40 (2012): 165–96.

Shaw, Jo. 'EU Citizenship: Still a Fundamental Status?'. In R. Bauböck (ed.), *Debating European Citizenship*, 1–17. Springer International Publishing, 2019.

Sheldon, R. 'Hannibal's Spies'. *International Journal of Intelligence and CounterIntelligence* 1 (1986): 53–70.

Sheldon, R. *Intelligence Activities in Ancient Rome—Trust in the Gods, but Verify*. Routledge, 2005.

Shiffrin, S. V. 'Lockean Theories of Intellectual Property'. In S. R. Munzer (ed.), *New Essays in the Political Theory of Property*. Cambridge University Press, 2001.

Shiffrin, S. V. *Speech Matters: On Lying, Morality, and the Law*. Princeton University Press, 2014.

Shin, P. S. 'Treatment as an Individual and the Priority of Persons Over Groups in Antidiscrimination Law'. *Duke Journal of Constitutional Law & Public Policy* 12 (2016): 107–34.

Shklar, J. *Ordinary Vices*. Harvard University Press, 1984.

Siddique, H. 'GCHQ's Mass Data Interception Violated Right to Privacy, Court Rules'. *The Guardian* (25/05/2021).

Simpson, T. 'The Morality of Unconventional Force'. In J. Galliott and W. Reed (eds.), *Ethics and the Future of Spying*. Routledge, 2016.

Sims, J. E. 'Foreign Intelligence Liaison: Devils, Deals, and Details'. *International Journal of Intelligence and CounterIntelligence* 19 (2006): 195–217.

Sims, J. E. 'The Theory and Philosophy of Intelligence'. In R. Dover, M. S. Goodman, and C. Hillebrand (eds.), *Routledge Companion to Intelligence Studies*. Routledge, 2014.

Sims, J. E. 'The Future of Counter-Intelligence: The Twenty-first Century Challenge'. In I. Duyvesteyn et al. (eds.), *The Future of Intelligence—Challenges in the 21st century*. Routledge, 2015.

Singer, A. A. *The Form of the Firm—A Normative Political Theory of the Corporation*. Oxford University Press, 2019.

Singer, P. W. and A. Friedman. *Cybersecurity and Cyberwar*. Oxford University Press, 2014.

Skerker, M. 'Interrogation Ethics in the Context of Intelligence Collection'. In J. Goldman (ed.), *Ethics of Spying: A Reader for the Intelligence Professional*, vol. 1. Scarecrow Press, 2005.

Skerker, M. 'Moral Concerns with Cyberespionage'. In F. Allhoff, A. Henschke, and B. J. Strawser (eds.), *Binary Bullets*. Oxford University Press, 2016.

Skerker, M. 'A Two-Level Account of Executive Authority'. In C. Finkelstein and M. Skerker (eds.), *Sovereignty and the New Executive Authority*. Oxford University Press, 2019.

Skerker, M. 'The Rights of Foreign Intelligence Targets'. In S. Miller, M. Regan, and P. Walsh (eds.), *National Security Intelligence and Ethics*. Routledge, forthcoming 2021–22.

Smart, J. and Williams, B. A. O. *Utilitarianism: For and Against*. Cambridge University Press, 1973.

Smilansky, S. 'May We Stop Worrying about Blackmail?'. *Analysis* 55 (1995): 116–20.

Smith, H. M. 'The Subjective Moral Duty to Inform Oneself before Acting'. *Ethics* 125 (2014): 11–38.

Solove, D. J. 'Privacy and Power: Computer Databases and Metaphors for Information Privacy'. *Stanford Law Review* 53 (2001): 1393–462.

Solove, D. J. *Understanding Privacy*. Harvard University Press, 2008.

Spielmann, K. 'I Got Algorithm: Can There Be a Nate Silver in Intelligence?'. *International Journal of Intelligence and CounterIntelligence* 29 (2016): 525–44.

Steiner, H. 'Individual Liberty'. *Proceedings of the Aristotelian Society* 75 (1974): 33–50.

Stemplowska, Z. 'Feasibility: Individual and Collective'. *Social Philosophy and Policy* 33 (2016): 273–91.

Stocker, M. 'Dirty Hands and Ordinary Life'. In P. Rynard and D. P. Shugarman (eds.), *Cruelty and Deception*. Broadview Press, 2000.

Strandburg, K. J. 'Monitoring, Datafication, and Consent: Legal Approaches to Privacy in the Big Data Context'. In J. Lane, V. Stodden, S. Bender, and H. Nissenbaum (eds.), *Privacy, Big Data and the Public Good—Frameworks for Engagement*. Cambridge University Press, 2014.

Sussman, D. 'On the Supposed Duty of Truthfulness—Kant on Lying in Self-Defense'. In C. Martin (ed.), *The Philosophy of Deception*. Oxford University Press, 2009.

Tadros, V. 'Permissibility in a World of Wrongdoing'. *Philosophy & Public Affairs* 44 (2016): 101–32.

Tadros, V. 'Unjust Wars Worth Fighting For'. *Journal of Practical Ethics* 4 (2016): 52–78.

Tadros, V. 'Duress and Duty'. In S. Bazargan and S. Rickless (eds.), *The Ethics of War*. Oxford University Press, 2017.

Tadros, V. 'Localized Restricted Aggregation'. In D. Sobel, P. Vallentyne, and S. Wall (eds.), *Oxford Studies in Political Philosophy—vol. 5*. Oxford University Press, 2019.

Tadros, V. *To Do, To Die, To Reason Why: Individual Ethics in War*. Oxford University Press, 2020.

Thompson, D. F. 'Democratic Secrecy'. *Political Science Quarterly* 114 (1999): 181–93.

Thomson, J. J. 'The Right to Privacy'. *Philosophy & Public Affairs* 4 (1975): 295–314.

Thomson, J. J. 'Imposing Risks'. In *Rights, Restitution, and Risk - Essays in Moral Theory*, Harvard University Press, 1986.

Topping, A. 'Top Secret Australian Government Files Found in Secondhand Shop'. *The Guardian* (31/01/2018).

Tuchman, B. *The Zimmermann Telegram*. Penguin Books, 1958.

Turner, S. 'Intelligence for a New World Order'. *Foreign Affairs* 70 (1991): 150–66.

Tzu, S. *The Art of War*. Edited by S. B. Griffith. Oxford: Oxford University Press, 1963 [sixth century BC].

Valeriano, B., B. Jensen, and Maness, R. C. *Cyber Strategy—The Evolving Character of Power and Coercion*. Oxford University Press, 2018.

Van Puyvelde, D., Coulthart, S., and Hossain, M. S. 'Beyond the Buzzword: Big Data and National Security Decision-making'. *International Affairs* 93 (2017): 1397–416.

Veliz, C. *Privacy is Power—Why and How You should Take Back Control of Your Data*. Bantam Press, 2020.

Veliz, C. *The Ethics of Privacy*. Oxford University Press, forthcoming.

Vitoria, F. 'On the Law of War'. In A. Pagden and J. Lawrance (eds.), *Political Writings*. Cambridge University Press, 1991 [1539].

Voorhoeve, A. 'How Should We Aggregate Competing Claims?'. *Ethics* 125 (2014): 64–87.

Waldron, J. 'Can Communal Goods be Human Rights?'. In J. Waldron, *Liberal Rights—Collected Papers 1981–1991*. Cambridge University Press, 1993.

Waldron, J. 'Safety and Security'. In J. Waldron, *Torture, Terror and Trade-Offs: Philosophy for the White House*. Oxford University Press, 2010.

Walen, A. *The Mechanics of Claims and Permissible Killing in War*. Oxford University Press, 2019.

Walsh, P. F. and S. Miller. 'Rethinking "Five Eyes" Security Intelligence Collection Policies and Practice Post Snowden'. *Intelligence and National Security* 31 (2016): 345–68.

Walzer, M. 'Political Action: The Problem of Dirty Hands'. *Philosophy & Public Affairs* 2 (1973): 160–80.

Wanis-St John, A. *Back Channel Negotiation—Secrecy in the Middle East Peace Process*. Syracuse University Press, 2011.

Wark, W. K. (ed.). *Twenty-First Century Intelligence*. Routledge, 2005.

Warrell, H., C. Cookson, and H. Foy. 'Russia-linked Hackers Accused of Targeting Covid-9 Vaccine Developers'. *The Financial Times* (16/07/2020).

Warren, S. D. and Brandeis, L. D. 'The Right to Privacy'. *Harvard Law Review* 4 (1890): 193–220.

Wege, C. A. 'The Changing Islamic State Intelligence Apparatus'. *International Journal of Intelligence and Counterintelligence* 31 (2018): 271–88.

Weinberg, G. L. *A World at Arms: A Global History of World War II*. Cambridge: Cambridge University Press, 1994.

Weiner, T. *Legacy of Ashes: The History of the CIA*. Penguin Books, 2007.

Weiner, T. *Enemies: A History of the FBI*. Penguin Books, 2012.

Weiss, M. 'The Hero Who Betrayed His Country'. *The Atlantic* (26/06/2019).

Wertheimer, A. *Coercion*. Princeton University Press, 1987.

Wertheimer, A. *Exploitation*. Princeton University Press, 1996.

West, R. *The Meaning of Treason*. 2nd. Macmillan/The Reprint Society, 1952.

Westin, A. *Privacy and Freedom*. Atheneum, 1967.

Wijze, S. de. 'Dirty Hands: Doing Wrong to do Right'. In I. Primoratz (ed.), *Politics and Morality*. Palgrave Macmillan, 2006.

Williams, B. A. O. 'Politics and Moral Character'. In S. Hampshire (ed.), *Public and Private Morality*. Cambridge University Press, 1978.

Williams, B. A. O. *Truth and Truthfulness: An Essay in Genealogy*. Princeton University Press, 2002.

Williams, G. 'Blackmail'. *Criminal Law Review* (1954): 79–92.

Willsher, K. 'France Summons US Ambassador over "Unacceptable" Spying'. *The Guardian* (24/06/2015).

Wilson, J. 'Could There be a Right to Own Intellectual Property?'. *Law and Philosophy* 28 (2009): 393–427.

Wolfe-Robinson, M. 'Classified Ministry of Defence Papers Found at Bus Stop in Kent'. *The Guardian* (27/06/2021).

Wolf, M. and McElvoy, A. *Man Without a Face: The Autobiography of Communism's Greatest Spymaster*. Time Books, 1997.

Wood, A. W. *Kantian Ethics*. Cambridge University Press, 2008.

Wood, A. W. 'Coercion, Manipulation and Exploitation'. In C. Coons and M. Weber (eds.), *Manipulation—Theory and Practice*. Oxford University Press, 2014.

Zimmerman, M. J. 'Intervening Agents and Moral Responsibility'. *The Philosophical Quarterly* 35 (1985): 347–58.

Zimmerman, M. J. *Living with Uncertainty—The Moral Significance of Ignorance*. Cambridge University Press, 2008.

Index